GREENE KING

A Business and Family History

GREENE KING

A Business and Family History

R. G. WILSON

THE BODLEY HEAD
&
JONATHAN CAPE

British Library Cataloguing in Publication Data
Wilson, Richard G.
Greene King: a business and family history.
1. Greene King – History
2. Brewing industry – Suffolk – History
I. Title
338. 7′6633′094264   HD9397.G74G/
ISBN 0-370-30548-5
ISBN 0-224-01375-0 (Cape)

© R. G. Wilson 1983
Printed in Great Britain for
The Bodley Head Ltd
9 Bow Street, London WC2E 7AL
Jonathan Cape Ltd
30 Bedford Square, London WC1
by St Edmundsbury Press, Bury St Edmunds
Set in Linotron Sabon
by Rowland Phototypesetting, Bury St Edmunds
First published 1983

CONTENTS

ILLUSTRATIONS

ILLUSTRATIONS

between pages 210 and 211

viii

PICTURE CREDITS

The author and publishers wish to thank the following for kind permission to reproduce illustrations: Mr John Bridge for Plates 7 and 11; Mr Martin Corke for Plates 9, 13 and 20; Mrs Hugh Gilson-Taylor for Plate 6; Sir Hugh Greene for Plate 29; the late Dr Raymond Greene for Plates 3, 4, 5, 10 and 12; Greene King and Sons, Bury St Edmunds for Plates 1, 8, 15, 16, 17, 18, 19, 22, 23, 25, 26, 27, 28 and 31; Greene King (Biggleswade) Ltd, for Plate 21; Sir Alfred Munnings Art Museum for Plate 14; the National Buildings Record for Plate 24; the Suffolk Record Office, Bury St Edmunds, for Plate 2; and Universal Pictorial Press and Agency Ltd for Plate 30. The maps were drawn by Mr B. J. Clarke (Greene King and Sons) and Mr D. Mew (University of East Anglia), who also drew the diagram.

Preface

The decision to write a business *and* family history of Greene King was not dictated by the survival of papers, as few remain concerning Greene's brewery in the pre-1887 period, but because various Greenes have achieved distinction in the worlds of business and banking, literature and broadcasting in the nineteenth and twentieth centuries. Therefore I have traced in some detail the background of this remarkable family to show the way in which the brewery and their other economic interests sustained their thrusting social and political ambitions. The result provides a classic example of the upward mobility of countless families engaged in business and commerce in the century before 1914, a microcosm of a significant slice of our social history in those years. And the Kings, very Suffolk and successful on their own terms, provide a good contrast with the Greenes.

Of course, I have focused much of the story upon the Greene and King breweries, their differences of style in running them, and the way in which, after the amalgamation of 1887, the firm grew by careful management and modest expansion. For over 100 years now they have absorbed competitors, throughout East Anglia and the South Midlands, so that Greene King has emerged in the 1980s amongst the dozen largest breweries in Britain. Tracing this development of a single firm is also useful in that detailed economic histories of breweries are rare.* Like many

* Two comprehensive ones exist: P. Lynch and J. E. Vaizey, *Guinness's Brewery in the Irish Economy, 1759–1876* (1960), and K. H. Hawkins, *A History of Bass Charrington* (1978). See also Appendix 1, A Note on Sources.

business histories the sources have dictated that it is largely a view
of the owners, and, later, the Board at work. But in breweries,
where they held such sway over their small workforces, the
approach is defensible as well as inevitable. To place both the firm
and the families that have nurtured its growth in context I have
also included a good deal of material about Bury St Edmunds and
East Anglia, especially during the nineteenth century. I hope that I
have preserved a reasonable balance between these various
aspects of this study – the firm and the brewing industry, the
owners and their business, social and political interests, and
developments in Bury and West Suffolk. Some statistical material
is included in tables in Appendix 2.

When I considered writing the history of Greene King friends
told me that firms were invariably 'difficult' and that colleagues
wrinkled their noses at *business* history. They were quite wrong,
for I have received so much encouragement both from Greene
King and economic historians at the University of East Anglia that
my task throughout has been enjoyable. Amongst those at the
former I must mention the joint managing director, Martin
Corke, whose unenviable, although I believe self-imposed, task
was to see this volume into print. The chairman, John Bridge, and
his fellow directors, Bernard Tickner, Jonathan Clarke, John
Banham, Simon and Timothy Redman, Timothy Bridge and the
company secretary, H. G. (Dick) Lines, the group accountant,
John Barnes, and retired head brewer, O. H. Heyhoe, have aided
me at various stages in my work. Some of them read my manuscript, at least in part, and made many useful suggestions, especially about the last chapter. Ken Page, at the Biggleswade Brewery, allowed me to see the results of his many years' work on the
history of Wells and Winch. My colleagues, Terry Gourvish, Bill
Mathew and Michael Miller read and commented upon my work.
The former, who is writing a history of Steward and Patteson, the
one-time Norwich brewers, gave me the benefit of his knowledge
of the brewing industry and nineteenth-century business history,
while the latter two, both Scots, provided me with insights into the
niceties of accountancy, punctuation and spelling that my incomplete education in England had never provided. To them all I owe
my grateful thanks.

Sir Hugh Greene, as my publisher and a former chairman of

Greene King, gave me the friendliest support as did his son, Graham, and brother, the late Dr Raymond Greene. Over the years Dr Greene collected a mass of material relating to his family. It has been an invaluable source in writing this book. His brother-in-law, Rodney Dennys, Arundel Herald of Arms, allowed me to see his genealogical work on the Greenes, and he also read and discussed Chapter 1. His research assistant, Mrs Karen Proudfoot, helped me with the Greene family tree I have provided.

Mrs Rosemary James and Mrs Anstace Gilson-Taylor let me see papers in their possession concerning the Molineux-Montgomerie and Blake families, which are the basis for parts of Chapter 2. The staff of the Suffolk Record Office at Bury St Edmunds were invariably helpful. If there were a *Guide* to good archives, it would receive a five star rating. I must also acknowledge help in various forms from Professors Frank Thistlethwaite, Robert Ashton, L. S. Pressnell and Howard Temperley, and from Mr K. H. Hawkins of the University of Bradford, and Mr A. Burns at the Brewers' Society Library in London. I am also grateful for the help Jill Sutcliffe and Valerie Buckingham of Jonathan Cape Limited have given me in the production of this book in its later stages. My thanks are also due to Judith Sparks and Mary Gurteen who, in typing my manuscript, overcame the illegibility of my handwriting with remarkable cheerfulness. My family has lived with Greene King longer than they care to remember. For years now on journeys in East Anglia they have pointed out – usually at the last minute when traffic seemed busiest – the precise location of many Greene King houses. My wife has provided a great deal of practical help and has read and criticised the various drafts of these chapters. I can only hope that my book in some measure reflects all these sources of aid, trust and encouragement.

R. G. W.
Hethel, October 1982

1

Benjamin Greene,
Bury and Brewing, 1799–1836

There is some uncertainty about the date when Greene King and
Sons was founded. Nowhere is this stated more clearly than on the
Westgate front of the head offices in Bury St Edmunds. The date
above the front door boldly asserts 'Founded 1800', while to the
left of the same door the plaque carrying the Greene King emblem
proclaims—'Fine Suffolk Ales 1799'.[1] Curiously neither date is
strictly correct. Nor is 1798, the year in which William Buck and
Benjamin Greene supposedly acquired the Westgate brewery
from Messrs Wright, who in that year gave up business after
occupying the premises for most of the eighteenth century. These
dates, 1799 and 1800, probably indicate the year Benjamin
Greene first came to Bury on the completion of his training at
Whitbreads, the great London brewers. The eighteenth century
was neither so accurate nor so obsessive as the twentieth about
dates, and when the brewery flourished after 1860, Edward
Greene, needing a foundation date for publicity purposes, selected
the year he recollected his father had arrived in Bury. The first
positive evidence of a Greene connection with brewing at Westgate in fact comes from an advertisement in the *Bury and Norwich
Post* in April 1806, when Messrs Buck and Greene

> begged leave respectfully to inform the public that they will be
> ready by the first week in June, to execute any order they may be
> favoured with for Table Beer, and will as soon as possible

announce when they shall be able to supply such Ale, Porter and Old Beer, as will give complete satisfaction to their friends, and secure their own reputation, particularly in private families.[2]

The newspapers repeated the advertisement throughout the summer of 1806.

Neither of the original co-partners of the firm was a Bury man and neither fitted the contemporary image of a brewer—rich, Anglican, Tory and locally well connected. When the latter first came to Bury around the turn of the eighteenth century he had not yet attained his majority and he possessed none of these attributes. He was a Midlander, a Nonconformist and without close connections in Bury. Much later, family tradition provided a gloss on Benjamin Greene's origins that obscured his family's long participation in the textile business in Bedfordshire and Northamptonshire.

The 'legend' appears in print for the first time in 1875 in a long article that the *Bury Post* published on the Westgate Brewery.[3] By this time the brewery was a prosperous concern and Benjamin Greene's third son had become the town's Conservative M.P. Not surprisingly in an age when successful businessmen were looking at ways to take the raw edges off their riches—and in a county like Suffolk, dominated by old landowning families, this search for genealogical respectability was intensive[4]—some of the details about the family of the brewery's founder were confused. The account maintained that although the Greenes were 'unflinching Nonconformists', they were a branch of a family—the Greenes of Green's Norton and Drayton House—which was 'one of the most ancient in the county of Northampton'. The roll call of the family and their manors that followed included Lords Chief Justice, High Sheriffs, the mother of Katherine Parr, and, more topically, the Greenes who owned the famous Stag Brewery in Westminster.[5] Any careful genealogist would have detected a vagueness about the precise links and chronology of the pedigree, and it is significant that the lineage of the Bury Greenes which eventually found its way into Burke's *Peerage* and *Landed Gentry* traced Benjamin Greene's ancestry no further back than his father. Yet the 1875 article held that 'during the last century, a son of Sir Thomas Greene of Oundle went to the West Indian colonies, where he became a wealthy planter, eventually returning to this country, and from this gentleman are descended the member for Bury and his elder brother, the ex-governor of the Bank of England'. This is certainly a confusion of later events. As often, the truth is more intricate and interesting than the fiction.

I

Benjamin Greene was born in Oundle in 1780. He may have shared common ancestors with the Northamptonshire nobility, but his recent forebears were substantial Bedfordshire tradesmen. His great-grandfather Edmund Greene (d. 1724) had been a well-to-do draper in Ampthill and earlier generations of Greenes had carried on the same occupation in nearby Husborne Crawley, a village largely owned by the Dukes of Bedford and adjacent to Woburn.[6] Drapers were prosperous men, not simply selling goods across a counter in a shop, piled high with rolls of cloth, but travelling across wide stretches of the countryside trading their wares, wholesale as well as retail. Fees paid for apprenticeships show that amongst the largest sums that parents had to raise for their sons' training were those demanded by the leading drapers and mercers of any sizeable market town. When Benjamin Greene I (1693–1751), the brewer's grandfather and a draper and chapman in Ampthill, took George Gurney as an apprentice in 1743 he accepted £100 from Gurney's parents. Clearly to attract a premium of this size Benjamin Greene I was a tradesman of repute. And he had several relatives, also drapers, who formed a network across the South Midlands from Hitchin, Bedford, Woburn and Wellingborough. Here, as drapers invariably were elsewhere, they would be reckoned amongst the most well-to-do members of their communities.

The few facts we know about Benjamin Greene I are riddled with ambiguity. It seems likely that he succeeded to the Ampthill property, although his father's will, proved in February 1724, gives no precise clues. Recently having moved to Bedford from Ampthill the latter split his property in a way that anticipated dispute. For he left only very modest bequests to five of the six children who survived his two marriages and shared the bulk of his wealth between his second wife and the eldest son of his first marriage. Presumably Benjamin, the only son of his second

3

marriage, received his mother's support. He certainly carried on the Ampthill business, whereas his elder half-brother traded from Woburn and Bedford. In 1724, already married and with a young family, he was admitted to membership of the Independent Church in Bedford, an institution made famous by its associations with John Bunyan.[7] For the next twenty-five years—like many other fellow members—he travelled into Bedford from the countryside regularly for Sunday services. And like so many Dissenting tradesmen he appears to have prospered. But in 1751 things went badly wrong for Benjamin Greene I. The chapel minutes for the 13 November of that year record that he had recently become a bankrupt and that 'he should be suspended from the communion of this Church till his affairs can be more particularly enquired into'.[8] The chapel elders did not proceed far with their investigations. Benjamin Greene was dead within a month, possibly by his own hand.

It is uncertain how many children he left. Among them was Benjamin II, born about 1732. Around the difficult time when his father died he left Ampthill, for in 1757, when he married Sarah Baggerley of Oundle, he was described as a draper of the same town. She died ten years later, having produced eight children in a hectic, wearying decade. Within two years he married Rebecca Ashton, a thirty-year-old spinster from Kettering. But Benjamin Greene II's ascent in the world owed less to the dowries of his two wives, who supplied him so profusely with offspring, than to the fact that he inherited the Wellingborough property of his aunt, Sarah Rodick, who died in 1760. Sarah Rodick, his father's youngest sister, was a woman of some talent. She married twice: both times to drapers. Her second husband, John Rodick, was a very wealthy Dissenter from Northampton.[9] When she married him in 1738 she made the stipulation that should she die without issue—a not unlikely event since she was within a few days of her 43rd birthday—she would bequeath her estate to whomsoever she wished. It was from this arrangement that Benjamin Greene II, who had probably joined his aunt when left penniless by his father, benefited when she died 23 years later.

Yet he continued to support his large, young family from two marriages principally from his drapery business in Oundle. The brief entries of the diary of John Clifton, the Oundle Parish Clerk and cabinet maker, made several references to supplying 'Mr. Green' with ell wands besides repairs to his shutters and furniture.[10] It is clear from this source that Benjamin Greene II had also become a dealer in worsted yarn during the difficult years of the War of American Independence. As the war drew to a close, he died in February 1782. Suddenly the confined prose of the parish clerk is extended by the morbid excitement aroused by Greene's appalling end.

This morning Mr. Green the Draper Died after a Short but most Amazing Illness and he Bled in all parts of his Body, which looked as if he was Mortified and he was in a state of Putrefaction before Death. Mercy O Lord!

He was buried, fashionably, by torchlight, on a bitter March night three days later. Clifton, slipping back into his normal terse style, wrote: 'He has left a great family of children.' More than both hands of the parish clerk could count, for 13 survived their father.

Benjamin III (1780–1860), who eventually came to Bury St Edmunds, was the youngest, a mere 22 months old when his father died. Family circumstances had greatly improved since his grandfather's bankruptcy thirty years earlier and the children of the first marriage were all at least in their teens. Yet the family's moderate affluence, although it enabled all the children to receive a sound education and the sons a good business training, was no guarantee of perpetual success. For the remarkable thing about Benjamin Greene II's three young sons was the advance they each eventually made in the world. Clearly their father was a man of ability, extending the family draper business to include that of worsted yarn manufacture. These abilities were inherited. The eldest son, Thomas Baggerley Greene (1762–1834), carried on the family interests in Oundle, eventually making a considerable fortune. John, Benjamin Greene III's full brother born in 1777, was a banker in Birmingham after spending a brief period in Bury St Edmunds and Cambridge.[11] If inherited ability was one feature of their success, another was undoubtedly their strict Independent upbringing and the business opportunities that membership of the Dissenting elite brought them. Indeed it is a constant feature of the family's solid progress across the eighteenth century.

What enticed Benjamin III to brewing and Bury St Edmunds is

not entirely clear. The family had no previous connections with commercial brewing. Presumably his father's executors selected the occupation because they considered it to be a lucrative one. But the choice of firm for his training—Whitbreads, the most celebrated of the great London porter brewers, where Benjamin III was a trainee brewer in the late 1790s—was no accident.[12] In the late eighteenth century the descendants of Edmund Greene's first marriage were prominent in Bedford, and Samuel Whitbread owned a nearby estate at Cardington and was well known at the Independent Bunyan chapel. And in an age when even remote family connections possessed real strength, Benjamin III was introduced into the world of the Whitbreads, John Howard, the prison reformer, and his future father-in-law, the Revd Thomas Smith, who all worshipped together in Bedford. Yet there seems to be no apparent reason why on the completion of his apprenticeship around 1800 he should migrate to a quiet corner of East Anglia where he had no known relatives.[13] There are two possible explanations. One rests with the worsted yarn trade. His father, towards the end of his life, moved into its sale whilst it was still of course in its hand manufactured stages. Bury St Edmunds was in the eighteenth century a famed centre of yarn production, particularly for the Norwich worsted industry. There was possibly some business connection between Oundle and Bury that Benjamin Greene's father and brother, John, had exploited. For family notes suggest that the latter was in Bury St Edmunds some time during the 1790s. The other interpretation is that Benjamin Greene migrated via the Independent network. His religion was extremely important to him during his first few years in the town, the cornerstone of his business career as well as of his private life.

Whatever the explanations Benjamin was living in Bury in 1801, the year he came of age. Two pieces of evidence survive. Firstly, the Whiting Street Chapel accounts show he paid a quarterly subscription of half a guinea for the first time in early 1802, to provide himself and his servant with a pew. The second is more puzzling, since it is always stated that he formed a partnership with William Buck. Soon after his marriage (see below) he was ill, and went to recuperate with his mother at Oundle in the summer of 1804. His sister-in-law wrote, he has consulted a friend of the family who pronounced his disorder as inflammation of the lungs, but hopes to do him good—it is really distressing—Mr. Cl. continues to Brew himself—he had behaved the most unlike an *human Being* to Mr. G. in the affair—my father says Mr. G. wrote a very proper answer to him. Unfortunately for Mr. G. he entered into a three years' engagement with him and there is no chance of his being angry enough to wish to break it—Mr. G. has been sorry ever since.[14]

From this letter it is clear that Benjamin had entered a three year agreement with 'Mr. Cl.' which was working very badly. So badly that Benjamin never again referred to it in any accounts about himself or his brewery.

'Mr. Cl.' was without doubt John Clark, a brewer in Guildhall Street.[15] And here the old Bedfordshire–Ampthill connections of the Greenes creep in. This brewery was sited in what had once been the extensive yarn shops of James Oakes. Buckley and Garnish refitted them 'at great expense' and opened them in 1790 as an up-to-date, common brewery, with its plant 'constructed upon the most approved plan'.[16] In spite of the brewery's modernity their reign was brief, for in the autumn of 1792 they were bankrupt. James Oakes noted in his diary,

> The Brewery late Buckley and Garnish sold this Day by Auction at the Bell to a Morris of Ampthill for his nephew Mr. Clark at £2,500—It is suppos'd full £500 under its real value. He likewise bo^{t.} the Two Brewers at £500 . . . and the Unicorn at £420.

Some nine years later Benjamin Greene, on the completion of his training at Whitbread's, had entered a formal connection, perhaps as brewer, with John Clark who had, like Benjamin, relations in Ampthill.

These various explanations account for Benjamin Greene's move to Bury around the turn of the eighteenth century. Nevertheless, the choice of occupation and town for a very young, Midlands Dissenter remains curious. And it is an enigma that is not entirely dispelled when we look further at Bury and the brewing industry in Suffolk around 1800.

2

When William Cobbett visited Ipswich in 1830, and tactfully sang its praises, those inhabitants he talked to brushed his remarks aside and 'asked me if I did not think Bury St. Edmunds the nicest town in the world'. This was a touching local pride. But a host of more seasoned travellers than Cobbett's Ipswich informants were moved to similar eulogies. Leland in Henry VIII's reign was enchanted by its physical setting, 'a city more neatly seated the sun never saw, so curiously doth it hang upon a general descent, with a little river on the east side.' Almost two centuries later Daniel Defoe, attempting to capture 'the pleasure and agreeable delightful show of the town of Bury', found it 'crowded with nobility and gentry, and all sorts of the most agreeable company; and as the company invites, so there is the appearance of pleasure upon the very situation; and they that live at Bury, are supposed to live there for the sake of it.'

When Benjamin settled there the town was still renowned for its good society, the salubrity of its situation and the excellent classical education provided by its grammar school.[17] Yet in 1800 the town was small, not so much in comparison with other East Anglian market centres (except Norwich), but certainly with those towns in the Midlands and North which were beginning to enjoy industrial prosperity. Moreover in the preceding 25 years —and this was unusual at a time when the population everywhere was beginning to increase quite rapidly—the number of its inhabitants hardly grew.[18] What little industry it had enjoyed was now in decline. Throughout the eighteenth century the town produced yarn chiefly for the Norwich worsted industry, but after 1750 this market was increasingly supplied by imported Irish yarn and eventually machine spun yarn from the West Riding. By the 1790s the Norwich industry itself was in a state of stagnation, and this together with the inability of the Bury spinners and combers to meet Yorkshire's competition meant that yarn production slumped in the town. Early trade directories, available from the 1780s onwards, reveal very few yarn manufacturers and wool combers in Bury, and by the early nineteenth century most accounts of the town and county bemoan the lack of industry.[19] Several leading yarn firms like those of James Oakes in 1795 and William Buck around 1805—a decade that marked a sharp decline in hand spinning in Suffolk—switched their capital to other business ventures, Oakes to banking, Buck to brewing. When Oakes's Bank was forced by a new competitor in the town to allow 3 per cent interest on current accounts in 1801 the senior partner wrote in his diary,

> this was never known to be done on *running accounts* in this county and are well aware not to be afforded on account of the very limited situation of Business in this Town and Neighbourhood—it certainly has been the practice of the Norfolk and Norwich bankers for years back and in large commercial cities and sea ports this may possibly be done.

One inhabitant writing in 1831 described the town as,

> this comparatively quiet, non-manufacturing nook of our island. Here are no great interests on which the destinies of empires hinge: here are no rivalries of commerce to uphold—no manufacturing energies to quicken—no material advantages of any kind to secure.[20]

Even after the railways improved communications in 1846 (river navigation by the Lark reached no nearer Bury than Fornham, three miles away) and Suffolk experienced agricultural prosperity in the first half of Queen Victoria's reign there was little industrial activity. This lack of development was the despair of the compiler of the *Official Illustrated Guide to the Great Eastern Railway* (1865) who was looking for advertising revenue. Gloomily, admist all the obligatory verbiage he had to include about the Abbey, he wrote, 'there is not any branch of manufacture carried on . . . Bury St. Edmunds is not a commercial town'.[21]

Bury's prosperity had always been largely dependent upon its position as the market and social centre of West Suffolk. This reflected the setting of the town and its buildings which were in part a legacy of the great Abbey. More than most county towns in England Bury acted as a social palliative to ease the boredom of rural existence. Every visitor commented on the activity and gaiety of its social life, the unusually large numbers of country houses in its neighbourhood which then supposedly constituted the basis of 'good' society, and the way the town drew in the gentry of Suffolk and even Norfolk and Cambridgeshire during the great October Fair revels. Mothers found the brief season invaluable for launching into matrimony daughters who had not found husbands in the more competitive routs of London and Bath earlier in the year. Bury tradesmen were specialists in supplying the needs of the local gentry and farmers, and by 1800 the town had become almost solely a market and social centre whose prosperity was linked entirely to the state of agriculture in West Suffolk. This accounts for the slow growth of the town, especially when the yarn industry began to contract in the last quarter of the eighteenth century.

Not surprisingly, in view of this economic base, society in the town in 1800 was very traditional. Nowhere is this more revealed than in the closely written volumes of James Oakes's diaries.[22] Oakes (1741–1829) was for half a century before his death the doyen of the corporation in Bury. A man of enormous energy —four times Mayor, a member of an old, wealthy family whose fortune had been made in yarn manufacture, a neighbouring landowner (although he always lived in the handsome town house Sir John Soane designed for him in Guildhall Street[23]), a banker and receiver of the land tax and Justice of the Peace—he had his finger in every Bury and West Suffolk pie. Above all he was at the centre of the activities of the Corporation and the town's numerous charities, operating a web of power and patronage. His omnipresence gives his diaries an unrivalled prospect of Bury at several levels. Two of these views reveal the problem a Dissenter and newcomer would experience in the town around 1800. One exposes the workings of the Corporation, the other the lines of social demarcation which the inner elite operated.

At one level the way forward was not difficult. The Corporation was composed of an Alderman (or Mayor as he was in effect), 12 capital burgesses, and two dozen common councilmen. The Alderman and capital burgesses tended to be recruited from the town gentry and the most well-to-do businessmen like James Oakes, but the majority of the common councilmen were largely culled from the more affluent Anglican tradesmen on the nomination of the small ruling clique that ran the town's affairs. Before 1835 Nonconformists were excluded from the Corporation. The chief plum in its gift was the right its members exclusively possessed before 1832 to elect the town's two M.P.s at the

Guildhall.[24] But actual representation in the Parliaments of Georgian England was too important a source of power and profit for this to be assumed by two burgesses from a small market town, and in the event Lord Bristol and the Duke of Grafton shared the nomination of Bury's Members of Parliament. For longer than anyone could remember the M.P.s were invariably members of the Harvey and Fitzroy families. The detailed management of their interests and elections was left to zealous, pushing Bury men like James Oakes. When the reform party in 1827 attempted to secure the election of John Benjafield as Recorder in opposition to the Oakes's candidate Benjafield admitted 'he might as well expect to be appointed Emperor of the Turks'.[25] In political scrums of this sort Nonconformists like Benjamin Greene had little room.

Neither was its society more open. For at another level the diaries reveal the precise social distinctions that were observed in Bury. No one could measure up the company in a dining room or meeting more accurately than James Oakes. To him society consisted of four classes: the neighbouring landowners and clergy with their families; the town's own numerous gentry (often related to the former), clergy, surgeons, etc. who occupied the more prosperous houses of Northgate Street, Guildhall Street, Angel Hill, Westgate and St Mary's Square; those Bury tradesmen who were admitted to the Corporation and the financial management of the town and its charities on sufferance; and the rest. At every meeting and every social function he noted implicitly this differentiation. Occasionally he observed that the arrangements of segregation broke down. At the dinner in the Guildhall after the Mayor's installation in 1807 he commented, 'there still appears to want more regulation in placing the Gentlemen and Strangers at the first Table which ought to be managed if possible—many Tradesmen of the Town taking the place of the first Gentlemen.' Social control at the town's assemblies was easier since no one outside the town's well-defined social elite joined the county in their jollifications. A Suffolk *Guide* of 1829 reckoned:

> the three balls held annually during the great fair are in general attended by numbers of the first rank and fashion, as are also the four or five winter balls; but trades people, however respectable, are always rigorously excluded.[26]

An edition printed a few years earlier was even more sweeping in its denunciation of social customs in Bury, 'there is not perhaps a town in the kingdom where the pride of birth even though conjoined with poverty, is so tenaciously and so ridiculously maintained as at Bury.'[27] In this air, where Anglican, socially conservative values so filled the atmosphere, breathing for a young thrusting Midlands Dissenter was not easy.

3

Like the choice of a refined backwater for his venture Benjamin Greene's selection of career is odd in that brewing and Nonconformity were unnatural allies, although the union was not entirely unknown especially amongst Quakers. The occupation, however, was a fitting one for an ambitious young man. When Dr Johnson was involved in the sale of Thrale's brewery he enthused, 'we are not here to sell a parcel of boilers and vats, but the potentiality of growing rich beyond the dreams of avarice.'[28] Few brewers, especially outside London, inhabited this El Dorado, but the knowledge that an excellent living could be made from a successful brewery attracted many entrants to the trade. In fact in no other industry were there greater disparities in the scale and profitability of enterprises. Attention to the brewing industry in Georgian England has so far centred on the emergence of the eleven great breweries in London—producing porter, not ale —and which, like London itself, were largely unrepresentative of developments in the provinces.[29]

Before 1800 brewing fell into three broad categories. It is simplest to isolate them by looking at the principals involved —the home brewer, the brewing victualler, and the common brewer. Each deserves a moment's attention. The home brewer in the eighteenth century has few parallels with today's species, young men—often of the middle class—struggling with beer kits in their bathrooms. Then most gentlemen and all farmers who employed much labour, as well as institutions such as Colleges and Poor Houses, brewed their own ale. All these establishments possessed a set of brewing utensils, and their servants brewed —almost always without recourse to thermometer or hydrometer —ale of variable strength and goodness. The scale of this home brewing varied from the big institutions and the households of the great, producing large quantities regularly, to the cottager mashing molasses in a tea kettle. But in every type of household consumption was high, since supplies of water were often unsafe. Arthur Young reckoned that at the turn of the eighteenth century the average Suffolk labourer had an allowance of two pints of beer a day, three in summer, and five when employed in the harvest. And this was merely the ration constantly doled out by employers. A glimpse of middle-class supply is indicated by James Oakes in Bury. When in 1800 he cleared out the house of his aged father-in-law, Richard Adamson, he discovered thirteen hogsheads of beer (about 830 gallons). Adamson supposedly lived quietly. Oakes himself was able to brew four coombs of malt a day in the new brewhouse he built for himself in that year at his Guildhall Street house.

Of course not all beer was brewed at home, although we are uncertain about the proportion that was.[30] Beer had been sold retail for centuries in the alehouses of every parish and town in England. Many of these inns were supplied by the landlords themselves, mashing in their outbuildings a few bushels of malt every ten days or a fortnight on a scale that was no different from those country houses or institutions where large amounts of beer were brewed regularly. Normally they brewed no more than was consumed on their premises and by their private trade. In 1800 these publican brewers were especially numerous in the Midlands, the South-West, Wales and Lancashire, whereas in Surrey, Middlesex, Berkshire, Hertfordshire, Oxfordshire, Hampshire, Sussex and Kent there were virtually no publicans who brewed their own beer.[31] Here the ascendancy of the common brewer, that is a brewer who sold beer to other publicans, was complete. For centuries in London, with its great concentration of population, brewing had fallen into the hands of common brewers. Indeed some of the largest of all eighteenth-century industrial enterprises were London porter breweries. With a large consumer demand in the capital these brewers benefited from economies of scale which were derived from handling huge quantities of beer. And they went a step further in the organisation of their enterprises when they began to 'tie' their retail outlets by either acquiring outright ownership or, more frequently, making loans to those publicans who took their beer. Growth in the size of breweries was dependent upon the control of retail outlets in this way.

London took the lead in all these developments, but as towns everywhere grew with the population explosion of the late eighteenth century—an increase not confined to the industrial Midlands and North—similar, but less spectacular, transformations in the scale of brewing took place everywhere. The extent of these changes appears to have been dependent upon two factors. First, the size of breweries around 1800 was inhibited by carriage restrictions since beer, of great bulk and low value, was uneconomic to transport any distance along even the best roads of Georgian England. Therefore any appreciable changes in the scale of provincial brewing relied upon the concentration of demand that only a large, urban market provided. Secondly, as we have already noted, there were very marked geographical differences in the spread of common brewers between roughly the East and South on the one hand and the Midlands, Wales and some Northern counties on the other. These differences seem to be best explained by reference to the barley and malt trade. All good malting barley was grown in the dry eastern and south-eastern counties, and those brewers—certainly the majority in the east of England—that produced malt as well as beer derived benefits from this duality of business which allowed their breweries to expand. Already by 1800 there were towns in East Anglia, like King's Lynn, Norwich, Yarmouth and Ipswich, where common brewers were doing a trade of several thousands of barrels annually, owning their own maltings and many public houses. Rate books and insurance registers chart the rise of these substantial breweries like Bagges in King's Lynn and Steward and Pattesons in Norwich. Good water carriage was clearly important. Lacons at Yarmouth provides a good example: by the end of the Napoleonic Wars the family owned three maltings (in 1790 they had managed no fewer than 17 in the town before the export of malt to Holland declined), two breweries and forty-five 'tied' houses in Yarmouth alone. And they must have supplied many other inns in the surrounding countryside. Lacons was at the top end of the scale of East Anglian breweries in the early nineteenth century, but throughout Norfolk, Essex and Suffolk there were common brewers busily extending their breweries and retail trade.[32]

In Suffolk the process whereby the common brewer was gradually absorbing the production functions of the home and publican brewer, an absorption that is the central theme—especially in the South and East of England—in the history of brewing after 1750, was well advanced by the early nineteenth century. It had not proceeded so far as in Essex and Norfolk. In 1826 there were 35 common brewers who produced 26,113 barrels of strong beer and 212 victuallers who brewed 30,370.[33] These figures show the small size of the average Suffolk brewery and suggest, because total output was small, that private brewing was still widespread (see Appendix 2, Table 1). Certainly in Bury itself concentration was less forward than in the largest towns in the East Anglian region. Several factors were responsible: the relatively small size of its population; the number of farmers and local gentry themselves brewing with abundant supplies of local malt; the heavy dependence of the town on road transport so that little Bury beer was sold beyond a radius of ten or twelve miles; and, perhaps most significantly, the emergence of Bury as an important malting centre. Therefore the connection between malting and public house ownership was stronger than the links between common brewing and 'tied' property. Indeed in 1833 Greenes and Braddocks held only 3 out of a total of 54 inns and public houses in the town, although they leased and supplied many of the 20 or so of those that had no brewhouse, besides some that did, as well as a number of country inns and beer houses.[34] Nevertheless even thirty years earlier, when Benjamin Greene began his career, the changes we have noted in the relationship between common, home and victualling brewers were beginning to gain momentum. Acceleration was provided by fast-rising raw material prices and unprecedented increases in the malt tax and beer duties during the French Wars (1793–1815). High costs—notably advancing in the first decade of the nineteenth century—forced many home brewers and publicans to give up brewing and turn to the supplies of the common brewer.

There had been a brewery on the Westgate site throughout the eighteenth century. It was owned by three generations of the Wright family. In the course of their occupancy they became prosperous from brewing and farming, allying themselves with the Suffolk and Norfolk gentry by marriage, and becoming prominent in the affairs of the town after 1750. Matthias Wright was also a landowner at nearby Barrow, a Justice of the Peace and four times Alderman before his death in office in 1805. His son, Walter Rodwell Wright, poet and former consul-general of the Ionian islands, was elected Recorder of Bury in the same year. Because the Recorder made his own way successfully in life, and he himself spent more and more time at Barrow, Matthias Wright, who had been employed with his brother in the brewing and malting trade for thirty years, decided to sell the Westgate brewery, malting office and public houses in the late summer of 1798.[35] There was no quick sale. The populace of Bury celebrated Nelson's victory at the Battle of the Nile later that year with a dozen hogsheads of Wright's strong beer. Yet even by the standard of protracted property sales in the eighteenth century, the brewery was on the market for an exceptional length of time. Two years later it was no longer in use, and although Wright found a tenant for the brewery house, which his family had occupied for so long, it was not until the winter of 1805–6 that his executors finally sold the brewery to the partnership of Benjamin Greene and William Buck. In the St Mary's rate book Greene's name is pencilled in for the February 1806 assessment, showing that he had just become the occupier of Wright's 'brewing office' and house valued at £26 10s. per annum.

The clues to the Buck–Greene connection, indeed to what little we know about Benjamin's early years in Bury, are to be found in the records of the Independent Chapel.[36] There had been an Independent or Congregationalist meeting in Bury since the Civil War. Its size and zeal fluctuated a good deal over the next century and a half. Like the Anglican church, after the upheavals of the seventeenth century, many Dissenting chapels passed through a long quiet phase in the eighteenth. The Independent Chapel in Whiting Street was no exception. Then quite suddenly the respectable congregation of businessmen and shopkeepers, tranquillised by seventy years of spiritual lassitude, was reawakened by the exertions of a stirring Evangelical Yorkshireman, the Reverend Charles Dewhirst, who was appointed to the chapel in 1800. The revival quickly manifested itself in bricks and mortar. No sooner had a new gallery been completed to provide additional seating, than the chapel was entirely rebuilt in 1802. Not satisfied with reinvigorating the spiritual life of his Bury congregation, setting up thriving Sunday schools for children and adults alike, and a sick man's friendly society, Dewhirst spread his message to the neighbouring villages.

Benjamin Greene, whose father and grandfather had both been Independents, was immediately drawn into the infectious activities of the Bury meeting when he came to the town around 1800. As in all Dissenting congregations the financial aspects of chapel life—so important since ministers and chapels were entirely supported by subscriptions—were handled by a small caucus of wealthier members. It meant in practice that these chapels were often far from egalitarian in organisation, although they were frequently radical in political outlook. Moreover their members had a close knowledge of each other's financial worth, which is one reason why so many important business partnerships during the Industrial Revolution were forged in chapel meetings. In Bury Charles Dewhirst's work was founded on the financial support of five local businessmen: Simon Cumberland, a member of an old and wealthy Bury family that had liberally supported the chapel for over a century; George Paul, an ironmonger; William Buck and Abraham Maling, who were yarnmakers and John Corsbie, who was related to both Cumberland and Buck. It is possible that Buck and Maling, through their trade and religion, were already known to Greene when he came to Bury. Certainly this small coterie of well-to-do men welcomed him with open arms and launched him into the business and religious life of the town.

As we have seen, Benjamin Greene first made a quarterly subscription to the chapel in the spring of 1802, paying two guineas a year to provide himself and his servant with seating. Clearly chapel life was very important to him, for within twelve months he married Abraham Maling's third daughter, Mary, who was a Sunday School teacher at Whiting Street. Benjamin felt at home in the Maling family for, like his own, it was a large and pious one. Although the Malings were relative newcomers to Bury, Abraham was a deacon and a principal financial pillar of the Independent chapel, and a member of the town's business elite. He earned his living, somewhat precariously as the Suffolk textile industry contracted, as a yarnmaker in Long Brackland, later, after a brief period in London in 1810, moving to Westgate Street.[37] He and his wife had known great sorrow, since no fewer than seven of their children had died in infancy. And Mary caused them equal grief. For within a year of her marriage, whilst Benjamin was away in Oundle recuperating from his own illness, his young wife, who had still not attained her majority, died of a rapid consumption.[38]

1804 was an appalling year for Benjamin Greene. But the strength of his friendship within the Whiting Street congregation was such that there was no question of his leaving Bury.[39] Fortunately the following year was a much more auspicious one for the young widower. For two central events in Benjamin Greene's life took place in the year of Trafalgar. He remarried and he agreed to form a new partnership with William Buck. On 5 October 1805 he wedded Catherine Smith. She was the 21-year-old daughter of the late Reverend Thomas Smith, who had been minister for many years of the Howard congregational chapel in Bedford.[40] This chapel had seceded from the Bunyan meeting where Benjamin Greene's grandfather had worshipped over half a century previously. But this link was less consoling than the fact that Smith had been a celebrated and prosperous preacher. For years he had been the closest confidant of John Howard, the prison reformer, who, like another influential friend, the brewer Samuel Whitbread, lived at nearby Cardington. His wife Elizabeth was the daughter and heiress of Zachariah Carleton, a London banker. Catherine Smith herself was accomplished besides being prosperous and well connected. Their marriage placed Benjamin Greene close to the centre of the English dissenting elite. Moreover she brought him great conjugal happiness. Even by Greene standards of fertility she did well, for over the next 22 years she bore him 13 children, of whom all but three survived infancy.

About the time of his second marriage Benjamin, possibly with part of his wife's marriage portion, made an agreement with

William Buck to take over Wright's old Westgate brewery. The connection was a more propitious one for Greene than his first venture into brewing with John Clark. Unfortunately the partnership deeds do not survive although a good deal is known about William Buck (1747–1819). He had been a yarnmaker in Westgate for many years, although he originated from Rotherham in Yorkshire. His connections there and in Bury were impeccable.[41] Through his wife he was related to the Cumberlands, who were eminent yarnmakers in early Georgian Bury, and William found his way into this trade when he married the grand-daughter of Simon Cumberland. But by 1800, as we have seen, worsted yarn spinning was fast contracting in the town. In 1803–4 William Buck converted his own combing shop and warehouse into a tenement of six houses. Thereafter he was looking for alternative ways of utilising his capital and supporting his four sons. He was prominent in establishing the Suffolk and General Insurance Office after 1803.

Buck—himself of Anglican descent—had warmly embraced the Independent faith when he married into the Cumberland–Corsbie clan and the chapel records show his increasing involvement in its life after the 1790s. In December 1792 he chaired the meeting of Protestant Dissenters in Suffolk which declared its 'attachment to the Constitution'. Therefore it is not surprising that when Benjamin Greene first came to Bury in 1800, he should have formed a close connection with so prominent a chapel member as William Buck. For years Buck, who lived in comfortable style opposite the end of Guildhall Street (now 24 Westgate), surveyed Wright's empty brewery as he walked down Westgate.[42] Then after a long period of discussion with Benjamin Greene, they together decided in late 1805 to reopen it. William Buck brought into the partnership a lifetime's experience in business, a sound reputation and standing in Bury itself; Benjamin Greene contributed youth, enthusiasm, and above all a brewer's training, acquired in one of the most up-to-date breweries of the day. Both men were closely tied by their religious convictions and practical Christianity.

Moreover the Buck–Greene partnership was intellectually more exciting than either the chapel or business connection at first sight suggests. William Buck's elder daughter Catherine was vivacious and talented. Henry Crabb Robinson's *Diary* and *Reminiscences* recall how, in the early 1790s, she and her friend Sarah Jane Maling, who later became Benjamin Greene's sister-in-law, enthusiastically discussed with him and Capel Loft, a Whig landowner in Suffolk, the impact of the French Revolution and Godwin's *Political Justice*. In 1795 she married the great slavery reformer, Thomas Clarkson. For a brief period they farmed in the Lake District, where Catherine became the lifelong friend of the Wordsworths and Samuel Taylor Coleridge.[43] When they returned to Bury in 1805—they lived in St Mary's Square within sight of Catherine's father's Westgate brewery—they entertained a constant stream of visitors eager to discuss the evils of slavery and the need for its reform. No doubt their talk enlivened the provincial tedium of the closely-knit Buck, Maling and Greene families who lived down the road in Westgate although, as will be seen in Chapter 2, Benjamin accepted few of the Clarksons' high-minded views.

5

Since few business records survive before the Greene King amalgamation in 1887 little is known about Buck and Greene's brewery. Two sources are moderately helpful, the *Bury and Norwich Post* and the evidence Benjamin Greene gave before a Parliamentary enquiry into the use of molasses in breweries in 1831. The former provides from its advertisements occasional glimpses of the brewery's trade. Public houses as far distant as Newmarket and Barton Mills were supplied with porter, ale and old beer. Direct ownership of public houses was apparently very limited. Payne's 1833 survey reveals that the only public house the firm owned in Bury was *The Dog* tap house in Angel Lane. Certainly Greene's attempt to convert his own house into a tavern had been unsuccessful. Early in 1806 he and his young wife moved into the Wrights' house in Crown Street. Although it was now surrounded by the appendages of a country brewery, it was famous in the annals of the town (see plate 2) for it was here that the last Abbot of Bury had resided, after eviction from his palatial quarters in the Abbey. By the early nineteenth century it was, not surprisingly, in poor shape and in 1819 Benjamin moved, with his large young family, into the fine new house, no. 6 Westgate, which the architect William Wilkins had just built next to his new Theatre. Benjamin, never slow to take an opportunity, converted Abbot Reeve's house into the *Theatre Tavern*. There was always criticism that the Theatre was not sufficiently central in the town, and the tavern, with two competitors in Crown Street alone, clearly was going to have difficulty in attracting large custom. Greene had three tenants in 18 months, applied for a rate reduction, and then finally abandoned the project in 1822.[44] Subsequently he let the old house to a succession of clergymen who were seemingly not averse to the sights, sounds and smells of a busy brewery in their backyard.

In the surrounding countryside Buck and Greene's ownership of public houses was slightly more extensive, but it was on a scale that would have provided any brewer with only a modest living. In fact they supplied many more public houses than they owned, besides possessing a large private trade. It was customary in the early nineteenth century for brewers to lease public houses from their owners—often petty, rural investors in property like farmers, builders and widows—and sub-let them to tenants. Probably the majority of Buck and Greene's 'tying' arrangements were of this sort. In 1831 Benjamin Greene reckoned he brewed 5,000 barrels of beer and 2,000 of 'small' and table beer each year.[45] The average Suffolk inn sold little more than two barrels a week around this time, and discounting the small beer, which was largely sold to private families, it suggests that even after 25 years in business the Westgate brewery supplied no more than 45 public houses with their beer. Whatever the local reputation of its beer it was not much larger than the average country brewery in Eastern England, and a good deal smaller than the bigger regional breweries in Colchester, Norwich and Yarmouth which could ship their beer to London.

Westgate, in the first quarter of the nineteenth century, was almost entirely residential, except between Bridewell Lane and Sparhawk Street. At this point the neatly spaced, capacious Georgian houses were broken by the Westgate brewery and Maulkin's maltings (see pp. 98–100), the largest in the town. The original site of the brewery—a constant problem throughout —was confined. It ran along Westgate from Crown Street to Bridewell Lane, occupying a piece of ground a mere three-eighths of an acre in extent into which Abbot Reeve's house, a malt office, brewery, beer house, stable, outbuildings, counting-house and yards were crowded. Opposite the brewery house on the other side of Crown Street, behind Maulkin's maltings, Benjamin Greene owned a small piece of ground, always used as a garden for the brewery house. A study of the rate books in this period shows the Westgate brewery to have been no larger than its two Bury competitors, Stutter and Gallant of Guildhall Street and the Southgate brewery of Henry Braddock.[46] The rateable value in 1821 of the brewing office was fixed at £10, £15 on the malting, and £4 10s. on a two acre paddock Benjamin rented in Westgate for the brewery horses. In fact the rate books suggest that Stutter and Gallant's brewery was rather larger, rated at £37 for their brewery, maltings and a tenement, whilst Henry Braddock's was estimated at £42 10s., although this included his fine house in Southgate. There is some evidence that Buck and Greene were maltsters on a scale beyond that necessary for their own brewing operations. In 1813–14 they extended the maltings in the brewery yard and rented one, and sometimes two, additional maltings in the town. Although it is unwise to press comparisons too closely when using rate books for this period, it is instructive to reflect that the *Angel Hotel* was rated at £65, the Assembly Rooms and Theatre each almost as highly, and the houses of the Bury gentry from £30–£40 apiece. Nevertheless although rates show some rough estimate of property values, they tell us nothing about profits derived from different establishments. Yet the recollection of Edward Greene in 1875, that the brewery of his childhood was a small affair, is accurate.

From the outset it is clear that Benjamin Greene played the dominant role in the partnership of Buck and Greene. William Buck was close on 60 when the partnership was formed. And he, in search of eternal riches, turned increasingly to religion, not business.[47] In 1810 he succeeded Abraham Maling as chapel deacon and undertook his pastor's proselytising work with a ready zeal before his death in 1819. Nor were his sons more active in the brewery. John the eldest (1775–1839)—five years the senior of Benjamin Greene—was a stockjobber in London. His three younger brothers all farmed in the Bury neighbourhood: Samuel (1778–1852) at Hawstead Hall; William (1785–1838) at

Fornham All Saints; and Robert (1787–1860) at Nowton Hall Farm. They were solid gentlemen-farmers and all bachelors. The independence of their means and status allowed Benjamin Greene to obtain sole control of the brewery soon after their father's death.

Although the evidence suggests no great expansion in the first thirty years of the brewery's history these were momentous times for all brewers. Buck and Greene, on the surface pursuing their activities so quietly in Bury, were inevitably caught up in the changes that enveloped the industry. Novel price trends, the use of substitutes and adulterants in brewing and the 'freeing' of the trade in beer were the most important of these.

The French Wars were one of the great inflationary periods in British history. Brewing materials did not escape the sharp advance that all foodstuff prices experienced. The price of the fairly typical Hertfordshire pale malts that had averaged 36s. 8d. in the 1780s and 43s. 4d. in the 1790s, advanced to 70s. in the 1800s and 83s. 2d. in the 1810s. And the price of hops, always highly variable in the days before effective fungicides and insecticides controlled diseases, showed even greater increases. Although they did not display the same strong upward movement as malt prices, disastrous seasons like 1799 and 1800 saw brewers paying three times more than in normal years. Similar increases were witnessed in 1816 and 1817. But difficulties did not stop here. Both the duties paid on malt and beer were caught up in the general escalation of taxes that paid for the war effort. In 1802–4 both were increased sharply: beer duties by 25 per cent, the malt tax by over 300 per cent.

In the short run brewers found it difficult to advance their prices to meet these steep increases because they had kept prices stable for decades in the eighteenth century. Clearly tradition had to be upset and the consumer experienced sharp advances in beer prices especially in the years 1802–4 when duties increased. The price of a quart pot of ale was raised from 4d. to 6d. and kept close to this upper level throughout the rest of the war years. Brewers said that their profits were modest. Most, although their estimates were vague since accounting practices were in their infancy, reckoned they were fortunate to return between 7 and 10 per cent, after they had made an allowance for interest charges on their capital.

Critics were sceptical. They believed that the brewers—especially between 1804 and 1810—had made large profits because they had not reduced prices when those of their raw materials eased. This was much less true after 1809 when the price of malt rose again and hop prices were generally high between 1813 and 1818. Consumption was certainly checked, but this was hardly surprising in the years of falling money wages and uncertain employment prospects after 1813. Yet duties on beer and malt were not relaxed since government debt charges remained long after the wars were over. Problems were particularly acute in the depressed rural areas of the South and East.

In these difficult years after 1810, when profit margins were sharply squeezed, the production of beer was brought into greater public disrepute than had ever been known before as brewers and publicans alike experimented with a whole range of cheap substitutes.[48] The evidence relates chiefly to London although malpractices were common throughout the country.[49] The big London brewers maintained that their hands were clean, and it was generally accepted that the worst excesses of adulteration occurred amongst the smaller brewers and landlords of tied houses. They seem to have had a wide battery of adulterants at their command. Many had long been in use by publicans of dubious reputation, although not all were inherently harmful. This was especially true of the use of molasses (the skimmings and waste of cane sugar) which, in years of very high barley prices, were a partial substitute for malt. But in normal years their use was prohibited by an Act of Queen Anne's reign. The landed interest especially was opposed to the introduction of molasses since they had no desire to see barley prices undermined by a foreign substitute. The other common practice, although not deleterious to health, was certainly disreputable and difficult to detect by the excisemen. This was the practice by brewers and publicans of mixing strong and table beer (which paid a much lower duty) and retailing the mixture as strong beer.

The rest of the malpractices were again supposedly ubiquitous amongst small brewers and publicans alike. Certainly the evidence of excisemen and the many fines levied suggest that they were widespread. Some, like the use of vitriol and copperas, were used to bring beer into condition more quickly; others, like liquorice, quassia and wormwood, were added to impart the flavour of hops; coculus indicus and opium supposedly increased the strength of beer. The use of additives—isinglass only was permissible in law—was especially prevalent in porter where they often escaped detection through its high colour, properly achieved by the use of roasted brown malt. But even in the production of beer and lighter ales—both after 1800 achieving greater popularity vis-à-vis the heavy stout-like porters—additives were used. Excisemen were increasingly anxious about large numbers of travelling chemists who pushed them to country brewers. The laws prohibiting the use of adulterants and the means of enforcing them were inadequate in this period of minimum consumer protection and amateur chemical analysis. Nevertheless offenders sometimes went beyond the limits of a tolerant law. One small brewer thought it simpler to leave the country rather than face charges of adding coculus indicus, vitriol and guinea pepper to his beer. And Professor Andrew Ure, the well-known political economist and chemist, and far too serious to tell a tall Glaswegian story, recalled that the amount of opium added to the beer sold in one Clyde paddle steamer was so excessive that he could have carried out a 'post mortem' on its victims without their realising what was happening.

Adulteration was at its height between 1812 and 1818. The problem was aired widely in the House of Commons in 1818 and 1819, but in the next decade it was the general fall in prices that most affected brewers. Although they reduced beer prices after 1820 they were unable to do so sufficiently to stimulate a rise in consumer demand whilst the duty on beer remained at war time levels (although the malt tax was almost halved after 1822). The long post-war recession, particularly acute in non-industrial areas such as Suffolk which were badly affected by falls in cereal prices, found brewers examining two solutions—the use of permissible substitutes and the repeal of the duties on beer and malt. In both these issues Benjamin Greene involved himself with a vigour that was untypical of the average country brewer. Events show him employing a strange mixture of ability and imperceptiveness.

He was particularly involved in discussions about the use of molasses in brewing. His interest is easily explicable. Around 1825 he had acquired a large sugar estate in St Kitts and he subsequently worked others which he leased (see Chapter 2). In 1831, as a witness before the House of Commons Committee on the Use of Molasses in Breweries and Distilleries he admitted, three-quarters of the way through his evidence, that he owned property in the West Indies. Like other proprietors he was deeply concerned about the sharp decline in the price of sugar and molasses after 1825 and was looking for more extensive market openings as well as a reduction in duties. For although molasses were used extensively in gin distillation, and as a cheap sweetener in Lancashire, their use in brewing was prohibited and it was this great industry that Greene wanted to open up. He became their most prominent advocate. He wrong long, carefully argued letters to the press. He waited on Ministers and Members of Parliament. And as a practical brewer he was heeded. In fact his evidence before the 1831 Committee was unimpressive.[50] Whilst he could show from experiments he had conducted in the Westgate brewery, that molasses provided a cheap substitute for malt in producing saccharine matter, he revealed that it was possible to do so only in small quantities, especially in warmer weather, before the quality of the beer deteriorated. In brewing its chief use was as a colourant in the production of porter, which was largely monopolised by the eleven great London breweries.

Although its uses were clearly limited, Greene's proposals were like red rags to landed interest bulls, for the equivalent prices of malt and molasses (both paying substantial duties) were in 1831, 66s. and 47s. Even the use of small quantities would aid the brewer and consumer, but agriculturists were totally opposed to any substitute that might lower the price of malting barley. And although Greene conceded that no molasses should be introduced in brewing until barley was 34s. a quarter, his pleas about the plight of West Indian proprietors fell on deaf ears. No action was taken on the findings of the 1831 Committee. In Bury, the centre of some of the best barley growing country in England, his proposals were coldly dismissed. They cannot have made him a popular man amongst neighbouring landowners and farmers.

In the debate about the Beer Act of 1830 Benjamin Greene's role was less prominent. The Act, which effectively freed the beer trade, provides a strange episode in pre-1832 politics.[51] Its passage aroused the passions of numerous political and economic interests, especially in a county like Suffolk. And its application was a central feature in the brewing world between 1830 and 1870.

The debate about 'free trade' in beer had two major strands. One was the mechanism of licensing public houses, the other the profitability of brewing and farming ventures. Since the 1550s the licensing of inns, taverns and alehouses had been controlled by magistrates, informally at first, and then in annual brewster sessions after 1729. In certain periods their administration was very lax and in none ungenerous, but what Reformers after 1815 disliked was the capricious way in which the magistrates arbitrarily exercised their powers to create and withhold licences. Any two magistrates granting a licence conferred a substantial additional value on the newly-licensed property. In the provinces this might be little more than £100; in the metropolis it was nearer £1,000. To most Whigs the system was one more instance of the corruption that was ubiquitous in central and local government alike.

The other point from which pressure was exerted for change was the depressed state of brewing and agriculture after 1815. Already we have seen that the beer and malt taxes were continued at high levels long after the French Wars were over, and, although raw material prices fell, brewers were unable to lower prices sufficiently to sustain consumption.[52] The double duties, adding, it was maintained, as much as 170 per cent to the materials used in brewing, fell particularly on the poor, whereas the well-to-do, who owned their own brewing utensils, were able to evade the beer duties. The situation was exacerbated in 1825 when duties on spirits were reduced—supposedly to abate illicit trading—whereupon spirit sales increased sharply in the next five years, and gin shops flourished. The ruling classes were shocked by the excesses of spirit drinking amongst the working classes and were anxious to revive beer drinking, universally held to be more wholesome, more British, and more beneficial to the economy. In late 1829 and early 1830 there were numerous county meetings to petition Parliament about the depressed state of agriculture. The Suffolk meeting considered 'the unparalleled distress of all classes dependent on Agriculture'. Foremost amongst suggestions for relief were the unrestricted sale of beer, and remission of the beer and malt duties.[53] The Wellington government, anxious to court political popularity, hastily convened a committee which, although it presented the case for the brewers and licensed victuallers, glossed over all differences, concentrated largely on the London trade, and recommended—as had been anticipated from the outset—the freeing of the beer trade.

The Beer Act was passed in July 1830, after a series of lively, if somewhat uninformed, debates. All historians subsequently have been puzzled, not by the government's ready acquiescence in removing the beer duty (that on malt was retained), but by its decision, arrived at so nonchalantly, to free the trade. The answer seems to lie in the fact that contemporaries believed that if the price of beer was to be reduced substantially—the real aim in 1830—then this could only be achieved by free competition. The brewers, controlling so many of the retail outlets through the tying of public houses, were not to be trusted. The government was concerned with prices and the stimulation of agricultural production. With these aims in view it declined to anticipate the social consequences of the Beer Act.

The act created a fourth type of public house, the beer house. Inns, public houses or taverns, alehouses (i.e. possessing no spirit licence) still came within the surveillance of the magistrates, but any householder who paid rates might apply for a two guinea excise licence to sell beer on his premises. The number of establishments in this fourth category—immediately represented as the most squalid of drinking outlets—grew rapidly. Within six months no fewer than 24,342 new beer sellers had paid the excise fee, a number that rose to 33,515 in 1832 and to 45,917 in 1838. In 1830 almost all licensed victuallers and some brewers were horrified at the prospect of free trade. Calculations were made about the reduction in values of existing inns and public houses, although most large brewers accepted change as the price of the removal of beer duty. They insisted that they could produce a better and cheaper beer in any market situation.

Benjamin Greene was one of this group. His letter to the Chancellor of the Exchequer on the subject began in fine style,

I had the honour of corresponding with my Lord Goderich ... and I have recently been in communication with the Duke of Wellington and pressed upon his Grace's consideration the advantages which the poor, the agriculturists and the brewers would derive from a repeal of the duty on beer, and a remission of those restrictions to which its sale has been subjected.

He admitted the present licensing system created a monopoly but argued that successive Parliaments had allowed its creation and that brewers felt 'themselves entitled to a recompense for the injury they would sustain' by its removal. Their compensation must be the repeal of the duty on beer.[54] Two months later an editorial, in the newspaper Benjamin had recently acquired, argued that repeal of the duty would remove the inclination to adulterate and would inject a healthy competition. And he rounded his case out with a plea—especially applicable in rural Suffolk —that it was

> questionable policy to deprive the mass of poor, honest labourers of almost the only article of luxury that comes within their reach for the sake of preserving the questionable morality of a few sots.[55]

It was influential letters like this that informed thinking behind the controversial Beer Act.

The results of the Act for a brewer such as Greene were mixed. Of course beer sales increased—Benjamin Greene admitted his advanced by 50 per cent the following year—but brewers had to be prepared to write down the valuations placed on public houses they owned and wholeheartedly exploit new opportunities. Certainly Benjamin was quick off the mark. His newspaper informed its readers:

> Mr. Greene, the Brewer of this Town, intends lowering the price of the best old beer and stout porter 21s. per barrel on the 11th October at which period better and stronger beer and porter will be sold at 3d. per quart than is now sold for sixpence, and excellent table beer at a half-penny per quart.[56]

But in Bury St Edmunds, already amply supplied with public houses, many of which were free, there seems to have been only a handful of new beer houses, chiefly in the working-class Long Brackland area. In neighbouring villages beer shops were numerous. In 1840 there were no fewer than 577 in Suffolk, compared with 700 fully licensed houses. The former were brewing over 15 per cent of the county's total beer production in the 1840s and early 1850s (see Appendix 2, Table 1). In Suffolk, as elsewhere in the South and East, they were thought to be a root cause of rural unrest in the 1830s and 1840s. They never lost their seedy reputation in the eyes of the gentry and clergy. In 1861, Wortham, a straggling village in North Suffolk, was served by four public houses and a solitary beer house. Only the latter called forth the Rector's strictures. It was, he wrote, 'one of those low public houses where people meet on the Roadside and sit at the Gate.'[57]

Undoubtedly the retailing of beer experienced a great shake-up in the early 1830s with new outlets and a price war. Many breweries and public houses changed hands. Benjamin Greene and his son Edward, who took over the brewery in 1836, completely reviewed their policy of public house ownership. Yet around 1840, at least in Suffolk, the brewing trade settled down again as agricultural prosperity slowly returned.

<h2 style="text-align:center">6</h2>

By the 1830s Benjamin, the Midlands Dissenter, had made a name for himself in Suffolk. It was almost in spite of his brewery. Tucked away in landlocked, slowly expanding Bury it remained small in comparison with regional leaders in the industry. Only the railways, the decline of home brewing and a much greater agricultural prosperity could invigorate its affairs. Yet Benjamin, who was exceptionally ambitious and capable, pushed his way forward. He was undoubtedly aided by a good second marriage and William Buck's friendship. It was Buck also who saw that he was included in the Grand Jury lists for the Liberty of Bury each year. At its meetings he met the leading men in West Suffolk. And as we shall see in the next chapter he had obtained property in the West Indies in the 1820s. This gave him further assurance, since he then became a prominent spokesman on brewing and West Indian affairs. The government had recognised this by appointing him to two of its committees of enquiry.[58] In politics and religion his views shifted a good deal. As the hold of Dissent, once such a prop to his existence, weakened, his inherent conservatism took on a new intensity. The realisation grew that the real prizes in life were not to be won in the Whiting Street chapel. With these various forces shifting, his position in Bury and the trade became controversial. And like most moderately successful brewers, he had never viewed brewing as the only feature of his activities. Yet whereas others usually took to hunting and agricultural and military matters, Benjamin began to inhabit the much more unusual world of provincial newspaper proprietorship and West Indian affairs.

2

The Greenes'
West Indian Venture

In 1836 Benjamin Greene, well into his middle age, retired from all active involvement in his small brewery to begin a second career as a merchant in London. The break was less dramatic than it appears. But it hides an unusually interesting story of the political and economic involvement of a country brewer in the 1820s and 1830s and demonstrates the key role of chance in everyone's affairs. Any account of the Greene family fortunes in the nineteenth century would be hopelessly incomplete without a description of their commercial ventures in London, the West Indies and Mauritius. For the brewery, left under the sole control of Benjamin's third son Edward when he came of age in 1836, held a relatively minor part in the family's business strategy until his successful management of it became evident in the 1860s. This summary of Benjamin's subsequent career in London—he died in 1860—and the brief accounts of those of his five sons provide a fascinating example of the steep upward social mobility of a pushing Victorian middle-class family. With the stress on wealth and status, and a brief view of the acute psychological strains such a family could generate within itself, it is *The Forsyte Saga* in reality.

I

From 1805 to 1819 Benjamin Greene apparently led the simple life of a pious country brewer with a large young family. What is certain is that Benjamin's ambitions, circumscribed by the Tory Anglican elite in Bury on the one hand, were in no way satisfied by the management of the brewery itself on the other. Even William Buck's death in 1819 gave them no fillip since Benjamin had long run the brewery's affairs. But in that same year he found a new outlet for his abilities. It would be wrong to pretend that, hemmed in by the lack of opportunities of his small brewery, he made some great entrepreneurial leap into the dark. The reality, as so often, was more homespun. For he acquired a stake in the West Indies almost by accident.

Ever since 1806 when he had moved into the Westgate brewery house, his neighbours across the yard in Crown Street had been Sir Patrick and Lady Blake. Confined as the baronet was by the brewery on one side and the *Dog and Partridge* on the other it was not a contiguity likely to lead to lasting friendship. The Blakes were West Indian nabobs of Irish descent with extensive properties in St Kitts and Montserrat.[1] When Sir Patrick Blake's father became M.P. for Sudbury in 1768 and married the daughter of Sir William Bunbury he bought the Langham Hall estate some nine miles north of Bury. The second baronet, Benjamin Greene's neighbour, married the heiress of another St Kitts sugar planter, James Phipps. By the close of the Napoleonic Wars the Blakes, who had made a great stir in late eighteenth-century Suffolk society, were in financial difficulties. Langham Hall was let from 1805. Nevertheless their household, although reduced in size, was a source of wonderment to the young Dissenting couple and their children. And since the Blakes had no children themselves they made a great fuss of Benjamin's young family. There were endless stories to tell of Sir Patrick's visits to St Kitts in the 1780s and 1790s, pictures and maps of the estates to pore over. He played them tunes on his old violin nicknamed 'the Jew'. And the tales were colourful for, even by West Indian standards, Sir Patrick's sojourn had been extravagant. On no other plantation were entertainments more prodigal and Sir Patrick, a one-time officer in the 10th Dragoons, had, to the wonderment of his neighbours, drilled his slaves in the military routines of the day.

Above all the Blakes enjoyed Benjamin Greene's lively conversation, and eventually his advice was sought about Sir Patrick's troubled business affairs. As was common amongst the Georgian

33

gentry, both the Suffolk and West Indian estates were entailed and Sir Patrick and his legal heir (his brother James) were tenants for life. And, as with other landowners, debts were inherited and fresh ones added to them. Especially was this true in the Blakes' case, for the traditional extravagance of the West Indian grandees was not curtailed overnight. Most serious of all was that income from the Suffolk rentals declined after 1813 and profits from St Kitts sugar contracted sharply after 1814. By 1817 the position was serious. When Sir Patrick had married in 1792 the estates already carried two mortgages of £17,500 and these were still undischarged twenty-five years later. And in the intervening years further charges were made against the estates. On Sir Patrick's death affairs would be further exacerbated because his widow was entitled to an annuity of £1,500 and his brother could then charge the estates with a similar amount for his wife and £15,000 for the benefit of his seven younger children. Beyond letting Langham Hall few sensible economies were made. Sir Patrick's generosity was proverbial. No effort was made to manage the West Indian properties more efficiently or any steps taken to introduce his younger brother, who lived in Sussex, into the management of either the Suffolk or the St Kitts properties. Instead in 1817 he made Benjamin Greene a trustee of the 1792 marriage settlement. Of the other trustees, the original one was advanced in years—in fact he died early in 1819—and the other, most unusually, was an aged spinster. Clearly when Sir Patrick himself died in July 1818 Benjamin already held a key position in his affairs. This ascendancy is further revealed in the will of Sir Patrick and in that of Lady Blake, who died in 1823.[2]

As a life tenant Sir Patrick had no direction in the disposition of the Blake estates, but he left some £18,000 including extraordinarily generous bequests to his servants and £910 to Benjamin Greene and his eldest son.[3] Five years later his widow died and although she left little property in England to dispose of she gave Benjamin, after even more generous benefactions to her housekeeper and lady's maid with a life interest for two aged spinsters, a half share of her money and West Indian properties. His portion was an estate at Nicola Town, St Kitts and a smaller property on Montserrat. By 1826 he was—albeit on a fairly small scale—a West Indian proprietor. This acquisition by devise was entirely fortuitous: Benjamin had struck up a warm friendship with his grand neighbours; Lady Blake had no close blood relatives.

But his West Indian interest was not limited to the ownership of these properties alone. For he also became the manager of the Blakes' other estates both in St Kitts and in Suffolk. The financial clouds fast gathering towards the end of Sir Patrick's life finally broke when his affairs were wound up. Not only were there the family debts and charges discussed above—running at £4,170 a year alone on interest charges and annuities for Lady Blake, the servants and a former mistress—but Sir Patrick owed considerable sums to the assignees of James Wildman, the merchant and St Kitts proprietor who had consigned the Blakes' sugar and lent them substantial sums against it. What was worse was that Sir James Blake had to meet the claims of his brother's executors, including Benjamin Greene, and that he himself 'was otherwise indebted to a considerable amount'. With the consent of his son a settlement was patched up to raise a further £21,800 on mortgage.[4] Sir James agreed to write down the claims of his own family and together they consigned the estates to three trustees to effect these transactions. The trustees were two landowning relatives of the Blakes—John Gage of Roegate in Sussex and Henry Adeane of Babraham in Cambridgeshire—and Benjamin Greene, acting as Sir Patrick Blake's executor. Since neither Gage nor Adeane took a close role in affairs and since Sir James continued to live in Sussex, the active management of the Blake estates was left in the 1820s to the man on the spot, Benjamin Greene. After 1821 he was empowered to keep the accounts of all their properties.[5] He was therefore the manager of over 2,000 acres in Suffolk, three good estates on St Kitts—Sandy Point and the adjoining Penels and Diamond Point in Basseterre parish —and one on Montserrat. Quite suddenly the horizons of the modest country brewer were dramatically extended. He had become a gentleman of consequence in Suffolk and a West Indian proprietor.

Beyond the piecing together of the legal records of these transactions which pushed Benjamin into prominence, few further papers have survived for the 1820s and 1830s. The firm with which he and his eldest son were associated lost all their records in an air raid in 1941, and the family papers of this senior branch of the family have not survived. Therefore the first view we have of his new prosperity comes in 1828 when he acquired a newspaper in Bury St Edmunds. For the next eight years he was extremely active as a supporter of the West Indian interest in the discussion about the abolition of slavery, and as a Tory reformer. Politically it was a far cry from his Dissenting position of twenty years earlier and shows how far his views had swung since 1817. In fact Benjamin never held any of his opinions quietly for there was a disputatious streak in his make-up. Family tradition remembers him at the end of his life standing before the fireplace of his house at 45 Russell Square pronouncing on every subject and reciting long passages from Shakespeare. With active opinions on trade and industry, especially on beer, sugar and agriculture, it was not entirely surprising that he acquired the *Bury and Suffolk Herald* in 1828.

2

Like many provincial newspapers the *Bury and Suffolk Herald* boasted no past and held out little promise for the future. It had been in existence for only fifteen months when Benjamin Greene acquired its ownership in June 1828.[6] From its inception it had been ultra-Tory in its views: anti-Reform, anti-Canning, above all anti-Catholic Emancipation. It exactly suited the requirements of the new proprietor. During the next few months he launched his views with a rare zest. The paper gained a reputation for the liveliness of its political stance and its excellent coverage of local news. There was no great editorial consistency, for it followed no slavish party line and dealt too much in personalities to achieve any detached impartiality. Indeed it was involved in no fewer than three court actions in 1833–4, such was Benjamin Greene's predilection for polemics and personalities. So acrimonious was one suit against the rival *Bury Post* that he lost all credibility and it was in no small measure responsible for his decision to leave Bury and the brewery in 1836. Up to 1834, however, his controversial proprietorship and the views he propounded on the free trade in beer (see pp. 26–9), reform in Bury, and above all the slavery question brought him a reputation in East Anglia as a Tory propagandist of ability.

The amazing thing about the whole episode of Benjamin

Greene's proprietorship of the *Herald* was the extraordinary position of his own stance. Here was a Dissenter, albeit by the late 1820s in name only, opposing religious toleration, preaching free trade in beer, upholding slavery in the West Indies, wavering on the question of political reform. It was a unique tightrope that he fashioned and walked. The peculiar inconsistencies of his politics were at once evident. The Duke of Wellington's ministry could neither be trusted nor forgiven for allowing Catholic Emancipation. But the paper's hard face of reaction to religious toleration was softened in Bury by its view of the Corporation. Benjamin had long held opinions about its venality and Anglican exclusiveness. Not surprisingly, therefore, tucked away in the minute print of the *Herald* were to be found disparaging references to the Corporation. The members were represented, not very consistently, as 'dictators', 'dummies', mere pawns of Lord Bristol and the Duke of Grafton.[7] The pigs at the Corporation trough fed well off the spoils. The *Herald* preached these themes until 1831.

Meanwhile it shifted its position on national reform. One of the principal props of Benjamin's argument about 'free' trade in beer was that it would benefit the labouring classes. Given their poverty in West Suffolk it was a natural conclusion, but in the autumn of 1830 when the 'Swing' riots ravaged southern England and there were real fears of a rural rising, the *Herald* continued its pleas for conciliatory measures in dealing with the appalling plight of farm labourers. The Wellington ministry was attacked for its inept handling of agricultural affairs and its complete inability to pursue cohesive social policies. Holding these old-fashioned, paternalistic views of the rural world, the *Herald* was forced to shift its position about reform when it reviewed the bleak aspect of national affairs in late 1830 and the record of Wellington's ministry. It began to advocate moderate reform 'approached with great care'.[8] In the election of 1831 Benjamin was prominent in organising—he was not a member of the Corporation and therefore possessed no vote in Bury—the candidature of Philip Bennet, Junior against the Bristol–Grafton interest. But Bennet's taste for reform was as recherché as the *Herald*'s and he was not elected. Nevertheless the mere fact of his contesting an election was hailed in Bury as an unparalleled stance for independence.[9] No sooner had the *Herald* swallowed the pill of national reform than it rejected the dose it had approved for the Corporation. Personalities were entirely responsible for this strange volte-face.

When the Blakes' house in Crown Street was at length sold in 1829 the purchaser was a Suffolk barrister, Francis King Eagle. He prided himself on his oratory and passion for reform. Within two years he had transformed politics in Bury. The old order of patronage and interest, of the Bristols, Graftons and Oakeses threatened to collapse in 1831–2. Benjamin Greene, living across the brewery yard from King Eagle, noted all his actions with increasing distaste.[10] There was no immediate alarm when King Eagle instigated an enquiry into the monetary affairs of the Guildhall Feoffment but Benjamin was incensed when he attacked the monopoly of the Bury coal merchants. Like most country brewers the Greenes were involved in this business themselves. Benjamin did not have to wait long for his opportunity to respond. In the election of December 1832 King Eagle stood for Bury in the Reform, anti-Bristol-and-Grafton interests. The abuse that the *Herald* unloaded on him was extreme, even by early nineteenth-century standards. He was represented as owning insufficient property to meet the qualifications for election, as being so impossibly disputatious that he was at law with his own brother, and that 'he was not admitted to the table of any respectable individual in the county'.[11] 'In firmness and integrity of purpose, in fortune and in everything he was "a beggar!"' Hundreds of placards and squibs about King Eagle were distributed from the *Herald* office and although he had the vehicle for a reply in his own newspaper, the *Bury and Suffolk Press* (which appeared briefly from March 1832 to June 1833), it was clear that in all this furore the proprietors of the *Herald* had sailed too close to the winds of libel. Somewhat belatedly, in February 1834 King Eagle brought an action before the Lord Chief Justice (Denman) in the Court of King's Bench against Frost, the *Herald*'s printer. The hearing of the case in London seemed very unnecessary but he was awarded 20s. damages and costs. In the heat of the political kitchen, Benjamin Greene, concentrating on personalities, quite forgot his old anti-Corporation ingredients. When King Eagle threatened to petition against the election of 1832 in which he was defeated, Benjamin embraced the Bristol cause ecstatically. He spoke at Lord Jermyn's election dinner, supported the Corporation against King Eagle's attacks, and attempted a total whitewash when the Whig Corporation commissioners carried out their investigations in Bury in November 1833.[12]

Benjamin's involvement in the politics of Bury reform was overshadowed by the notoriety of his stand against the emancipation of slaves. In the 1820s, although he never visited the properties he owned and managed in St Kitts, he became, at second hand, increasingly knowledgeable about the intricacies of West Indian affairs. And when after 1823 there was a resurgence of interest in the abolition of slavery itself, and the formation in many towns, including Bury, of local anti-slavery societies, Benjamin could not restrain himself from entering the heated debates.[13] He read Clarkson, the *Anti-Slavery Reporter*, the Parliamentary evidence, the outpourings of the missionaries who had returned from the Caribbean, and dismissed them all. He found, as he always stated, the traffic in slaves abhorrent, but the institution itself—and here he quoted Biblical precedents—was necessary. Conditions had, he argued from the fastness of his Bury study, greatly improved after 1815 with the passing of the Colonial Acts. Amelioration was the answer to the abolitionists.

He began to propound these views in a series of letters to the *Herald* in February 1828.[14] The first set the tone of the rest. Slavery was 'neither productive of misery, nor repugnant to the duties of religion'. In paragraphs that are forerunners of Richard Oastler's celebrated comparisons of the exploited Yorkshire factory workers with West Indian slaves, he pointed to the lot of agricultural labourers, chimney sweeps, and milliners' assistants in England. There, conditions of life and labour were worse. 'I may safely and confidently repeat my assertion', he wrote in the 17 March number, *'that the persons of the Negroes are protected by the most equitable laws*, and moreover without fear of confutation, that they are better clothed, better housed, and better fed, than the English agricultural labourer.'[15] The correspondence, anonymous, acerbic and able, continued until late April. Benjamin clearly enjoyed it and it was presumably a principal factor in his acquisition of the *Herald* in June 1828. Early in May he took up some comments Thomas Clarkson had made at an anti-slavery meeting in Ipswich and there began a second, and much longer, series of letters which continued throughout the summer of 1828.[16] Although Clarkson was now out of the mainstream of the anti-slavery movement and had always wielded a laborious pen, Benjamin treated him initially with great deference as a member 'from whose family [i.e. the Bucks] I have experienced continual acts of kindness and attention'. The correspondence, in letters often of 3,000 words and more, was a highly technical discussion of the working of the Colonial Acts, the reality of the slaves' sabbath, and whether they had sufficient time to cultivate their grounds for food. At the back of Benjamin's mind were fears about the continuation of the French and Spanish slave trades and whether the British islands could meet foreign competition if slavery were abolished. But Clarkson, sticking rigidly to his authorities, found his adversary difficult to tie down and, when in the *Herald* of 9 July, he accused Benjamin of seriously misquoting a letter of James Stephen, the correspondence took on a decidedly sharp note. Benjamin had the edge on the arguments. The extract from *John Bull* that the *Herald* so gleefully quoted—

> Mr. Greene manages his facts and arguments so well, and so easily to put down the veteran abolitionist that it is only necessary to read his letters to see the fallacy, absurdity and shuffling trickery of the ancient proser's mode of handling the question

—should not be taken too seriously.[17] Nevertheless Clarkson harked back all too often to evidence of the pre-1807 period and would admit of no improvement in the slave's position. In August 1829 the *Herald* published the letters, with a preface by Benjamin, in the form of a moderate-sized book.

Then for 18 months the topic slipped almost out of view in the *Herald*. There were interesting letters: one from Benjamin's daughter, another from his eldest son who went out to manage the West Indian properties in 1829. Both gave first-hand evidence of amelioration.[18] The latter's showed that eighteen months' residence in St Kitts had done nothing to diminish the firm imprint of his father's opinions. He concluded a long letter with the remark that

distress was unknown here amongst the lower orders
... their situation is extremely comfortable and could not be
bettered without raising them in the scale of society far above
the condition of the labourers.

Conservative views for a young man who had just reached his
majority.

But this lull in activity was a prelude to the stormiest period in
Benjamin's ventures into newspaper proprietorship and politics.
In November 1830, at the height of the agricultural labourers'
unrest in England, there was an attempt to reinvigorate the ailing
Anti-Slavery Society in Bury by a public meeting. Notices
appeared throughout the town that the meeting would be
attended by several speakers from the parent society in London.
Meanwhile Benjamin was warming himself for the fray. In October he had published a pamphlet, 'British Colonial Slavery compared with that of Pagan Antiquity'. This had led to a heated
correspondence in the *Herald* and a long editorial on 10 November explaining how the reform of slavery must be evolutionary.
But the prospect of the Anti-Slavery Society missionaries regaling
the Bury meeting with their tales of horror drove the proprietor of
the *Herald* to new excesses. He found 'it ... marvellous that the
good people who are busying themselves about this matter, do not
turn their bowels of compassion to their own countrymen,
and ... attempt to rescue from starvation and crime the suffering
thousands who surround them.'[19] In November 1830 this was
fair comment. His animadversions on the speakers at the forthcoming meeting, however, were not. With one exception they
were branded as 'rabble-rousers'; Joseph Phillips, who had spent
a period in gaol for his zeal and, Benjamin hinted, financial
embezzlement had a character 'which stands as low as any in the
community'. Worse was to follow. Two days before the meeting
he issued a further anonymous pamphlet attacking the reputations of the speakers. The libel about Phillips was repeated and
embroidered; (Sir) George Stephen held 'a lucrative situation in
the Share Registry Office'; the Revd J. Orton was branded by
'prospective damnation'. Readers should look at the next issue of
Fraser's Magazine to find serious charges laid against him. With
advance publicity of this nature the meeting at the Guildhall was

sold out. It lasted five hours and though there were graphic, rousing speeches on the conditions of the West Indian slaves, the effect of the pamphlet hung over its entire proceedings. The chairman denounced it as 'low trash', but the most dramatic moment came when the Revd Cornelius Elven asked the 'anonymous slanderer' to step forward. Benjamin had been summoned to his mother's funeral in Oundle. Rarely can family duty have called at a more opportune time. So Mr Elven had to be content with the measured revelation of the pamphlet's author, 'Is he *brewing* fresh mischief? . . . I understand that every retailer of beer is obliged to put his name over the door in letters three inches in length; and O that the authors of such pamphlets as this were obliged to offer their names to their slanders in letters as large and legible.'[20]

The meeting was the liveliest Bury had known for years. Thousands of readers throughout East Anglia perused the long, and very different, accounts in the next issues of the *Post* and *Herald*. Benjamin's reputation was blighted and his newspaper steered clear of the slavery subject until February 1833. Then there was a second major meeting in Bury as emancipation drew nearer. Elven, speaking again, maintained that Benjamin stood 'convicted of deliberate falsehood' in the matter of Orton and the *Fraser's Magazine* reference. For the attack had not appeared in the next number and when it did three months later had carried none of the damning material hinted at. It was a curious affair, for when in 1830 Orton had called on Benjamin for an explanation, he had accepted his account and the two had subsequently corresponded and lent each other books. Now in 1833 Benjamin, equally litigious and fiery as his adversary King Eagle, went round to the printer of the *Bury Post*, which carried a full account of the February meeting, to demand a public retraction of the phrase 'convicted of deliberate falsehood'. It was not forthcoming, so the following year Benjamin brought a highly technical libel action before a special jury against Johnson Gedge the printer.[21] It was so recondite and yet had such important implications for newspaper printers that it was subsequently referred to a Commons Committee. At the hearing Benjamin was awarded a farthing's damages and had to pay his own costs. But the summing up of the defence counsel and the judge was so damning about the plaintiff, who had blatantly libelled Orton but was not guilty of the 'deliberate falsehood' charge, that he lost any residue of public esteem he had held since the infamous publication of his second pamphlet in November 1830. The *Post* received many sympathetic letters enclosing guineas to meet Gedge's defence costs. In the eyes of all, Benjamin stood convicted of gross humbug. The judgment was the end of his incursions into the swirling waters of reform politics and slavery. This interlude in his life had been brief, notorious and, especially for a brewer, most unconventional. Reconstructing the story 150 years later from the files of old newspapers leaves no doubt about the strength of his convictions and his ability to wield an effective, if venomous, pen. His judgment is quite another matter. Now in 1836 with his family almost grown up—his eldest son in St Kitts, his second established as a solicitor in Bury, and the third, just of age and already running the brewery—he left the town at the age of 56 to begin the second phase of his career, as a respectable London merchant. It brings us back to his West Indian ventures.

3

By 1836 Benjamin was a planter in St Kitts on a considerable scale.[22] In addition to the Nicola Town estate acquired by devise from Lady Blake and the management of the Blake estates at Sandy Point he bought the Cranstoun and Belle Tete properties in the same parish and Spooners in Nicola Town so that the half dozen properties could be conveniently run together. And in 1829 he began a long connection, through his management of their estate which was contiguous to his Nicola Town properties, with the Molineuxs. Like the Blakes, they were old members of the island's absentee aristocracy. They also had settled on the Norfolk–Suffolk border, living colourfully beyond their means, with a string of illegitimate offspring and dabbling in county politics. Their acquaintance—they had long had connections in Bury through Francis Sandys (the architect of Ickworth)—further fed Benjamin's mind about the riches of the planters' lives.

In fact well before Benjamin ever acquired an acre of plantation on the West Indies the legendary wealth of its planters was being undermined. In St Kitts, one of the most fertile of all the West Indian islands, the peak of prosperity had already been reached fifty years earlier and although high prices for sugar ruled during the 1790s, the decline in profitability brought about by excessive monoculture, the abolition of the slave trade and eventually slavery, the growth of sugar production in Brazil, Cuba and Mauritius, and by the planters' own absenteeism, was not in the long run halted.[23] Benjamin Greene entered the world of West Indian planters when its sun was well past its zenith. Indeed this is why he acquired additional estates cheaply. But being a newcomer in the mid-1820s he possessed none of the seasoned planters' gloom and retained the memories with which Sir Patrick Blake had regaled him about the island's golden age. Any streaks of romanticism in his make-up were, however, overlaid by those of extraordinary ambition and business acumen. Already middle-aged and with a large and still young family it was out of the question for him to undertake the re-invigoration of the estates he owned and managed in St Kitts. Instead in 1829 he sent out his eldest son, Benjamin Buck Greene, who had just come of age. Very much in the mould of his father—intelligent, conservative, extremely hard-working and possessed of a diamond edge in business transactions, he was an ideal choice. He needed to be, for West Indian affairs had never been at a more critical juncture. Not only were the planters' interests thoroughly shaken by the imminent threat of abolition, but sugar prices, partly through Brazilian and Cuban competition, partly through the downward drift of all prices after 1815, collapsed in the later 1820s. In 1815 they had stood at 62s. 4d. per cwt in London; in 1831 they averaged 23s. 10d. The planters and merchants poured forth evidence of 'severe distress' before the 1831 Commons Select Committee.[24]

Nevertheless the two Greenes believed that by careful attention to costs they could transform the extravagant mode of production on their own plantations.[25] This was especially necessary in the period of transition between slavery and freedom known as apprenticeship (1834–8), and in its immediate aftermath when labour problems and costs were unknown quantities. But their reforms did not stop at slimming down costs of production.[26] They also intended to transform methods of cultivation and processes by the introduction of new farming methods and machinery. There had long been periodic experiments with ploughing (instead of the traditional 'holing' method) and using horses instead of oxen. Benjamin Buck Greene instigated a new round of these in the 1830s. There is an ecstatic account of a ploughing match on his Nicola Town estates in 1835 in the *Bury Post*.[27] Not only were horses matched against oxen, but also negroes against two Suffolk ploughmen. Benjamin had dispatched eight labourers and their families from the Duke of Grafton's Suffolk estates and there were plans to send out six more families in the spring of 1836 'as examples of skill and industry to the negroes and as protectors of their master's property in case of disorder'. He had also shipped two Durham shorthorn bulls and two Leicester rams to improve the island's stock and his son was experimenting with buffalo crosses. 'We are happy', wrote the *St Christopher's Gazette* from which the *Bury Post* report was taken, 'to see the enterprising spirit of this patriotic gentleman at this momentous period, coming forward, sparing neither time, trouble, nor expense in devising means and advancing improvements for the future prosperity of this country.' Even Edwin Pickwoad, a failed planter and sworn enemy of Benjamin Buck Greene, conceded that 'he had established in this island the greatest reputation as a planter'. The Greenes were also introducing horse-drawn weeding machines and above all steam engines to power the cane crushing mills. In 1833 there was only one in the island. In the following year Benjamin Buck Greene installed two on his father's estates and by 1837 when he left he had erected nine on the various properties under their management. Innovating so boldly to cut labour costs by mechanisation, believed to be essential in the post-abolition period, his fame spread amongst the planters and attorneys on the island's seventy or so estates. Briefly, in the mid-1830s, he was managing 16 to 18 properties on the island which, together, produced a third of the island's sugar exports for two years.

In the period of reasonably buoyant prices between 1831 and 1846 the Greenes did well. Profits were not on the old pre-1800 scale, but then neither was the price of West Indian property. Benjamin Buck Greene produced figures before the Sugar and Coffee Committee in 1848 to show that net profits on the Nicola Town and Cranstoun estates produced almost £3,000 per annum between 1838 and 1846 on average for his father in London. And in the late 1830s when prices peaked around 40s. a cwt, they had been considerably higher. Then (1838–40) five estates they owned and leased produced £10,277 per annum. On top of this there were commissions from the management of other estates and brokerage and shipping profits in London. William Greene wrote in 1853, 'my father whose original occupation was that of a brewer, but who for many years past had launched into and carried on an increasing trade with the West Indies with great enterprise and judgement, removed to London for the purpose of more conveniently managing his affairs which had now settled into considerable importance'. That had been in 1836; in the following year he and his eldest son had established themselves as West Indian merchants in Mincing Lane, already crowded with the offices of sugar brokers. By the 1840s the 'Court' sections of the London directories list him as 'Benjamin Greene Esq of 45 Russell Square and Bury St. Edmunds'. Family tradition remembers him going each day to Mincing Lane in his coach emblazoned, like his silver, with the armorials of the Greenes of Green's Norton. Benjamin had arrived in the ranks of the Victorian plutocracy.

Since the business papers of the firm of B. and B. B. Greene have not survived it is impossible to reconstruct the capital employed in their West Indian ventures. Even with the reduced values of the 1830s and 1840s it must have been considerable. The four estates Benjamin owned by the mid-1830s ran to 683 acres of cane land and 598 of pasture and waste land.[28] Around 1840 they were worth together as much as £65,000–£70,000. Moreover their shipping ventures were considerable for at the same time as they began the mechanisation of cultivation and production on their estates they bought several ships to carry their produce from St Kitts. By 1844 the Greenes had five sizeable barques registered with Lloyds: two on the St Kitts run, three to Jamaica.[29] Shipping costs were always highly contentious between planter and merchant and the surviving evidence from both the Sugar and Coffee Committee and H. B. Blake's journal below shows that dissatisfaction with the Greenes' high charges on both passages was no exception. Any estate once it had debts with its London brokers and shipper was at their mercy in the matter of transport charges.

Yet however much the Greenes might believe their plantation could be transformed by the Victorian virtues of thrift and application, St Kitts was not to be tamed by them or by their steam engines and loyal Suffolk labourers. That society had roots running deep into a sore and troubled past. Two fascinating and fragmentary accounts survive which show their failure and take the history of the Greenes and their West Indian ventures a stage forward. One is the strange, expurgated passages of the auto-biography of William Greene (1824–81), Benjamin's youngest son, written in 1853;[30] the other the brief diary of the Revd Henry Blake (1820–73), which was scribbled down during his brief sojourn in St Kitts in 1845–6.

When Benjamin Buck returned in 1837 his place in St Kitts was taken by Benjamin's precocious fourth son Charles (1821–40). Edward Greene (1815–91) the third son, who ran Westgate Brewery alone after 1836, used to tell the story regularly when he became M.P. for Bury, with that mixture of patriotism and pomposity which was the lifeblood of Victorian provincial poli-tics, that his father offered him the job but that he turned it down on the grounds that 'old England was good enough for him'. Charles Greene's career was meteoric. Like all his brothers he attended Bury School. There under Dr Malkin he had received an excellent education, for the headmaster was liberal, encouraging boys in resourcefulness and independence—a fruitful area for venturers to the West Indies.[31] Charles was merely sixteen when he landed at Basseterre. Nevertheless he was immediately given the supervision of the family properties together with the manage-ment of three or four others. He lived at Nicola Town where 'for many years the estate had been under first class manage-ment . . . and its improvement was in advance of all others in the Island'. His eldest brother, too hardheaded to succumb to fraternal piety, reckoned him 'a very able manager'.[32] But Charles possessed 'a very affectionate nature' and although he carried out his father's instructions from London well enough he began to burn the candle at both ends. William, the fifth son and then only 15, came out to the island in 1839 after a year in his father's counting house. He helped Charles in the running of the estates, but his brother's other activities were largely kept from him. 'The land of fun and fever' took its toll on Charles as it had done on many a planter before him. When he died in August 1840, not quite 19 years old, after four days of yellow fever, the 'fun' account was also rendered. He left 13 illegitimate children. Today even though most of his descendants 'sank back into the anonymous mass of negro labour' some survive, with the unmistakable Greene gait and propensity for large families, and have achieved modest prosperity.[33] William wrote on his brother's death, 'My brother, whose shrewdness and maturity of judgement and consistency of conduct was marvellous, died . . . having filled the most responsible post that was ever entrusted to one so youthful. The genuine piety and retired virtues that formed the groundwork of his character had ripened him for the inheritance of a better world.' How much he told his father when he returned to England that autumn is unknown. Presumably with this view of affairs much could have gone unreported. William, however, was allowed to return to St Kitts in 1843 after 18 months with 'a well established and highly esteemed Commercial house of sugar importers'. By nature deeply introspective he was quite unsuited to trade and the demands his father made upon him. He began his autobiographical sketch with the imperishable words 'To whom it may concern, I first commenced my career of mortal strife and unknown destiny in the year of our Lord 1824 in the well known market-town of Bury St. Edmunds.' And much of his recollection was in similar vein. Yet he had found that first spell in St Kitts, 'the most cheerful, careless and happy period of my life'. He begged his father to be allowed to return. He was permitted no more authority than acting as attorney and manager of one modest estate for three years, a far cry from the responsibility thrust upon Benjamin Buck and Charles a few years earlier.

It is Henry Bunbury Blake's brief journal which shows the extent to which the management of the Greene estates declined after Charles's death in 1840. William Greene found them in poorer shape three years later, attributing this in part to drought. There was also a shortage of coal for the engines and most of the white labourers had fallen victims to the temptations of drink. Moreover the Blakes in Suffolk had heard rumours about the deterioration of their properties in 1843–4. Sir Henry Blake, now firmly in charge of his family's affairs, sent out his elder son the Revd Henry Blake (1820–73) to see things at first hand. The account is prejudiced, because like all absentee owners the Blakes believed that the Greenes, the managers of their estates and consignees of their sugar, charged excessively high commission rates and looked after the interests of their own affairs first. No doubt there was something in the catalogue of Henry Blake's suspicions, but he soon realised that the gross mismanagement of their estates—shameful at least in the eyes of a 25-year-old Suffolk clergyman—was due to the weakness of their attorney and the lack of application of their manager. The latter's morals, revealed chapter and verse in an anonymous letter, shocked Blake. But what brought home his mismanagement most was the fact that he was charging the estate with the keep of four fine horses which he and the attorney raced on Greene's Cranstoun estate. There the attorney had cleared several acres of cane for a race track. The manager was dismissed and Blake, like many a deluded planter before him, believed that a few months' exertion would settle the estates on a new course. The diary shows that even in well-run estates like the Greenes' things could deteriorate very quickly under the attorney system as soon as the owner returned to the metropolis. In fact Benjamin Buck Greene tried to prove otherwise.

With a large measure of absenteeism the plantation system of sugar production had always relied for its success on good management. For many reasons it was usually sadly lacking. Appearances could be deceptive: observers believed the estates the Greenes managed were still among the best run in St Kitts. Certainly this is the impression Benjamin Buck Greene conveyed in 1848 when he gave evidence before the Commons Committee once more looking at the plight of the colonial sugar interests. Greene spoke for the planters who were totally opposed to the Sugar Duties Act of 1846 which—in accordance with Free Trade policies—removed the preference on British colonial sugar during the following six years.[34] He engaged himself, very much in his father's tradition, in a lively controversy, which lights up the dull volumes of evidence, to show that the estates of the absentee proprietors of St Kitts were better managed than those of the diminished ranks of the island's resident planters. His approach was direct and polemical, although his proposition was also backed by an impressive range of figures and accounts. Much of the Committee's Report to the Commons consisted of comments on Greene's evidence. His opponent, Edwin Pickwoad, was 'unworthy of credence'; Benjamin Buck, however, was 'one of the best informed and most skilful planters examined by your Committee'. Powerful evidence like Greene's—driving home the consequences of the 1846 Act and the results of the commercial panic of 1847 on colonial interests—split the Committee, although in spite of the chairman's casting vote for a temporary continuation of colonial preference the free traders in the Commons insisted that it would be eliminated by 1854.

In fact this argument in 1848 was somewhat academic to the Greenes because they had already begun to pull out of St Kitts. There were several reasons. First, sugar prices declined sharply after 1843 and the effects of the Sugar Duties Act 1846 and the financial crisis of 1847 thoroughly depressed the West Indian sugar interests. Prospects of profitability were at an all time low in the late 1840s. Even innovators like the Greenes, who had believed that they could make the plantation system work in the post-abolition period, realised that with a further spell of low prices they were incapable of introducing technological improvements in the processes of manufacture, for recent inventions like steam-heated clarifiers, vacuum pans and centrifugal driers were quite beyond the resources of the estates on the smaller islands. They were forced to continue producing semi-refined muscovado sugar for the British refiners. Second, Benjamin Buck Greene entered a new partnership in 1846. On his return from St Kitts in 1837 he had married Isabella Blyth, the daughter of a wealthy Limehouse ship's chandler.[35] Her brothers James and Henry had in 1830 become shipping agents in Mauritius, acquired a large sugar plantation there in 1836 and, by the time of Benjamin's marriage, controlled most of the island's trade. They owned eight sizeable ships on the England–Mauritius–India run and had capital and credits of 'about £180,000 or £200,000 exclusive of shipping and other property' in 1845.[36] Benjamin, who had been involved with the Blyths in joint ventures to the West Indies for at least two years previously, brought considerable capital into the new partnership of Blyth and Greene, which from the outset was one of London's principal colonial merchant and shipping houses.[37] The firm decided, not surprisingly, to concentrate largely upon its Mauritius and Indian connections and run down the Greenes' less profitable St Kitts affairs. In 1845 they owned and leased fourteen estates; three years later there were only eight.

Soon after 1846 Benjamin, then aged sixty-six, withdrew from active business. He still retained the ownership of the Cranstoun and Nicola Town plantations, although Blyth and Greene assumed their active management. His retirement coincided with a further decline in profitability. In 1848 he was arguing about the size of rebate on the Molineux estate rental, telling the Molineux –Montgomeries in Norfolk that he had been offered properties at a peppercorn rental and that his losses on their estate equalled the rent he had paid them in the last two years. He forced them after 1846 to accept rebates of at least half the £700 rental agreed in the 1839 lease, and when the lease was renewed in 1857 the figure of £300, the sum actually paid for many years past, was finally agreed. In fact profits were improving. The three Nicola Town estates returned an average £1,080 per annum for 1854–7, double the level of the years 1848–54. Nevertheless in 1857 father and son stressed very forcibly that working expenses had 'enormously increased since the abolition of the Apprenticeship' and when the protection of British colonial sugar was withdrawn in 1854 it had 'reduced very considerably the profits of all Estates and brought very many to utter ruin'.[38]

When Benjamin died in 1860 he left his West Indian property to be divided equally amongst his very numerous grandchildren.[39] By the early 1890s there were over fifty beneficiaries sharing out a dwindling income. Overall control devolved upon the new *paterfamilias* of the Greene clan, Benjamin Buck, who delegated most of the routine arrangements to his firm, Blyth, Greene and Jourdain. Curiously, given his earlier vigour in their improvement, he seems to have cared little about their fate. His younger brother William had a far greater attachment to them. But his involvement was highly emotional and his father realised that he could never be entrusted with their administration, for unlike his elder brothers he made no progress in the wholly material world they inhabited. They viewed his failure to climb the greasy pole to success and financial independence with increasing unease.

William failed all the tests his family set him. He had failed in the West Indies in the early 1840s, failed in Blyth and Greene when he returned, failed as a farmer in Essex, failed as a Conservative party agent, failed as a country solicitor in the Fens. Only in his marriage was he successful. And then in terms of the Greenes' ambition he married beneath him. They, particularly the brewing branches, must have blanched if they read the lines Charlotte Smith's sister sent to the bride on the day that she married William:

> All hail the happy morning
> Let Joy and loudness reign
> Fair Temperance adorning
> Thy auspicious bridal train.
> There will be no drunken carols
> Upon thy Wedding Day
> It needs no brewers barrels
> To make thy Nuptials gay.[40]

In fact Charlotte Greene, the daughter of a Lincolnshire coastal shipping master, possessed abundant commonsense and provided a haven of calm for their nine children. William Greene was devoted to books and philosophy, although since his basic education was shaky he made inefficient use of either. Mrs Edward Greene, his daughter-in-law, recalled him, 'a nervous, highly strung man with no real occupation . . . being fond of walking he spent whole days wandering about the countryside with a volume of Plutarch or Bacon's *Essays* in his pocket, resting and reading from time to time in the shade of trees or hedges'. As his brothers pointed out, he could enjoy his books only because his father provided him with an income of around £750 a year (managed by his three brothers) which kept him and his family in genteel poverty. In the 1870s, when all attempts to establish him in a job had failed, they were living, like many a middle-class family, in Bedford for the convenience and cheapness of its celebrated schools. When this palled, his grandson Graham Greene wrote,

> The only occupation he followed for any length of time was based on a place he called on his letter-heads 'Bleak House, the Plains of Desolation' . . .
> He had become the only active (though none of his activities was very active) director of a peat company—his young partner committed suicide. He would disappear suddenly from Bedford, the large house and the large garden and the large family,

leaving no money behind, and the next they would hear of him
was from the overseer's hut, the only human habitation among
the black bogs . . . He took no genuine part in the enterprise,
but he would take long walks with a book in his pocket, and
then return at night to the unfinished tramway-line, the half-
built hydraulic plant, the rough food, the uneducated conversation in the lamplight and the narrow camp bed. He wasn't made
for the family life in Bedford . . .[41]

In 1881, unhinged further by the death of a friend, he went once
more to St Kitts. There he wandered over the island, lost in the
scenes and events of his youth. He soon contracted a 'low fever',
plunged himself one morning into a cold bath in the yard, and
emerged according to a laconic eye witness with an 'altered
appearance'. He died later that day. He was buried next to his
brother Charles. The family sent out two Portland stone slabs and
paid the Nicola Town clergyman £25 to see that the graves were
kept tidy. Benjamin Greene's boundless West Indian hopes of the
1820s had been very firmly blindfolded.

In fact, the agents of this bondage were economic as well as
personal. The Greenes' plantations had returned modest dividends for the beneficiaries of Benjamin's will in the 1860s and
1870s: from 1861–8 they averaged £3,025, from 1871–7,
£4,225 per annum. These reflected a rapidly increasing sugar
consumption in Britain and until 1874 customs dues had favoured
muscovado sugar. Costs were contained and the results of the
mid-1870s highly satisfactory but after 1874 there was complete
free trade in sugar and the threat of continental beet sugar,
encouraged by bounties, materialised very quickly.[42] By 1882
beet sugar inroads into the British market spelt real distress for the
West Indies. And now with free trade and lower prices for the
consumer than ever before the West Indies interest found no
support. Prices fell dramatically in 1884: from 20s. to 13s. per
cwt. The Greene plantations, like many others, folded under this
pressure. No dividend was declared in five years out of six
between 1883 and 1889. The value of the estates fell from
£37,000 in 1883 to £23,000 in 1890. Cranstoun remained in
reasonable condition, but the lands of the Nicola Town plantation, once the best managed in St Kitts, were in 1890 in 'a

wretchedly starved condition', the 'buildings much decayed' and the livestock 'very poor'. Many of the Greenes hardly cared, but the effects for the widow and children of William Greene were the stuff of those Victorian novels in which the family's reversal of fortune was sudden and catastrophic. William's family moved from the roomy Bedford house to a confined affair in Hampstead: his widow's allowance, doled out by Benjamin Buck and Edward Greene, declined from £60 a month to £16 5s. between 1881 and 1890.[43] Her family saw the irony, for her son noted that Edward left £350,000 in 1891 and Benjamin Buck £470,000 in 1902 —enormous fortunes by Victorian standards.

The latter was less than half hearted about the fate of the St Kitts plantations in the 1880s and 1890s. He poured cold water on the plans of those members of the family who wanted to form a limited company in the 1880s to run the estates, and in the 1890s he brushed aside all schemes for their rescue in his haste to dispose of them. The prices they realised showed the total collapse of small West Indian properties. Nicola Town was sold to the Molineux–Montgomeries for £7,000 in 1893; Cranstoun was virtually given away in 1897 for £3,500 after a decision had been taken to abandon it if necessary. Those heady days of the 1820s and 1830s when Benjamin Greene had believed that they could transform the old slave plantation system by steam engines, immigrant white labour, agricultural improvements and the drive of their own management were long forgotten. Benjamin Buck, always the financial realist, apparently never cast them a thought. The Greenes had been caught, yet more English victims claimed by the West Indies.

4

With the exception of William's family the Greenes had long since ceased to depend on income from St Kitts. In the brief concluding section of this chapter a sketch of the other interests of Benjamin Buck Greene, his brother John's career, and a passing reference to Edward's extremely successful management of the brewery (see Chapter 3), outlines the family's extraordinary success in the second half of the nineteenth century. The motivation and whole ethos of its triumph reveals the core of Victorian entrepreneurship and the social advancement of its industrial and commercial leaders. In this atmosphere the wilting of tender plants such as William Greene is less surprising.

It would be easy to ignore the career of John Greene (1810–67) altogether. On the surface it was most conventional: country lawyer, Justice of the Peace, Mayor of Bury in 1841 and 1852, governor and secretary of many institutions in Bury and West Suffolk. But for the advancement of the Greene family it had more significance. In public John Greene did things well. At Bury School, where he was captain, he outshone his brothers; when he led the Tory revival in Bury and became the first post-Reform Conservative mayor he was magnanimous enough not to turn out all the Whig office holders; he married well;[44] his firm of solicitors flourished. And he attended not only to material affairs: he lectured on Magna Carta and Bury Abbey; he read his New Testament daily in Greek; he gave poetry readings. He seems not to have read his own in public, although the friend who wrote a fiercely loyal obituary suggests that he should have done so—

> In his youth time, his muse was prolific. Some of his compositions at that period are evidences of great taste, feeling and refinement. There is also a classical humour in some of them which evinces the elasticity of his genius.

In 1865 he was proposed as Conservative candidate for Bury (see p. 85), but his health was so indifferent that he declined in favour of his brother Edward.[45]

Benjamin Buck Greene was the most successful of the Greene brothers. The drive he brought to the management of their St Kitts plantations in the 1830s was transferred to the running of Blyth and Greene after 1846. The firm prospered, for he and his brother-in-law, James Blyth, were amongst London's ablest merchants.[46] The hub of their business was importing sugar from the East and West Indies, India, France, and above all Mauritius. The latter was their initial centre of operations and they were prominent in creating its brief spell of prosperity as a coaling station and important sugar producer between 1835 and the opening of the Suez canal. As well as sugar they handled the imports of coal, fertilisers, textiles and machinery to the island. In the process they became considerable ship owners on the Cape –Mauritius–India run. Over 100 letters survive between the two brothers-in-law in the summer of 1860 although most of the firm's papers were destroyed in the Blitz. In 1860 Benjamin Buck went out to sort out the affairs of Blyth Brothers, the Mauritius subsidiary in which two of the local directors had mishandled the agency for Peruvian guano. The letters are remarkable in a number of ways. They show the great warmth between the correspondents and the powerful network of the Greene, Blyth, Currie clan[47], their will to succeed and their application. When Benjamin Buck descended on the firm's ledgers, his eye for detail drove the two miscreant partners to take to their beds. But the letters reveal more than a ruthless efficiency; they show that he was also judicious and possessed the utmost probity. The instructions he left about sugar purchases, imports, shipping and remittance are models of clarity. The correspondence reveals all that was best in Victorian business ethics, and these qualities were widely recognised in the City. He was a director of the Bank of England for over fifty years after 1850, acting as Governor in 1873–5, and on the Board, eventually vice-chairman, of the Atlas Assurance Company for almost as long.

Contemporaries, as historians have since, recognised Benjamin Buck Greene as one of the ablest Bank directors in the second half of the nineteenth century. Sir Reginald Wilby at the Treasury reckoned him in 1891—when he was almost 83—'the second best man at the Bank'.[48] He had two great triumphs. When he was Governor in 1873, according to Professor L. S. Pressnell, he avoided 'by promptly and determinedly raising [the Bank's] rate' the financial crisis that swept West Europe and America. With Henry Hucks Gibbs he subsequently formulated what Pressnell had called 'the Greene–Gibbs policy' of bankers' balances which argued that 'clearing' balances could virtually be ignored—thus flying in the face of the pre-1914 preoccupation with the weekly Bank returns—when considering the potential claims on the Bank's gold. Secondly he played, at the age of 82, a crucial role in the Baring crisis which rocked the City and Government in November 1890. He, with Bertram Currie of Glyn, Mills, Currie and Co., provided the Governor with a report on Baring's affairs. Greene prepared the key report, 'working pretty late at night without any clerical assistance'. In its recommendations it broke new ground. For it recognised the necessity of a massive rescue operation by the Bank to avert a crash that would have had spectacular repercussions in the City.

In his period as Governor he prepared a book of tables, 'Periodical Fluctuations', (updated in 1890) which showed the seasonal influx and outflow of coins to and from the Bank within Britain. The Court of Directors on his death in 1902, recalled this 'profound study . . . which has been since its inception in 1875, and no doubt will always be, of the greatest use to the Court'.[49] As late as 1894 he prepared a report disarmingly entitled, 'Relieving Directors of Mere Clerical Duties', which in fact improved financial checks on staff after the misdemeanours of the Chief Cashier in 1893. Both on his retirement and his death the Bank's Court of Directors paid unusually warm tributes to his great care for its interests—'even after his retirement . . . almost to the day of his death' and his 'eminently high character' and 'unvarying kindliness and courtesy'. By his death in 1902 he reminded them of old values somewhat out of currency. His old school put it nicely: 'he left behind him a good report as a pattern of what an English merchant should be, and though he left a large fortune, had nothing in common with the modern millionaire.'[50]

But the success did show. In 1856 he bought Midgham House in Berkshire with nearly 1300 acres.[51] He was a model landowner: no money was spared on the improvement of the house, the estate, the church, parsonage and school. He served as High Sheriff of the county in 1865, and as a Justice of the Peace there and in London. Around the same time that he bought Midgham he moved to a grand town house, 25 Kensington Palace Gardens. From here he controlled family affairs. Even before his father's death he played, according to Edward Greene, a crucial role in family councils. Later the whole Greene–Blyth clan were summoned to discuss their prospects. He proffered advice and made loans (at 5 per cent interest) to the great-nephews and great-nieces who needed them for worthy projects. When in 1900 there were three Greene members in the House of Commons he was overjoyed. But most of those that came to Kensington Palace Gardens were overawed both by the house and their distant relative. A delightful account of a visit survives from Eva, the wife of Edward Greene (1866–1938).[52] The young newly married couple had just arrived in England from Brazil. Used to the sun, they were appalled by the near darkness of the house on a bright July day in 1901. They were four at luncheon, waited on in the gloom by the butler and three footmen. The conversation with Benjamin Buck was about Brazilian shares and with Miss Greene, who had had an unsatisfactory affair with an impoverished curate many years previously, 'about Religion and God and my Soul'. In the interlude before tea they were treated to 'carriage exercise' in the Park. Two dalmatians, specially trained, ran between the back wheels of the impressive equipage.

As well as the aura of solemnity and chilliness surrounding the completely successful Victorian man of business, Benjamin Buck possessed a sense of scrupulous fairness. His wealth, which he himself had so laboriously accumulated, was neatly partitioned into great parcels of shares and property for division amongst his five children.[53] No one was forgotten. There were generous bequests for servants and needy relatives and the host of great-nephews and great-nieces and all their children, Blyths as well as Greenes, were left modest sums. The dismemberment of this great inheritance, however, provides a grim footnote on the imperma-nence of wealth and underlines the fact that entrepreneurial talent is not heritable. His eldest son Benjamin (1839–1916), who after a short spell with Blyth and Greene trained as an architect, was given to good works. He underwent religious conversion and zealously preached total temperance for many years in Switzer-land and, much more improbably, Lyons. The second son Fred (1841–1914) followed in his father's footsteps, holding direc-torships with the Atlas Assurance Company, the Standard Bank of South Africa and the Colonial Security Trust Company, but he had none of his father's or grandfather's ability and drive.[54] Only the third son, Henry David (1843–1915), seemed to abide by Greene rules. He was a barrister, Recorder for Ludlow, and Conservative M.P. for Shrewsbury, between 1892 and 1906. He married the heiress of a wealthy banker and Shropshire land-owner and they lived penuriously on great riches.[55] Their children —the only grandchildren of Benjamin Buck Greene—were chro-nic epileptics and both he and his wife failed to make watertight wills, in spite of the fact that he was the Lord Chancellor's Visitor in Lunacy. When the children eventually died they had no rela-tives closer than second cousins and, being themselves incapable of making wills, an estate of almost two million pounds passed to the Treasury. It was a sad conclusion to what had been in the nineteenth century the brightest chapter in the Greenes' book of success.

3

Edward Greene,
1815–91

Edward Greene, Benjamin's third son, was born in 1815. Like all his brothers he was educated at the Bury Grammar School. When a mere thirteen years old he entered the family brewery. Although many years later he claimed that he had twice declined to run the West Indian estates it is clear—since he did not achieve the same academic distinction at school as his two elder brothers—his father's plan was that he should take over the brewery when he came of age. Edward was never to work elsewhere, or live more than half a dozen miles from Bury. Unlike his father, his vision was entirely a Suffolk one. As Benjamin Greene grew older the brewery became a minor, receding satellite of his world. The West Indies, Mauritius, and the great whirl of London commerce drew him eagerly into a larger system. For Edward the brewery always remained at the centre of his existence. Not narrowly so, but its ownership provided the openings in his long life. Hunting, farming, membership of Parliament and the acquisition of a country estate: these were all made possible on a generous scale by his creation of a notable enterprise. After 1865 when he entered the House of Commons he drew the lessons of these experiences into a lively, empirical philosophy that reconciled his thoughts on the expansion of agriculture, the role of the Church, landownership and the labouring classes with the view of the role of business in Victorian England that he had acquired in over thirty years as a bustling country brewer. The result was a highly successful recipe that returned him to Parliament for a quarter of a century. He became the best known, most popular man in West Suffolk. When he died in 1891 it was claimed that there were more prints of Edward Greene than of Queen Victoria in its public houses. And by no means all of them were owned by his brewery. Yet from 1830 to 1865 Edward Greene's world was entirely that of a country brewer.

I

His training was confined to the Westgate brewery. This was somewhat surprising, not only in that brewers usually gained valuable experience through apprenticeship in another brewery before running their own, but also that his father had acquired a first-class training at Whitbreads. Edward shaped up well in these years for he was already managing the brewery in 1834 and on his coming of age two years later,

> his father handed over the brewery stock, plant and everything connected therewith at a given price, every shilling of which the son was able to pay within the period originally fixed.[1]

1836 was an inauspicious year for a young man to acquire a brewery. Eager as Benjamin Greene was to show Bury his heels, he must have possessed great faith in the capabilities of Edward to pull through the recession that had hit East Anglian agriculture. Corn prices again fell to low levels in the mid-1830s and, although this meant low costs for brewers, beer consumption—so dependent in Suffolk upon the prosperity of arable farming—stagnated after its rapid advance in 1830–1. For the 1830s were poor years for agricultural labourers: wages were low; there were high levels of under-employment, especially acute in the winter months; and migration to London and emigration overseas was a regular feature of working-class life in the region. Moreover, as we have seen, the Beer Act of 1830—allowing the creation of 40,000 beer houses within a decade—thoroughly upset the interests of brewers. Those in East Anglia, many of whom had carefully built up their stock of tied houses since the last quarter of the eighteenth century, now faced a situation in which any ratepayer could open a beer house on payment of the two guinea licence fee. Of course the majority of these outlets (see Appendix 2, Table 1) were supplied by commercial brewers, but there is evidence that the region's breweries took a sharp knock in the 1830s. With free trade competition was fierce. Many publicans went bankrupt, and in 1836 and 1837 an unprecedented number of breweries themselves came on to the market: at Harwich, Colchester, Eye, Thetford, Sudbury, Wisbech and Cambridge.[2] Most of these were bigger than Edward Greene's brewery with its annual 3,000–5,000 barrel output—those at Colchester, Wisbech and Cambridge had 40 or more public houses attached. Although the advertisements held out numerous blandishments, ranging from 'a desirable opportunity for embarking a moderate capital with considerable advantages', to the Sudbury brewery, 'in which a splendid fortune of upwards of £100,000 was lately realised', none of them was sold as a going concern. They were split into lots, with brewers and private individuals in search of traditional property investments driving up the prices of the public houses to levels that surprised those closely connected with the industry. Perhaps by 1837 buyers realised that the bottom had been reached in the post-war depression of agriculture and that the rate at which beer house licences were created had slowed down after 1834.

Edward Greene was not among those who acquired these public houses in 1836 and 1837, although many were within a close radius of Bury. In fact quite the reverse occurred, for when he acquired control he put on to the market those few public houses which the Westgate brewery owned. It was a surprising move even in unsettled times. 'All the "tied" houses belonging to the firm were disposed of excepting one which was retained as a memento of the past.' In 1865, when he first stood for Parliament, he transferred his action into a creed:

> I have clung to no monopoly, I am a Free-trader, and was so long before Free-trade was greatly thought of. I hold no public houses, and have not for the last seven years held an agreement for any man to deal with me for beer, even if he occupied my own houses. When I commenced business I nailed my colours to the masthead, feeling, that if by industry I could give the public such an article that they could not do better elsewhere, they would come to me.[3]

These were bold words and very quickly swallowed when he began busily to acquire public houses in the late 1860s.

Now from the scanty records it is impossible to re-create Edward's free trade moves.[4] Certainly in the 1840s and 1850s when 'free' houses were very numerous, and commercial breweries in Suffolk generally small, it was possible to make headway without 'tied' house protection. This was especially true before 1850 when country inns in Suffolk faced tough competition from the new beer houses.

At the outset of his career as a country brewer, therefore, Edward Greene was bereft of the conventional market of tied property which his rivals in the East of England had acquired during the French wars and still retained. It was of little consequence. They had never been a complete umbrella for the small Westgate brewery, since it had always largely relied on sales to free and leasehold houses in the Bury neighbourhood, and now, in the changed climate of the 1830s, his experience of providing fine beers to the free trade stood Edward Greene in good stead. It was exactly the formula by which after 1840 the Burton brewers and Guinness launched their conquest of the mid-Victorian beer market. They did so without the aid of any tied houses. Like them assisted by the railways and the rapidly increasing consumption of beer between 1840 and 1880, Edward's plans for survival and eventual expansion had to be entirely based on the sale of beer to any outlets that could be persuaded of its superiority.

When we turn to examine this challenge in detail the evidence is lacking before the 1870s. It is possible to examine in outline at least the physical growth of the brewery and the means by which Edward Greene increased his sales twentyfold in the forty years after 1836. And fortunately towards the end of his life he talked a great deal about his business philosophy and experiences. It is impossible, however, to provide a detailed view of the growth of the Westgate brewery from a small affair to one of regional importance across this period without letters and account books. First, however, we must briefly consider brewing practices at the beginning of Queen Victoria's reign in order to gauge the technical problems facing Edward Greene and the brewers of his day (see Diagram 1 for a representation of the modern brewing process).

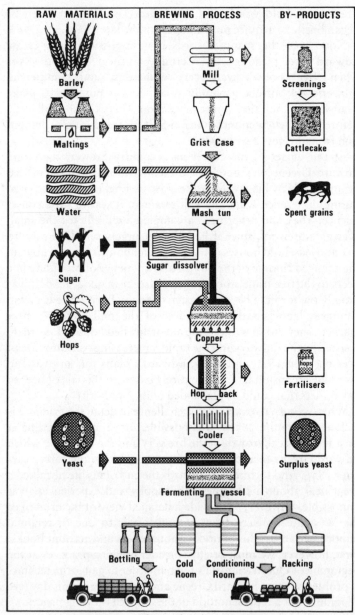

Diagram 1: The modern brewing process

2

Everyone in early nineteenth-century England must have seen beer being made, whether at home, at their employers', in an institution, or commercially in breweries and public houses. Knowledge about the intricacies and problems of brewing was widespread in a society so much closer to the soil than our own, and in which beer drinking was universal. Yet widespread as knowledge was, brewing remained until the 1870s an inexact science. It was a mystery in which secrets were carefully handed down from generation to generation. Scientific understanding of the key processes, especially fermentation, was in its infancy. All brewers relied on their empirical knowledge and a handful of brewing manuals—correct enough in many respects, but riddled with the idiosyncrasies of centuries of folklore—and when things went wrong there were no certain rules to follow. Therefore because the science of brewing was revealed so slowly, the pace of change was more leisurely than in any other major industry (except perhaps coal) in the century and a half before 1870. Had the Wrights reappeared in 1836 they would have found little to set them pondering in Edward Greene's brewery: nothing more than brief puzzlement at the constant use of thermometers and hydro-meters, piped hot and cold water to control temperatures more effectively at all stages, more complex pumps and gearing to move malt, liquor and worts[5] more easily. In fact Edward installed a small Cornish-type steam engine for these tasks in 1836.[6] But basic processes remained unchanged and the scale of brewing, although this was not true in London and the largest industrial cities, grew only slowly in the country before the Railway Age.

Any brewery had to possess a good water supply. This was believed to be important for giving beers their special flavour. It was thought, quite wrongly, that good porter could only be brewed with water from the Thames, although the excellence of Burton ales—in enormous vogue in Victorian England—*was* derived from special salts in the town's water supply. Greene's brewery relied on a 120-feet-deep well in the yard where the water had been filtered through a generous layer of chalk, a geological association always prized by brewers. It allowed Edward to brew a pale bright bitter that imitated the Burton beers.

In best practice breweries, usually those in London which first

65

popularised the 'tower' principle, water (or liquor as it is always known in brewing) and ground malt were pumped and elevated the height of the brewery. Then the liquor, malt and hops fell by gravity as they underwent the various processes that converted them into beer. But few country breweries were custom-built before 1850 and their layout caused adverse comment from the writers of brewing manuals. This was certainly true of the Westgate brewery, which had grown haphazardly over the years on its restricted site.

The liquor was heated in the copper and pumped to the great oak mash tun and there, when cooled to the correct temperature, the ground malt was added and, in Edward Green's time, mashed with power-driven 'flies' that had come into use in the early nineteenth century. Almost simultaneously, certainly by 1835, sparging or top sprinkling was introduced for adding heated liquor at subsequent stages in the key mashing process, in which starch in the malt was converted into fermentable sugars. The malt was sparged two or three times, each at different heats and for different lengths of time, producing worts of varying strengths for the different qualities of beers. These worts were drained into the underbacks before being boiled with hops (which gave the beer its bitter taste and preserving qualities) or in scientific terms the extract achieved biochemical and biological stability. After reduction through boiling in the copper for one to two hours, the wort passed through the hop or 'jack' back where the spent hops were extracted. Then the wort was cooled as quickly as possible in big open coolers before passing to the fermenting vessels or 'working squares' or 'guile tuns' as they were variously known in the 1830s. There brewer's yeast was introduced, assimilating the sugars dissolved from the malt and turning them into alcohol, and after several days' fermentation the beer was skimmed and fined. Since the taste in Suffolk in the mid-nineteenth century was for old strong beers, it was 'cleansed' in pontoons and stored in giant oak vats until in good condition. Some of the strongest ales were stored for a year or more. It was then racked and fined with isinglass. In the case of light ale and table beers, however, they were usually fined at once and put straight into casks after mixing with a proportion of 'old', returned beers.

There were three critical points in the whole process: malting, mashing and fermentation. Here success depended largely on the brewer's knowledge and experience, and each of them prized and fiercely guarded his own secret, inherited skills.[7] Malting was usually considered the easiest area in which to achieve competence. Edward Greene always used malt that the firm made itself in its various maltings. He was fortunate that amongst the best of all English malting barleys were those grown on the light Suffolk soils. Clearly its quality varied from harvest to harvest and the maltster had no control of this beyond careful selection of his samples. But subsequent success depended entirely upon his skill in steeping the barley, encouraging an even, unchecked germination, stopping growth at the correct point and drying the malt according to its type. Since the process took two to three weeks, depending on the barley and temperatures outside, there was ample time for error in the various processes. But all brewers recognised that good beer was not made with poor malt. It was false economy to use anything other than the best malts. The eventual reputation of Edward Greene's bitter beers was founded on his skill as a maltster.

Mashing, and above all fermentation, caused brewers more problems than malting. In these processes the brewer's skill was paramount. The early brewing manuals, which every brewer possessed, were helpful, especially those by Richardson and Black.[8] Yet since both authors were practising brewers—as were almost all writers on the art of brewing—they tended not to disclose the closer secrets of their skills. They were therefore vague about the all-important temperatures and times in mashing, and when it came to describing the critical fermentation process they were unable to do so with precision, not only because they did not understand the scientific basis of its mysteries, but also because they were unable to do so in a concise language that brewers could follow. Nevertheless there were significant advances, especially in mashing. Two simple innovations of the late eighteenth century, the thermometer and hydrometer (for testing the specific gravity of worts and beers), gave the brewer some control over both processes. The thermometer allowed him to mash and ferment at *known* heats. The hydrometer made it possible to ascertain the correct 'length' or quantity of beer of a given strength that could be brewed from a certain quantity and quality of malt. It was useful, especially in fermentation. As one itinerant brewer who visited Bury to instruct publicans and brewers claimed,

> by strictly attending to the use of it, during the progress of attenuation in the gyle, the cleansing point is discovered for beers of all densities, so that the artisan may ensure an uniform transparency in 8 or 10 days.[9]

These were important steps forward in the production of anything like a standard brew. The old folklore about finger testing the heat of mashing liquor, and uncertainty about ascertaining the subsequent strength of beer, except through taste, now slowly disappeared as most brewers tried to overcome the complexities of using the hydrometer at different stages in production. In 1813 John Baverstock believed almost all brewers used both hydrometers and thermometers, although he admitted results still varied according to individual skill and judgment. By then it was certainly considered extravagant to brew without them.[10]

Nevertheless the most vital and difficult part of the whole brewing process, fermentation, was not understood in any scientific way before Pasteur's work in the 1860s and 1870s became generally known. The best brewers could do was pay meticulous attention to cleanliness. Most manuals, and especially William Black's widely used book, first published in 1835, insisted upon this, but it was difficult to achieve with the wooden tubs or 'backs' that were used at all stages in the brewing process. Bacteriological infection, producing unstable worts and worst of all 'foxing' the beer in fermentation, was most frequently introduced in the big open coolers in which the wort rested before passing to the fermenting squares. There it too often imbibed acidity, especially in hot weather, causing bad flavour and loss of keeping qualities. Steam from the coppers invaded other parts of the brewery, condensing on dust-laden beams, and fell into the open backs and squares. One of the most important innovations was for brewers to cover the cooling squares and introduce 'refrigerators' and attemperators—nothing more than piped cold water—to lower temperatures in the cooling and fermenting squares as speedily as possible.[11] The high temperatures at which fermentation took place encouraged bacteriological infection. At temperatures above 75°F (24°C) infection was difficult to restrain, which was the principal reason why brewers before the late nineteenth century only exceptionally brewed between early June and the end of September. Warm weather stimulated 'foxing' and the production of 'wild' yeasts. Then the brewer had to stop production, scour all his equipment, and obtain a fresh yeast strain from another brewery. When temperatures were too low fermentation was difficult to achieve without the constant use of rousers. Unless absolute cleanliness was insisted upon and fermentation was properly controlled a 'sickly' beer was produced which some brewers attempted to cure by the use of various drugs. English brewers, entirely guided by consumer preference, insisted on top fermentation at temperatures between 60° and 75°F. This ensured secondary and tertiary milder fermentations during storage which, with heavy hopping, gave British beers their strength, colour and special character. The continental method of bottom fermentation at much lower temperatures was far safer, but it produced a lighter, 'bright', lager-type beer that found no favour with the beer drinkers of Victorian Britain.

It is somewhat surprising that breweries witnessed only modest technological developments before 1870 because the scale and prosperity of brewing certainly increased after the mid-1830s. There were three main reasons for this improvement in the industry's fortunes. The first was that the removal of beer duties in 1830 and 'Free Trade' lowered prices and increased consumption. The yearly average output of beer in England advanced from 13·6 million standard barrels in 1831–5 to 28·4 million in 1874–8 and *per capita* consumption in the United Kingdom rose from 22·0 gallons to an all time peak of 33·7 gallons over the same period.[12] The second was that the English economy experienced a strong upward trend for thirty years after 1843, growth associated with the maturity of the textile, iron, coal and engineering industries, expansion of exports, and the creation of the railways. Most members of the working class were better off, with rising money wages and hence more to spend on food, drink and leisure. And middle-class values that preached the virtues of abstinence and control in matters of sex, alcohol and violence were not yet entirely pervasive. In the first flush of its modest economic liberation the working class in early Victorian England turned in its celebration to beer. Of course there were regional differences in beer consumption patterns. From the evidence of the drunkenness statistics, rural areas were always more sober than their urban and industrial counterparts, although, since policing was easier in towns, the drunkenness/consumption figures are difficult to reconcile satisfactorily. Nevertheless consumption in Suffolk certainly did not match the national trend, because population in Suffolk, largely due to out-migration, grew so slowly after the 1840s.[13] But as the home production of beer contracted rural brewers quickly captured the market. The third reason was that the coming of the railways meant that the market of country breweries was no longer confined by the inadequacies and high costs of existing road transport. Good beer, like the famous Burton ales and Guinness stout, could travel anywhere. Ambitious brewers were suddenly emancipated—in Edward Greene's case in 1846, when the Bury St Edmunds–Ipswich railway was opened.

3

Already in 1845 Edward Greene had anticipated the coming of the railways by building a new, extensive School maltings in Bridewell Lane and reorganising the brewery itself. At first after 1836 there had been few new developments beyond the installation of a steam engine. Money was tight. He had agreed to repay his father the purchase price of the brewery within nine years. Edward Greene always remembered these as hard years in his struggle for success. Between 1830 and 1842 he recalled that, 'he never, save on one occasion, missed being the first in the morning in the brewery to superintend the commencement of the day's labours.'[14] When he married in 1840, although his young bride was the daughter of a Huntingdonshire parson and magistrate, and socially a cut above the Greenes, he had to settle into Abbot Reeve's decrepit house in the brewery yard (plate 2), whilst his father's fine home, 6 Westgate, was let to a succession of tenants including the essayist, William Bodham Donne. But it would be misleading to suggest that Edward's shortage of funds led him to run the brewery in Benjamin's way, for his livelihood depended totally upon it. He had no prospect of sharing his father's and eldest brother's commercial success in London. Indeed their achievement was a spur to his endeavours. Moreover he was fortunate that economic conditions in Suffolk began to improve slowly after 1837. In the brewery, expansion came in the early 1840s. Initially it was unspectacular. In 1841 Edward rented McL'Roth's maltings in St Andrew's Street; in the following year an additional small malting in Westgate Street—Bury was crowded with malting houses—and two years later a more extensive one in Southgate. The three rented maltings were retained for many years. As soon as he had repaid his father, he realised more ambitious plans in 1845–6. The malting house in Bridewell Lane was an important departure for two reasons. Not only was the School maltings large for its day[15] (it still survives), but it was built across Bridewell Lane on ground that Edward bought from the Guildhall Feoffment. It was the first building outside the original Westgate site that Buck and Green had acquired in 1805 (see Map 1, page 74). Also in the same year he advertised 30 hogshead casks and other equipment for sale 'in consequence of the proprietor altering the Brewing plant'.[16]

Our knowledge of the brewery before 1887 is derived from fragmentary sources, but the decade of 1846 to 1856 appears to have been one of quiet consolidation. Certainly there was no further major building. For Edward the period was also one of personal tragedy. In 1848, shortly after giving birth to their fifth child, his first wife died. The 1851 census lists him with five young children and four servants, employing a typically modest labour force of eighteen men and three boys. He remained a widower for many years, absorbed more than ever in the vigorous management of his brewery. In 1854 he moved his young family across Westgate to his father's house with its spacious garden next to the Theatre. Abbot Reeve's house, where Edward had spent his own childhood and married life, was demolished, and the site used to extend the brewery. Between 1856 and 1858 there was 'a large extension of the premises in Westgate Street and the completion of the spacious malt house'.[17] When it was finished Edward reckoned the business had increased tenfold since he had taken over the brewery (i.e. producing 20,000 barrels a year). Three years later he was employing forty-five men and five boys in his brewery and farm, more than a doubling of his workforce ten years earlier, and at home the four maids were joined by a butler and governess. Greene's ales had become popular throughout

West Suffolk and the bordering counties, and when demand increased further in the prosperous 1860s Edward, now joined in business by his son Walter, again extensively altered the brewery. In October 1866 he gave a great celebratory dinner for 350 in the Theatre for his workmen and those of Robert Boby and George Cornish, the Bury engineers.

> During the past year [the *Bury Post* reported] many extensive alterations and improvements have been effected in the brewery, which has been considerably enlarged and a number of modern appliances introduced whereby the conduct of the various operations connected with brewing has been greatly facilitated.[18]

The improvements at Westgate included the installation of a second steam engine, a 10 h.p. model made by George Cornish.[19] Edward, who had been elected M.P. for Bury the previous year, spoke with great pride about all the work being completed by Bury workmen. The dinner was a remarkable event not least because, with its long speeches about progress, self-help and good labour relations by the two chief architects of Bury's industrial renaissance (Edward Greene and Robert Boby), it locates precisely the revival of the town's economic fortunes. It also reflects that brewing, both by publicans and private individuals alike, was fast contracting in Suffolk after 1850. Twenty years later the twenty-three breweries in Suffolk were responsible for around three-quarters of beer output in the county.

In fact, even after extensive alterations and additions in 1845–6, 1856–8 and 1865–6, Westgate brewery was never a model one. It might have been the source of great local pride, but it did not appear engraved in the brewing journals of the day or in Barnard's four-volume *Noted Breweries of Great Britain and Ireland* (1889–91)—sure tests of a brewery's modernity. For there was no complete rebuilding with the advice of brewing architects and engineers. Plans were always those of Edward Greene himself, executed by Bury firms when needs became acute. The result as a whole was physically unimpressive (see plate 8). A long article in the *Licensed Victuallers' Gazette* in 1875, conveyed a sense of perplexity when it compared Greene's brewery with others it had described.[20] By this time, although it was medium-sized in terms of output (around 40,000 barrels a year), its layout remained compressed. This was the result of the original cramped site. Even when the two big malting houses were constructed across Bridewell Street, and Abbot Reeve's house was demolished, the brewery was extremely tight for space. An article on the Westgate brewery, in a series the *Bury and Norwich Post* ran on Bury industries in 1884, commented,

> its distinguishing feature is its compactness, although the multi-tudinous arrangements appear to an uninitiated person somewhat complicated as he stumbles about between mash tuns, under Archimedean screws and Jacob's ladders . . . or finds his way about the cellars and encounters casks of ale in transit in narrow tunnels.[21]

Although compactness was no fault in a brewery's layout, manoeuvring waggons, carts and drays was not easy in the small yards. There was no solution to the problem, however, because the original site of just over one acre was restricted by roads on three sides and the *Dog and Partridge* (not owned by Greene's until 1872) and residential buildings on the fourth. Even the malthouses between Bridewell Lane and College Street were hemmed in by two schools and a set of almshouses (see the brewery plan, c. 1890, on p. 74). The only solution—never contemplated until the 1930s—was to build a new brewery on a much larger site. As a result the huddled conglomeration of buildings, surrounded by no fewer than four schools and two groups of almshouses, did not add up to the brewing journals' standard illustration of a modern brewery. For temperance workers, appalled by the fact that generations of Bury children had had their senses dulled by the emanations from Greene's brewery, the prospect was infernal.

The narrow confines of the brewery disguised a surprising feature, for Edward ran 'in a sense two breweries in one as it contains a double plant, complete in every particular, the one being a forty quarter and the other a twenty-five quarter plant'.[22] This curious arrangement reflected the piecemeal growth of the brewery. Inside the buildings the reporter for the *Licensed Victuallers' Gazette* noted the contrast between old and modern practices. Edward, harking back to views held in his youth, had an

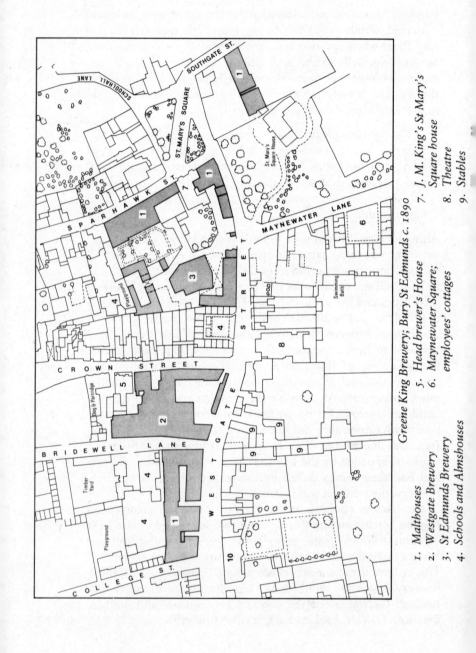

Greene King Brewery; Bury St Edmunds c. 1890

1. Malthouses
2. Westgate Brewery
3. St Edmunds Brewery
4. Schools and Almshouses
5. Head brewer's House
6. Maynewater Square;
   employees' cottages
7. J. M. King's St Mary's
   Square house
8. Theatre
9. Stables

objection to the use of slate and metal in the construction of mash tuns, cooling and fermenting squares, in spite of most brewers' preference for these materials in the 1870s.[23] He insisted upon the use of wood, more likely to harbour infection and more difficult to cleanse. Even the 'coppers' were of wood heated by steam coils and the use of wooden pontoons for skimming old ales was abandoned by modern breweries in the 1880s. Moreover, unlike many of his competitors he still stored most of his beer to mature in oak vats. One of the best features of the brewery was its extensive cellarage—most of it still existing and dating from the Wrights' day—and in 1884 it was filled with 50 vats each holding between 100 and 600 barrels each, in all accommodating 11,000 barrels of ale.[24] In the largest a traditional supper had been held on its completion. The use of wood and the insistence on maturing beer were somewhat old-fashioned features by the 1870s. On the other hand, equipment in use like Colman's patent coolers, Morton's refrigerators and Sorrell's mashing machinery was of 'the most approved constructions' and steam heat obtained 'scrupulous cleanliness'. In fact Edward's predilection for out-of-date ways did not matter. Whereas his attitude might well have spelt ruin in an industry where leaders had to keep abreast of technological developments, in the brewing world his old-fashionedness, in comparison with up-to-date practices in London and Burton, was a virtue. For he recognised that breweries were judged on their beer and its price, not by the newness of their plant and the convenience of their layout. Even the 1875 reporter, restrained in his comment about the brewery and its equipment, was convinced that he had never met with better bitter ales. They were, he noted, 'of the most marked excellence, best of all to our taste being the stronger bitter ale, the price at which this is sold fairly astonishing us.' Praise enough of Edward's skills as a brewer and his view that the end was more important than the means.

It is impossible now to discover the sources of capital for these periodic extensions of the brewery. As in so many Victorian businesses ploughed back profits and the assistance of banks and family funds were central props of financial structure. The industry was so highly liquid in terms of funds that many brewers were themselves bankers. Indeed Edward was for many years a partner in a banking and wine-merchants venture in Bury—Huddleston,

Cooper, Greene and Co. The bank was overshadowed by two larger rivals and the brewery was probably more important to its existence than *vice versa*. Certainly by the 1850s the brewery was doing so well that Edward could afford improvements and extensions to the brewery out of current profits. Moreover the building was modest in cost. The entire brewery and malthouses were valued only at £19,033 in 1877 and the largest malting house erected in 1880 (still standing in Westgate with a dated keystone) cost a mere £4,500. Of course building was only one part of capital cost. Machinery, casks, horses and drays together well exceeded building valuations and the chief costs of any brewer were in providing circulating capital to hold stocks of malt, hops and beer.[25] Here problems were not acute because the brewer's sales were usually steady and regular, with few bad debts. Only in one year (between 1877 and 1886) was a modest sum owing to the bank when the firm's annual accounts were struck.

In the late 1860s the firm began to acquire public houses as competition in the free trade became stiffer. Within twenty years it bought around ninety (see p. 104 below) and this became the brewery's major area of capital expenditure. Again this was almost entirely met from current profits. But there are earlier indications that the brewery was not straitened for cash and could itself provide enough for Edward's expansionary programme, which allowed the brewery to increase its capacity from around a mere 2,000 barrels in 1836 to 40,000 forty years later. In the mid-1860s he bought and rebuilt Westgate House, the grandest dwelling in the street, and several other Westgate properties. He also acquired cottages for his workforce, took over the mastership of the Suffolk Hunt, and in 1865—to set the seal on his return to Parliament—leased the Ixworth Abbey estate and began farming on a much more extensive scale—before eventually buying the 850-acre Nether Hall estate in 1874. Without the aid of large loans and mortgages, the brewery was a highly effective wealth-generating mechanism which not only financed its own further expansion, but also yielded funds for the acquisition of public houses and an increasingly expensive way of life for its proprietor.

4

The Westgate brewery's breakthrough to success, its transformation from a small country brewery to one of regional significance, came in the 1850s and 1860s. The background to Edward Greene's achievement was general economic expansion, rising standards of living, the creation of the railway system, and the growth of commercial brewing. Nevertheless, without his enterprise the brewery could easily have stagnated. Hundreds of country breweries, the equal of his in 1850, did so. Later in life he explained his success in terms of hard work, an excellent work force and good labour relations, and an eagerness to supply the public with the best beer. In many ways Edward's analysis was like any other Victorian businessman's standard account of the path to prosperity, but his discussion of the springs of his actions is sufficiently precise and different for us to dwell on it briefly here.

The cornerstone of his business philosophy was application. 'We must all be busy', he told the Y.M.C.A. in Bury, 'idleness is not a feature in God's work.'[26] Every account of his life included as an illustration the fact that, except on the single occasion of his marriage, he was the first to arrive for work in the brewery between 1830 and 1842. Until he became an M.P. at the age of fifty he never relaxed his work routine. Living either in the brewery yard or across at 6 Westgate, little escaped his notice. In politics he was celebrated for his energy and loud voice, features clearly acquired in running the brewery. But his stern attitude to work—the cornerstone of Victorian enterprise and individualism —was softened by the stress he placed upon honesty and avoidance of the narrowness of purely commercial pursuits.

Edward Greene was a Christian, professing vigorously a simple, very Protestant faith, on the one hand strongly opposed to any whiff of ritualism and neo-Catholicism in the Anglican church and on the other to non-conformity with its strong temperance associations. He, like all his brothers and sisters, abandoned centuries of inherited Dissent for the 'Lowest' form of Anglicanism, theologically common ground for brewers harassed after the 1830s by the temperance lobby. When he entered the House of Commons his fellow Conservative M.P.s were amused by his homely views about business and the Anglican church delivered, with frequent reference to biblical texts, in a rather harsh, Suffolk voice. Always he was insistent that his Christian principles were the basis of his business life. 'Whatsoever ye would that men should do to you, do ye even so to them' was a favourite text. Another saying he remembered from childhood, expressed in an apt metaphor for a brewer, was 'an ill-gotten sixpence will rot a bushel'. At the same Y.M.C.A. lecture in which he extolled the rewards of hard work he warned them that 'falsehood will one day be found out—fraud will soon destroy credit—and gain gotten by evil doing brings no blessing with it'. These principles informed his actions in brewing, in farming, and in politics. Religion can become a cover for hypocrisy, but in Edward Greene's case his simple faith, honesty and plain speaking carried total conviction with his employees and his electorate to the end. Of course Christian principles did not stop him pursuing a hard bargain. He expected from his side of any contract a proper day's work and the same standards of business integrity he himself pursued. Occasional court cases show that he was not easily deterred.

Although he had well-formed views about work and honesty, and had achieved success through vigorous toil for thirty-five years he reckoned 'it a very grievous evil when a man suffers his business to become his master and he begins to serve it as if he were a slave'. For his workmen he advocated recreation and religion and for himself the recipe was not dissimilar. Throughout his life he had a passion for hunting and horses and after 1865 his own experience broadened, comprehending the activities of a country gentleman, magistrate, politician and noted agriculturalist. He practised what he preached for after he entered Parliament the day to day running of the brewery was given over to his son (Walter Greene), nephew (E. W. Lake), and manager (William Pead). Then Edward's vision widened. He stood back from the brewery that had been his world for thirty-five years and talked in a homely way, that was so well understood in late Victorian Suffolk, about the prosperity of Bury, working-class housing, agriculture, and religion. He had a genius for communication. A fine figure of a man, partly self-made, never given to obscure profundities but concentrating on essential Suffolk issues in a style that owed something to an Evangelical preacher, he was completely understood by all classes from Lord Bristol to the poorest agricultural labourer. Indeed it was his attitude to the working class—forged in the brewery itself—that won him his widest support.

5

Breweries have never been large employers of labour in relation to their capital investment. In 1851 Edward ran the Westgate brewery with only eighteen men and three boys, and although it claimed to be the premier firm in Bury, employing ninety men by the early 1880s, this was well under half those working at Boby's, the agricultural engineers. And after the mid-1850s Edward's labour total always included those men who were employed on the farm and in carting barley to the maltings, for there was a seasonal exchange of men between the farm and brewery just as there was of horses and feedstuffs, of beer and barley. It was in his tightly run family firm that Edward formulated his views about labour relations. In the background was the plight of the agricultural worker in Suffolk which remained acute for much of the nineteenth century. In large measure this was due to a constant oversupply of labour, exacerbated during the long periods of agricultural depression. All Edward had to do in this situation was offer a higher wage, traditionally reckoned to be two shillings per week over farm wages, for his general labourers. Then higher differentials were paid to foremen and skilled craftsmen like coopers. Yet Edward went further than a simple manipulation of wages. The core of his views about labour relations was a heavy, almost pre-industrial paternalism, and a belief—much rarer amongst employers—in the necessity of good housing for his workforce.

Paternalism existed in all sorts of ways. It was Edward's practice after 1836 to 'meet together once a year with those who had aided him during that year in the progress of his affairs'.[27] On these occasions—a continuation of the old harvest supper on Suffolk farms—he lectured his audience after they had fed well and the songs had died away. Year after year his themes hardly varied: the rewards of diligence, the march of material progress, the need for religion and decency in everyday life. But the speeches were always enlivened by passages in which Edward went beyond the conventionalities of the archetypal Victorian businessman. He could achieve nothing 'if he had not men about him in whom he could place the utmost confidence and whose best energies were devoted to his service'. He liked men about him whose faces he knew, men whom he could help in old age.[28] Such sentiments were well received and as a result the brewery possessed a highly loyal workforce, many of whom had been employed by Greenes all their working lives. From the outset there were 'dynasties' of workers as closely identified with the brewery as the owner himself.

Linked with his paternalism was his practice of management:

> it says something for the characters alike of employers and employed [wrote the *Licensed Victuallers' Gazette* reporter in 1875] that the large majority of these are old servants, all the heads of department particularly having been in the firm from boyhood. Mr. Greene is certainly fortunate in being well served, but perhaps the system he adopts is in part measure answerable for the happy result. The various heads of departments he gives absolute power in their own provinces, with responsibility only to himself; and thus, while knowing at once whom to blame for any shortcoming, he keeps all the strings, so to speak, of the business in his own hands.[29]

On other occasions the paternalism seems to us less deftly done. At the birth of an heir and on the marriages of Edward himself and of his children, beef, tea and gowns were distributed and a similar routine was followed each Christmas when the managers supplied half stones of beef and a pound of tea to every employee.[30] When Edward died the *Bury Post* carried a long obituary, later produced as a booklet, which attempted to summarise his life's work. Writing about his attitude to his workmen it concluded,

> Men who did their work well secured a rise in their wages; old servants when incapacitated were pensioned off to spend the remainder of their days in peace; and in case of death the widows of those who had been long with the firm . . . were allowed a weekly remittance. The effects of this policy in keeping alive a good feeling between employer and employed

may be heard on every hand, and Mr. Greene's popularity with the working classes is consequently very great.[31]

Edward's old-fashioned views about his workforce were reinforced by more practical notions about their housing. At first the brewery owned none, since resources were scarce, and the dozen or so married employees rented accommodation in the terraces of small cottages which speculators like William Steggles created on all sides of Bury in the 1820s and 1830s. By the late 1850s, when funds were more abundant, Edward himself began buying and building property. The first—still surviving in Crown Street —were commissioned in 1859, and over the next twenty-five years a further 40 were acquired so that by 1887, when the amalgamation with King's brewery took place, over half his workforce were housed in brewery cottages let at low rents. All were built or converted to three bedrooms and those in Greene's Square off Maynewater Lane were considered, in Suffolk, model examples. Edward spoke on the hustings and in Parliament about the need for decent working-class housing:

> my idea is that the legislature should interfere, and that every cottage should have at least three bedrooms. I will not own a cottage with less for the occupation of families. I bought ten cottages the other day, and although they were very respectable looking outside, I found, to my astonishment, that they had only two bedrooms each. I have given orders for a third to be added. How can you expect morality among the poor if you put them in hovels only fit for pigs? I hold it to be every man's duty to look to his cottages. The first who have partaken of my prosperity are my poorer neighbours.[32]

In a rural county like Suffolk, where, except on a handful of large estates, labourers' cottages were grossly inadequate, Edward's insistence on and publicity for decent working-class housing was an important factor in the very gradual improvement of conditions after 1870. He always claimed that although he held no brief for trade unions he had 'ever sympathised with the working man'. He preached the self-help gospel for the amelioration of their conditions and thought that their independence should be sacrosanct. And he certainly believed in high wages, although he had difficulty in spelling this out. It was easy for his critics to conclude from his message that as a brewer he was only interested in selling more beer. Moreover his farming constituents, who were not compensated by high grain prices after 1870, saw wage increases very differently indeed from Edward.

With these advanced views about housing, encouraging a paternalism that elsewhere in Victorian industrial England was in decline, and paying wages above the average of neighbouring farmers, Edward Greene achieved exactly what he wanted: a devoted workforce with a low turnover and a reputation as a good employer throughout his twenty-five years in Parliament. There was never an aspersion cast on his record as an employer and more surprisingly, none about his beer. If he accounted for his own entrepreneurial success in terms of hard work, decent business principles, and the support of a loyal workforce, his aim he always maintained was simply to produce good beer.

The growing regional reputation of the Westgate brewery after 1850 was built upon two types of beer—old ale and bitter. The former, very sharp and strong, was a Suffolk speciality and greatly esteemed in the county. Newcomers found it an acquired taste, like Roquefort or olives. There was an old saying, 'Suffolk cheeses are as hard as stones but Suffolk ales are sharp enough to cut them with.' And Greene's old ale illustrated the adage perfectly.[33] Yet Edward Greene's real pride was his best bitter. 'For without flattery', wrote a consumer in 1875, 'this ale is equal to any of the kind we have tasted, and though, of course, not possessing the exact flavour of the Burton beers, which is just now fashionable, is full of a character and flavour of its own, which to many palates would be even preferable.' Presumably few publican brewers could match this beer consistently. When Edward died in 1891 the *London Star* maintained,

> He was one of the first country brewers to discover that beer need not be vile, black, turgid stuff, but brewed a bright amber-coloured liquid of Burton type, which he sold at a shilling per gallon, and made a fortune.[34]

By the early 1880s the brewery produced eight different beers: four old ales of varying strength, two bitters, a mild Burton-style ale and a stout. Edward Greene remained his own brewer for

1. Benjamin Greene
(1780—1860), the
founder of the brewery.
2. Westgate Brewery
House in 1839.
Benjamin Greene
occupied it from 1806 to
1819 and his son
Edward from 1840 until
1853. It was demolished
to make space for
brewery extensions in
the mid-1850s.

3. *(above left)* Edward Greene (1815–91) in about 1875 when he was M.P. for Bury St Edmunds and a very popular Suffolk figure. He was responsible for the first real expansion of Greene's brewery after 1850.
4. *(above right)* Benjamin Buck Greene (1808–1902) in 1895, for fifty years a director of the Bank of England. In 1890 h was reckoned to be 'the second best man a the Bank'.
5. *(left)* William Greene (1824–81), Benjamin Greene's troubled fourth son. H spent several years in St Kitts, fathered a typically large Greene family, but, to the dismay of his brothers, never settled into any regular occupation.

about twenty years, then in the mid-1850s employed and apprenticed a succession of brewers so that in 1875 he could boast of having trained the brewers at George's in Bristol, Mann and Crossmans in Burton, Charringtons at Mile End, and 'one of the largest breweries in Ireland'. This instruction and placement of brewers in noted firms elsewhere was the beginning of a long tradition at Greene King.

As we have seen the great breakthrough in production from 2,000 barrels a year in 1836 to 40,000 in 1875 was achieved without the protection of tied houses but by a network of agents and travellers throughout East Anglia, in London, and even the industrial Midlands and North. By the early 1880s the firm owned stores in Haverhill, Stowmarket, London, Sutton (Ely) and Wolverhampton. Bury beer had found its way as far as San Francisco, Natal and Australia, and a reporter on the *Bury Post*, carried away by the list of far flung places, where Greene's ales might be found, quipped that 'we might do worse than attempting to solve the Sudan difficulty by presenting the Mahdi with a barrel of XXXX' (strongest old ale).[35]

The town's pride in its biggest brewery was natural enough, but the centre of gravity in its sales was more local. By the early 1870s Greene's ales had become 'the accepted and most popular "tap" from Watton and Wymondham in the north to Colchester and Bishop's Stortford in the south, and from Ely and St Ives in the west to Framlingham and Woodbridge in the east.'[36] This regional domination had been achieved gradually in the previous thirty years by travellers and agents assiduously pushing lighter, Burton-type beers at competitive prices on a sharply rising market. At the centre of this expansion was Edward Greene's drive. His success was achieved unaided. He was endlessly ambitious—a feature in his character clearly inherited from his father—yet a fair employer, tireless before 1865 in the pursuit of his business, confident of a fund of commonsense, and secure with the rewards of hard work and the support of his Lord and Maker.

6

Before Edward Greene became Conservative M.P. for Bury St Edmunds in 1865 he had achieved little outside the brewery itself. Certainly that was unrecognisable from the affair his father had sold him thirty years earlier. His record here was noted in the town, as was his reputation as a good employer and a prominent supporter of charitable effort in mid-Victorian Bury.[37] Yet his standing was less than that of his two elder brothers and, in some ways, of his father. Benjamin Greene had been, throughout his stay in Bury, a controversial figure, irascible and yet very able, and Edward's eldest brother, Benjamin Buck Greene, had gained great distinction in the world of London business—feats always reported in the Bury press—and John Greene, twice Mayor of the town, was regarded throughout Suffolk as a Conservative politician and solicitor whose talents were never fully realised in Bury. Edward, as at school, remained somewhat in the shadow of his two clever brothers. What time he spared from the brewery he devoted to his family, for when his young wife died in 1848 he was left to bring up five children, all under the age of seven. He had the aid of a devoted governess, chosen, as his grand-daughter recalled, so that her looks would not ensnare the well-to-do widower. But there seemed little danger at home or elsewhere, for he took no part in Bury's social round, avoided its winter assemblies and never entered the Theatre, despite living next door. He was an active churchman and after the mid-1850s pursued a growing practical involvement in agriculture. Even his great recreation, hunting, was undertaken in no lighthearted way. All his exploits from youth with horse and hound stress his energetic zeal. On one occasion, 'when he was master of the harriers, after having them out at five in the morning, and tiring them, he went 24 miles to Watton, and hunted with Mr. Villebois' hounds for several hours, and then rode home in the evening.'[38] In politics, however, he was apparently uninterested. He never bothered to stand for the Town Council and avoided the blandishments of the Guildhall Feoffees, the central points of power in Bury. Although his support for the Conservatives was well known, it came as a surprise that the Conservative elders in Bury seriously considered him as their candidate in 1865. Then, as always, he maintained that he was without political ambition.

When the 1832 Reform Act was passed the electorate of Bury increased overnight from the 37 councilmen of the Corporation to between 600 and 700 townsmen. As in so many small boroughs the electoral interests of neighbouring territorial magnates did not wither overnight and until the 1860s the Duke of Grafton and the Marquis of Bristol were considered still to possess considerable influence in returning the town's *two* M.P.s. Indeed the Herveys' representation of the borough was unbroken for 260 years. But their present nominee, Lord Alfred Hervey, was reckoned to have behaved very badly. As often as not he had voted with Lord Palmerston and the Whigs and he had, to the chagrin of the Bury Conservatives, voted for the abolition of church rates. When Parliament was dissolved in the summer of 1865 the Bury Conservative party was determined to run an orthodox candidate against Lord Alfred. Their first choice was Edward's brother John, but when he declined through ill health, they selected Edward.

The resulting contest was fascinating in that, although their decision automatically ensured the return of the *other* Member, the Essex brewer J. A. Hardcastle, who sat as the Liberal, the Bristols' ancient interest was under real threat. The tension was highlighted by the two Conservative candidates. Lord Alfred, aristocratic but not arrogant, saw no reason to account for his conduct in the House of Commons to the electors of Bury and as the inheritor of two and a half centuries of automatic nomination he had little relish for a fight. He stood on the hustings with a scurrilous broadsheet (attacking his place-seeking) in his hand, 'scarcely know[ing] whether I don't degrade myself by alluding to it.'[39] In contrast, Edward Greene, acknowledged by his two opponents as an able businessman, and a generous supporter of good causes, seemed earnestly brash. Standing as a Progressive Conservative, and stressing his independence of mind and means he displayed, if somewhat obscurely, his political armoury. Central to this was the part he had played in reviving Bury's economic fortunes, for within the past year he claimed that he had, almost single handed, attracted the Royal Agricultural Society's show to the town and instigated the Bury and Thetford Railway. He also talked about the prosperity of Free Trade, and about labourers' dwellings (thereby anticipating Disraeli's programme of the early 1870s to improve the conditions of the working class). As in all Edward's speeches, however, the political content was less important than the way in which they were delivered. Their infectiousness is ephemeral, but their directness and fund of jokes with a basis of agricultural metaphors clearly engaged the audience. In comparison with the cold distinction of Lord Alfred Hervey's utterances they possessed a homely illogicality.

The contest was clearly seen to be between new and old conservatism, between the aristocratic and capitalist interests: a perfect microcosm of the struggle fought out between the two groups in the nineteenth century. Edward Greene recognised it to be exactly this. There was no aggressive attack on the Bristols, but he recalled later how his father had begun the onslaught on aristocratic influence in Bury in the 1820s, and he considered himself a worthy heir in 1865. At the election in July Edward was easily returned. Hardcastle headed the poll with 331 votes, Edward came second with 300 (including 192 single vote 'plumpers', compared with Hervey's 44) and Lord Alfred lost his seat with 266. Edward, the well-to-do brewer and sound Conservative, was the archetypal representative of the new wealth of the 1860s.

Although he represented Bury for twenty years, in terms of election contests, the excitement of 1865 was never recaptured.[40] The election of 1874 which returned the Conservatives to power after years in the wilderness marked the highwater of his popularity when he not only topped the polls, as he had in 1868, but also saw Lord Francis Hervey returned for Bury in the Conservative interest. For Edward it was the culmination of nine years of hard work as a back-bench M.P., years in which he was assiduous in his attendance in the House, where he spoke on a variety of issues, and in West Suffolk, where he was in great demand as a platform and after dinner speaker. He was at his best when he talked about Suffolk issues. When he tackled a complex national subject like reform in 1866–7 the inconsistencies of his views and the heaviness of his political footwork were quickly revealed. He learned the novice's lesson and thereafter restricted himself to matters he understood.

His exertions were suddenly halted in November 1878—he had just celebrated his Golden Jubilee with the brewery—when he suffered a bad fall in the hunting field. There was gloom in Bury. The Conservative Association Banquet was postponed three times for the universal feeling prevailed that no gathering of the Conservative Party in Bury would be complete unless Mr. Greene was present, not only because he is looked up to as the natural leader of the party, but because his well-known *bonhomie*, tact and energy are so well calculated to ensure the success of any gathering at which he may preside.

This was by no means his first accident, but he was now 63 and his recovery was apparently very slow. For almost five years he rarely appeared in Parliament or at functions in Suffolk, and when he did so he was clearly way below his old form. Although he was returned to Parliament in 1880 it was with a much reduced majority and he came well behind Hardcastle (the former Liberal M.P. who had been turned out in 1874) in the poll. Edward could take comfort from the fact that his defeat owed less to his enforced inattention to his constituency than to the general unpopularity of the Conservative government, which appeared ineffective in its handling of the widespread depression of industry and agriculture in the late 1870s.

Since no personal correspondence survives, it is difficult to understand why Edward's recovery was so painfully slow. Partly it was due to family dispute. In 1870 Edward had at last remarried. His wife was the widow of an impecunious admiral and baronet, Sir William Hoste, who had rented Westgate House from Edward for some three years before his death in 1868. His young widow remained in Bury and saw a good deal of her landlord (almost twenty years her senior) whom she married two years later. The match had advantages for both parties: for Dorothea Hoste it meant the end of possible financial worry; for Edward his wife brought him new claims to acceptance amongst the old Suffolk gentry, given that she belonged to a leading Cornish landed family, the Prideaux Brunes. Lady Hoste had two children by her previous marriage and a third was born to her and Edward in 1872. For a time they lived at Ixworth Abbey, which Edward had rented since 1865, until in 1874 he bought the Nether Hall estate from J. A. Hardcastle, the ex-Liberal M.P. for Bury. The Jacobean house was largely rebuilt and extended, and Edward was able to indulge his passion for agriculture and horses on a new scale. He was also a Justice of the Peace and deputy lieutenant and master of the Suffolk Hunt for four years after 1871.

Impressive as all this might look in the county, there were problems. Lady Hoste—she never dropped her title and style —was a small woman of determination. All Edward's first family were now married and in their thirties and they resented the new regime—no one more than Walter Greene, Edward's only son. He had been taken into the firm as a partner in 1862 at the age of 20, and although he had neither his father's application nor capacities for business, being aggressively addicted to the chase, there was a deep affection between them. Animosities were never pursued in the management of the brewery, but in 1880 there was a robbery at Nether Hall in which £6,000 worth of gold and silver plate was stolen. The whole affair was hushed up and Walter Greene accused Lady Hoste of protecting the culprit, whom he believed to be a member of her family. It was the culmination of years of ill feeling: the tide ran so high that in 1883 he moved his young family to Worcestershire, rented Wolverton Hall and took over the mastership of the Croome Hunt. The public reason was his wife's health, but the real cause was the rift with Lady Hoste. For a man so attached to Suffolk and so devoted to his father's interests it was a move that showed the intensity of the family dispute. In this atmosphere it was perhaps not surprising that Edward's recovery in the early 1880s was protracted.

By 1883 he was again appearing at events in Suffolk. Something of his old energy and interest returned. In November he was attempting to ride in the park at Nether Hall a new tricycle, down an incline rather too steep for a heavy man of advancing years. He was badly thrown and broke his arm.[41] This time his recovery was rapid, although his attendances at Parliament were never resumed on the old scale and he seldom spoke in the House. Since he was approaching 70 his inattention to political affairs was excused and in the summer of 1885 he declined—even so a little reluctantly—to stand again in the coming election. To the electors he expressed his gratitude for their having borne so patiently with him for the past few years and spoke of 'circumstances over which I have no control'. Whether he was referring to old age, family difficulties, or the fact that Bury was reduced by the Reform Act of 1884 to returning only one M.P. he did not make clear.

The Parliament returned in 1885 was one of the shortest and most troubled on record. Neither party had a clear majority and both the Conservative and Liberal Governments failed to secure Home Rule for Ireland, the former because Lord Salisbury had no desire to split his party as in 1846, the latter since Gladstone, who did not accomplish the necessary proselytising for his 'mission', was left with no option but to split his. Chamberlain and Bright led 93 Liberal Unionist M.P.s through the lobby with the Conservatives. Gladstone resigned and went to the country on the Home Rule question. Edward Greene at 71 decided to come out of retirement: his health somewhat improved, he was unable to resist the pressing invitation to stand for North-West Suffolk. He himself did little campaigning. The fight was left to Walter Greene and E. W. Lake, who made forays each evening into the villages to put over their views to the Suffolk labourers, only recently enfranchised (1884) and unused to such attentions. It was in some ways fortunate that Edward could plead advancing years, for the intricacies of the Home Rule question did not suit his simple Suffolk style. Indeed he was unconvinced about its central place in the campaign. One irate Liberal at Walsham-le-Willows insisted 'he knew no more of the subject than a bull'. Therefore, when Edward spoke, he wandered on to his old themes of class cohesion, insisting that the labourers had been mischievously duped by Radical promises in 1885, which had led them to believe that 'animals and acres were going to be handed round like buns at a school treat'. Cohesion would be achieved by trust, not rash promises, and worked out in questions like allotments and free education. Edward himself was paraded as the grand old man of Suffolk politics, 'the man who had never been beaten', the supporter of the working man—'for he had gained their esteem, their confidence by his unremitting friendship to them'.[42] Although the formula worked, and in line with the national Conservative swing he was returned with a comfortable majority, the agricultural labourers were thought to have largely abstained from voting in North-West Suffolk.

Edward represented the constituency until his death in 1891. He recaptured some of his old zest for making speeches, not in the House itself, but in Suffolk, although even on home ground he was becoming increasingly out of touch. There was little in his speeches: they were 'studded with the usual party platitudes'. Political and economic realities were largely ignored. His world was that of the Suffolk of his youth. For 'blind, thick and thin Bourbon like Toryism' the *Bury Free Press* thought he had no equal in 1890.[43].

Edward's success in business was there for all to see. What do we make of his career in politics? Was it anything more than the conventional role of the typical Conservative businessman M.P.? In one sense it undoubtedly was. Edward achieved little distinction beyond the confines of West Suffolk. Even in brewing and agricultural affairs where he was an acknowledged expert his talents went unrecognised at Westminster. The most he did was to become a member of the Select Committee on Artisans' and Labourers' Dwellings (1866), and give evidence to a Committee of the House of Lords on the supply of horses in 1873.[44] The latter was a curious affair in which Edward presented his opinionated observations on the position in Suffolk in response to the vacuous questioning of the Prince of Wales, the Duke of Cambridge and the horsier members of the peerage who formed the Committee. Six years later illness prevented his inclusion in the important Richmond Committee which examined the acute depression in agriculture. Nevertheless although his spell in politics brought none of the conventional rewards—though there were rumours of a baronetcy shortly before he died—he was held in affection by the House for his short, anecdotal speeches, transparent honesty and old-fashioned manners.[45]

In Suffolk there was no such condescension. Here, it is clear, when the outpourings of an unquestioning and obsequious local press have been reduced to essentials, that his position in county affairs was unique for a quarter of a century. There are several explanations. Edward had been a new force in Suffolk politics, a mainly self-made man in a self-help age. Yet his position as the representative of the new monied class hardly threatened the old landed interest which had hitherto dominated politics in the county. Not only did he increasingly adopt their way of life but he also spoke their language on key issues like agriculture, religion and education. Even his independence was something reserved for the hustings, for in the Commons, as his opponents quickly pointed out, he maintained total party docility. Yet he was able to

extend the narrow repertoire of politics that suited Suffolk agriculturalists to include material that brought him unflinching
working-class support. To us his message of class cohesion and
individualism seems crude but audiences a century ago received it
differently. Partly this was because he was a model employer, a
man of unquestionable honesty in an era of increasing chicanery
in business life. In most matters he discussed he could convey
conviction, commonsense and often practical involvement, not
only on questions such as farming, employment and housing but
also on religion and education, where he himself had for years
provided instruction for the young employees on his farms and
brewery. Disraeli might scoff that he was the 'fiercest Protestant in
the House',[46] but in Bury his practical experiences recounted with
directness and good humour and devoid of any wider theory and
grasp, exactly suited the working classes, barely emancipated in
either politics or education. Even on the controversial drink issue,
forced into the forefront of attention by the various temperance
movements, and a minefield for brewer-politicians, he could point
to his own moderation—a drink once a day at dinner—and his
firmly held belief that the working man's way out of the trap of
poverty and drunkenness that gripped the Suffolk of his youth
was the improvement of housing and a decent wage. He wanted
them in this way to share in the increased prosperity of the period
and to enjoy their recreations after a hard day's labour, drinking
good beer in moderation (drunkenness he abhorred) in a comfortable public house. He was convinced in the 1870s that social
habits were changing and people were drinking less. It was a
sensible standpoint that faced the reality of working-class life far
more effectively than the narrow prescriptions of the temperance
movement. Undoubtedly his ability—something quite rare
amongst politicians—was to catch the mood of all classes, Liberals often as well as Tories, in the 1870s and 1880s. This knack,
well concealed behind the homely front, made him the most
popular man in Suffolk politics in the late Victorian period.

7

In fact Edward's most lasting contribution to Suffolk life was in
agriculture, not politics, for he deserves a reputation as an innovator in the High Farming period between 1840 and 1880. Suffolk

farming, like agriculture throughout the East of England, suffered periods of depression in Edward Greene's youth. After real surges of prosperity during the French Wars (1793–1815) falling cereal prices after 1813 meant difficult years for farmers, especially in the early 1820s and mid-1830s. Then in the late 1830s the recession lifted. Rising standards of living for a fast growing population, advancing prices even after the Corn Laws were repealed in 1846, the widespread use of new fertilisers, the coming of the railways, the inability of foreign producers to exploit the British grain market in the 1850s and 1860s, all played their role in the prosperity of these years. Success for individual farmers, however, depended upon their skills in adapting traditional practices to the changing situation. Those who attempted to produce more corn and beef by increasing their investment in farm buildings, the new machinery and fertilisers did best. Amongst leaders in the High Farming movement in Suffolk was Edward Greene.

He began farming in 1854 when he leased Stone Bridge farm within the boundaries of Bury St Edmunds from Lady Cullum of Hardwick for twelve years. At first the 138-acre holding seems to have been no more than an adjunct of the brewery, providing additional horse feed to that supplied by his meadows that ran down to the river behind his house. Soon, however, in all sorts of ways the brewery and farm were integrated, not only in the supply of horse feed and malting barley but also in the consumption of malt dust and spent grains on the farm and in the sharing of workmen and horses. Stone Bridge farm gave Edward a taste for farming. When in 1865 he leased Ixworth Abbey he took with it 400 acres of light land, and from 1874 he himself farmed over 500 acres at Nether Hall. Partly his interest matched his new role as Member of Parliament and county Justice of the Peace. But his involvement went much deeper than those ventures of M.P.s who were anxious to exploit a concern for agricultural affairs, for he took to farming with his characteristic energy. Of course, his first-hand knowledge of agricultural problems in East Anglia was invaluable to his political career in Suffolk, but he made a contribution to Suffolk's agriculture in two notable ways beyond this.

The first was through the Ixworth Farmers' Club. In 1870 he was largely responsible for its foundation and for the next twenty-

one years remained its president. Meeting monthly for papers
and discussions amongst neighbouring landowners and farmers
it encouraged experiment and after 1875 considered how best to
face the great depression in farming.[47] Edward addressed it on a
number of topics which he repeated at other farming clubs and
agriculturists' dinners. Most of his material was culled from
observations on his own farms, but he did stress key issues like
capital investment and the necessity for all farmers to keep proper
accounts. His active interest ensured support and speakers so that
the Ixworth Club was soon the liveliest and most successful
farmers' club in Suffolk, an important influence in the diffusion of
agricultural knowledge. Edward was also prominent in the
formation of the West Suffolk Chamber of Agriculture in 1867
and for a time was a delegate to the National Chamber in London.
But the more grandiose Chamber never met with the popular
success of the Ixworth meetings at the *Pickerell* Inn. The second
major contribution Edward made was in taking the lead in steam
ploughing experiments in Suffolk in the 1860s.[48] The promise of
steam motive power—the mainspring of early Victorian industrial change—was largely unfulfilled in agriculture. Certainly
steam powered threshing sets were invaluable innovations after
the 1860s, but steam's application to ploughing—potentially
invaluable in replacing the limited energy of the horse to carry out
the task more speedily, and work heavy soils more deeply—was
disappointing. The problem was cost and the great weight of the
early traction engines. Edward carried out experiments in the
1860s and attempted to bring the notice of agriculturalists
throughout Suffolk to the importance of steam power in farming.
He claimed that not only was it economic in comparison with the
use of horses, but that Suffolk labourers could work the engines
without trouble and it had enabled him to grow two crops a year
by quickly enabling him to break up his stubbles in early September and plant a green crop for his sheep to consume in spring. At
one time in the middle 1860s he was pursuing plans to set up a
joint stock steam ploughing company. But conservative farmers
were not convinced by the advocacy of a newcomer to their ranks,
one to whom money was apparently limitless. Even Edward
admitted later that repairs were heavy, and depression in the
mid-1870s and the immobility and weight of the ploughing sets

curtailed their general introduction even amongst the largest farmers. But as an innovator who experimented with new crops and breeds and invested heavily in machinery, as a noted publicist who possessed faith in agriculture, even in the darkest days of the 1880s, he deserves a place amongst the leading 'High Farmers' of Victorian England.

Together with his reputation as the advocate of progressive farming in Suffolk Edward was credited with having revived Bury's economic life in the 1850s and 1860s. Since he was responsible for the expansion of its best known firm this was inevitable, but his participation in the town's modest recovery went well beyond this. He never missed an opportunity to talk about the importance of bringing development—largely agricultural engineering and malting—to Bury, and stressed the need to improve its market facilities for West Suffolk and South West Norfolk in the railway age. His mission was only partly successful. Robert Boby's engineering works, founded in the mid-1850s, initially expanded rapidly, but since it came to specialise in malt screens it never joined the first flight of agricultural machinery manufacturers. Although big new maltings were built, these were small employers of labour. Consequently Bury's population grew only very slowly from 13,900 in 1851 to 16,255 in 1901. There was no sustained industrial 'take-off' following the activity of the 1860s and early 1870s. Bury basically remained a sleepy backwater. Its predicament as market centre of an agricultural region which suffered severe depression after 1875 was epitomised by Edward's close involvement in the Bury and Thetford railway between 1865 and 1878.

Bury was already served by three lines: to Ipswich (opened 1846), Newmarket (1854), and Long Melford-Sudbury (1865). In effect, this switched Bury's port of supply to Ipswich from its centuries old connection with King's Lynn (by the Ouse and Lark navigations). This transfer had caused rumblings in Bury about the monopoly of the Great Eastern Railway and its high freight charges. Moreover there was a desire to bring the Breckland around Thetford back into Bury's hinterland. Therefore, in a 'mania' of railway promotions between 1863 and 1866, an Act was obtained in 1865 to complete a railway from Bury to Thetford. By other branch lines through Watton and Swaffham, this was planned to link up with King's Lynn to provide an alternative outlet to Ipswich. Edward and his brother John were responsible for obtaining the 1865 Act. The former was chairman of the Bury and Thetford Railway. The directors included his banking partner, Peter Huddleston, Robert Boby, and a barrister, Hunter Rodwell of Ampton Hall. Although the quartet might look impressive in Bury they were unable to secure much interest beyond the town. Edward, with no railway experience beyond owning a score of shares in a Welsh railway, was twelve years in raising the £100,000 necessary to complete the thirteen miles across the easiest terrain. Twice a year he addressed a handful of shareholders and the local press on the benefits that Bury market would receive from the West Norfolk link and attempted to conceal an embarrassing lack of progress.[49] Blame was attached to the financial crisis of 1866 and poor times in farming after 1870.

These were clearly important, but it is also an indication of the lack of enterprise and real wealth in Bury that Edward was so long in gouging £90,000 from the pockets of its leading inhabitants and a few neighbouring landowners. He and Lord Bristol had to dig deeply into their own before any progress was made. For once Edward's ability to publicise his ventures failed, although it was widely acknowledged 'it was in a great measure to the confidence which everyone had in him that the successful completion of the railway was due'. As soon as the railway was finished in 1876 it was transferred to the G.E.R. As a line it brought few of the rewards Edward had struggled so hard to secure.[50] Bury remained in the shadow of Ipswich and Norwich as a regional centre, never well positioned with direct rail connections, whilst the Breckland area was perhaps the most depressed of all agricultural areas in the country in the 1880s and 1890s. The Bury and Thetford railway was one of Edward's failures. He declared it always to have been 'uphill work'. Yet his involvement in an unprofitable line was undertaken in the belief that he was pushing Bury into a new era of prosperity. Apart from this, his public service was characterised by enormous energy, commonsense and success.

4

Fred King and
the Amalgamation of 1887

I

King's St Edmunds brewery was established in 1868, a mere nineteen years before its amalgamation with that of the Greenes. Yet its founder, Frederick William King, could claim on his own and his wife's behalf a longer connection with the brewing industry and farming in the Bury area than the Greenes. The King family originated from the other side of the county at Moulton, a village nine miles due west of Bury on the Cambridgeshire border. Then, around 1750, they moved to the next parish, Gazeley. Twenty years later they were renting Desning Hall, the largest farm in the village, which was set well away from its centre, in gently rolling chalkland. In 1783 its young occupant John King —Fred's grandfather—married a minor, Lucy Cornell, the daughter of a well-to-do family who farmed in the adjacent parishes of Higham and Cavenham. During the next twenty-four years the couple were blessed with fourteen children. In 1809 John King died. His widow kept on the 600-acre farm. Initially her four young sons could provide little help. The eldest was nearly 16, but the three youngest were all under ten years of age. Yet she survived all the crises that the birth and death rates of her time could inflict.[1] It was inevitable that her sons in their turn would farm. James, her second son to survive, rented a farm in Higham shortly after he came of age. He married soon afterwards, and produced three sons in quick succession. The youngest was

Fred, born in 1828 at Bramfield near Halesworth where his parents briefly rented a farm. In 1833 James King moved back to Desning Hall when his elder, bachelor brother died. His joy in returning home was shortlived, however, as his wife died later that same year.

It is necessary at the outset of this chapter to dwell briefly on Fred King's family because the account contains two features which are essential to any understanding of his subsequent career. The first is the family's total involvement in agriculture. Not only were the Kings active at Gazeley—they occupied three farms there in the 1850s—but they were eventually involved in farming enterprises in Norfolk, Cambridgeshire and Suffolk.[2] Thus Fred King's background was quite different from the Greenes'. The blood of commerce and Dissent ran deep in their veins whereas his experience was confined to the world of a very insular Suffolk famly totally committed to the land. Secondly, his mother's death was a shattering experience. He was barely five at the time. A year later his father remarried and his second wife quickly produced two further sons. From an early age it became clear that he and his two full brothers could expect no part of the Desning inheritance, for when his father retired his younger half-brothers carried on the family farms at Gazeley. It was this realisation that partly explains his drive and certainly his obsession with will-making; when his own large family grew up he was determined, so far as was legally possible, that they should all possess an equal start in life and fair share of any fortune he made.

Whatever he felt about his father's second marriage, Fred, as the youngest son of the first, had his own living to make. As was usual practice in the King family, he became a farmer. When he came of age—unfortunately there is no evidence about his education—he rented a farm at Kirtling just across the border in Cambridgeshire. Whilst he was there he saw a good deal of his King cousins at nearby Brinkley Hall and their neighbours the Maulkins. In 1852 Fred, then 23, married Emily, the eldest daughter of Robert Maulkin of Brinkley Grove. It was this connection that brought him to Bury St Edmunds in 1855, for the Maulkins were one of the best known business families in Bury at the turn of the eighteenth century.[3] Their property interests in the town were still considerable in the 1850s.

The founder of their fortunes in Bury was Joseph Maulkin, Emily King's great-grandfather. He was a maltster who, in 1765, acquired a large malthouse and granary on the Sparhawk Street corner of Westgate, adjacent to Wright's (later Greene's) brewery, and lived on the premises, in adjoining St Mary's Square (then the Horsemarket). It was this complex of buildings that later provided the site of the St Edmunds brewery. He prospered, for in 1778 he was elected Alderman, six years after joining the Corporation, and when he died in 1782 he left a fair amount of scattered land in Bury and the nearby villages, including a 175-acre farm at Bradfield St George, a £200 annuity to his widow and good legacies to his four sons. Three of them were prominent in Bury affairs in the next half century. Their occupations show a variety which reflects how far businessmen had to diversify in middling market towns to make a reasonable living in the eighteenth century. Joseph (1748–1827), the eldest, inherited his father's property. It is unclear whether he farmed much of this land himself, although he paid rates on thirty acres in Bury and mentioned his farming implements in his will. His main occupation, however, was running the maltings and a coal merchant's business in Sparhawk Street. Throughout his working life, which exactly spanned the golden age of coaching, he provided a coach service to London and Norwich from the *Six Bells*.[4] Two other sons, Thomas and Robert (1753–1829), were wholesale grocers and wine merchants in Market Hill and the latter was a founder of the Suffolk Assurance Company. Then there was an uncle who was a yarn merchant whilst the fourth son of Joseph Maulkin, Solomon, managed, and presumably brewed at, the *Six Bells*. After the *Angel* this was the busiest inn in Bury, although James Oakes never found its food and arrangements for public dinners anything more than moderate. Joseph and Robert together were active in the political life of Bury for over half a century, both of them serving the office of Alderman.[5] They frequently appear in James Oakes's diaries although he could approve neither of their political standpoint—they were part of the small caucus that opposed the Oakes' interest—nor of their total involvement in Bury business which excluded them from the narrow social elite of the town.

When Joseph died without issue in 1827 his business interests and much of his property devolved upon Solomon Maulkin's elder son, Robert (1791–1875), who was Emily King's father.[6] On the surface the inheritance seemed splendid—the largest maltings in Bury and its working capital,[7] four public houses in the town and two in the country (which Joseph had acquired through his close ties with brewing victuallers), 38 acres in Bury and over 200 in the county, and £3,400 in 3½ per cent Consols. The reality was, however, rather different. Some of the property had been recently purchased with substantial mortgages, including the *Castle* and adjoining Moyse's Hall in 1828, and Joseph Maulkin, who had married twice, had left numerous sizeable annuities charged against his estates. Robert Maulkin also bought two more inns in Bury in 1831 on mortgage and raised a further £1,700 on the maltings, so that during the recession of the mid-1830s he faced difficulties in meeting the heavy interest charges on his loans. The situation was greatly exacerbated by his extravagance. Whereas his uncle had worked hard and lived simply, when Robert inherited his property he felt restraint unnecessary. Matters soon went from bad to worse. In 1834 a trust was set up to provide his wife (who belonged to the Jonas family, leading farmers on the Cambridge–Essex borders[8]) with £300 a year which would be beyond his debts and control. Other clauses provided for his family in case of his death or whenever he gave up business. He managed to keep up a good face in Bury, for late in 1835 he was re-elected as a Conservative councillor in the reformed Corporation. Then in the next year the real reckoning came. Just before Christmas he had to sell the contents of his St Mary's Square house. The sale revealed the taste and lavishness of his home. The three-day sale included furniture in the most recent fashion, 300 ounces of plate, paintings by Gainsborough and Reynolds, and 'an excellent town-built Britchka by Gower of London nearly new'.[9] Yet the trustees of the 1834 settlement managed to keep the properties intact largely because they were charged with Mrs Maulkin's income. They persuaded Robert to take George Beeton as a partner in the malting business and he ran its affairs for twenty years. Robert soon afterwards went to live out of harm's way at Brinkley Grove, where he spent the next thirty years in economical seclusion with his family of three daughters.

Thus, when Fred King married Emily Maulkin in 1852, her
family, despite comparatively reduced circumstances, still held
valuable property in and around Bury which eventually provided
the basis for his malting and brewing venture. For three years he
continued farming at Kirtling until at Michaelmas 1855 he gave
up his tenancy to join George Beeton, who appears to have run the
Maulkin maltings on his own account after 1850. Within two
years Beeton had been eased out of the partnership and for the
next eleven Fred King managed them alone. The rate-books
suggest that there was no expansion and what had once been the
largest maltings in Bury were now overtaken in size by Edward
Greene's adjacent buildings. Yet it is unlikely that he ran them in
the same lackadaisical fashion as his father-in-law and his partner
had done; that was not in his nature. He revived the wine
merchanting business of the elder Robert Maulkin and like many
maltsters he combined a coal merchant's business with his trade.
Indeed he opened a new coal depot at the railway station. But in
neither of these enterprises was he likely to make a rapid fortune
in Bury. Clearly he did well enough: the 1861 census shows him
living comfortably in the Maulkins' St Mary's Square house with
three servants. Moreover when Gladstone removed the duties on
wines in 1860 national consumption doubled in the next six years.
Nevertheless with a family of eleven children to support he looked
for a new outlet for his enterprise and capital. Farming was always
a possibility—something he certainly undertook after 1875—but
his next venture was bolder. In 1868 he became a brewer. At first
sight the move appears a strange one. Through his wife's family he
could claim to be a fourth generation maltster and wine and spirits
dealer, but the Maulkins, even when running the busy *Six Bells*,
had never been common brewers. He himself had no brewer's
training and managing a malting house, although providing
obvious enough connections, gave few insights into the actual
mysteries of brewing. Moreover, Greene's Westgate brewery was
next door. By 1868 it was so thriving that all Suffolk realised the
fortune that could be made by an energetic country brewer in the
railway age. Yet to most men the threat of such obvious and
overwhelming competition would have been a deterrent. Not
Fred King. He based his move on several calculations. First, it was
clear that the economic climate was right. Beer drinking was

almost at its zenith in the prosperous 1860s. Second, it was well known that Edward Greene had made his fortune in the free trade. Why not emulate his success? Third, malting on the old pattern, as public house brewing declined, possessed an uncertain future. Wines and spirits, after the burst of the 1860s, had a limited market in low income, agricultural West Suffolk. Lastly, through the Maulkin inheritance he had the protection of eight public houses. Nevertheless, overshadowed as he literally was, by Greene's brewery, then at the height of its Victorian expansion, his venture was a brave one. To a more cautious man there would not have seemed room for two thriving breweries in the same street of a sleepy market town.

Again that there are few records that cover the 1868–87 period for King's St Edmunds brewery beyond five stray balance sheets and those that record certain legal provisions.[10] Even so Fred King's drive clearly emerges through their dull restraint. It forces itself through at three points: in his building of the St Edmunds brewery; in his acquisition of public houses; in the vigour of his management.

2

When he had taken the decision in early 1868 to begin brewing there were two immediate problems: to find a brewery and a partner who knew the beer business.[11] He solved the latter first. In June 1868 he inserted a notice in the Bury newspapers that he had 'entered into a Partnership Arrangement with Mr. Francis Phillips, late of the Stowmarket Brewery, and that to the present business of Wine Merchant, Maltster, etc., it is intended to establish a Brewery as soon as arrangements can be made for suitable Premises'.[12] In the following month Fred King purchased the Maulkins' maltings and St Mary's Square properties for £5,300, which he raised by obtaining a 5 per cent mortgage for the full value of the properties from the trustees of the family trust. The purchase allowed him to redevelop the Maulkin property which had remained so long unchanged. It was clear that the maltings could be neither cheaply nor satisfactorily converted and within the next few months he built a new brewery and counting house in grey brick on the Westgate corner of the maltings site. It was not large but it was constructed on the up-to-date 'tower' principle, tall but not quite high enough to cast a shadow over the adjacent almshouses on to Greene's brewery. The new brewery, built without adequate foundations as it transpired in the 1920s, was in production by Easter 1869. Two years later it was valued at £2,000 with plant reckoned at £1,747. Maulkin's maltings were extended, a further set rented in 1871 and another malting house built in 1872. Early advertisements (Fred King, unlike other brewers, made regular use of these) maintained that the St Edmunds March-brewed beers kept well throughout the summer. In the trying season of 1876 not a single barrel was returned. A letter even appeared from the Public Analyst for Norfolk highly recommending the beer. Mild was retailed at less than a shilling a gallon (32s. for a 36-gallon cask) with I.A. and B-3 stock (presumably an Old Ale) selling at 44s. and 54s. a barrel respectively in the 1870s.[13] By 1874 Fred King was receiving such 'handsome support . . . in the arduous undertaking of establishing the brewery' that he was 'again obliged to ENLARGE AND ADD NEW MACHINERY to meet the rapidly increasing demands.'[14] From its foundation, the brewery gained a reputation for its beers, especially stouts, and its owner's brisk business methods.

The completion of the St Edmunds Brewery was accomplished easily enough: the creation of a market for its output was a far more difficult and prolonged operation. Certainly it was founded in the middle of a strong upward movement in beer consumption. National figures of annual consumption indicate a rise from around 23 gallons per head of population in the late 1850s to a staggering all-time peak of over 33 gallons between 1874 and 1878. Too much should not be read into these, especially since they do not necessarily reflect East Anglian patterns, where beer consumption, as in all rural areas, was lower than in London and the industrial Midlands and North. But rising real incomes achieved by money wages outstripping price rises in agricultural areas in the late 1860s and especially in the early years of the 1870s, when advances were achieved by the farm workers' union for the first time, meant that working-class demand for beer increased even in areas of traditionally low consumption. Nevertheless it would be wrong to conclude that Fred King's new enterprise was swept effortlessly along on a flood tide of rising consumption.

There were apparently two ways open for him to break into the Greenes' near monopoly of common brewing in the Bury area: he could engage in a price war in the free trade or purchase public houses to provide himself with a protective umbrella. In fact the first option was not really a possibility. For the retail price of beer remained remarkably constant between 1870 and 1896 and price lists of the early 1870s show the two breweries marketing a virtually identical range of beers at prices that varied by no more than a shilling per 36-gallon barrel. Any significant cut could only come about by a deterioration in quality. As it was, he had to retail a beer that was not noticeably inferior to that of his rivals. Of course using brisker business methods than his competitors, especially giving loans to the free trade, would extend his sales and possibly increase his profits. But they were risky and in themselves they could not ensure his survival. Therefore Fred King turned to the most reliable form of aid, the acquisition of a string of public houses. This decision led him into head-on rivalry with the Greenes and was a key reason for the ultimate amalgamation of the two firms.

As we have seen, Edward Greene's success, and the much more sensational expansion of the Burton brewers after 1840, was achieved in the free trade. But their example, at least in East Anglia, was unusual. Here most of the large and old-established breweries owned a substantial number of houses that had been acquired before 1830. It is possible that in the free trade era between 1830 and 1870 they bought few more, for with monopolistic tendencies so shaken by the new beer houses, and with a steady expansion of demand anyway, there was little apparent advantage in doing so. Unlike Edward Greene they did not sell their pre-1830 stock of houses, for even the smallest breweries that came on to the market between 1830 and 1870 were invariably advertised with the benefit of at least a handful of public houses. They also relied strongly on leasing arrangements—the regional variation of the London loan-tie agreements. This mixed situation continued until the 1880s when, as is well known, 'the retailing end of the brewing industry underwent a fundamental transformation.'[15] Then breweries everywhere began the wholesale acquisition of public houses, after the decline in *per capita* consumption set in from 1878 and free trade in licences came to an end with the restrictive legislation of 1869–72. The movement to acquire tied houses also reflects the fact that commercial brewing was absolutely in the ascendant by 1880. At that date the brewing victualler and beer house keeper had been routed (see Appendix 2, Table 1). Common breweries had grown for forty years by absorbing their production. Now when the two species were virtually extinct, the likes of Edward Greene had to secure their trade in perpetuity by purchase and lease.

Table 1: Inns, public houses and beer houses bought by Edward Greene and Fred King, 1868–87*

	Before 1870	1870–4	1875–9	1880–4	1885–7
Edward Greene					
Purchases	4	17	27	31	12
Stock at end of period	4	21	48	79	91
Fred King					
Purchases	1	13	27	5	6
Stock at end of period	1	14	41	46	52

* This table has been constructed from incomplete legal records. It shows trends, however, clearly enough. It should also be remembered that the two firms in addition also *leased* houses. There were possibly between 40–50 in this category by the mid-1880s.

What is unusual in the Greene and King examples is that their purchases of public houses began so early. It is clear that in Fred King's case he was buying public houses quite freely after 1869 to establish his market and this forced the Greenes to match his moves. Within ten years Fred King had acquired no fewer than forty public houses. Thereafter the rate of purchase was much slower.

From the outset he worked with the knowledge that a minimum safety net for his operations was formed by the eight public houses belonging to his wife's family trust. Obviously it was inadequate, and neither King nor his wife was a trustee. Moreover when he began brewing in 1869 the tenants already had their own arrangements. Also it was apparent that when the septuagenarian Robert

Maulkin died the Trust properties would be sold for the benefit of his widow and daughters. Since Fred King could not wait upon these events, he began in 1869 the purchase of his own small empire. Within five years he had bought eleven assorted public and beer houses: four in Bury, and the rest in the villages to the west. On average they cost him £470 apiece. They were purchased partly out of the new brewery's current profits, partly on mortgage.[16] In 1875 he began more extensive purchases, again often with loans. Further property in St Mary's Square and two inns at Haverhill were purchased with the aid of £2,000 from the Revd W. Wayman; Fred King's spinster sister found £500 for the *Crown* at Fornham; and when in 1876 the entire Maulkin trust was dispersed at public auction he purchased four of the public houses and immediately mortgaged them, with two others recently acquired in Bury, for £5,000 to the Maulkin trustees. In 1878 when he took his eldest son James Maulkin King into partnership, the deeds listed forty inns and beer houses. No fewer than fourteen of these properties were in Bury itself and by the late 1870s fierce competition with Edward Greene in their acquisition had noticeably driven up their price. Whereas in the early 1870s they were costing him around £470 on average, by 1877 two country inns in Hopton were each bought at over twice that sum.

For many years the bigger regional brewers such as Cobbold's, Tollemache's, Steward and Patteson, Lacon's and the Colchester Brewery, all with their satellites of tied houses, had defined 'spheres of influence'. So had Edward Greene, although with his free trade principles he was perhaps less well placed than most of these. He nevertheless supplied many public houses in Bury and West Suffolk, North Essex, Cambridgeshire and South-West Norfolk. By the late 1860s this was accepted by other regional brewers to be Greene country. But after 1869 it became a battle-field between Greene's and King's for the acquisition of its public houses. From 1869 they raced neck and neck together until 1875–6, when Fred King, acquiring no fewer than twenty-one houses in two years, briefly outdistanced his more substantial rival. Then his pace slackened. Acute agricultural depression again hit all grain growing areas in the late 1870s—1879 was the worst year on record for farmers—and national consumption of beer faltered. In Suffolk the recession for farmers was very serious, although labourers' real wages increased as food prices fell. In these conditions brewers with lower raw material costs did not necessarily suffer, but the Greene accounts (see Appendix 2, Table 2) show that the early 1880s were leaner years than had been experienced in the 1870s. It is unlikely that Fred King's fortunes were different.

On paper King's brewery looked sound enough: the 1878 partnership valuation reckoned the stock, trade debts and farming capital alone were worth £35,739. Besides this there were forty public houses, the brewery, maltings, and the goodwill of the business, all of which Fred King retained and rented to the partnership for £2,985 per annum. The valuation of these assets, albeit somewhat inflated after 1879, was around £50,000. His resources—ample enough on paper although always more limited than those of his competitor—had, however, been stretched even in the buoyant market of the mid-1870s. After 1879 there was no further expansion on the old scale. As Greene's acquisition surged forward Fred King and his son bought only a further twelve public houses before the 1887 amalgamation. Half of these were bought in 1886 alone.

Yet it would be wrong to assume from this fragmentary evidence that King's brewery went through some sort of crisis between 1879 and 1885.[17] The key to these years, as in so much of Fred King's career, was his family. His eleven children were becoming financially increasingly burdensome. Not only was their education expensive—for his sons he thought in terms of Oxford or Cambridge, although none of them went there—but from the late 1870s he was also having to find substantial sums to launch his daughters into matrimony and his five sons into business. The eldest, J. M. King, became a partner in the brewery and the third was trained in the brewing business,[18] but it was impossible to find room in the firm for all five sons. At first their father turned to the old family involvement, farming. Throughout his long life the urge to farm ran very deep in his veins. In the early 1870s he rented his father-in-law's Bradfield St George farm and also made bricks there. When it was sold in 1876 he rented, on an annual lease, the 350-acre Vicarage Farm at Great Barton. This was a first class farm which he ran on the best mixed farming principles.[19] Two years later he was also farming Rushford Lodge on the Norfolk border; a big farm of about 1,200 acres, its marginal, Breckland land can hardly have been profitable in the years he occupied it (1878–97). The chief attraction for Fred King was its excellent shooting and a rambling, beautifully secluded house on the Little Ouse, all within a dozen miles of Bury.[20] He also rented other farms: Ashby Hall in Cambridgeshire, and one at Dalham. In the mid-1880s he was farming almost 2,500 acres, a quite exceptional farming venture for this time. All were rented. His accounts show that he had £15,500 invested in them in 1886. They were managed by his second son Frank, although after 1880 he relied increasingly on the advice of his son-in-law, George Blencowe, the leading land valuer in West Suffolk in the late nineteenth century.[21] Even on this scale farming in East Anglia was an uphill struggle throughout the 1880s and 1890s so Fred King cast wider for opportunities for his sons. His next move was almost as bold as his venture into brewing.

In 1881 he invested £8,000 in a cement and brick manufactory, in the Caledonian Road in North London. He knew something of brick-making but nothing about cement manufacture. Again it shows his vision for with house-building booming in and around a rapidly expanding London, prospects in this business for his second and fourth sons, Frank and John, seemed excellent.[22] In the same year Fred King invested £3,500 in purchasing the Great Tithes at Pakenham. Not surprisingly he was writing in December, 'I may perhaps want to deposit my deeds as a temporary security with my Bankers until I can realise some of the money employed on the Farms . . . next Michaelmas.' In the event he continued farming but, with expenditure on this scale, he was withdrawing money from the brewery that might have been used in the purchase of tied property had family circumstances been different. The 1878 partnership agreement, which allowed a rental of almost £3,000 per annum for all the brewery property as well as a seven-eighths share of its profits, was being utilised to provide his family with the economic security that he felt he had never possessed in his own youth. Although it was possible to commandeer funds during his lifetime in this way, his death would have badly upset the strategy. Therefore after 1876, when his solicitor described him as 'in a large way of business', he attempted by a series of very detailed wills to devise a trust fund in

the event of his demise which would ensure the survival of the
brewery intact and yet allow sufficient income to keep his widow,
educate his children and launch them liberally into the world. It
was this desire to provide for his large family that drove Fred King
to make the arrangement with the Greenes in 1887. The background was partly the recession in beer sales in the 1880s and
uncertainties about agriculture, but also changes in company law
in the previous twenty-five years which allowed limited liability
of the private company. He saw that if the two firms were amalgamated his share of the new firm's capitalisation could be
fairly divided amongst his family; at the same time it would in
no way prejudice James King's position as a director of the
new venture, or that of the son he could additionally expect to
have admitted on his retirement or death. Amalgamation
achieved the exact purpose he had been puzzling over since the
early 1870s.

Before we examine the way in which Greene's brewery faced
the changes of the 1870s and 1880s and its reasons for amalgamation we must briefly look at Fred King's business techniques, for
they show in their typically Victorian recipe of hard work, thrift
and bustle, a good contrast with Edward Greene's more conscious, carefully publicised ventures into business management.
We have already seen evidence of his great drive. By 1886 his
assets in the brewery, farms, cement business and investments
(largely foreign) were valued at £135,000, returning him a gross
income of £14,154 in that year. For the man who had been sent
thirty years earlier to rescue his father-in-law's ailing maltings it
was a notable achievement. Fortunes like this were not often made
in Victorian Bury. In business he combined vision, a terrifying
decisiveness and a remarkable attention to detail. The force of his
ambition was his desire to provide for his family and the urge, in
the best Victorian tradition, to create a fortune. He was obsessed
by the disposition of property and money. Even in the 1930s his
activities were remembered in the brewery. By this time they had
degenerated into tales about his parsimony. The one most current
was of the lad sent into town for a kipper for Mr King's breakfast
after an early brewing session. He brought back a pair, was
soundly lectured about extravagance and smartly sent back to
return one to the fishmonger. Such tales illustrate one side of Fred

King's character, but they should not obscure his wider business talents.

Clearly there was an awkward side to his personality. He could be alarmingly brusque on occasions, which when carried into business or family affairs could have sharp consequences for those closest to him. His first partnership with Francis Phillips was a curious affair. It was advertised in the Bury newspapers and a bill for the legal work survives. But there were problems about Phillips's release from his previous partnership at Stowmarket and he worked as King's brewer's assistant for three years before he threatened legal action about his status in the firm.[23] Fred King consulted his lawyer about the 'alleged claim' and excluded Phillips from the brewery. Since no more was heard of the claim, presumably legal right was on Fred King's side. When he married his second wife in 1889 she must have been somewhat anxious about the unusual way in which he completed her marriage settlement post-nuptially. At all times Fred King was unnervingly decisive. There were continually sharp exchanges with his travellers, tenants and solicitors. All matters had to be sorted out quickly, cheaply and made legally watertight. No one got the better of him in a bargain. When it came to valuations at the expiration of a tenancy, or the finer details of a contract, he was the match for any tenant or solicitor in Suffolk or London. Effective measures were taken against bad debtors. Loyal work-men were fairly treated and given pensions on their retirement, but even here he could be engagingly idiosyncratic. When he left £25 a year to his coachman, it was made clear that 'payments shall cease immediately on his becoming tenant of a Public House or Beerhouse or Hotel Tap'. It was typical of Fred King that when he fell out in 1886 with William Finch, who had been his traveller and head clerk for seventeen years, there was a dispute about whether he was legally entitled to restrain a traveller from work-ing with another firm.

Nothing captures the flavour of his approach better than his correspondence over a barn at Great Barton which he rented from the Vicar after purchasing the *Crown* Inn there in 1872. Four years later the rent was suddenly increased from £1 to £9 a year. Fred King refused either to pay or quit and said it was a matter entirely to be decided by his sub-tenant. After a sharp letter from the Vicar's solicitors he told them bluntly they were lying. By return he received a curt note: 'We beg to acknowledge the Receipt of your most insulting letter of yesterday's date, giving us the lie direct—of course we can hold no further communication with you.' The envelope was addressed to 'Mr F. W. King, Common Brewer, Bury'. Fred King was a match for the lawyer, replying,

> 'I am obliged to answer your wrathful letter rec$^{d.}$ this day. It was not my intention to discuss the matter but merely to impress upon you that I could not accept your statement. Had I been aware Mr. Isaacson's ire was so soon excited I would have worded it otherwise. I am not ashamed to subscribe myself The Very Common Brewer, Fred$^{k.}$ Wllm. King.'

It was left for King's solicitors, Partridge and Wilson, to sort out the affair. They, enjoying his extensive business, came to live with his curt notes written on the cheapest squared paper. Others were incensed by his peremptory instructions and observations. When the Maulkin trust was being wound up its smart London solicitor, Alfred Jonas, a cousin of the first Mrs King, found 'he appeared to discredit my information and to know more about my business than I did.' When he tried to raise £5,000 by note of hand, Jonas, alarmed by his attempts to shortcircuit the accepted legal route, tartly commented, 'The method Mr King proposes to adopt is new to us but these are times for startling innovations in the transfer of land.'

Fred King's life was devoted to business. He had little time for politics in Bury and none at all for its social round. He never made a public statement, even on farming. He seldom attended any meeting, never held any sort of office in the town, and never joined the Farmers Clubs which were so popular in late Victorian England. When he died at the age of 87 in 1917 the *Bury Free Press* commented, 'The deceased gentleman has not identified himself with local public work.'[24] His public appearances and charity were limited to attendance at and support of St Mary's Church. Shooting was his sole recreation. Even after a day's sport with the Duke of Grafton at Euston—an event which would have moved most rising brewers to some effusion—Fred King could report the event in the same style he would have used for a communication with his tenants. The contrast between his career and Edward Greene's was total. They shared little beyond a common occupation and abundant energy. With Fred King the latter never waned: even after he went to live at Rushford in 1880 the St Edmunds brewery was conscious that its driving force had not been removed. Each Wednesday, market day in Bury, he descended to view his staff, his books and his beer with alarming thoroughness. Even after he returned to Rushford, that 'benighted place', the flow of missives was never reduced.

3

When Edward Greene became M.P. for Bury St Edmunds in 1865 he could no longer devote time to the everyday management of the Westgate Brewery. For thirty-five years he had nurtured its growth, been constant in his daily attention to its affairs and lived either in the brewery yard or within earshot at 6 Westgate. Now parliamentary duties meant increasingly long absences from Bury. He usually rented a town house for the sessions of the House of Commons, and even when he was in Suffolk he lived at Ixworth. His county responsibilities burgeoned. As an M.P., county Justice of the Peace, master of the Suffolk Hunt (1871–5), prominent Low Churchman and High Farmer, he addressed countless meetings between 1865 and 1878 on a great variety of subjects. Of course he still dictated overall brewery policy and when he was at Ixworth and later Nether Hall he rode to Bury each Wednesday to attend the Market and visit the brewery for a weekly meeting. The close supervision which had been the root of his success was, however, now left to others. Already he had devised a system of management which devolved some responsibilities to heads of departments. This solved management problems at the lower level, although with such a devoted workforce operating in the context of an oversupplied market for agricultural labour, they were not great. Much of the work in breweries and maltings is routine in nature, and they have always been relatively small employers of labour. Real success in Edward Greene's day was dependent upon a clever brewer, and a management which could provide sufficient impetus to meet the challenge of expanding consumption within the changing framework of retail outlets, producing and efficiently marketing reliable beers. After 1865, when Edward could no longer supply this type of regular drive, it was essential for the brewery to find a replacement.

First choice fell automatically upon his only son Walter.[25] Born in 1842, Walter Greene was always destined to run the brewery. He grew up in its environs, and the experiences of his childhood were circumscribed by its activities, noise and odour. Yet the family circumstances of his infancy and youth in the 1840s and 1850s were more affluent than those of the previous generation in the 1820s. Whereas his father and uncles had received excellent educations at the Bury Grammar School, when it failed to make the transition into a first-rate public school, Edward removed him, after only a term there, to the most publicised of all the reinvigorated Victorian educational establishments, Dr Arnold's Rugby. Not that Walter achieved any greater academic distinction there than he would have done at Bury, for he had throughout his life little time for books. Later his daughter recalled that he always told her not to bother her head with books: Surtees and the Bible had been enough for him. There was no pressure to attain the academic competence that would have carried him, like so many scholars at new public schools, into the professions, for he had no need to look beyond the brewery for an ample livelihood. Rugby gave him easy manners, a scrupulous conscientiousness to carry out his responsibilities, and an extensive range of social acquaintances. He was good looking and the apple of his widowed father's eye—although his four sisters, who had to play second fiddle to their only brother in most matters, found him distinctly spoilt. From his earliest days he liked and expected his own way. After Rugby he went to Paris to learn foreign languages, travelled extensively in Europe, and then completed his brewer's training at Brighton with a 'noted firm'.[26] In 1862, just before he came of age, his father took him into partnership. Two years later he married the daughter of a well-connected Staffordshire clergyman. His father bought Westgate House and the young couple moved into the old family home, 6 Westgate.

Therefore when Edward Greene was returned to Parliament he, like his father in 1836, had visions of new opportunities and plans to hand over the management of the brewery to his son. Walter, however, never showed the aptitude for work and business that Edward and Benjamin had possessed. In many ways he was the archetypal third generation businessman whose example gives support to those historians who believe entrepreneurial failure underpins Britain's gradual economic decline after 1870. His prospects were always too settled, his education and tastes un-suited to the dull routine of everyday business. Ideally he should have been a colonel in a good cavalry regiment with ample opportunities for fox hunting in the Shires. There, with a proper concern for his men, his horses and his hounds, he would have been superb. Instead he had to centre his life in Bury and the brewery. He neither resented nor shirked his business responsi-bilities—his upbringing at home and training at Rugby prevented this—but he had little to offer in a positive, dynamic way to the management of the brewery. His interests were always elsewhere.

Walter was extremely sociable and an excellent sportsman: a first class shot, a keen yachtsman, and a bold driver of a four-in-hand. From the age of seventeen he was active in the Suffolk Militia.[27] His greatest passion was hunting, 'Given a bright winter's morning, a pack of well-bred hounds and a good field he was in his *métier*'.[28] He remembered following his father's beagles as soon as he could run and on one occasion, at the age of nine, hunted hounds himself. In 1864 he began to hunt at his own expense a pack of harriers and briefly some staghounds before joining his father in the mastership of the Suffolk Hunt (1871–5). Then in 1875 he suffered a very serious accident when his four-horse drag overturned on a steep Derbyshire hill. He was lucky to escape with his life. His spine was badly injured and most of the next five years was spent recuperating. At one stage in his slow convalescence he spent several months travelling in India with his young family. By 1880 he had recovered sufficiently to hunt the Suffolk hounds again before leaving in 1883 to become master of the Croome Hunt in Worcestershire for five years.[29] Suffolk by the 1870s was not ideal hunting country. There was too much plough and preserved game to achieve anything like the fast runs of the Shires. Therefore at times between 1867 and 1871 and from 1891 to 1899, Walter kept his own pack of staghounds to enjoy a more exciting sport two days a week. His commitment was total, for he always hunted hounds himself. Indeed critics in the saddle thought he was over zealous in his vocation, too inclined to lift hounds from their scent. But Walter was immensely

proud that for thirty-four years, often at his own expense, he
hunted with genial success harriers, fox and staghounds.

Visitors to the Westgate brewery were intrigued. For even in the
nineteenth century the juxtaposition of a thriving brewery with
hunt kennels and stables was unusual. When the reporter of the
Victuallers' Gazette in 1875 inspected the latter behind 6, Westgate he had expected to find 'some splendid specimens of the dray
horse' but he was surprised to find also a stud of seventeen
hunters, carriage horses and cover-hacks and then to come upon
the 'kennels where some fifty couples of foxhounds are discours-
ing most musically'. It was a sound that advertised the profitability of breweries, the ample leisure of brewers and the real interests
of Walter Greene.

Walter's preoccupation with rural sports which coincided with
the brewery's busy season did not lead to tensions with his father.
The latter was proud of his son's prowess in the hunting field and
his predilection for sporting and military matters. He believed his
activities gave the Greenes lustre in the County. Moreover Walter
was immensely loyal to his father, and politically they saw
completely eye to eye. Yet Walter's sporting interests, to say
nothing of his frequent incapacity through injury, meant that
Edward was forced to find a more active manager for his brewery
—especially after 1869 when the competition from Fred King's
new brewery began to make itself felt. At first he turned to
William Pead (1831–1903) who had joined the brewery from
school in the mid-1840s.[30] Twenty years later he had become
manager. From around this date he seems to have enjoyed a share
of the malting's profits, for the post 1876 partnership accounts,
although they omit him as a fully profit sharing partner, show that
he was paid a share of the malting's profits and a small proportion
of those of the brewery. In addition he drew a fixed salary of £800
as general manager with 'supreme control of the office and the
books, with a supervising power over the whole establishment'.
Although he clearly fulfilled a vital role in the brewery's management in the decade after Edward entered Parliament, his power
was more apparent than real. For Edward was extremely hesitant
to allow control in any measure to slip outside the family, even if
he interpreted family to include the large clan of Benjamin Green's
grandchildren. He trained two Burrell nephews in the firm during

6. 'A North View of the Buildings on the Sandy Point Estate of Sir Patrick Blake Baronet' (c. 1790). Benjamin Greene and his son Benjamin Buck managed this, and other St Kitts' estates, in the 1820s and 1830s.

7. Fred King and his young family in 1866, two years before he founded his brewery. The photograph was probably taken in the garden of their St Mary's Square house, the site of the present bottling stores. James King, joint managing director of Greene King (1887–1915) stands at his father's elbow,

8. This panoramic view of Westgate Brewery in the early 1880s conveys its compact, almost domestic features. The malt houses of 1855 and 1880 are shown on the left.

9. 'The Rushbrooke Arms', Little Welnetham, from a card posted in 1906. Greene King owned scores of similar village public houses in East Anglia, although few were more picturesque than this one.

10. Nether Hall in about 1900. The estate was bought by Edward Greene in 1875. The house had a seventeenth-century core which was almost entirely obscured by his refenestration of the house, and Walter Greene's wholesale alterations and extensions after 1891.

the 1860s and when (in 1864) his histrionic eldest daughter Emily married a somewhat impecunious Yorkshireman, Fred Machell Smith, he found him a partnership first in his bank and then in his thriving wine and spirit business. Fred Smith was a gentleman of uncertain temperament, greatly given to photography, and although he played the churchman, hunting and agricultural-interest games according to Greene rules he was always over-powered by their family and was never offered a partnership by his father-in-law. In 1885 his wife, bored by 'dull Bury', per-suaded him to find emancipation in London.[31]

Seemingly, neither the Burrells nor Fred Smith had the neces-sary qualities to be absorbed into the brewery's upper manage-ment. Instead in 1869 Edward took another nephew, Edward Lake, then 19, into the firm. In fact the arrangement was merely to help his sister, the widow of a London solicitor. Edward Lake was the youngest of her eight children and his uncle agreed to give him a brewer's training. For two years he worked in the office and was then appointed to assist the head brewer, R. J. Symonds. After a further couple of years his uncle found him a place with a brewery in Kent, but just before he was due to move Walter Greene suffered one of his numerous accidents in the hunting field and Edward then decided to keep his nephew at the brewery. For from the outset he had shaped extremely well, possessing real financial and management acumen. He did everything his uncle wanted. With a young man's energy he absorbed himself in Bury life. He was a keen member of the Athenaeum debating society, a good footballer—he formed the first team in the town—and a left arm bowler with the Bury and West Suffolk cricket club.[32] By 1875 he held 'an important place in the brewery' and his uncle rewarded him in the 1876 partnership by a one-twelfth share of its profits. Edward had solved the problem of management continuity. Ownership and, indeed, overall direction was still firmly retained in his own hands, but he could at last turn his attention fully to Parliamentary and County affairs, confident that however much time he spent in London, or Walter might devote to his hunting and yachting, the management was safe with Edward Lake. Giving him his head so quickly was one of the best moves Edward ever made. It is good testimony to his sound judgment.

4

There had already been a major switch in policy after 1871 when Edward Greene turned from his much publicised free trade position to begin buying public houses throughout West Suffolk. Undoubtedly the motive was competition from King's neighbouring St Edmunds brewery. At Greene King it is still recalled that the 1887 amalgamation was the result of the breakneck race to acquire public houses by both breweries.[33] In essentials the recollection is correct enough.

Edward's first purchase for over twenty years took place in August 1868. The precise chronology is important. In March 1868 Henry Braddock, who had run the Southgate brewery and had been prominent in Bury affairs for almost half a century, died. Both his politics and his brewery were old-fashioned: he was a Whig and, since he was an old man with no sons, the brewery went unmodernised. It was nevertheless valuable for it included eleven public houses, possession of which the auctioneer at the sale in July joked provided 'a stepping stone to a seat in Parliament'. Edward had to acquire it not so much to protect his electoral position as to stop any rival brewer buying it. For only in June, Fred King, possibly seeing the gap that Henry Braddock's demise provided, had announced his plans to commence brewing. Therefore Edward bought the Southgate brewery for £7,000 and immediately began its dismemberment. The brewery, with its fine house, was sold to his manager William Pead and brewing there ceased although the *White Hart* maltings provided an additional source of malt as late as the 1930s. Within the next few months seven of the eleven public houses were sold. Edward was not yet convinced about the need to acquire every public house within range, although he was certain about the desirability of restricting competition by undermining his rivals. The break-up of Braddock's brewery, however, in no way stemmed Fred King's enterprise and there seems to have been genuine uncertainty about the next move in the Westgate camp. Greene's bought the *Dog and Partridge* in 1870, which was sensible enough since it adjoined the brewery yard, but it was only in late 1871 after Fred King had bought five public houses, as well as obtaining control of the eight belonging to the Maulkin trust, that Edward initiated a systematic policy of leasing and purchasing public houses to match that of his rival. In the next five years he bought twenty and leased thirteen more.

The expansion of the Greene empire before 1887 is reconstructed from three sources, all of which are incomplete. First, the debenture trust deed of December 1887 provides a detailed list of acquisitions by both breweries with precise dates. It is incomplete in two respects: it provides a list of those houses held by the firm in December 1887, although already there had been some sales of unwanted houses; the solicitor's working papers for the amalgamation suggest it does not include a handful of mortgaged houses, although it includes others that were. From its schedules of free and copyhold property—the security for debenture holders—a total of 91 public and beer houses are shown to have been purchased before 1 June 1887 (see Table 1, p. 104). Second, the partnership accounts which run from 1 May 1876 to 1 May 1886 provide annual figures of the acquisition of public houses. These seem rather low, since they appear to exclude the Stowmarket Brewery houses bought in 1883. In 1886, a year before amalgamation, these accounts show the Westgate brewery owning seventy-six inns valued at £51,835, a sum that had doubled during the ten years of the partnership and which now almost equalled that invested in machinery, plant, drays and stocks of malt, beer and casks. Third, some of the firm's legal papers survive to flesh out, albeit unevenly, the skeleton of these statistics and provide a list of Greene leases in operation when the firms merged.

This survey of the Greene public houses is interesting at two levels: it shows how a middle-sized country brewery expanded in the 1870s and 1880s in attempting to restrict competition; and the legal papers that have survived for these transactions reveal a fascinating vignette of Suffolk's social history for the previous half century. The world of country inns, beer house keepers and the ways in which they made their modest living, their indebtedness, and their response to pushy brewers such as Edward Greene and Fred King is a theme that historians have neglected.

First let us look at the motives behind Edward Greene and his partner's extension of their market after 1870. Most accounts of the brewing industry in the late nineteenth century maintain that the brewers' scramble to obtain their own public houses was in response to the tightening up of licensing after 1869 and the downturn in *per capita* beer consumption from the late 1870s. Neither was initially significant in the Greene impetus, for licensing restrictions had little bite in Suffolk before 1902 and whatever happened to *per capita* consumption, total output rose until the turn of the century. What is clear is that throughout the twenty years before the 1887 merger the Greenes were attempting to expand their market by stifling competition. It was a natural response to Fred King's threat to check their growth. The dismemberment of Braddock's brewery in 1868 was the first manifestation of this fear. But there are others.

As we have seen, Edward Greene proudly maintained in 1865 that for the past decade he had eschewed all forms of legal ties with publicans to supply his beers. He was soon eating his words. Not only did the firm begin the regular *purchase* of houses after 1871 but he was also keenly *leasing* them.[36] Of 20 leases in operation in 1887, 13 were contracted between 1871 and 1874, some of which had previously been let to other brewers. After 1874 the rate slowed down for only a further 6 were contracted.[37] Either the supply of leasehold houses had dried up or their owners were being persuaded by good offers to sell them. In a period of increasing competition a lease gave the brewer imperfect protection. It normally ran for seven years and, although clauses restricting sales to his beers and spirits were binding enough, there was no guarantee that at the end of the period the owner would withstand the blandishments of a rival brewer. Moreover, the advance in public house property prices in the 1870s induced many owners to place their investments on the market. By 1875 Edward Greene seems to have acknowledged that the way forward was not to be achieved by the traditional leasing arrangements. Henceforth purchases were more usual.

The scramble to acquire public houses was intensified when breweries themselves came on to the market. In Suffolk they were not usually worthy of the name, being little more than busy inns producing their own beer. The 1876–86 partnership accounts show that the mortgage account never exceeded £4,000 except when the purchase of the Stowmarket brewery sent borrowing requirements rising. Then £26,450 was raised; but largely by the sale of its unwanted houses this debt was reduced to under £10,000 within three years. Of course, like all brewers, Greenes were aided in the expansion of their tied houses by the low raw material costs and interest charges which ruled after 1873. In every year except 1879, when the partnership balance was struck on 1 May their account was in credit at the bank, although it is likely that when purchases of hops and barley were at their peak in autumn the position was different. Most similar sized firms would have envied Greene's financial stability, with profits in excess of 12 per cent and a good cash flow, in this period of growth and innovation.

The collection of legal documents relating to the acquisition of public houses by Edward Greene and Fred King before 1887 can never provide, like a firm's letter book, a detailed picture of the ownership of public houses and the relationship between brewer and tenant in the Victorian period. Yet they show something of the changes taking place in this interesting, unexplored corner of our social history. Many of the public and beer houses bought by the two firms were owned by petty investors—farmers, builders, shopkeepers, country craftsmen, and widows. Their owners had bought them when the savings of these rural classes found their way into either property or loans. And of course some had been acquired, often on mortgage, by publicans themselves. Frequently they were in poor repair, old, and constructed with bad building materials. Sometimes they included adjoining cottages and shops. The *Castle* Inn at Bury St Edmunds though 'most prominently situated' in the Cornhill was a glorious confusion: its 'Large and Handsome Club Room' ran under Bury Police Station, which seems to have occupied part of the ground floor annex of the inn, whilst three of its bedrooms were above the police offices.[38] This rare contiguity of premise use must have provided an exacting test for publican and police alike. Invariably, when purchased, houses needed money spending on their repair. In the country they seldom sold more than two or three barrels of beer a week. The bigger inns in Bury plied a brisker trade and were often used as lodging houses. Many attracted custom through the use of their club rooms and these were becoming a feature of the busier country inns. Most possessed brewing facilities and probably made some of their own beer until annexation by one or other of the two breweries. When the eight Maulkin houses were sold in 1875, although all were 'held by Mr. Frederick W. King, whose

Tenancy expires on first day of May next', seven possessed brew houses and five of these still had 'brewing plant'. The *Bushel* Inn in St John's Street enjoyed 'a large reputation for Home-brewed Beer. There is a capital Brewing Plant upon the Premises.' From this evidence many tenants were still brewing a proportion of their own beer until the 1870s.

Of course most tenants, to make a living, held other occupations. Publican cum dealer was a frequent affiliation. An inn with a few acres of grass was the ideal venue for a cattle jobber to do business. *The Manger* at Bradfield Combust, sold with 20 acres of land in 1875, was 'especially attractive . . . to Publican and Dealers' being within four miles of Bury market. Others, especially beer houses, often had facilities for baking bread and selling groceries and meat whilst the publican of the aptly named *Horse and Shoes* at Stanton ran a blacksmith's shop. Many country inns had cottages and parcels of land adjoining. The Whepstead *Greyhound* had 10 acres and a brick kiln and the tenant of the *Rose and Crown* at Stanton farmed 43 acres.

Yet duality of occupation did not give the publican independence of the brewer. If the former brewed extensively then this did, but the tendency after 1830 was for victuallers to buy at least some of their beer from nearby common brewers. It was more convenient, sometimes cheaper, and usually of more reliable quality. Yet when a publican began to take beer from a brewer he invariably became indebted to him. Many of the beer houses acquired from publicans eventually fell into Greene's and King's hands because they had failed to settle their accounts. When Edward Death sold a beer house at Rattlesden for £580 to Edward Greene in 1882 he received only £140, for £300 was due to the mortgagor and £140 to Fred King for the supply of beer.

From the brewer's viewpoint the new arrangements ensured conditions of greater certainty and reliability. Leases, and especially outright purchase, brought tenants into line. When the brewer became the landlord he could enforce his policy more effectively than when the publican was independent or was the lessee of another owner. Brewers forced tenants into line by two means. First, they devised legal agreements which were binding in respect of valuations about fittings, internal decorations, the licence, and of course the exclusive sale of their beers, mineral waters and often spirits. Second, conformity in these areas was enforced by the regular visits of the brewer's clerk and traveller. Edward Greene and Fred King relied on three: Robert Spalding, Robert Carliell and William Last.[39] All were well paid, respectable, and devoted to the interests and politics of their masters. They not only took orders, collected cash and negotiated the details of rents and fittings, but they assessed the tenant's credit worthiness, industry and cleanliness. Every detail was reported back to Bury.

If wholesale purchase of public houses imposed a new order in the relationship between brewer and tenant the old haphazard arrangements that existed in Suffolk up to the last quarter of the nineteenth century are well brought out by the case of the Stanton *Rose and Crown*. The inn with 43 acres was owned by a neighbouring landowner, leased to Edward Greene and in turn tenanted by a feckless farmer, William Kinsey. Greene's supplied Kinsey with ale and beer and nominated the supplier of spirits and wines. Kinsey was badly hit by rapidly falling agricultural prices in the late 1870s and by dwindling custom. His debt with Greene's increased. In 1880 he agreed with their traveller to sell all his greyhounds except a bitch, 'which paid them well'. Unfortunately the contraction of his kennels did nothing for the state of his account. He tried the good offices of the firm's traveller in January 1881, thanking him for 'great kindness for interceding with the firm on my behalf . . . my wife and self very much regret the state of affairs but hope that by perseverance and Economy we may overcome the difficulties occasioned by the late bad Seasons . . . our study is to comply with the wishes of the firm in all transactions.' Good Victorian intentions, yet the debt still grew. Greene's men came out from Bury that autumn to take the harvest from the fields. Even so Kinsey owed the firm £122. In the following spring bankruptcy proceedings could be staved off no longer. The whole affair was messy, but not altogether untypical of those existing between brewer and publican in the days before breweries owned most of their houses. Certainly outright ownership, the more careful selection of tenants and greater control by the brewer and his clerks and travellers were all partial solutions to problems illustrated by William Kinsey.

Control of tenants then was an important aspect of acquisition.

Moreover in terms of investment public houses were sensible speculations in themselves, especially in the early 1870s and again when prices fell in the 1880s. For not only did they provide protection from competition but their rentals produced a return that was reasonable in comparison with most real estate. The evidence suggests that rentals (the 'dry' rent) were not excessive and that it was, of course, the 'wet rent', i.e. the profit of 11 shillings on barrels passed to tenants compared with the 6 shillings profit on those sold to the 'free trade' that provided the real economic justification of public house acquisition.

Even with price falls after 1880, agricultural depression in Suffolk and licence restrictions, these houses bought before the boom of the mid-1890s remained sound earning assets. Within little more than a decade Fred King and Edward Greene had joined the ranks of the largest property owners in the county. The latter, in the name of his firm and himself, between 1870 and 1887 had acquired an 850-acre estate, further property in Bury and over ninety public houses—assets valued at around £150,000. Both men were great joys to their solicitor, whose Guildhall Street offices became cluttered with their deed boxes.

5

Although the rapid acquisition of public houses by Greene's and King's breweries after 1870 gave both firms a more extended and better protected market, they could not guarantee the permanently high profits many brewers anticipated. For the prosperous conditions of the late 1860s and early 1870s were not repeated in the early 1880s. Sales figures for Greene's running from May 1876 to May 1886 (see Appendix 2, Table 2), show a check in 1880, stagnation in 1881–2, and a sharp fall from late 1884. The causes were the onset of deep agricultural depression after 1879 and, to a lesser degree, a low rate of population growth in East Anglia. Of course malt prices were low when cereal prices declined sharply (with the exception of hops in 1882–4) and continuously after the late 1870s so that profitability, although 'sticky' throughout the 1876–86 partnership, always remained at a healthy 12-plus per cent. National figures suggest a similar stagnation in output in the 1880s.

Table 2: Beer output, consumption and real wages, 1850–1914*

Years	Beer output (million barrels)	Consumption per head (gallons)	Average real wages (1850 = 100)
1850–4	16·1	21·1	101·2
1855–9	17·2	22·0	96·2
1860–4	19·9	24·7	105·8
1865–9	24·3	28·8	111·6
1870–4	27·6	31·1	127·4
1875–9	31·0	33·2	132·0
1880–4	28·5	29·1	137·2
1885–9	28·7	28·3	149·4
1890–4	31·5	29·7	164·0
1895–9	34·6	31·2	176·4
1900–4	35·2	30·2	175·2
1905–9	33·2	27·3	173·0
1910–14	34·1	26·9	171·2

* Source: B. R. Mitchell and P. Deane, *Abstract of British Historical Statistics* (1962), pp. 343–5 and G. B. Wilson, *Alcohol and the Nation* (1940), pp. 333–5.

There was, however, a paradox in the brewing trade which the annual reviews of the trade clearly bring out. Although they often categorise years in the late 1870s and 1880s as 'quiet', 'dull' and 'bad', they always concluded that the industry was, in comparison with all others, constitutionally very healthy. The *Brewers' Journal* commented that

1879 gave brewers no reason to complain . . . when the fact is considered that the large brewing companies go on paying 10, 14 and 18 per cent, it will be perceived that the business is a remarkably good one. If we were of a mercenary frame of mind we would now prefer the lot of an extensive holder of brewery shares to that of any other individual.

Discussing the previous year it came to the view,

however much people may be disposed to economise in other directions, it is evident that they will not do without the national beverage.

Nevertheless the hesitancy in Greene's sales and profitability after 1880 was a disappointing reward for their large-scale purchase of public houses. No doubt it was concluded that without them they might easily have done worse, yet even so by the 1880s their rate of profit was at best static and they were clearly worried about Fred King's competition. These are the classic motives behind the amalgamation of firms. We can only surmise that they were cogent with Edward Greene and Edward Lake, since little correspondence for the 1887 Greene King merger survives, except for a few letters from their London legal advisers. This is hardly surprising since the negotiations were rapid and secret between four principals who shared adjoining premises. Nevertheless there was clearly a defensive element in the Greenes' thinking.

The other factor in the background of the amalgamation was the great activity in the flotation of brewery companies by the mid-1880s. There were four main strands to this:[40] changes in company law going back to the mid-1850s which gave those firms that registered under the Acts limited liability and corporate status; the profitability of the trade; the tendency towards 'monopoly' by the elimination of the competition of the small brewer[41] who was unable to meet the many costs of technology and transport; and lastly, the rush to buy public houses after licence restrictions, the fear of hostile legislation from a Liberal government, and above all the drive to restrict competition. In the mid-1880s these various strands fused to carry a high voltage of speculative activity in the industry. Previously the breweries with their tight family control and very adequate finances had not been among the front runners of those firms which went public or, more usually, sought only the benefits of limited liability by registration.[42] But a comment in the *Bury Post* in 1882 typifies the growing interest in the flotation of brewery shares. In that summer the Bow Brewery went public with a share capital of £450,000:

> the Prospectus shows that the other London breweries owned by Limited Private Companies have declared large dividends, and the shares stand at high premiums, and anticipates the like prosperity for the projected undertaking.[43]

When conditions of real prosperity returned in 1886 there was dramatic speculative interest in the brewing industry. It was really launched by the spectacular public conversion of Guinness's brewery late in the year. This £6m. issue was over-subscribed several times; 'for weeks it was', the *Brewers' Journal* noted, 'the theme of universal interest and discussion'. Suddenly the biggest brewers, company promoters and financiers realised that the flotation of companies could yield big capital gains. The boom was on. In 1886 alone, twenty-eight firms, with a capital of £9.5m., changed from partnership status to limited liability as other leaders of the industry, Ind Coope, Samuel Allsopp, Whitbread and Courage, followed Guinness's lead. Many of them, even if their preference and ordinary shares were not marketed publicly, used money raised by debenture issues to purchase public houses, stimulating wholesale acquisition usually known as the 'Brewers Wars'. Where the supply of free houses was already small or when stocks dried up firms grew by amalgamation.[44] Of course the brewing interest welcomed the public's attention, for, given the hostile attitude of the Liberal party, they were anxious that ownership and involvement in the industry should be more widely spread.

The speculative mania even reached East Anglia. Late in 1886 the Norfolk and Suffolk Brewing Company sought to raise £200,000 to take over the Eye Brewery and the Falcon Brewery, Ipswich. Early in 1887 the Colchester Brewing Company merged Stope's and Cobbold's Colchester breweries. From the outset it was overcapitalised with a £300,000 mortgage and debenture debt so that, although the new company controlled 323 tied houses, by 1890 it was in serious financial straits. Morgan's Brewery Company in Norwich amalgamated breweries in Norwich and King's Lynn with a total capital of £185,000. Both the Colchester Brewing Company and Morgan's Brewery just predate the Greene King amalgamation of 1 June 1887.

From the correspondence that survives it is clear that Edward Lake was central to the plans to seek limited liability for the new company. Not only was he much more abreast of the rapid changes in the industry than his co-partners, but his brother Benjamin, an alert London solicitor, gave him invaluable advice about company flotation.[45] Of course Edward Greene and Fred King were eager to merge. As we have seen, Edward Greene, now in his seventies, wished to make provision for his family and was perturbed by the renewed activity of Fred King in buying public houses in 1886–7. Also profitability had been somewhat disappointing in the mid-1880s so that, listening to Edward Lake's advocacy of the benefits of amalgamation and corporate ownership, he opted for limited liability. In the fray King's had proved to be the leaner and fitter contestant. Although its output was only half that of its bigger rival, it had a quicker sales turn-round, lower unit costs, and its profits, at least from the evidence of the 1886–7 accounts, were two-thirds those of Greene's. In the latter respect it is significant that Fred King had from the outset used a firm of London accountants;[46] Greene's did so only when the amalgamation made them essential. Like Edward Greene himself, the firm had become somewhat ponderous in the 1870s and the 1880s. Yet for Fred King, with a family of eleven grown children and limited resources for his brewery's future expansion, the merger was equally attractive. In a letter to their accountant J. M. King admitted the advantages of a linkage with a business twice their size and he advised him to watch 'the Managing Partner (E. W. Lake) . . . a particularly smart man'. The size of the enterprise, Edward Lake's entrepreneurial qualities and the Kings' economical management would be a force to be reckoned with amongst East Anglian breweries.

The merger was agreed very quickly in early May. Edward Greene and Fred King gave their formal consent and the details were worked out by Edward Lake. For other principals such as the secretary, William Pead, the new status was something of a mystery. Pead was excluded from the negotiations except 'where they affect him'. Rowland Wilson (Greene's solicitor) wrote to Edward Greene in London, 'Edward Lake desires me to assure you that the contents of these documents [the Memorandum and Articles of Association] have been kept private from everyone except King himself and myself.'[47] Walter Greene, living in Worcestershire, was not involved in detailed negotiations. And Rowland Wilson, whose experience was confined to legal practice in backward Bury, was so unused to the workings of the Companies Act that even the most routine aspects of the amalgamation were referred for Benjamin Lake's opinion. Except for his brother, Benjamin clearly believed no one at Greene's or King's properly understood the business. He wrote insultingly from London at one stage, 'the Secretary [Pead] will no doubt understand that the Minutes are to be entered in the Minute Book and duly kept up'.

Nevertheless, the merger was pushed through with amazing speed. On 16 May there was no complete list of tied house property available and the senior partner of Partridge and Wilson had gone away for a month's holiday, taking the keys of all Fred King's deed boxes with him. But after frenzied efforts Edward and Benjamin Lake were able to complete the necessary documentation for registration of the new company on 1 June 1887. Its capitalisation was £555,000 which made it the second largest of the twenty-nine breweries which sought limited liability in 1887, and on these terms it was comparable with other regional leaders like Phipps' of Northampton and Smith's Tadcaster brewery.

There is no doubt that this capitalisation was generous and allowed for considerable future growth. Greene's tangible assets in May 1886 were valued at almost £218,000. King's accounts are more problematic. The partnership in 1886 was reckoned to be worth only £50,100, for the firm's stocks of beer were only one-eighth those of Greene's. These accounts included twelve public houses and the Suffolk Hunt Kennels, but they did not value the St Edmunds Brewery, maltings and thirty-nine public houses which Fred King rented to the partnership. Including a £6,000 goodwill valuation, these assets were valued in his private accounts at £44,879. Together the assets of the two firms were worth £343,000 in May–June 1886. In the speculative boom of 1886–7 they were somewhat undervalued, especially since both partnerships had been running for eight or nine years and valuations had not been increased much since their commencement. In May 1887 these assets were written up by rounding out tangible ones at £360,000 and placing a generous one-third or £180,000 estimate on the firm's goodwill. This notional figure supposedly represented the value of the free trade of both partnerships in order to balance the credit side of Greene King assets. The first balance sheet makes this clear (see Figure 1).

The allotment of shares followed a formula which valued the Westgate Brewery and its goodwill at £370,000 and those of St Edmunds at £170,000. As Greene King was a private company this generous valuation of its assets was unimportant. Voting rights were restricted to ordinary shares and, in the unlikely event

Dr.	£	Cr.	£
Capital		Freehold & leasehold	
20,000 Preference		properties	229,395
shares of £10 each	200,000	Goodwill	180,000
20,000 Ordinary			
shares of £10 each	200,000		
Debenture Stock	155,000	Plant, Machinery (less	
Sundry creditors	13,308	5% depreciation)	55,167
Sundry items	738	Casks	12,573
Profit after payment		Horses	2,571
of Debenture Interest		Mineral Waters,	
and Dividends	17,701	Stores etc.	13,000
		Debtors	21,962
		Loans to customers etc.	5,052
		Farm valuations,	
		rents owing	4,866
		Stocks of beer, malt	
		etc.	42,909
		Cash at Banks	19,252
	£586,747		£586,747

Figure 1: Greene King Balance Sheet, 31 May 1888

of a serious rift in policy, the Greene–Lake interest held the whip hand. Ownership of the company, with the exception of £5,000 worth of ordinary shares distributed to William Pead and £400 shared among four senior employees, was restricted to eight individuals. Two of these, Fred King's sisters-in-law, were being compensated for the £5,000 mortgage they held on the old Maulkin properties; and George Blencowe's shares were held in trust for Fred King's six daughters. Thus effective ownership was confined to the five partners of the two firms, who now became directors. Restrictions were placed on the sale of shares outside the Greene, King and Lake families. At the same time the Company issued £155,000 worth of debenture stock. Unlike so many breweries, which issued debentures to raise further funds for public house purchase, the Greene King issue was a paper transaction (although it went through all the necessary legal forms) to compensate the old partners for their firm's free trade.[48] It followed standard accounting practice whereby loans did not exceed one-third of total share capital. It also, of course, gave its owners the security of a first charge on the assets of the new company should it run into bad times. In addition to the £140,000 allotted to the Greene and King families in debentures, £14,300 was raised late in 1887 from individuals in and around Bury to pay for the purchase of the Kedington brewery.

Table 3: The capitalisation of Greene King and Sons, December 1887

Owner	Value of 5% preference shares*	Value of ordinary shares	4% debenture stock
	£	£	£
Edward Greene	85,900	80,750	59,300
E. W. Greene	34,400	34,300	23,800
F. W. King	28,500	30,900	21,500
E. W. Lake	17,200	17,150	8,700
J. M. King	14,000	14,000	9,000
G. Blencowe & E. M. King	17,500	17,500	12,000
M. E. & L. E. Maulkin	2,500	—	2,500
W. Pead	—	5,000	—
Others	—	400†	17,500
Total	£200,000	£200,000	£154,300

* Preference and ordinary shares were of £10 denomination, debentures (redeemable from 1917) were initially of £1,000 each, although when £14,300 was issued to 'others' late in 1887 allotments were as small as £200.

† Ten shares each were allotted to Greene's brewer (R. J. Symonds), two clerks and the head traveller.

The new company placed Greene King amongst the largest country brewers in England. Their adoption of limited liability was comparatively early. Although there was a defensive element in the amalgamation, their actions in 1887 suggest they were front runners in the industry. Now we must examine whether the new arrangements brought about profound changes in the management, production and policies of the brewery.

5

The New Company and
Edward Lake's Regime, 1887–1920

The amalgamation effected minimal changes except in the financial arrangements of the company. Brewing continued quite separately on both sites under the charge of a first and second brewer, and workmen still felt their affiliations were with 'Westgate' or 'St Edmunds' rather than with Greene King. Physically the breweries developed much more slowly after 1887 than they had in the two decades before. There were immediate minor alterations in 1888 to bring the St Edmunds brewery up to scratch, but casual passers-by would scarcely have noticed any changes as they walked down Westgate in the 1890s. For the annual capacity of the two breweries together—around 65,000–70,000 barrels in the mid-1880s—needed virtually no expansion to meet demand in the years before 1914,[1] although there were improvements in machinery and plant as the technology of brewing underwent significant changes in this period.

Nationally, growth in the industry slowed down after the 1880s. The process was not uniform: there was a surge in activity between 1894 and 1900, and there were always differences between the prosperity of the urban and country trades. Overall, however, there was a feeling in the industry that the heady days of mid-Victorian expansion were over. From 1900 there was constant gloom when real wages fell and the Liberal governments after 1905 seemed determined to pursue a policy of hostile legislation taken straight from the Temperance handbook. The basis of deceleration, however, appears to have been a gradual change in people's spending and leisure habits. Real wages continued to rise until the late 1890s but already it was being observed that, in contrast to the 1860s and 1870s, a smaller proportion was being spent on the national drink.[2] Other consumer industries, just coming to prominence with the development of a mass market in ready-made clothing and shoes, machine-produced furniture and packaged foodstuffs, attracted the spending of working-class families. Moreover as music halls, football and cheap railway excursions proliferated, the public house, that old citadel of working-class leisure, declined somewhat in popularity. These social changes were far more important in reducing drink consumption than the Temperance and Non-Conformist attacks on liquor. Even rural Suffolk, where social habits changed more slowly than in the great cities, was not immune from these forces. At a directors' meeting in 1904 Edward Lake noted,

> a long discussion took place with regard to pushing the private trade of the Brewery in view of the fact that there seemed a tendency among the public not to use the Public Houses as formerly.

When we examine the firm's record in the context of the changing fortunes of the brewing industry after 1887 three aspects stand out: the steady accumulation of tied property between 1887 and 1904; the strength of Edward Lake's financial management; and the modest degree of change that the merger brought about in the running of the brewery.[3] Before we turn to these, however, it is necessary to look a little more closely at the economic and political climate between 1887 and 1914 within which Greene King operated. It will allow us to see how far the experiences of a major regional brewery with a largely rural outlet coincided with those of its parent industry and also to outline the types of problem the firm faced in these years.

I

No sooner had Greene's and King's merged than their fortunes were caught once more in the web of agricultural recession which caught the arable farmers of the South and East in the last quarter of the nineteenth century. The lull of the mid-1880s was short-lived. When the firm came to assess the results of amalgamation in its first annual report it found no cause for concern about profitability since it had 'quite equalled their expectation', but the level of output was worrying. In spite of buying no fewer than forty-one public houses during the first year production declined by over 1,300 barrels. The directors blamed the agricultural depression and saw no relief so long as it continued.[4] Figures for production and profit suggest that there was—except briefly in 1890—no recovery until 1895, for not until the year ending 31 May 1896 did either exceed pre-amalgamation levels. Nationally the figures of output and *per capita* consumption show a modest recovery in the early 1890s which accelerated after 1895, whereas the trade journals, perhaps reflecting too closely the ebb in the public capitalisation of breweries, maintain that the 1890–3 period was 'generally depressed'. Nevertheless the brewing industry nationally did not experience conditions as bad as those in Suffolk, where the agricultural depression was exceptionally severe.

Then the economy began to pick up in 1894. Prosperity was slow to percolate into West Suffolk, but by 1896 there are clear indications that Greene King was enjoying a greater buoyancy than at any time in the past twenty years. Output increased by 10,000 barrels between 1895 and 1899 (see Appendix 2, Table 4), profits and reserves assumed so healthy an aspect that the net profits available for distribution increased more than two-and-a-half times in the same period and the reserve fund quadrupled in the five year period ending in 1900. In that year the managing directors were given good honorariums and £50 went to the head brewer, R. J. Symonds, for 'the excellence of his beers'. Even the thin prose of Edward Lake's annual reports cannot subdue the jubilation about the improvement in their position. Raw material prices remained low and a modest degree of prosperity returned to agriculture so that unusually in 1902 and 1903 the firm's 'country' trade was more buoyant than its 'town' counterpart.

These good years for the firm, stretching from 1895 to 1903, were ones of Conservative rule.[5] With their party in office brewers felt far less exposed to political attack. Admittedly there were important enquiries into the trade with the setting up in 1896 of the Royal Commission on the Licensing Laws and the Departmental Committee on Beer Materials. Yet the trade believed these leisurely paced exercises gave it a pause and that interference, given the splendid contribution brewers made to Conservative Party funds, would be reluctant. The high water marks of prosperity for the whole 1887–1914 period were the years 1899 and 1900. The old century passed, the *Brewers' Journal* noted in an unusually rapturous phrase, with 'an exceptionally brilliant and prolonged summer'. This paradise for brewers, on the evidence of Greene King's figures, continued in the Suffolk trade until 1903–4.

In the brewing industry generally, however, it was agreed that prosperity began to contract two years earlier. Brewers blamed additional taxation imposed during the Boer War and 'a wane in spending power'. By 1902 the heyday of company flotation in the industry was over and the recession gathered momentum across poor summers (1903) and good ones (1904) alike. The industry felt the pounding of 'teetotal waves' and lamented 'a decrease in healthy and sober drinking'. Although it was not opposed to the compensation clauses of the Licensing Act (1904) the levy (see pp. 142–4) on the breweries meant an additional financial burden. Brewers, like farmers, are old hands at publicising their plight, and sceptics simply pointed to the profitability of brewery shares. By 1905, however, it was clear that the industry was in more difficulty than at any time since the 1830s. There was an almost 12 per cent decline in output since the peak of 1899–1900 and hop prices had risen sharply in 1903–5. One journal, comparing the prosperity of the cotton industry with the difficulties of the brewing trade, maintained the tied system had brought benefits to no one.[6] There was truth in the analysis in that brewers in the 1880s and 1890s, in their scramble to acquire public houses, had driven up prices and paid for their purchases largely by the creation of preference shares and debenture issues. Now when there was a sharp drop in output and profits, those companies that had over-extended themselves in the stampede had, in some cases, to pass over dividends on their ordinary shares. The London and Burton brewers were especially ailing.[7] Several of them 'staggered on the edge of bankruptcy' in the early 1900s. In 1907 Allsopps and Ind Coope paid no ordinary dividends and two years later the latter was in the hands of the Receiver. Charringtons paid no ordinary dividend between 1907 and 1911. The Burton brewers were being gradually undermined by every brewer in the country who could imitate and bottle Burton-type beers; those in London suffered from a dwindling output, which exacerbated debt charges on the public houses they had bought at grossly inflated prices in the 1890s. In East Anglia large breweries such as Bullards of Norwich fared no better.

In this atmosphere company flotations ceased. When Lord Faber introduced a deputation of brewery debenture holders to the Chancellor of the Exchequer in November 1907 he maintained,

> For some years past it has not been possible to deal with brewery stocks: one could not sell debenture stock, could not deal in ordinary and preference stock.[8]

In the climate of reduced demand after 1900 there was no chance of increasing beer prices. For beer after 1880 was relatively expensive. Whereas the price of most foodstuffs fell appreciably, brewers, with their increasing grip on outlets and 'understandings' about pricing, had not followed suit except for allowing —largely in the London area—the 'long pull' or extended measure. Now, in the present climate of dwindling demand, raising prices was out of the question. More than ever the importance of good management showed in the novel situation in which the industry found itself after 1900.

Not all breweries were equally affected by the recession in the industry. It was not simply that competition, unemployment, declining real wages, Temperance and Non-Conformist activities varied across the country, but that some breweries had in the past twenty years pursued more cautious financial and economic management policies than others. Amongst those in this category which withstood the storm easily were Greene King. Mitchell's and Butler's in Birmingham, Phipps' in Northampton, Cameron's in West Hartlepool and the Hull Brewery Co. had good records too. But the plight of East Anglian breweries such as Morgan's and the Colchester Brewery, with overvalued properties and big mortgage debts, passing over their ordinary shares or paying a very beggarly 1 or 2 per cent, showed the other side of the Edwardian brewing coin.

Moreover the recession of 1904–5 lasted. There were hopes that it had reached its bottom in 1906, but the slight improvement of early 1907 was not maintained and 1908–9 witnessed new agonies for brewers. Of course the brewing interest was so incensed by the depredations of the Liberal government, when it had to rely on the House of Lords to throw out in December 1908 a Licensing Bill threatening 'confiscation' by a 'teetotal-ridden government', that it was unable to provide any reasoned assessment of prospects: 1908 'was the worst [year] that the brewing trade has experienced within modern times at least'; 1909 'will undoubtedly go down to history as the blackest, without exception, in the annals of the brewing and licensed trade'. The licensing proposals in the 1909 budget were capped by one of the wettest and coldest summers on record. Behind the furore caused by the Liberal Government's actions many breweries faltered. For Greene King the year ending 1908 saw a decrease of 2,400 barrels produced. The directors blamed

> the cold, wet summer, general dullness of trade and slackness at work at Messrs. Boby and Co. due to the Licensing Bill and the decreased consumption of drink amongst all classes.

In the following year trade was 'still dull' especially in Bury and Colchester. Only in 1910 did conditions gradually improve and by 1912–13 the industry was again enjoying modest prosperity. In Suffolk Greene King production levels for the year 1913–14 reached almost the level of their 1903 peak.

2

When Edward Greene and Fred King merged their firms, they together owned 148 houses. The acquisition of these had been the cornerstone of both men's policy for almost twenty years and, when Edward Lake and J. M. King assumed the management of the new firm, the rate of purchases was intensified. Indeed it was the chief objective of the merger in Edward Lake's scheme to fight competitors and secure healthy development. He and his co-directors seem to have been guided by three criteria. First, they should concentrate their activities in an area roughly running from a line drawn through Ely, Thetford and Walsham-le-Willows in the North across thirty miles of East Cambridgeshire, Suffolk and North Essex to a base that joined Braintree and Colchester in the South. Second, small breweries with their handful of tied houses in this area were particularly attractive since they brought new trade, whereas the purchase of previously leased houses did not do so whatever other reasons might compel their acquisition. Lastly, property should be paid for out of the brewery's reserves for this purpose except where the takeover of another brewery was beyond the scope of the fund. Only then should there be resort to the creation of new debenture stock. There were exceptions to these guidelines, but we should examine each more closely.

The restriction of operations to this big rural pentagon reflected existing methods of distribution from the two breweries. The greatest concentration of public houses was in Bury St Edmunds. In 1902 the brewery owned and leased no fewer than 70 public houses and off-licences in the town and 180 in the surrounding area—always known as 'the Country Trade'—which were supplied directly from Bury.[9] In addition 128 houses were served by beer stores at Sutton near Ely (11), Fakenham (11), Colchester (41 and 3 off-licences), Haverhill (41) and Stowmarket (24).[10] Beer was supplied to these stores by rail from Bury. There were also thirty agents in towns scattered throughout the four eastern counties: in 1901 they handled around 3,000 barrels a year but this trade was evidently well in decline for by 1910 it had diminished by almost a half. Before the coming of the motor lorry on the eve of the First World War, easy accessibility to Bury and the beer stores dictated the pattern of public house acquisition. Only the purchase of Charlton's Fakenham brewery with eleven tied houses in North Norfolk in 1891 defies explanation, for it was sixty-five miles from Bury. The problem of its distance clearly changed policy in the mid-1890s, for when Pinchin's brewery at Fakenham was offered in 1899 the directors declined. And when in 1903 Page's Framlingham brewery—only fourteen miles from the Stowmarket store—was on the market they showed no interest since 'it was so far off'.

Accessibility was one criterion of policy: the other was trade. Houses where turnover was under 75 barrels a year were not

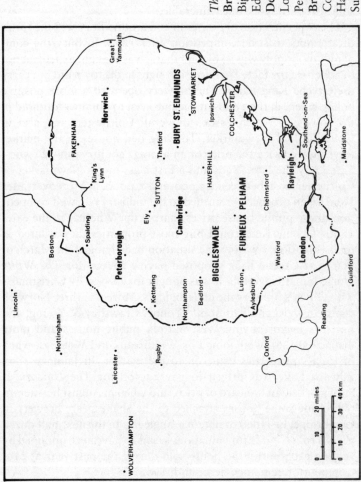

The Greene King Region
Breweries in 1983: Biggleswade, Bury St Edmunds, Furneux Pelham. **Depots in 1983:** Cambridge, London, Norwich, Peterborough, Rayleigh. **Brewery Stores in 1900:** Colchester, Fakenham, Haverhill, Stowmarket, Sutton, Wolverhampton.

considered. The average annual trade of all Greene King houses was 135 barrels in 1903, although there were a dozen houses where trade was under a barrel a week. The urge to keep rivals out of their region meant that the firm acquired properties on occasion whose turnover was only marginally economic. For the same reasons, in many villages around Bury it kept open an excessive number of inns—Ixworth with four; Barrow, five and Mildenhall, five, provide good examples—so that when licensing restrictions operated effectively after 1904 and consumption was static some properties became vulnerable.

The concentration of houses in and around Bury was the result of attempts to stifle competition after 1870. In Bury the company's monopoly was so blatant that it was thought expedient not to advertise the fact. Therefore inn signs in the town did not carry the Greene King name. The brewery operated a more positive policy when, in the 1890s, it became keen to obtain a foothold in the towns of North Essex, above all Colchester, and also in Haverhill and Newmarket. Thriving tied houses in the market towns were twice the price of an average country inn—£1,500–£2,000 by the late 1890s and a first class inn in Newmarket or Colchester cost between £3,000 and £4,000.[11] Moreover after 1896 when prosperity returned to the industry renewed competition drove public house prices sharply up. Whereas in the early 1890s Greene King could buy most properties they wanted at their valuation, by 1897 the situation had changed. In March of that year Greene King proposed paying £1,300 for *The White Horse* Inn at Haverhill. It was bought for £1,900 by Christmas's with Oliver's brewery the underbidders. Moreover three Norwich firms, Steward and Patteson,[12] Young, Crawshay & Young, and Bullards began buying West Suffolk public houses and more menacingly still were joined by Whitbreads and Watneys, when first class properties came on to the market. In January 1897 Edward Lake was driven to pay £3,500 for *The Unicorn* at Stowmarket, an unheard of price, and when in August he attempted to buy some houses attached to the Shakespeare brewery in Cambridge, he failed to obtain a single lot. In the next half dozen years a rough guide for valuations seems to have been obtained by valuing each barrel the house sold during the past year at £10. Competition remained fierce until 1904.

It would be misleading to stress that purchases exactly mirrored the firm's prosperity, for no clear pattern emerges from 1902. There was a heady start in 1888, but the only strong upward trend between 1896–9, when the brewery bought sixty houses, is in fact not far above the average of 13·6 public houses added each year between 1887 and 1902. Basic policy during this period was the procurement at a sensible valuation of any reasonably flourishing house that came on to the market within range of the brewery and the stores in Suffolk, Cambridgeshire and Essex. By the 1890s 'free' houses were becoming rare and since 'new' trade was not secured by converting existing leaseholds into freeholds the best prospect for Greene King was the purchase of those small breweries that still survived in the large market towns of East Anglia. The rate at which they were acquired therefore provides the best explanation of the growth of the firm's tied houses between 1887 and 1920 (see Appendix 2, Table 3).

In all cases except at Bocking, Haverhill and Sudbury[13] brewing was discontinued and the premises sold for other uses. Like many of the bigger breweries that Greene King bought either post-1918 or in the 1950s and 1960s, those acquired before the First World War, although small, had interesting histories on their own accounts. Most had known a hand to mouth existence in the agricultural depression of the 1880s and 1890s. The Goslings had a longer connection with their Bocking Brewery than the Greenes at Westgate. And Miss Moody's Newmarket brewery, well known to the racing fraternity through its five houses in the town, had had a chequered history in the nineteenth century. In 1869 her brothers were bankrupt. The ways of the racing world had clearly rubbed off on to Messrs Moody. When their debts of £6,000 were examined it was disclosed that they had rented a shooting-box in Scotland and had expended large sums in sporting pursuits. One of the brothers provided a marvellous, typically East Anglian, explanation. He denied renting moors in Scotland but 'admitted he had indulged in pigeon shooting'.[14] Perhaps not surprisingly with its principals displaying ingenuity of this degree the Moodys' brewery survived until 1896.

The high point of 'tied' house acquisition before Christmas's Haverhill brewery was taken over in 1918 was reached in 1905 when the firm owned 365 houses and leased a further 24. In the next ten years there was a net loss of 33 houses. Why was the policy of 1887–1904, that had been so important to Greene King, reversed? There are two explanations. Houses became increasingly expensive between 1895 and 1902. Therefore when trade ceased to grow after 1903 and property values fell there was little point in adding to the stock of houses in anything but the most selective way. Secondly, the Licensing Act of 1904 changed the conditions within which the 'tied house' market had previously operated.

3

Rapacious Chancellors of the Exchequer and Temperance reformers alike were old spectres in brewing demonology. Above all brewers resented central government's tampering with the magistrates' supervision of licensing affairs and Liberal threats to limit opening hours, impose Sunday closing and restrict the number of licences.[15] Bruce, Gladstone's Home Secretary, had had to drop a major Licensing Bill in 1871, although two years previously he had brought the beer houses licensed under the 1830 Act under stricter magisterial control and in 1872 passed an Act which tightened up licensing procedures and limited opening hours, especially on Sundays. But then for thirty years, in spite of annual bills from the tiny block of Temperance M.P.s, the trade saw few additional restrictions. What the legislation of 1869–74, temperance publicity, and a series of High Court judgments (especially Sharp v. Wakefield, 1891) achieved was a marginal fall in the number of licences at a time when the urban population at least was growing. The result was that the number of persons per on-licence increased from 223 to one in 1875 to 324 to one in 1906. The total of pre-1869 beer houses in fact fell sharply. Although partly compensated for by a rapid growth in off-licences between 1874 and 1882,[16] beer houses were always the most marginal of outlets and the decline reflects more the brewers' lack of interest in them than magistrates' vigilance. Full licences fell only very marginally from 68,358 in 1869 to 67,071 in 1902. It is against this background of restriction, modest but real, that 'the Brewers' Wars' were fought. Of course the number of licences declined at different rates in different areas depending upon magistrates' policy. In the four East Anglian counties the fall in the total of full and beer house on-licences was small (see Table 4).

This reflects not only a scattered population but also that Anglican landowners and clergymen were much less restrictive magistrates than their Non-Conformist counterparts in some of the big boroughs. Of course, Suffolk was amongst the five most sober counties according to the statistics for drunkenness prosecutions. In Bury itself only one house between 1883 and 1903 lost its licence.[17]

Table 4: The reduction of licences in East Anglia, 1875–96

	1875	1896
Cambridgeshire	1,532	1,450
Essex	2,404	2,356
Norfolk	2,751	2,684
Suffolk	1,698	1,672

Source: G. B. Wilson, *Alcohol and the Nation* (1940), p. 379.

If the pace of licensing restriction was very easy between 1872 and 1900, the trade was conscious of the threat of increasing pressure for the rate to be speeded up. Even if *per capita* consumption waned after 1880, drunkenness did not. Nor did Temperance propaganda. When the Royal Commission on Licensing reported in 1899 both the majority and minority reports favoured further restriction. Of course the brewers were not opposed to limited restriction: it kept property prices high, especially when trade faltered after 1900. But they supported the policy only so long as adequate compensation for lost licences was offered. Although the Royal Commission had studied the problems of compensation, when the Conservative Government in 1902 passed a further Licensing Act which attempted to deal with habitual drunkenness and the registration of clubs, it ducked the crucial issue of restriction and compensation. In the same year Farnham magistrates refused to renew nine out of the forty-five licence renewals before its brewster sessions. In Birmingham and Liverpool, where all parties recognised that there were too many public houses, this process had been going on for several years, but when the zealous Surrey magistrates decided to operate the full letter of the 1872 Act and impose restriction without compensation, the interest of

every brewer in the country seemed threatened. In 1903, 240
licences in England were refused—well above the average of the
past five years.[18] Threats of 'confiscation' and hopes of 'compensation' filled the pages of the brewing journals. The Government promised legislation and in 1904 passed a major Act which
offered proper compensation for further restrictions. The powers
of Justices of the Peace were now limited and they had to provide
real reasons for closure, for example ill-conduct or structurally
unsound premises. Otherwise closures had to be compensated
from a fund levied on all licensed premises by the compensation
committees of quarter sessions.[19] Although the Government
made wild estimates about as many as 2,500 houses being closed
annually, and the brewers themselves were alone responsible for
the levy they had to pay on each of their houses, it was soon
obvious that the limits of the compensation fund would in future
entirely dictate the pace of public house closure. Indeed the Act
was immediately represented as a 'Brewers' Endowment Act'. The
Temperance Non-Conformist wing of the Liberal party was incensed.

Certainly the evidence from Greene King suggests that they, like
the trade in general, warmly welcomed the Act. In public they
grumbled about the levy, but it provided a settled state of proper
compensation. Between 1905 and 1914 the pages of the firm's
minute book are filled with the details of the Act's workings—for
it allowed the company, in difficult trading years, to rid itself of
some of its least profitable houses.

Greene King surrendered some three dozen public and beer
house licences between 1905 and the outbreak of war to the
compensation authorities set up in 1904 within their area. What
once would have been a difficult exercise was now, in the context
of a stagnant industry, achieved amicably, with the firm's directors
becoming increasingly enthusiastic about offloading some of its
least economic houses. Of course the exercise was more complex
than this and its rules could not be bent to achieve these ends. The
firm paid appreciable levies on all its houses which amounted to
over £1,500 a year and there then followed delicate negotiations
between the clerks of the magistrates, acting upon police information, and Edward Lake, who was the brewery's representative in
all licensing affairs. Knowing the size of the compensation fund in

any year the magistrates submitted a list of houses they could afford to close down, and Edward Lake, along with other brewers, suggested the names of those houses they would not object to seeing closed, if the magistrates were to withdraw their licences. The lists by no means coincided, and after 1910 the firm had to lodge formal objections to a number of houses the various benches of magistrates wished to see delicensed. In Clare in 1913 there was a proposal to remove licences from three of the village's Greene King houses. Not surprisingly Edward Lake fought strongly—and successfully—against their closure.

The whole process was aided by the fact that Edward Lake, like three of his four co-directors, was a magistrate.[20] They knew the procedure and their fellow Justices, although none of the directors sat when licensing matters were being discussed. And the West Suffolk magistrates, like most rural benches, were not Temperance gospellers. Their sympathies were with the brewers—in 1910, when the Suffolk brewers complained about increased licence duties, they dropped the compensation levy for a year to ease the burden on the trade. Even relationships with the police seem to have been eased by the annual presents of game, made in the name of the firm's Chairman. There is evidence of these gifts in the 1880s, although they had probably ceased by the 1900s, when the Temperance climate hotted up. It also helped that John Greene, a cousin of the Greenes and Lakes, was clerk to the Bury sessions. These relationships aided negotiation: they in no way affected the number of licences referred and the amount of compensation paid. This was entirely regulated by the size of the compensation fund. The actual sum paid was worked out by a formula of multiplying the annual barrellage of a referred house by ten shillings (seven and sixpence after 1909 when adjusted for the fall in licensed property prices) and reaching a final sum by extending this figure over twenty years. The compensation authority seems to have usually settled at a figure rather below the Greene King estimate, although after 1912 the firm found, rather belatedly, that it always paid to contest the local valuation and have compensation fixed in arbitration by the Inland Revenue valuers in London.[21] Nevertheless the firm was well pleased, like most breweries, with the workings of the 1904 Act. In December 1911 Edward Lake, an addict of statistics in pre-pocket-

calculator days, could not resist supplying the following information to the directors' meeting. Since the introduction of the Act the
sale of delicensed properties had realised £17,034–£11,071 in
compensation and £5,963 for their subsequent sale. In the same
period only £10,527 had been spent on buying new houses. The
compensation levy amounted to £9,299.[22] These were neat sums
in difficult years.

The conflict between the Liberal Government and the drink
trade had been at the centre of the constitutional conflict in 1908
and 1909. When the budget proposals of 1909, which contained
a still fiercer attack upon the brewers' tied houses, were defeated
in the House of Lords an election was inevitable. The first priority
in the new Government's 1910 budget was—'in a spirit of vin-
dictiveness' as the breweries represented it—to raise steeply the
licence duty on public houses. There were the gloomiest predictions about 'hounding the trade out of existence' and levies of £5
million on the industry. In the event the old pre-budget licence
revenue of £1.9 million was merely doubled and brewers found
salvation by contesting all the rating valuations of their public
houses on the grounds that their value was diminished with the
additional licence duty which now equalled half the annual value
of the premises. In some cases rate reductions were as much as
increases in duty. Greene King evidence shows that although the
firm was perturbed at the prospect of the new duty—at one stage
taking the unprecedented step of inviting all their tenants to lunch
at Bury to discuss the implications of the working out of the new
rating assessments—it caused nothing more than short-term
problems. Reductions were generous in its region. The case in
which the Poor Law Guardians at Newmarket reduced *The Star's*
assessment by only £28 although the licence had been raised by
£57 seems to have been an exceptionally ungenerous abatement.
Once more the company was grateful for Edward Lake's common
sense and efficiency in easing a new threat quickly and effectively.

4

Greene King's acquisition of public houses after 1887 and its
success in riding out the storm of the Liberal Government attack,
licensing reform and falling beer consumption after 1900, gave it
a reputation for excellent management in the East Anglian busi-

ness world and amongst brewers generally. Most of the credit for his achievement rightly went to Edward Lake. His reputation partly stemmed from the fact that after 1883 he put Bury St Edmunds' borough finances on a modern footing when he was elected Chairman of its Finance Committee. Bury soon acquired a name for being amongst the best run small towns in England. Although this work brought him a wider experience and authority, his expertise was gained at Greene's in the 1870s. The ledgers and minute books reveal a model of sound finance. Eventually his reputation spread, for when the directors of the Cheltenham Original Brewing Company were in trouble in 1905 they sought

> the expert advice of the Managing Director of an important brewery in the East of England . . . Mr. Lake. They hoped by the aid of his expert knowledge of brewery management . . . to introduce reforms and retrenchments in the management and expenditure of the brewery that would augment its profits and increase its future prosperity.[23]

Edward Lake learnt his accountancy in the days before firms had to produce accounts for public consumption and in the infancy of the accountancy profession. His training related to the businessman's traditional compilation of an annual statement of profit and loss in their private notebook from the firm's cash books, journals and ledgers. As firms grew in size and took joint-stock status in the last quarter of the nineteenth century they had to provide annual figures for their shareholders as well. Now it is difficult to reconstruct the precise meaning of entries, especially the final profit figures, and ascertain whether they give 'a True and Fair View' of the company's finances. This is still a key problem in accountancy. Knowledge of today's sophisticated practices is not necessarily very helpful in the historian's task of interpreting figures about a company's performance close on a century ago. For without notes about their compilation it is, to be honest, a hazardous exercise. In the case of a firm such as Greene King this is especially true, since Edward Lake produced his figures for no wider audience than his four fellow directors who together owned 97 per cent of the firm's ordinary shares. The merger brought some changes in accounting practice. Josiah Beddow, Fred King's accountant since 1868, came down to Bury from London each June and made various suggestions.

When the figures for the 1887–1914 period are examined two features stand out: the creation of a large reserve fund, and the payment for public houses out of current profits with little further debenture creation. The two items are closely linked. The firm's gearing—that is the ratio of debentures to share capital—was well within accepted margins, but as we have seen, in order to balance the generous capitalisation in preference shares and debentures the credit side of the balance sheet contained a large valuation of £180,000 for 'goodwill'. This was traditional accounting practice adapted to brewing, to place a notional value on the 'free' house connections and the expertise of the two firms. That it was so high might have worried a company relying on public subscription with taunts about 'watered' capital. Even if, expressed as a proportion of other assets, goodwill was within safe margins, it represented in terms of the number of years' purchase of earnings a generous valuation in comparison with other brewers.[24] Edward Lake, therefore, took the conventional response of writing it off by the creation of a reserve fund. These reserves were the sums retained each year after profits were distributed. Clearly with only four fellow directors to convince he could ask them to make a generous provision for this fund and restrict the impulse to distribute too high a proportion of profits as dividends on the ordinary shares, which was a feature of the firm's finances before 1895 (see Appendix 2, Table 5). In many years after 1895 when the company was doing well the sum added to reserves was in excess of two-thirds of the sum paid on the ordinary shares. Edward Lake was proud of his achievement. In 1898 he wrote in his annual report,

> It is interesting to note that during the eleven years which have elapsed since the formation of the Company no less than £157,602 has been expended on the purchase of 157 Houses. Only £41,000 of this has been met by debentures. The rest of this amount has been found net of Profits and by the amount written off Machinery and by the reduction of Capital in Book Debts, Beer, Malt, Hops etc.[25]

11. *(above)* F. W. King (1828–1917) in active old age. After the amalgamation of 1887 he advised the brewery about its investments and continued a life-long interest in farming.

12. *(below)* Sir Walter Greene (1842–1920). Created a baronet in 1900, Sir Walter was addicted to hunting, shooting and a succession of steam-yachts.

13. E. W. Lake and his six sons after their return from the First World War. Four of them were decorated together by King George V, 'the large assembly . . . applauded heartily as the four stood on the dais and were decorated and congratulated by the King'. *Back row:* Nevile, Alan, Basil, Ronald. *Front row:* Lance, Edward Lake, Harold.

14. *(above)* Sir Raymond Greene (1869–1947) was a director of the brewery for well over half a century but he never involved himself closely with its management. He is seen here when he was a keen follower of the Cottesmore Hunt in the 1920s.

15. *(below)* The Bottled Beer Boys in the early 1920s. Greene King, unusually, employed neither girls nor women and the boys were selected for their sporting prowess at school. Frequent broken glass and caustic soda made working conditions unpleasant at times.

16. Greene King transport fleet around 1930. Motor transport, introduced before 1914, made great strides forward in the 1920s. Some of the older employees recall with great nostalgia their adventures with the early lorries.

17. 'The Roaring Donkey', Holland-on-Sea, c. 1935. Formerly the 'Princess Helena', it was rebuilt in 1934 at a cost of £5,700.

By the mid-1890s even major purchases required no new loans. When Miss Moody's Newmarket brewery was bought with its ten houses for £22,500 in 1896,

> the purchase money [was] partly defrayed from the reserve fund, and partly from the amount written off for depreciation, the balance [£6,400] being carried forward to be defrayed out of the current year's income, and thus no fresh Debentures will be required.

The fact that the firm acquired its tied house empire out of current earnings and reserves meant that when sales contracted after 1903 the brewery did not find itself paying poor dividends, like so many who had expanded their tied property holdings by the wholesale creation of debentures and preference shares. Ordinary dividends were pegged at a steady, unspectacular 10 per cent until 1915, a level and evenness of performance many other brewers envied in these years. When new acquisitions dried up after 1905, Edward Lake was able to remove the £180,000 'goodwill' valuation by 1912. He then used 'reserves' to create a large investment fund. Even after the amalgamation Fred King had been allowed to indulge his old hobby of playing the Stock Market[26] and the firm always held a few thousand pounds worth of stocks and shares in the 1890s. After the rush to acquire houses in the late 1890s, however, their value in the ledgers stood at an all time low of £460 in 1902. Then, as the purchase of tied houses dried up, the fund was increased very rapidly. In 1914 it reached a record £118,000.[27] Most of the shares, invariably bought on Fred King's advice, were held in foreign railways and state and city public loans, so that the Company's holding looked like that of any wealthy Edwardian *rentier*.[28] One aspect of this move was a diversification of the risk of brewing, another was that the firm was generating more income than it could reinvest in those years before 1914. Returns from railway and government bonds, preference and debenture shares were, however, unspectacular and after 1910 a decision was taken to repay the 1887 debenture loan due in 1918. By the outbreak of war it had been reduced from £181,000 to £121,000. Although the firm, acquiring a good portfolio of foreign investments, might be seen to be absorbing functions normally carried out by its owners on their own accounts, the principal shareholders could hardly protest that Edward Lake's management was depriving them of income. The return on the equity might look unimpressive in modern accounting terms, but the directors had only to look at the fate of shareholders in many breweries after 1900 to appreciate their own good fortune. Sir Walter Greene after 1902 drew an annual income of £18,000—more than twice that which his father was withdrawing from the 1876–86 partnership. Fred King (who had already distributed a good part of his assets to his children), J. M. King and Edward Lake also drew annual dividends averaging £3,000 each. Even the junior director, Raymond Greene, who at this time relied on his father's generosity to advance his political career, had £1,300.

The creation of healthy reserves to extend the tied house holding was Edward Lake's overall aim, but consistently high levels of profit reflected the meticulous detail of his management. The reputation he enjoyed publicly for his superb control of Bury's purse-strings and policy was equally deserved in the brewery. Nothing was too small to escape his attention in the constant pursuit of efficiency. This attempt to squeeze costs to improve performance was especially important when sales were static after 1903. Bad debts for many years had been virtually non-existent, and brewing materials, especially hops, were carefully purchased. There was no cash flow problem. Each November and May the directors were told that there was a sufficient balance at the bank to pay the half-yearly dividends. Gurneys and Oakes Bevan were only too keen to provide any credit the firm might require, a useful facility although the firm seldom borrowed. An interesting and unusual departure was Edward Lake's creation of a fire insurance fund to cover the firm's tied houses and cottages. The company first put away £300 under this head in 1888. Between then and 1914 it was assiduously built up so that its investments were valued at £33,300 on the outbreak of war. It also covered the loss of licences on properties and, after 1902, Workmen's Compensation insurance.[29] It is possible to argue that a brewer's lot was simple in comparison with that of most industrialists. But Edward Lake had Greene King in such excellent shape that, when slimming for most breweries became essential with the ill-health of the industry after 1900, he had to take no action. His conservative financial management after 1887 paid handsomely.

5

In its acquisition of public houses and the soundness of its financial management Greene King had few equals. Yet when we examine its response to the 'scientific revolution' that brewing in Britain supposedly underwent in the last quarter of the nineteenth century, the picture is by no means so clear.[30] In fairness the obscurity that surrounds the application of science to brewing extends to most breweries. It is *terra nova* for the historian.

The scientific revolution in brewing had two main roots, in Pasteur's work on fermentation (published in English in 1879) and in the research carried out by Horace Brown and G. H. Morris at the great Burton breweries after 1870. They converted Pasteur's findings into everyday practice and carried out equally important work on understanding the best conditions for the conversion into sugar by the diastase enzyme in malt extract. There was also Hansen's work on pure yeast at the Carlsberg brewery in the 1880s and research on the nitrogenous content of different barley types supported by Guinness between 1901 and 1906. Some of the earlier findings were summarised in Moritz's *Science of Brewing* (1891). 'No more valuable treatise on brewing science has ever been published', enthused the editor of the *Brewing Trade Review*, and all the journals looking back in 1900 on advances made in the previous century reckoned that the application of science to brewing had been the great feature of the post-1870 period. The quips of 'empiric soup-making' and the adage that 'any old woman can brew', they maintained, were fast losing any meaning.

Yet when we look more closely at the revolution in terms of its application in the average country brewery it becomes more difficult to accept the force of its impact in the way that either the importance of the research or the enthusiasm of the brewing journals suggests. The gap between research, even when carried out within an industry itself, and shop-floor practice is always difficult to measure judiciously. In this case it is especially so since Pasteur's work related to the continental 'bottom' method of fermentation whereby the process was completed at temperatures about 25°F (12°C) below British practice. Continental beers were then stored, expensively, at very low temperatures. Beer drinkers in this country much preferred the taste of a heavily-hopped 'top' fermented beer. At one level the failure to adopt up-to-date findings was a question of established tastes, at another it was undoubtedly the slow acceptance of change by practising brewers, for they were as notoriously conservative in business practices as they were in politics. Much of the journals' enthusiasm for science failed to rub off on to their readers although there are not enough studies of individual breweries to know exactly what happened. And when a business like Greene King is studied firm conclusions from the surviving evidence are difficult to draw.[31]

Two clues suggest that the firm made little advance in terms of scientific practice between 1887 and 1914: the rating dispute of 1898–9 and O. H. Heyhoe's recollections of the brewery in the early 1920s. In 1898 the rating assessment of the brewery was sharply increased. There had been no change for almost a decade and the Board of Poor Law Guardians, observing the brewery's prosperity in the late 1890s and holding possibly some resentment against Edward Lake's brisk management of the town's finances, went for a 75 per cent rise.[32] It was an unheard of advance. The details of the case—Greene King won its appeal with costs at Quarter Sessions on the way in which the valuer was paid on commission for advancing the assessment—are unimportant but it provides significant evidence about the brewery's modernity. Like most evidence it is seriously slanted. All those valuers who appeared for the company tended to write down the sums placed upon building and plant for obvious reasons (it being fortunate that the company's profits were not known outside the board room), yet even so they made some startling observations.

The Greene King position was that the assessment was excessive because the brewery was inconveniently sited for the railway (its requiring a large number of horses to cart goods over a mile to and from the station);[33] its duplication of premises and lack of integration meant high running costs; and some of the maltings, especially Braddock's complex, were outdated. There was a real discrepancy in valuing the brewery's machinery, partly depending upon whether it was reckoned 'in use' or at scrap prices. The Poor Law Guardians' valuer maintained the Westgate plant was worth £6,587, the firm's valuers agreed sums around £3,000. Behind the smokescreen of differences between valuers it is clear that much of the plant was antiquated in 1899. There had been little new investment on any scale since 1870. The three boilers were all at least thirty years old and some of the refrigerators and attemperators were in poor condition. When C. A. Spelman, the firm's valuer from Norwich, commented on the brewery he

> was astounded by two things, first the great want of apparatus of a modern type and secondly the appalling array of old vats which were never used now.[34]

In the maltings the position was no different. J. M. King maintained

> some of the maltings were very old and bad and he thought it would be a very great godsend if someone would burn them down.

No insurance company blanched at his invitation to arson—curious for a Justice of the Peace—since the maltings were not insured.

Even allowing for the circumstances in which this evidence was produced it is obvious that amalgamation had not meant modernisation. The two sites remained largely distinct, Westgate producing bitter and 'old' ales, St Edmunds stout and mild beers. In comparison with the new model breweries built in the booms of 1885–90 and 1894–1900, often designed by Adlam's, the Bristol brewing engineers, both of Greene King's breweries and their maltings were distinctly old fashioned. The situation did not change much in the next thirty years. When O. H. Heyhoe joined the firm as third brewer in 1920 he found it full of old plant. Certainly the machinery had depreciated during the First World War, but some of it, for example the beam engine Edward Greene installed in 1836, the vats dating from Benjamin Greene's days, and the fermenting vessels, was decrepit long before. Except for pumping beer no electric motors were used. Moreover there were problems with the beer in 1920. Due to the shortage of materials and government directives about the strength of beer the head brewer had been running too much liquor over the mash tuns, so that the resulting wort was very unstable. When Edward Lake asked the new young brewer (just arrived from a post-war training course at Cambridge Laboratories) what should be done, Heyhoe bravely suggested that they 'build a new brewery'. 'You talk like a fool', replied Edward Lake, 'storming out of the room'.[35] On another occasion E. L. D. Lake, Edward's son, and managing director after 1919, told him 'Oh! we don't believe in chemistry. Send a sample of malt to two people and you get two different answers.' Although O. H. Heyhoe was allowed to set up a makeshift laboratory in a corner of the Westgate brewery, it is clear that the 'scientific revolution' made no great headway at Greene King's before the 1920s.

Of course much of its message had been absorbed empirically and unspectacularly over the years. There was a wide spectrum of brewing practice which allowed brewers to go their own way and not conform to scientific theory in precise, textbook fashion. Most brewers, especially in the country, retained their own mysteries, prizing dented coppers, using false thermometers, and relying on the lore of the firm. At the Panton Brewery in Cambridge (taken over by Greene King in 1925) the brewer always brought the mash within a few degrees of boiling point. It was unheard of practice, the absolute negation of expert advice, but its beers won the gold medal at the Brewers' Society Exhibition in 1929 and 1931 and, perhaps a greater tribute, were secreted into the Greene King bowling club at Bury to unsteady the opposition's truest eye and surest hand.

All brewers knew that it was the end, not the means of production, that was important. From about 1880 onwards, as brewing methods became more scientifically controlled, Greene King would send samples of malt or beer to a London laboratory for analysis when something had gone badly wrong at the brewery. With advice obtained in this way, and with the résumé of brewing research which the journals provided, brewers were gradually put on the right track. It is evident in 1883 that there was a real preoccupation with cleanliness, for all the liquors were heated by steam coils to protect them from infection and there was a constant use of refrigerators and attemperators to control fermentation. In a practical sense, given the use of good materials, Greene King's brewers could do little more. Certainly the results were excellent. In 1899 'returned' beer was a mere 300 barrels out of 71,000 and even more impressive levels were achieved in the next decade. These are figures far below the astounding 7,000 barrels returned to the Colchester Brewing Company in the early 1890s which spelt bad brewing practice and management.[36] Yet at Greene King the means to this end are not clear beyond the attention to cleanliness and Edward Lake's impeccable attention to detail.

The minute books reinforce the evidence of the rating assessment dispute in showing that there was little new investment to adapt the brewery to the recent scientific innovations. There was a round of constant repairs and minor alterations by the brewery's bricklayers. There is occasional reference to extra expenditure such as 'the considerable alterations' to St Edmunds fermenting rooms in 1888 or 1893 when the St Mary's Square maltings were rebuilt. In 1908 Adlam's installed new pressurised coppers at a cost of £353.

The two major innovations of the 1887–1914 period were the introduction of bottled beers and the use of motor transport after 1908. Bottling beer was nothing new, but the practice was almost totally inhibited by the problems of cost and keeping qualities. These were solved in the 1880s and 1890s by the introduction of mass-produced glass beer bottles, crown corks and an understanding of pasteurisation and chilling. In addition there was a switch in taste towards a lighter, more gaseous beer. The brewing journals first discuss bottled beer in the boom of the mid-1880s, but Vaizey maintains that it remained an unimportant aspect of trade before 1914.[37] His conclusions seem sweeping. On the basis of percentage of volumes brewed and in comparison with post-1918 growth his comments about bottling are correct enough but an important pioneering stage was completed in the twenty years before 1914. Greene King began bottling beer in 1897, four years after their leading Norwich competitor, Steward and Patteson. What expertise Greene King possessed had been gained in the mineral water branch of their trade over the previous forty years, and in bottling Guinness and Bass. The venture proved an immediate success. Figures survive only from 1905 onwards (see Table 5). Yet by 1904 the trade was considered sufficiently profitable for the firm to build a new bottling store, and in 1911 there were further additions including a chilling plant, based upon the installation at Taylor Walker's Brewery. By 1910 the directors considered it an important branch of their business—not surprisingly, since after 1905 it was the only area in which, year after year, the directors could look for growth. Moreover, it was important in that its development led to the second major innovation, the introduction of motor transport.

Table 5: The growth in bottled beer at Greene King, 1905–13

Year ending 31 May	No. of standard barrels bottled
1906	2,495
1907	2,648
1908	2,854
1909	2,903
1910	3,103
1911	3,722
1912	4,343
1913	5,045

In contrast with other East Anglian breweries such as the Colchester Brewing Company, Greene King was an early user of motor transport.[38] In November 1908 it hired two Foden lorries and was well pleased with their introduction throughout the winter of 1908–9. They were especially useful in carrying crates of bottled beers, mineral waters and spirits, and, in addition to saving rail costs, Edward Lake found he could do without two horses and a man at Bury and a horse at Colchester. Moreover in the Bury area it became possible to make two deliveries in the day. Soon the lorries were a familiar sight on the road to Stowmarket, Colchester and Haverhill, where rail connections were poor. In 1909 when it was shown that the firm was at least 'breaking even' on its use of motor transport it entered into a contract with the Eastern Motor Waggon Company to hire three steam driven lorries for two years, at a cost of £40 each a year. But three rural district councils opposed this 'extraordinary traffic'. In February 1910 Clare R.D.C. took out an injunction against Greene King, restraining it from using roads within its jurisdiction, and demanded £1,450 in costs and damages. However, this opposition to 'steamers' was only a temporary halt in the firm's increasing reliance on motor transport. In 1913 it bought two Leyland motor lorries for £725 apiece, and Sir Walter Greene, at the age of seventy, terrified his family, servants and passengers when he, like Toad, became a zealous convert to motoring. He was keen to buy more, although his fellow directors dissuaded him until they had tried the other two a little longer. When part of the stabling in the yard between 6 Westgate and Westgate House was demolished in 1913 to make room for garaging the lorries, it was the outward, visible sign that Greene King had entered the twentieth century.[39] Edward Greene's peaceful world of horses and old ale had passed.

Having written off its 'goodwill' valuation and begun its repayment of the 1887 debenture loan the firm was in a good position, when the brewing industry's prosperity revived just before the First World War, to begin an extensive modernisation programme. In 1913 the present head offices were built at the top of the stable yard at a cost of £4,500 and the first directors' meeting was held in the new board room in November 1914. Any architectural pretensions the building might have are entirely due to Sir Walter Greene's insistence that an architect should elaborate upon the mundane design of Frost's, the Bury builders. Also in 1913, at a similar cost, a barley store and drier—very advanced for its day—was erected, with Boby's installing the machinery. If working continued night and day it was reckoned that it was capable of drying all the barley the brewery used. It was the largest addition since Edward and Walter Greene had built a new malting in 1880. It is likely that had not the war intervened further extensive works would have been carried out.

The impression is then that the brewery was very economically run between 1887 and 1914. Edward Lake consistently sought savings, and any tendency towards extravagance by Sir Walter Greene was restrained by the opposition of Fred and J. M. King to major programmes of expenditure. In 1890, when Edward Lake, supported by Walter Greene, wished to install electric lighting, they were opposed by the Kings and Edward Greene, then a very old man, who gave his chairman's casting vote against. It is the only time a contentious vote is mentioned in the minutes but it neatly illustrates the balance of power and outlook of the directors. Not until 1901 was electric lighting installed. Premises and plant were kept in reasonable order, but the period, except in

1913–14, was not one of major expansion as were the 1860s and 1870s. And whatever the impact of the 'scientific revolution' on brewing practice during these years, it was easily contained at Greene King within narrow bounds of expenditure.

6

In terms of management the 1887 merger again introduced few fundamental changes. Unlike some large manufacturing firms that went public in the late nineteenth century and began to separate ownership and management, making possible the attraction of new talent into industry and the gradual creation of a managerial elite, the two functions at Greene King, as in most breweries, entirely overlapped. In no other big industry, due to its special amalgam of conservatism, great wealth and the gentlemanly conduct of its activities, did owners maintain such a jealous control of affairs. When Edward Lake and J. M. King were appointed joint managing directors all this did was effectively release Walter Greene and Fred King from any close management involvement. They continued to attend the directors' monthly meetings and the stamp of both is evident: Walter Greene was a voice on the side of progress and expansion; Fred King was tireless in his preoccupation with economy and the investment of the firm's surpluses. But their involvement was not sufficiently onerous to stop Walter Greene, still only forty-five at the time of the merger, perfecting the lifestyle and itinerary of the Edwardian plutocracy, or Fred King continuing farming and making a second fortune. There was nothing new in this. Senior partners of firms had for generations eased themselves of responsibility by relying on their sons and juniors for the running of day-to-day business so that they could devote themselves to rural pleasures. Usually, as in the case of Greene King, there was no question of new blood being introduced, and so long as someone as competent as Edward Lake continued the drive of Edward Greene and Fred King it did not matter. In this section we shall briefly examine the activities of the directors after 1887, for they tell us a good deal about the world of the late Victorian businessman. In their contrast is also revealed the hazards of making generalisations about the entrepreneurial role of businessmen in history.

When Walter Greene returned from Worcestershire on his

father's death in the spring of 1891 he expected to step straight into the latter's shoes in the county. Those at the brewery had long been occupied by Edward Lake and except when Walter drove his coach and four with great ceremony into Bury every Wednesday morning for his weekly meeting with the managing directors he allowed his cousin to run the brewery without much interference. As Chairman until his death in 1920 Walter gave him support in the acquisition of public houses and assumed his father's role of encouraging good relations with his workforce. With so much time on his hands and money in his pockets[40] he was free to indulge his passion for sport and rural pursuits on a new scale. His staghounds were revived, an order was placed for a new 300-ton steam yacht, and by the mid-1890s he had adopted the annual migration pattern of the super-rich.[41] Christmas and the New Year were spent hunting and shooting in Suffolk, then in March or April he was ready for a jaunt to the Continent, often Monte Carlo. June was spent at Cowes and in July he sailed for the West of Scotland, where each year he rented an estate for grouse shooting and deer stalking. In September he was back in Suffolk for the partridges, racing at Newmarket and the beginning of the hunting and shooting seasons. Frequent visits to London were inserted into this calendar so that for weeks on end he never went near the brewery. If his lifestyle so closely resembled that of the new-rich who surrounded the Prince of Wales, he never launched himself into the 'fast set' whose doings filled the columns of the popular press. A staunch faith—he was a great patron of Thurston Church, and, during the First World War, himself conducted services in the 'Tin Tabernacle' at Pakenham—devotion to an ailing wife, a Victorian uprightness and an abiding delight in Suffolk life kept him from its clutches. But he loved having people around him. Nether Hall was modernised and extended for a second time in 1891, and the park 'improved' by a large lake that provided work for scores of labourers in the winter of 1891—2.[42] Soon the Hall's guest rooms were crowded with a succession of visitors. When he was High Sheriff in 1897—8 he gave the most splendid ball the county could remember, and a dazzling stream of entertainments was kept up throughout his year of office. Nether Hall was the envy of the Suffolk gentry, who had fared so badly since the agricultural recession set in during the 1870s. Even in

1918, when he was living alone at Nether Hall, he had ten servants and five horses in the stables 'while', wrote his daughter in her diary, 'restriction and rigid Economy is the War-Order of these days'. Before 1914 his establishment had been far more extensive. Its basis was the income of around £18,000 per annum which he drew from the brewery in the 1900s. With it he could indulge his passion for expensive sports, farming and the lifestyle of the Edwardian rich on a scale quite beyond the old gentry. In Suffolk there were few more conspicuous representatives of the new aristocracy of industrial and commercial wealth, whereas the landed families of his grandfather's youth who had been so influential in the county, or those like the Blakes and Molineux-Montgomeries which also enjoyed West Indian properties, were now in acute financial difficulties when their rent rolls contracted sharply after 1880.

Although Walter Greene, who in 1900 was granted the baronetcy that had been promised to his father just before his death, was never happier than when playing the role of the country gentleman, he did so with none of the serious purpose of Edward Greene. Christopher Isherwood, his great-nephew, recalls him as

> a practical joker of the kind called infantile by those who are not amused and surrealistic by those who enjoy seeing others made ridiculous. He had been known to give specially designed fireworks to his guests instead of cartridges, when they were going shooting. The Smoking Room at Nether offered explosive cigars and trick lighters. And there was a stuffed rabbit which a concealed gamekeeper would drop across the lawn on a wire. 'There's that confounded rabbit again!' Walter would exclaim when the drawing-room was full at tea-time; whereupon the male guests excused themselves, ran to the Gun Room for weapons and blazed away.[43]

His daughter, Mrs Pell, remembered an occasion when the surrealism went too far. Walter had been out hunting with Raymond, his eldest son. When they arrived back at the stables he had two grooms carry Raymond prostrate on a door past the drawing room window at Westgate House. The effect on Mrs Greene, whose nerves were never strong, was so devastating that the irresponsible Walter promised a moratorium on practical jokes. When Mrs Pell came to live at Nether Hall after her husband's death in 1915 she represents Sir Walter in her diary as self-centred, tactless and irascible. But he was an old man in poorish health, and she was too shaken by her bereavement, and too anxious about the disposition of Sir Walter's estate to recall his geniality and probity. The essence of his odd charm is best captured by a vignette of 1898. That December he took his house party to perform at the Thurston Cricket Club entertainment. Walter led the festivities, playing 'The Lost Chord' as a cornet solo.[44]

If Sir Walter Greene was known throughout Suffolk as a first rate sportsman and a generous employer and landlord he never —and this grieved him—successfully inherited his father's political mantle. No sooner was Edward Greene buried than Walter was invited to stand as Conservative candidate in his North West Suffolk seat.[45] The contest was pure Trollope, a marvellous epitome of the changing relationships within the power base of late Victorian politics.[46] The Liberal candidate was a Portuguese, some said Austrian, Jew, Viscount Sydney de Stern, a millionaire, Cambridge-educated stockbroker. Already four times unsuccessful in his attempt to obtain a seat in the House of Commons during the 1880s he had nursed the constituency for three years in an improbable attempt to attract the agricultural workers' vote. He did not own a blade of grass in Suffolk and was unable, his critics averred, to distinguish a mangold from a turnip. The contest was seen entirely in terms of an honest Suffolk-bred patriot fighting a foreign interloper. It seemed perfectly to illustrate a current rhyme about new style M.P.s:

> Brewers and bankers men of hideous omen
> Auriferous fellows of immense abdomen
> Flash directors with their diamond rings
> Such is the sum of our six hundred Kings.

National issues such as the Irish Question, allotments, free education and the Salisbury Government's record were lost in the welter of abuse about de Stern—although Walter Greene, to his credit, kept clear of personalities. In the end the by-election hinged on a misquotation and a telling cartoon. During the 1886 election,

Walter Greene, in a speech supporting his father's candidature, had said that all the land a working man could expect to obtain from the radicals was a plot six feet long by two. In 1891 the Liberals quoted this out of context and however much Walter Greene might claim to have inherited his father's desire to aid the working classes and talk about allotments, education and high wages he could not suppress the Liberals' calumny. The agricultural workers, who now decided the outcome of rural elections, largely voted for Stern, who won by a majority of 214 votes.[47]

General surprise in the country and county was nothing compared to Walter's shock. Yet his political ambition did not entirely cool, especially since in 1895 his son Raymond was elected member for West Cambridgeshire, and his cousin Henry Greene was member for Shrewsbury, so that when he was invited by the Bury Conservatives to stand as their candidate in the 1900 election he could not resist the opportunity of becoming the third Greene Conservative member in the House.[48] In the event he was returned unopposed. He proved to be a poor member. He had neither his father's gift for communication nor his application. His speeches in Bury were empty of serious content and seemed ill prepared. In the House he very seldom spoke. In 1905 he decided not to stand again for Parliament.

Fred King's retirement provides a strong contrast. When the two businesses merged he was 59 years old, with his family—he had been solely responsible for the upbringing of the younger ones since his wife's sudden death in 1880—at last grown up. Unlike Walter Greene he was quite without social or political ambition and even after remarriage in 1889 his ways remained unchanged. Having known nothing beyond the world of Bury business and Suffolk farming he made no attempt to break from its confines. He continued to live for a few more years at Rushford Lodge before returning to Bury in 1895, when he bought 5 and 6 St Mary's Square—opposite the Maulkins' old house and within a stone's throw of his brewery—to live out in comfort and convenience his long retirement.[49] But idleness, any sense of lack of purpose, was anathema to Fred King, and he began a third career as, and in his case there is no contradiction, a very active *rentier*. Almost every day between 1895 and 1917 his small, brisk figure could be seen making its way to the brewery or his solicitors in Guildhall Street to consult about Greene King or his own investments.

Much documentation about the growth and disposition of Fred King's wealth has survived. As we have seen, the central feature was an attempt to achieve an equitable distribution amongst his surviving children. It is present in his first will of 1869 when he visualised that his assets might have to be realised and invested in 'Colonial, Government securities or English railway shares' to provide for each of his children as they attained their majorities. It is still apparent in wills made forty years later. By then of course his wealth was both greater and more easily divisible. He achieved this essentially by his consent to the merger and capitalisation of his brewery and by the creation of two trust funds. In 1887 he settled £47,000 of Greene King shares and debentures in trust for his younger children. This was distributed amongst them when the youngest became twenty-one (in 1893) and two years later he set up a much more ambitious fund. Once more the motive was family provision with the incentive also of escaping recently introduced death duties. At first the 'King Securities Realisation Trust's' nominal £10,000 capital was based upon Fred King's two life insurance policies, £5,000 worth of promissory notes and sixteen parcels of foreign shares. Over the next two decades its holdings greatly expanded. When Counsel was consulted about its dissolution in the mid-1960s, he was informed by the Trust's solicitors that the company had been 'formed as a convenient way of making equal gifts to his ten children[50] and from time to time he transferred to the Company certain securities and this went on for many years'. Although Fred King admitted two sons and a son-in-law to the Trust's directorate he retained 'paramount authority' and the power to 'veto any proposition'.

Therefore after 1895 Fred King's great occupation was the purchase of shares for his family trust and for Greene King's investment fund. From 1868 he had sought the advice of Josiah Beddow, his London accountant, and, in all matters of real estate, his son-in-law, George Blencowe. Whatever the source of his advice Fred King was the principal agent in a build-up of Greene King's investment holdings, which stood at over £100,000 in 1910, and until his death in 1917, he regularly presented his own trust with numerous shares. By 1909 he had endowed it with most of his own Greene King shares and a valuation of that year reveals a list of sixty-seven lots of foreign assets, almost all in railway shares and municipal bonds. By this time the Trust's annual income was well in excess of £4,000 and it was growing fast, since during Fred King's lifetime 'the Company invested a large part of their income'. Thus by 1914 the trust was a principal shareholder in the brewery and in the inter-war years each of Fred King's surviving children was provided with a very respectable income.

But this was not all. In addition to endowing his family trust so liberally for twenty years he had also made a small fortune for himself. When he died in 1917 at the age of eighty-eight it was disclosed that he had, after the disposal of his Greene King shares (except for some debentures to provide for his widow) and his constant gifts to the King Securities Trust, accumulated a further £30,000, almost entirely in foreign shares and bonds. Like all his shares they had been bought in quite small amounts, month after month, from his savings. His establishment at St Mary's Square was modest in comparison with most successful brewers, but he enjoyed a comfortable home, the ministrations of four servants, and his great recreation, shooting. The meticulous attention to detail and the passion to save had never wavered and are well illustrated by his draft will in 1909. In the event of his death he made provision for his shoot to be continued for another season, and although he was content that the beaters should have their luncheons provided out of his estate, his sons, step-sons and their guests were 'in all cases to bring their own'. Not surprisingly when he died of influenza in 1917 his affairs were left in perfect order. There was virtually no cash in the house, and only the most trivial of debts were unpaid. He had achieved his lifelong ambition: a magnificent, controlled provision for his children.

His eldest son, J. M. King (1853–1917), who became joint managing director in 1887, is a more shadowy figure than his father in the brewery's history. He was educated at a private school in Bury, and joined the St Edmunds brewery shortly after its foundation. In the 1880s Fred King must have visualised for him a similar career in the county to that enjoyed by Edward and Walter Greene. The rivalry between the two breweries extended to the hunting field, for between 1884 and 1891 J. M. King was Master of the Suffolk Hunt.[51] Although he was a popular and proficient Master, like Fred King he eschewed West Suffolk politics. In the brewery after 1887 he looked after the tied property and the barley and malting side of the business. Here, as in the hunting field, he exhibited a steady competence. There was no hint of tension between the two managing directors, indeed they were both joint owners of Rayment's brewery which they bought in 1889. He was a quiet, unambitious bachelor, well content that his autocratic, supremely competent partner should assume day to day control of the firm. At some stage he acquired the 2,500-acre Bradfield St Clare estate, but he himself always lived modestly at Great Barton. Towards the end of his life he suffered from spinal paralysis, and retired from any active part in the firm's affairs around the same time as his father in 1915. He died tragically, racked with pain, and by his own hand, a few weeks before Fred King.[52]

7

The settled state of the brewing industry, when the threat of the 1906–10 Liberal Government subsided and the recession ebbed, was shortlived. It was just sufficiently long to lull the better managed breweries into a feeling of security. In 1912–13 Greene King had embarked on its first extensive building programme for over thirty years, and was planning the modernisation of some of its more profitable houses. In the summer of 1914 the firm's employees were given a Saturday half-day for the first time. Then the outbreak of war, which found the industry totally unprepared, brought changes and threats that were more far-reaching than any proposed in the darkest days of 1909.

The first of the Government moves were unexceptional. Patriotic brewers barely blanched at the trebling of beer duties from 7s. 9d. to 23s. a standard barrel, with the promise of a further rise of a shilling a year for the duration of the war, although they made the gloomiest predictions about their effect on output—the Chancellor of the Exchequer, Lloyd George, thought demand would be reduced by 35 per cent. But worries on this score were misplaced. For inflation, rapid from mid-1916, and full employment, ensured earning levels which kept demand well above either the Chancellor's or the brewers' own calculations. Much more menacing were the powers of the Defence of the Realm Act (DORA) and those given to the licensing Justices to close houses and restrict opening hours. At first they were used sparingly and achieved little more than 11 p.m. closing in London (it had been 12.30 a.m. before 1914), but when the munitions 'scandal' broke in the early months of 1915 Lloyd George, an old enemy of the drink trade, blamed supply shortages on the brewers. In a celebrated and often quoted speech he spoke

> of workmen in armaments works who refuse to do a full week's work for the nation's need. What is the reason? . . . It is mostly the lure of drink . . . Drink is doing us more damage in the war than all the German submarines put together.

The Temperance lobby was now able to wage its campaign more effectively than ever it had done in peacetime, for the control of drink had become the pursuit of the nation's survival. Therefore the Government devised from the spring of 1915 a far more savage set of restrictions than anything previously envisaged. The Central Control Board, established in May 1915, had sweeping powers to limit the production, sale and transport of drink. In the same year it enforced a drastic reduction in opening hours: from 16–19½ hours a day to 5½ with 9 p.m. closing required everywhere. Moreover, in 1916 and 1917, in its desire to conserve foodstuffs and shipping the Control Board limited output and dictated gravities. By the end of the war production was restricted in terms of standard strength to little more than a third of 1913–14 levels. In addition the entire industry was threatened with nationalisation from 1915. An advisory committee of the Cabinet recommended this step, although neither the Cabinet nor more especially the House was agreed on such a revolutionary move. As often, the matter came up against a financial stumbling block, in this instance the enormous problem of raising £300,000,000 of Government bonds to provide the necessary compensation. But if the central threat receded after 1916, the issue was far from dead. Until the early 1920s there was the fear of extending the 'Carlisle system' with its example of a swingeing reduction of public houses, the elimination of competition between brewers, and the benefit of its managed houses serving food and soft drinks as prominently as beer and spirits.[53]

As a result of much stricter controls drunkenness sharply contracted. The number of convictions fell from 183,829 to

29,075 in England and Wales across the duration of the war. Early closing, the shortage of beer after 1915, and its much diminished strength were principal causes. Indeed control of the industry was so effective that when there was an outbreak of unofficial strikes in the engineering and shipbuilding industries in 1917, the Whitley Commission found that shortage of beer and its poor quality were important factors in the unrest. The Government grudgingly recognised that the workers, employed for long hours in grim conditions, had a grievance, and they began to ease gently the Draconian restrictions on output to achieve greater industrial harmony. But the brewers' angry resentment at the Government's ham-fisted, Temperance-motivated interference with the industry—far more intrusive than anything that was to be devised during the Second World War, and cunningly garbed in the disguise of national need—was long-held. The way in which beer was forced into disrepute by both propaganda and enforced dilution was something the industry neither forgot nor forgave.

How did a regional brewery such as Greene King respond to Government control? Since it lay outside the main theatre of war preparations, it avoided the bigger dislocations of supply and demand experienced in the industrial North and Midlands. Agriculture witnessed a new prosperity, and until mid-1915 beer output held up. Moreover, there was no apparent shortage of labour or raw materials before the end of that year. The only crisis in fact was one of management. Sir Walter Greene, Fred King and Edward Lake were all old men in 1914: J. M. King was in increasingly poor health and Colonel Raymond Greene, M.P., had never been trained to involve himself closely in the brewery. In any case he joined his regiment at the outset of the war. The entire running of the brewery devolved upon Edward Lake, assisted by his son, E. L. D. Lake, and by Ralph King, who had both been admitted to the brewery as trainee managers in 1905. The latter, already forty and with an unsuccessful career as a stock-jobber behind him, showed little promise. Even when J. M. King and F. W. King, then eighty-six, resigned as directors in 1915 the problem was no nearer solution for, although both E. L. D. Lake and Ralph King were brought on to the Board, the former joined the Army in the summer of 1916 and the war effort revealed no further reserves in the latter. Indeed his health broke down at this juncture. Edward Lake was left to run the firm as the programme of government controls and restrictions burgeoned. Of course after forty years' outstanding service to the brewery and town he was well fitted, and constant hard work had never troubled him. He was now sixty-five, alone, controlling a skeleton staff of experienced hands—63 had joined the Army by June 1916 and the departure of a further 30 was likely—and coping with the totally changed conditions which the war imposed. Moreover, he was still involved in the affairs of the Cheltenham Original Brewery; he went over to Furneux Pelham fortnightly to supervise Rayment's Brewery, which he and J. M. King had bought in 1889; and he was the central figure in talks within the Norfolk and Suffolk Branch of the Brewers' Society about controls and price increases in 1916 and 1917. The work nearly killed him.

In the spring of 1917 he insisted that Greene King took over Clarke's Risbygate brewery in the town.[54] Although it brought a further twenty-eight public houses under the Greene King umbrella, and a thriving wines and spirits business (the well known Cupola House) and, although the negotiations were conducted against a background of discussions amongst East Anglian brewers about amalgamation as a way forward in the era of controls, the real reason was that Edward Lake needed Harry Clarke to run the malting and barley side of the business. His proposals to buy the brewery and appoint Clarke as a director were not welcomed by the Greene family. Mrs Pell noted that,

> Raymond came down from London for day [14 April 1917] to attend a special Brewery meeting re Taking Mr. Clark and Brewery into Managing-Directorship to which they apparently agreed to satisfy Ed. Lake against their better judgement.

In reality neither the Greene nor the King interest could answer Edward Lake's case that the critical state of the brewery's management at this juncture in the war needed an immediate transfusion of new blood.

The management crisis of 1915–17 did not impair the firm's performance because Edward Lake, although an overworked old man, still possessed a complete sense of reality and never allowed the Government's policies to shake his faith in the brewery's future. For years he had given sound advice to the East Anglian branch of the industry and he continued to be a source of commonsense in hard times. He seemed most concerned about prospects at the end of 1915. Output at Westgate was down 12 per cent in June–December 1915 in comparison with the previous year and the auditor was asked to do a quick forecast of profitability for 1915–16. The precaution was taken of limiting the interim dividend to eight per cent. Although barley restrictions were enforced much more effectively in 1916–18 and output fell by a quarter between June 1915 and June 1919 (much more in terms of barrels of standard strength) profitability was not a problem. Even if barley and sugar supplies were increasingly restricted and raw material prices rose steeply from early 1916, brewers, by meeting Government quotas, producing a much weaker beer (within bounds of 1,024–1,030 degrees, levels of unprecedented feebleness against the standard pre-1914 gravity of 1,055 degrees) and by raising prices several times from late 1916 onwards so that eventually they were two or three times their pre-1914 levels, brewers ensured that profitability increased.

As early as the autumn of 1914 Edward Lake was writing to the Chancellor of the Exchequer that the best way round raw material supplies and big duty increases was to produce a lighter beer that the less well paid sections of the working classes could afford. In the winter of 1914–15 Greene King was attempting to obtain royalties from other brewers in exchange for the secret of their light beer. But events soon overtook these early experiments, and all brewers were forced into producing beers of an undreamt of dilution. With raw material supplies cut to almost one-third of pre-1914 levels there was no alternative. Greene King's decreased barrellage (see Appendix 2, Table 4) hides this decline in strength. At the end of the war it was forced into running as much as eleven barrels of liquor to each quarter of malt in the mash tun instead of the usual half-dozen. This produced an unstable and weak beer, lacking in character.

Although the price of brewing materials advanced sharply after 1916 brewers were left with handsome profits because they adjusted beer prices to meet these increases and rising labour costs. Yet they produced roughly two-thirds of pre-war output with about one-third of the raw materials. Even with ample provision for Excess Profit Duty and Income Tax, breweries found towards the close of the war that they had big reserves to reduce debentures or buy War bonds and further tied property. In Greene King's case, since its loan finance was in such good shape in 1914, it could contemplate further takeovers. The industry believed that amalgamation was necessary to meet the threat of nationalisation, for it admitted that it was 'not run on the most economical lines' and that rationalisation was necessary. And Edward Lake was eager to convert these principles into action. In December 1917 he was conducting discussions to take over the only two sizeable breweries left in West Suffolk, Christmas's of Haverhill and Oliver's of Sudbury. Since Christmas's permitted a straight sale conducted by the trustees of the late F. C. Christmas, its purchase was completed quickly and without complication for £55,000—paid in cash and War bonds. Oliver's acquisition was a more protracted affair because the firm was run by two brothers, only one of whom was offered a directorship on Greene King's Board. The purchase was achieved partly in cash, and partly by the creation of a further 10,000 £10 ordinary shares.[55] Christmas's brought 49 houses and Oliver's 51 into the Westgate empire. Both were sensible buys, for the price of tied property advanced quickly in 1919 and early 1920; and since both breweries were kept open they extended Greene King capacity by around 37½ per cent at the point of peak Government restriction. When Edward Lake retired as Managing Director in June 1919 he could present his last report with great confidence. The brewery owned 460 public houses, three working breweries and boasted an output that topped 100,000 barrels.

Edward Lake's resignation in 1919 marked the end of an era at Greene King.[56] When he first joined the brewery as under-manager in 1873 it had owned half a dozen public houses and one small store at Haverhill. Now it was the largest brewery in East Anglia with almost 500 tied houses. Although the scale of changes seemed revolutionary its guiding hand was not, for Edward Lake adhered to the conservative ideals of his uncle. Growth was achieved by financial orthodoxy—'common-sense principles in business', as Edward Lake called it—the utmost probity and the old paternalism. Looking back on his achievement in 1919 he placed special emphasis on the latter with his constant attention to the men's welfare in the provision of medical insurance, pensions, bonuses and good housing.[57] A welfare visitor was appointed 'to visit the wives and families in their homes' and Mrs Lake inaugurated a Mothers' Meeting where wives could meet weekly at Westgate House. Trade Unions, he believed, given an open access to the management and in the context of these social facilities, were unnecessary intrusions. In his fifty years with the firm there were 'no serious differences of any kind' with its employees and tenants. When, during some wage negotiations in the First World War, Trade Union officials had attempted to obtain a toehold in the brewery Edward Lake had slammed the door firmly on them. He addressed the entire workforce

> and told them plainly that, while perfectly free to join any Union they chose, it was absurd for officials who knew nothing of the working of this business to come and arrange matters as between myself and them, and that I must decline in any way to permit such interference. I said I considered that the men must know their own business better than any men who had no experience in it, and in the same way I must be better acquainted with their difficulties and wants than outsiders. The men quite acquiesced, and I have never had any trouble since.

Here as 'in anything he had to do with he was an autocrat of the first order'. Not one of his family, fellow councillors or employees denied the trait, but as his political opponents readily conceded, this was combined with clear-sightedness, hard work and total honesty.

It was these qualities which he brought to his public work. Again his career in politics was an emulation of his uncle's principles. In fact, admitting its narrower range, it was far more successful. From his unusual entry to political life in Bury (being invited to become an alderman at the age of thirty-three) he brought those qualities that had already brought him recognition in the brewery—efficiency, economy and organised control—to every branch of municipal affairs. In the reform of council procedure and the 'centralisation of municipal work and offices', in the provision of electric light, modern sewage and water works, he dragged the old borough into the twentieth century. He was chairman of the town's education and finance committee and a county councillor from the inception of the West Suffolk council.

In education, at the West Suffolk Hospital, in the town's charities which he consolidated, he was the acknowledged financial expert, reducing accounts to the same clarity as the ledgers at the brewery. Although six times Mayor, given the rare honour of being elected the second honorary Freeman in the history of the post-1835 Corporation, and acknowledged on all sides to be the ablest figure ever remembered in the borough, he was never popular.[58] For in his desire to pursue economy and reform he met all his opponents, from whatever quarter, head-on. There were some widely publicised rows over seemingly dull subjects such as sewage and electric lighting.[59] And his autocratic manner won him few close allies. Nor was he afraid of taking on the council's officers on any matter. Nothing illustrates his lofty eminence in the town's affairs better than his role in the appointment of a full-time Town Clerk in 1904–5. Formerly the work had been done by a solicitor working from his own office. Municipal business had grown so much that this old arrangement was inconvenient and control was minimal. A majority of the council wished to appoint a full-time Town Clerk, based at the Town Hall. The incumbent, who was to be replaced by a new official, refused to acquiesce to the Council's proposals, and announced his intention of contesting the Abbeygate Ward. E. W. Lake, seeing that this would be awkward for the newly appointed officer, resigned both the mayoralty and his position as an alderman to contest the election. Lake was returned with a large majority. The action illustrates his fearsome standards and the reason why even his bitterest political enemies conceded respect for his steadfastness in ploughing a straight furrow in the uncertain loam of municipal affairs. Indeed his steely uprightness in the pursuit of order and reform led at times to estrangement within the town's Unionist party, of which he was chairman for over twenty years. 'Amongst the old Liberal Party he had many friends, and there was a time', the Liberal *Free Press* admitted, 'when the Liberals of Bury would have substantially supported him as a candidate if he stood for Parliament.'[60] Certainly no one was in doubt that his abilities in running the town and its biggest firm qualified him to do so. Unfortunately his commitment to both, and Walter Greene's own political pretensions, stood in his way. Yet his success in Bury was significant. 'Our present municipal position is largely what he has made it'

conceded the *Free Press* on his election as Freeman.[61] His financial
acumen was stamped on every important institution in the town.
In the trade his ability and probity were widely acknowledged.
'The late Mr. Lake', ran the *Brewing Trade Review*'s obituary,

> was an able man of great mental vigour, who thought things out
> thoroughly and always knew his own mind . . . his opinion
> and independent views were sought and respected, though
> they were not always in accord with the majority of his
> competitors.[62]

It has been necessary to stress Edward Lake's achievements not
only because they provide continuity with Edward Greene's
career, but also because their spirit was totally imbibed by his
eldest son, E. L. D. Lake, who succeeded as managing director in
1919. For the next quarter of a century his authority was stamped
on the brewery and Bury almost as firmly as his father's had been
in the forty years after 1880. This steadiness of thinking and
action, the total dedication to the welfare of the brewery, Bury
and West Suffolk across three generations, from the first stirrings
of Edward Greene's political consciousness in the 1840s to E. L.
D. Lake's death a century later, are key features in understanding
the inner reality of the brewery in these years.

6

Peace and War,

1920–45

_____

I

When the First World War ended, there was in the brewing industry, as elsewhere, a real desire to put the clock back to before 1914. Although brewers realised that peacetime prosperity could not perpetuate the profits bonanza of the last three years they contemplated the rapid end of government interference with total satisfaction. For a brief period the resetting of the clock looked possible. The summer of 1919 was a good one and the Christmas trade of that year the best ever experienced by many breweries. In 1920 the hated Control Board was wound up and restrictions —except in the area of Licensing (restated in the 1921 Act)—were relaxed. Yet as the nation painfully learned in the 1920s, the upheavals of the Great War were too far-reaching to allow affairs to settle easily again into the grooves of the Edwardian era. However much conservative brewers wished to re-establish their old world, a number of forces led to extensive changes in the conditions that fixed the well-being of their industry.

Above all, social change was rapid after 1920. The old heavy drinking that had coloured so much working-class life before 1914 never returned, even after 1919 when brewers were allowed to increase the strength of their beers again. The annual returns for drunkenness proceedings continued to decline sharply after the war. The preference was now for lighter, often bottled, beers. But brewers had to face a far greater change than the shifts in consumers' tastes. Their real difficulty was that consumption levels continued to fall or at best stagnate across the 1920s and 1930s alike.

Table 6: United Kingdom beer output and consumption, 1910–39*

Years	Beer output: million (standard barrels of 1,055°)	Consumption per head (gallons)
1910–14	34·1	26·9
1915–19	22·7	16·5
1920–4	22·3	16·4
1925–9	20·3	16·3
1930–4	16·6	13·0
1935–9	16·9	13·2

* Source: B. R. Mitchell, *Abstract of British Historical Statistics* (1962), p. 253.

It was a popular pastime in these years for brewery chairmen at their companies' Annual General Meetings to speculate about the reasons for declining consumption. They concentrated and varied their explanations around four themes. The principal reason for declining *per capita* consumption was that workers were increasingly hesitant to spend their wages—often cut in money terms between 1921 and 1923—on drink. The trend seemed strongest among the young. For this group there was a range of new alternatives—the cinema, the radio and recreational pursuits—which entailed either staying at home or family participation in leisure activities. An employer replying to a survey on drinking habits in 1931 stated the change succinctly:

> the younger men go in for bowling, tennis, cricket, rowing and cycling. Youths of 18 to 24 go in for smart clothes and are dancing mad. This type never mention public houses.[1]

New recreations in turn reflected the increasing amount of leisure time brought about by the shorter working hours introduced around 1919–20. The second explanation related the contraction in beer drinking to the high levels of unemployment which were a permanent feature of the interwar economy. Clearly since this was regional, and different levels were experienced in different industries, not all brewery chairmen were affected equally by its effects on their balance sheets. All in fact subscribed to the view that, except when unemployment was at its peak between 1930 and 1933, changing social habits were a more potent force in diminishing their output.

The third factor was one that chairmen had to handle more carefully. After 1919 the price of beer was universally acknowledged to be too high. Brewers blamed this upon two big increases in duty in 1919 and 1920 following hard upon those of the war years. By 1921 duties were fifteen times their pre-war levels —3¾d. per pint against ¼d. A modest rebate in 1923, resulting in the price of a pint falling by one penny to sixpence, was insufficient to allow brewers to fix prices at a level which stimulated consumption much. With diminishing output their profits were saved by falling raw material prices. This led the press frequently to point out, especially in the early 1920s, that high prices meant high profits; and the brewers had to run a constant campaign about duty levels in effect fixing prices, and the way in which any adequate reduction undertaken by themselves would have wiped out the industry's profitability.

At this point chairmen switched to their fourth explanation when they made the link between high duties and the Temperance animus which still infiltrated all the political parties. Given the pace of relaxation of old social codes in the 1920s the impact of the anti-drink campaign waned surprisingly slowly. It was still close to the centre of government, for, although Lloyd George was a spent force in politics after his defeat in 1922, the Home Secretary of Baldwin's second Government (1925–9), Joynson-Hicks, was a rabid teetotaller. And the Labour Cabinets of 1924 and 1929—31 were unknown quantities. At least the party was against Prohibition and the brewers soon realised that, whatever Sidney Webb[2] might write or politicians in public might say, the grass roots of the party had a more reassuring appraisal of working-class realities. Nevertheless, the second Labour Government set up a major Royal Commission on the Licensing Laws.

Some viewed it as 'the culminating point of 20 years of teetotal advocacy'. In fact its composition was a carefully balanced one, representing all the pro- and anti-drink lobbies interested in this key issue. Indeed it was so finely balanced that the brewers from the start predicted 'a sterile outcome'. After two years of deliberation, the Commission issued its inevitably divided recommendations. 'It consists', wrote the *Brewers' Trade Review*, 'in the main of recommendations of inappropriate remedies for evils which do not exist'. The Commission recognised the trend of increasing sobriety and the brewers' improvement of public houses, and dismissed Prohibition, Sunday Closing and Local Option. Even its positive recommendations about the more rapid closure of redundant public houses and an extension of the State 'Carlisle' system seemed out of touch in 1931. In any case the report's conclusions were lost without trace in the crisis of that year. The Government had more compelling priorities.

Of course the brewing industry, dispirited as it often was about the levels of duty, declining consumption, and attacks from various quarters, did not sit Canute-like as the new conditions of the 1920s washed over it. It made positive responses. The transformation programme had four main props: the modernisation of public houses; the re-equipment of plant to conform with scientific advances, developments in transport and, above all, the provision of extensive bottling facilities; amalgamation of firms to meet problems of surplus capacity by the rationalisation of production; and collective advertising to publicise the merits of beer. It is in these areas that we must focus the history of Greene King in the 1920s. Tucked peacefully away in East Anglia, they could not escape the forces of social change in the inter-war years. Nevertheless the quality of their management, the inheritance of Edward Greene's and Edward Lake's policy of sound growth, sound finance and sound beer, and the special nature of this largely rural market meant that they responded to the new challenges in a way that was different from other breweries.

2

Within five years (1917–22) the old guard of Greene King's second generation management—J. M. King, Sir Walter Greene and Edward Lake (briefly Chairman between 1920 and 1922)

—had gone. The next generation was untried, partly because of war service and partly because Edward Lake was temperamentally unable to relax his control of the firm. Moreover, with the exception of E. L. D. Lake, they had had no prolonged training in the industry. Ralph King had come too late to the task in 1905 and was never involved in the central running of affairs. Colonel Raymond Greene (b. 1869) and Captain Edward Greene (b. 1882), Sir Walter's two surviving sons, had always been encouraged to have ambitions beyond the day-to-day management of a country brewery. There was, therefore, in the 1920s and 1930s some tension between these principal shareholders of the firm[3] and the management, which had devolved upon E. L. D. Lake when he was appointed Managing Director in 1919 and upon his brother Harold, Company Secretary and a director in 1922.[4] In the past any potential strains had been avoided by the other directors' recognition of Edward Lake's abilities. He had held a special place as the chosen managerial heir of Edward Greene. Now after 1920 the situation changed. The old close working contacts between four intimates had gone and could not be re-created. Difficulties were exacerbated by personalities and the fact that Edward Lake had left six sons, all of whom at some time in the inter-war years were available for positions in the firm. Moreover the Lakes felt they were the inheritors of Edward Greene's and Edward Lake's honoured traditions in the firm and they shared a dual status. They were relatives and shareholders —although after 1922 Edward Lake's holdings were spread thinly amongst his twelve children—as well as managers.

At the centre of the new tension was Sir Raymond Greene.[5] Of this he was totally unwitting. He never enjoyed the pleasures that his father and grandfather derived from their position in the brewery, in the town, and in Suffolk itself. His education at Eton and Oriel College, Oxford, good looks and charm took him to the top of the social ladder which the Greenes had been successfully climbing for over a century. At first his career seemed to fit well enough into the family mould. He was appointed, soon after he came of age, a director of the brewery in 1891 on his grandfather's death—the first director to do so without any training in the business. In 1895 he was elected Conservative Member of Parliament for West Cambridgeshire, a seat he held until the Liberal

landslide victory of 1906. He served in the Boer War and was
Colonel commanding the Royal Suffolk Hussars from 1906 to
1911. Although he enjoyed military affairs and hunting he did so
without his father's warm, unthinking commitment. Indeed he
was always uncomfortable in Sir Walter's company. He disliked
his practical jokes and the Nether Hall regime. All this mattered
little in the brewery until after 1920,[6] although it was clear that
long before the First World War there was a parting of the ways
between father and son, contrasted in the cosmopolitan, political
set of Raymond Greene and the steam yachts, stags and partridges
that were central to Sir Walter's existence.[7]

Yet Sir Walter was proud of his elder son who, when out of
Parliament between 1906 and 1910, nursed the North Hackney
constituency by representing the borough on the London County
Council. He was Chairman of its Housing Committee in 1910, the
year he was returned again to the Commons. For the next thirteen
years he represented North Hackney in Parliament and was a
popular member both in the House and in his constituency. He
had an excellent career in the war: serving in the 9th Lancers,
commanding a battalion of the London Yeomanry, and winning
the D.S.O. He was, noted his sister in her diary, 'a rising man'. But
there was a fatal flaw in his political make-up as she conceded
when he lost his seat in 1923: he was 'entirely devoid of that
necessary Ambition which is essential for the rise to political
fame'. She also added, that like so many of his generation, his
health never recovered from the war.

The end of Sir Raymond's career in politics, coming shortly
after his appointment as Chairman of the brewery in August 1922,
did not lead to closer involvement at Westgate. For when his
father died in 1920 he immediately sold the Nether Hall estate. He
made it abundantly clear that he had no intention of fitting into Sir
Walter's shoes in the County. He showed provincial Suffolk a
clean pair of heels. His time was thereafter shared between his
London home in St James's Place and a hunting lodge in Leicestershire. From the latter he followed the Cottesmore until ill health
persuaded him in 1927 to sell his stable of hunters. At both
establishments the guests were smart and the food superb. Yet in
the centre of this stylish 1920s setting Sir Raymond seemed, at
least in his sister's eyes, to live without enjoyment. On Whit

Sunday 1924 she wrote whilst staying with him at Burrough-on-the-Hill,

> he went out in his motor after lunch to the kennels *alone*, a sad Bachelor atmosphere minus youth, zest or Future. My host somewhat silent—conversation uphill and not easy of selection. Health or lack of health seems to be his chronic study—I expect his nerves have never recovered from his shrapnel wound and hardship of the War—Restlessness always a symptom of nerve starvation—he lives on sips of water and fruit.

The aesthetic Sir Raymond was clearly putting up a good defence against his forceful, widowed sister, for elsewhere she noted his predilection for high society 'girl-friends'. They can hardly have been wooed by the type of reception he reserved for her.

Within eighteen months he gave up the chairmanship of the brewery, and though he remained its principal shareholder until his death in 1947, he took little active role in the business. He attended Board meetings when his health allowed and made a large loan on one occasion when the directors felt straitened for money after their purchase of the Cambridge brewery in 1925. His 'good advice and his sound wisdom' were something the Board valued for another quarter of a century. It must have been given behind the scenes for the minutes show little of this. One of his rare contributions was made in 1938 when he drove across from Leicestershire and was horrified by the posters of the Brewers' National Advertising Campaign: 'some of the figures on the hoardings were grotesque and the colouring frightful'. The quiet distinction of his charm when he visited Bury is still recalled in the brewery today. In reality, however, his inaction gave rise to the Greene–Lake rivalry in the running of the firm. For his younger brother, Captain Edward Greene, a director on his father's death in 1920, and Chairman after 1923, did not view events with equal detachment.

The trouble with Captain Greene was that he remained undecided about the level of his involvement in the firm. His attention to its concerns therefore fluctuated. After Eton and Oxford he undertook a brief training at Westgate. In 1904 there was 'a discussion about bringing the younger generation into the business'. E. L. D. Lake and Ralph King were paid £150 each as

18. *(above)* The New Brew House soon after its opening in January 1939.
19. *(below)* The first mash in the New Brew House, January 1939. *Left to right:* John Clarke (later Managing Director), G. N. Seton (Adlam's, Bristol), O. H. Heyhoe (First Brewer), E. L. D. Lake, Col. B. E. Oliver (Head Brewer and Director), Mark Jennings (Consultant Engineer), F. Reddish (Chemist), Martin Corke (present Managing Director), John Bridge (present Chairman).

20. *(above left)* E. L. D. Lake (1880–1946), Managing Director, 1919–1946. Passionately fond of cricket, his brewery and Bury, employees and tenants found his bark worse than his bite. 21. *(above right)* A. J. Redman, the vigorous chairman of Wells and Winch from 1920 until his death in 1948. He took over a number of breweries in the inter-war years and saw production quadruple. 22. *(below left)* John Clarke was Managing Director 1946–69, and Chairman 1969–71. 23. *(below right)* Sir Edward Greene (1883–1966) was a member of the Board, 1920–64, and its Chairman 1923–55.

24. *(above)* The fine façade of Simpson's Brewery, Baldock in 1950. Probably rebuilt around 1800 by the Pryor family, it was acquired by Greene King in 1954 and demolished fifteen years later.

25. *(below)* The Brewery Head Offices at the end of Frank Bevis's reign (1958), a jumble of high desks, stools and ledgers. There was not a single adding machine.

26. *(above)* 'The Nutshell', Bury St Edmunds. The smallest public house in Great Britain and probably the best known amongst Greene King's chain of 730. Its maximum dimensions are 15ft 10ins by 7ft 6ins.

27. *(below)* 'The Silver Jubilee', Peterborough, opened in 1977. Greene King have opened a new house a year on average since the late 1950s.

under-managers and Edward Greene £50 for his attendance at St
Edmunds brewery. The discrepancy in salary must indicate different levels of involvement. Certainly when the two under-
managers' salaries were doubled in 1912 there was no mention of
Edward Greene. The diversion of the Nether Hall calendar of
entertainments was not the best background for serious application to business. And in 1913 he was travelling extensively in
Canada, Japan and China. The war intervened,[8] and in 1921 he
was appointed comptroller to Lord Byng, the Governor-General
of Canada. When he returned the management of the brewery was
firmly in Lake hands. With two Lakes, Harry Clarke, and J. H.
Oliver running the Sudbury brewery, there was no opening for
another executive director. Moreover Edward Greene had a very
similar reaction to Suffolk and his father's ways as Sir Raymond.
Again he retreated to London. There from his house in Montagu
Street he enjoyed the same smart social round. After one of his
rare visits to his sister she scribbled in her diary, 'He has just been
much with the Queen of Spain during her autumn visit but of
course did not mention it.'[9]

Yet after he was elected Chairman in 1923 Edward Greene
attempted to direct events from London. His special interest was
business finance and it is clear that he talked a good deal about the
subject in his clubs and at dinner tables, so that he felt he could
give sound advice to the Lakes. For he believed that the financial
caution associated with Edward Lake and still pursued after his
death in 1922 was becoming out of date. He would have welcomed less of E. L. D. Lake's paternalism and more long-term
financial planning for the modernisation of the brewery. His
advice was not necessarily heeded. But the real conflict came over
the Managing Director's independence of action in matters the
Chairman thought should have been referred to him, and in his
criticisms about the continuation of brewing at Furneux Pelham
and Cambridge in the 1930s. More minor pinpricks were the farm
at Furneux Pelham, which the Lakes managed somewhat unevenly while the Company fielded the losses, and E. L. D. Lake's
generous list of charity donations. There was also a straight clash
of personalities. The Managing Director's passion for cricket,
Bury politics and West Suffolk charities reminded the Chairman
too much of the provincialism of the Nether Hall regime. It is also

clear that Edward Greene felt outnumbered by the Lakes, and that his distaste for E. L. D. Lake's sporting and political antics extended to the autocratic way in which he ran the brewery. Captain Neville Lake who managed Rayment's for many years after 1937 put the position succinctly: Edward Greene was jealous of the Lakes; E. L. D. Lake

> really was a very naughty number two . . . the Lakes are very bad number twos. They are much better as number one . . . and Mr. Bevis [Company Secretary] told me that the only real value of Ralph King to the brewery was that he kept the peace.

The squabble between the Chairman and Managing Director, never carried beyond the Boardroom doors, was important because it affected in some ways long-term planning in the brewery.

The central figure in the brewery's history between 1919 and 1946 was undoubtedly E. L. D. Lake, or Major Lake, as he was invariably known throughout West Suffolk. It is not easy to assess his career in the brewery for two reasons. First, except briefly between 1919 and 1921 and during the Second World War, the entire period was an awkward one for brewers. As we have seen, output stagnated or declined, and yet they had to modernise their tied houses and increase their provision for bottled beers. Although profits remained good for well-managed breweries, with the background of depression it seemed sensible for brewers to take a safe course, hang on to their trade, replace plant where necessary, and make modest provision for bottling facilities. This is exactly what Major Lake did. It worked well enough until the mid-1930s in an unadventurous way. Then he was much too slow in evolving long-term plans for new developments when the situation eased. Even when the plans were finalised for the new brewhouse built in 1938 they seem to have been pushed through by the head brewer, Colonel B. E. Oliver, with the Chairman's support rather than that of the Managing Director. And plans to extend the bottling stores and loading bays were too late to be completed before the war. The delay caused chronic problems after 1939.

Major Lake's policy—and in a sense this had always been done at Greene King—was to tackle problems in a piecemeal way as they arose, new fermenting vessels here, a bottle washer there. In his father's day this had not mattered since the plant was capable of meeting the demands placed upon it, and the chief plank of policy—extending the number of tied houses as financial resources allowed—was exactly right. After 1920 there were few further acquisitions of houses, with the major exception of Bailey and Tebbutt's Panton Brewery at Cambridge in 1925. But the Westgate Brewery itself needed extensive modernisation, and although there were always adequate finances for the purpose, this was only partially completed by the eve of the Second World War.

The conditions of the inter-war years largely explain Major Lake's hesitancy. A second reason necessary for consideration in any evaluation of his management is his father's heavy influence upon him. He continued Edward Lake's brewing philosophy in changed times in an unquestioning way. It was this that incensed the Chairman, Captain Edward Greene. When Major Lake left Uppingham he trained with Brakspear's Brewery at Henley-on-Thames and then—except for three years' war service—was under his father's surveillance at Westgate from 1904 to 1919. In that year, he was, although only thirty-eight, the automatic choice to replace him as Managing Director. He continued his father's policies in both the brewery and the town. In the former there was the same scrupulous attention to detail and an increasing tendency to run the company on military lines. In the operation he was well supported by Frank Bevis, the Company Secretary who supervised the office like 'a martinet'. Together they maintained a benign dictatorship. In the town and West Suffolk he continued the work of Edward Lake and Edward Greene. Their long tradition of municipal and county service was carried out entirely to the letter by Major Lake, greatly aided by his twin sister, Muriel.[10] A roll call of his offices would be almost identical to his father's: member of the town council from 1919, Mayor for nine years (six consecutively during the Second World War), a county councillor and long-serving member of Bury's Finance and Education Committees. He was also a Justice of the Peace, a great supporter of the Territorial Army, the West Suffolk Volunteer Hospital and the British Legion, a stalwart of the Bury and West Suffolk County Cricket Club, and Secretary of the Suffolk Hunt. When he died in 1946 St Edmundsbury Cathedral was crowded with 1,500 representatives of the business, social and charitable life of East Anglia. Although he inherited his father's enormous capacity for work and passion for voluntary organisations, he lacked his acute intelligence and political grasp. Edward Lake had been a man of steely reforming zeal. His son continued his work because he believed it was his inheritance to do so. He had all the integrity, the 'patent honesty', the lack of self-interest of his father, and although like him he was a passionate disciplinarian, he was essentially more emotional, more kind-hearted and more modest. When he received the freedom of the town in 1937 he believed that 'Bury was fifty years behind the times and none the worse for that'. The comment would have been inconceivable coming from Edward Lake. At times the same unthinking commitment is evident in the brewery.

In the 1930s and 1940s Major Lake had so many fingers in the Bury pie that the town was affectionately known as 'Lake District'. He also had a bigger role in the brewing trade than his father. Not only did he become Chairman of the Cheltenham Original Brewing Company in 1938, and keep a constant eye on his brother (Captain Neville Lake) at Furneux Pelham, but he was chairman of the Brewers' Society (1934–6) two years after joining its Council, and during the war Chairman of its Parliamentary Committee. There were few brewers who knew the Trade better and he was reckoned one of the best judges of hops in the country. At one stage he was so involved in Bury and West Suffolk affairs and national brewing matters that the Chairman insisted that he accept no more offices without his permission. But not for a moment was Greene King neglected and undoubtedly his years of overwork led to his sudden death in 1946.

3

In looking at these conflicts between the inherited traditions of the firm and the forces of change, between a part-time Chairman and autocratic Managing Director, and at the ways in which they shaped the development of the brewery in the inter-war years it is necessary to survey, very briefly, the four distinct sub-periods within these twenty years (1920–3; 1924–9; 1930–3; 1934–9) —for they were far from uniformly bleak. It is the fairly rapidly shifting experience from one to the other that explains the four

most obvious changes that took place between 1920 and 1939
—the closure of the Haverhill (1923) and Sudbury breweries
(1932); the purchase of the Cambridge Brewery in 1925; the
change in the status of the company; and the building of the new
brewhouse at Bury in the late 1930s.

The post-war brewing boom lasted well into 1920. In 1919
there was a feverish activity by brewers to acquire further public
houses that drove prices of them up as steeply as in the mid-1890s.
Greene King shared less obviously in the bonanza. They were still
assimilating the major purchases of Christmas's and Oliver's,
although there is evidence from the purchase of cottage properties, the construction of the Victory Sports Ground (see p. 206
below) and the increase in the strength of its beers (although well
short of pre-1914 levels), that the brewery enjoyed the common
prosperity. There were notes of caution: high levels of duty (the
1920 budget included a swingeing 30s. extra on a standard barrel)
and increases in costs, especially wages. Greene King sanctioned
four pay rises in 1918-20. This was fine so long as prices and
employment remained steady. But late in 1920 the mood of
optimism suddenly changed as the general industrial recession,
evident since spring, deepened. Negotiations for the purchase of
Coggeshall Brewery were broken off in November 1920[11] and the
figures for the year ending May 31 1921 revealed that beer sales in
the previous year had contracted by over 10 per cent—around the
national average. Now the Board realised they were caught by the
pincers of high duties and high costs. Duties shot up from 14s.
4d. per bulk barrel in 1918 to £3 2s. 3d. in 1921. Expenses
increased by a dramatic £44,068 between 1919 and 1921 and
expressed per bulk barrel from 24s. 4¾d. in 1920 to 30s. 8d. in
1921. Levels of duty could only be lowered by the brewers'
successful pressure on the Government, and expenses forced
down by wage reductions and a fall in raw material prices. The
decline in output continued well into 1923; sales fell from
109,318 bulk barrels in 1920 to 68,353 in 1923. It was the
sharpest contraction the brewery had ever experienced. The
reason for the recession in East Anglia was not hard to establish:
the collapse of agricultural prosperity after 1920, when the
Government rapidly withdrew its wartime support. Engineering,
the other major employer in Bury, was also badly hit. The

Managing Director of Greene King reported at the 1922 Annual
General Meeting,

> the decrease in sales is largely due to the fall in wages—at the
> present rate it is quite impossible for a working man to satisfy
> his legitimate requirements.

And, like all breweries, Greene King maintained it was powerless
to reduce prices whilst duties remained so high. Had it made the
smallest worthwhile reduction—24s. a barrel or 1d. per pint
—the *Brewers' Journal* maintained the industry's profits would
have been wiped out. Yet the apparent crisis of 1921 was averted
because breweries, like all other firms in 1922 and 1923, resorted
to wage reductions and the price of barley fell sharply. Greene
King's experience was not untypical. Profits fell from £84,161 to
£61,991 in 1920–1 and then stabilised over the next two years in
spite of further contractions in sales (although of course expressed
per barrel expenses stayed up). For the price of malt fell from
101s. 2d. in 1921 to 62s. 1d. in 1923. In the 1923 budget the
Government reduced duties by 20s. per bulk barrel after a massive
campaign by the brewers, so that breweries, finding the other 4s. a
barrel, reduced prices by a penny to sixpence a pint. It was not
enough to stimulate consumption much, but the worst of the
recession was over. For Greene King it had never been menacing
in financial terms, although the fall in production was alarming
enough. It led to the closure of the Haverhill brewery in late
1923—supplies could easily be delivered from Bury by lorry
—and Sudbury escaped only because the Chancellor of the Exchequer made his timely reduction in duty.

The rest of the 1920s marked new heights for Greene King.
Admittedly output did not improve spectacularly except between
1924 and 1926, and the directors were always aware that sales
would not burgeon so long as agriculture remained depressed
—which it did until the mid-1930s. But malt and hop prices
remained low and wage advances were minimal. Moreoever sales
of bottled beer—reflecting a change in consumer taste—
advanced spectacularly. In 1923 the firm had bottled 187,756
dozen; in 1928, 418,054 plus 125,278 crates at Cambridge.
Profits advancing sharply in 1926 reached new heights in each
successive year so that by 1928 they topped the £100,000 mark

for the first time. In 1929 dividends on the ordinary shares returned 18 per cent which compared very favourably with both regional competitors and the national breweries.[12] The management was justifiably proud of its record. Major Lake put its success down, when the summer was hot, to the weather, or when it was wet, to the public's appreciation of a good product. This was too modest and simplistic, for the Company pursued consistent policies of careful management and improvement. Gone were the days when every West Suffolk and Essex–Cambridgeshire borders public house of any size was snapped up. Houses were modernised and extended, particularly on the Essex coast and in the Newmarket area, and very few, except outstanding urban properties, were purchased. When the turnaround in trade came in 1924, the company had the good fortune to be offered Bailey and Tebbutt's Panton brewery in Cambridge. Its management had been latterly eccentric, not surprisingly, since Mr Tebbutt's affairs were handled by the Master in Lunacy, but it offered a foothold in Cambridge, where most of its forty-eight houses were sited, and a large (58 per cent) free trade. Its turnover was around a third of the Westgate Brewery. The deal was completed in February 1925: Greene King borrowing £149,000 of the £152,000 price, on unsecured loans of 4½–5 per cent from Lloyds and Barclays Banks. It proved an excellent buy. Brewing was continued at Cambridge although the brewery itself was very old-fashioned. At first the brewer, another Tebbutt, proved remarkably intractable to the Lakes' directives, but at the Brewers' Society show in 1929 it won the championship gold medal, the silver challenge cup and silver and bronze medals for its superb bitters and draught stout. Its profits were almost as delectable: in the years 1926–9 (inclusive) it returned on average £21,850. Other sizeable breweries were offered to Greene King—Phillips' Royston Brewery in 1926, Hudson's Pampisford and Fuller's Kelveden Breweries in 1929—but they were politely declined after discussions about their valuation although in reality they were turned down because they owned far too high a proportion of country properties.[13] Greene King had no wish to replicate its problems. In 1924 Major Lake disclosed that one of the reasons why recovery would be slow, was that the firm already owned far too many houses in villages, entirely dependent upon agriculture for their prosperity, and where population was still declining quite sharply. He reckoned that out of 322 'country' houses attached to Bury, 202 did a trade of fewer than two barrels a week. In Cockfield Greene King owned no fewer than five houses, each doing a trade of around one barrel a week. In extreme instances tenants needed help from the brewery. In contrast Bailey and Tebbutt's was so attractive—and this was rare in Eastern England—because it possessed a large free trade and most of its houses were in Cambridge itself.

The other key event of this period was that the brewery became a public company in early 1927. It did so because a clause of the Companies (Consolidation) Act of 1908 stipulated that any private company with more than fifty shareholders must adopt this status. When Sir Walter Greene and Edward Lake died in the early 1920s and settlements were made for their children and grandchildren, it was inevitable that numbers could not be restricted below fifty. In 1921 there were already forty-seven share-holders. Yet there were fears amongst them about the free transfer of shares, and the Managing Director

> hoped that it would not be necessary to publish a Balance Sheet in this period of trade depression when we are having to help our Tenants for the Profit might be misinterpreted.

It is clear from the minutes that Edward Greene thought very differently. He pressed several times that a public quotation of the company's shares and a further issue would be beneficial. He met with opposition both from the Lakes and Olivers. The real absurdity of the situation was revealed in 1924 when the company borrowed £149,000 for the purchase of the Cambridge Brewery. There was not the slightest hitch in raising the money and over the next two years almost half the principal was paid off, but Edward Greene argued that the creation of a further 50,000 ordinary shares would have rendered interest payments, of £7,000 a year initially, unnecessary and released funds for modernisation. The decision to seek public status was inevitable. It was taken in November 1926, although for the moment the conservative element within the directorate won on the decision not to seek any further issue of shares, and clauses about the restriction of share transfers in the 1887 incorporation were retained. The Chairman must have worked hard behind the scenes, for within a year both these decisions, in spite of a rearguard action by the Oliver family, were reversed. In December 1927 Cohen, Laming and Hoare marketed 53,250 additional ordinary shares—the denomination of all shares was altered from £10 to £1 when the company went public—which returned Greene King £101,175. The big loans from Barclays and Lloyds were wiped out overnight. The majority of these new shares was taken up by small investors in batches of 50 to 500. Holdings of 1,000 and more were rare. The Greene, King and Lake families took few,[14] although many of the new shareholders were Suffolk-based. Their names suddenly filled out the share register, but control still rested very firmly with the Greene and King families.

Greene King had fared better than the majority of middle-sized breweries in the late 1920s. Although agriculture remained depressed, unemployment in the Eastern counties was nothing like so severe as in the old industrial areas of South Wales, West Yorkshire, Lancashire, Tyneside and Central Scotland. And when the recession deepened in 1931–3, Greene King again came through largely unscathed. Indeed, until the Chancellor of the Exchequer, in his emergency budget of September 1931, imposed additional duties of 31s. per standard barrel, thereby raising prices by a minimum of 1d. a pint, the Depression had hardly affected Greene King. Profits in the years ending 31 May 1929–31 hovered around a record £107,000. Increased sales of bottled beer were reported, and, in November 1930, the firm bought Ogden's March Brewery for £50,500 with twenty-eight freehold and six leasehold houses. The brewery was immediately closed and the houses, although their beer sales were disappointing, helped to prop up the output of the Westgate Brewery. Much of the firm's success was owed to low raw material costs, first-rate financial control, good beers—the Cambridge Brewery won a further gold medal at the Brewers' Society Show in 1931—and a programme of steady improvement of public houses. The Cambridge Brewery, with its demand secured by a generation of students and dons more or less immune from the Depression, proved an excellent acquisition—at least until competition there increased after 1932.

Only in 1932 did sales contract sharply. Six months earlier,

Captain Greene had assured shareholders at the 1931 Annual General Meeting,

> in view of the general trade depression throughout the country, and when we see by the published figures what a very heavy decrease there has been in beer sales throughout the country, I think we must consider ourselves very fortunate.

The Chancellor of the Exchequer ended the brewery's run of luck in his September budget. By January 1932 the Greene King monthly trading figures were 'alarming'; and as soon as it was evident there was no relief in the April budget, the decision to close Sudbury Brewery was taken, and a 5 per cent cut in salaries and wages—to avoid redundancies—was made. By June output was reckoned to be 20 per cent down on the previous year. Tenants applied for aid and plans were discussed to close houses where they were too thick on the ground. The Managing Director was inundated with requests from other brewers: the Huntingdon Brewery, Phillips' (Royston), the Star Brewery (Cambridge), Yate's (Wisbech), Alston's (Manningtree), Maulden's (Sudbury), one at Kettering—to consider amalgamation or purchase. Inevitably and politely these were turned down. Mr Ogden of the March brewery had sought amalgamation initially, but he was content with a straight sale and appointment as joint manager of the Cambridge-March area. This was in 1930. In 1932 the flood of requests was frozen in that year's cold climate. Amalgamations with small, primarily country-based breweries offered few attractions. Of course there was plenty of spare capacity at Bury and Cambridge, but valuations were difficult in a collapsed market and the firm was very chary of adding to its string of houses selling two barrels a week and under.

The sole exception was the merger with Rayment's of Furneux Pelham. This was treated differently because it had been owned since its purchase in 1889 by Edward Lake and J. M. King.[15] They had each invested £10,000 in it and the former, by the purchase of a public house every few years and by using similar management techniques to those employed on a far bigger canvas at Bury, had built up a flourishing small country brewery with an excellent reputation for its beers. Before 1914 it returned net profits of around £1,300 on average. Yet like many small breweries in the

1920s, in spite of the Lakes' attentions and profits averaging £4,142 in that decade, it was ailing: although it possessed potential it lacked capital for further development. In the end the real problem was a managerial one. Alan Lake died in 1930 and his eldest brother decided that the best course of action was to merge Rayment's with Greene King. The autumn of 1931 was not a season for bold independence. Rayment's therefore became a subsidiary of Greene King by an exchange of 15,000 shares, although in fact it continued to be run almost independently of Bury. Edward Greene had to be content with asking searching questions about the rationale for its existence—and the continued losses of its 350-acre farm, which had failed to sell in the depth of the recession.

Until 1937 Rayment's was capably managed by Vice-Admiral W. J. C. Lake, a nephew of E. W. Lake. When he moved to the Panton Brewery he was succeeded by Captain Neville Lake, E.W.'s youngest son. For thirty years with a spell away during the Second World War, he ran Rayment's in a highly individualistic way. The brewing industry until very recently has always embraced a fair number of eccentrics. Few can have matched Captain Lake. His career in the Navy was largely confined to submarines. Thereafter he always expressed a strong preference for small ships and fiery admirals. Rayment's became the ship, he its choleric, outspoken admiral. He even brought his coxswain with him so that the air was perpetually heavy and blue with smoke and colourful naval language. The eccentricity was immediately observable to anyone who crossed his office floor. A large map of the environs not only revealed the whereabouts of Rayment's twenty-eight tied houses, but also in summer it showed the progress of neighbouring county council roadmen. When their tar boilers and steam rollers were reported to be approaching a Rayment's house, he drove across and welcomed them to a liberal amount of beer before concluding a bargain for the holes of the inn's car-park and yard to be repaired. His staff were devoted to him and Rayment's, after the doldrums of the mid-1930s, began to achieve an excellent reputation in the North London free trade for their first-rate service and good beers (see p. 203).

Steep as the recession was in 1932, Greene King's profits were not severely hit. In June 1933 output was declared to be 24 per cent down and profits 15 per cent down, figures around the national average for output and rather better for profitability. Production nationally fell from 25,000,000 bulk barrels in 1930 to 17,300,000 in 1933 and the *Brewing Trade Review* reckoned that the profits of some twelve big breweries fell between an eighth and two-fifths or about one-fifth on average. But by early 1933 there were modest signs of recovery, given a hefty fillip by the April budget. After eighteen months of pressure by the brewers, Neville Chamberlain, the Chancellor of the Exchequer, in consultation with the Brewers' Society and the Treasury, reformed the duties. The concept of a barrel of standard gravity of 1055° was abolished and duty was in future to be levied on the actual gravity of the beer. It was fixed at 24s. a bulk barrel of 1027° or less with an extra additional 2s. for every additional degree above this base. It halted the increasing demand for weaker beer, apparent since the late 1920s, a trend which had been intensified by the Depression of 1930–3.[16] More important, beer was reduced by a minimum of 1d. a pint. At Greene King there was an immediate turnaround: cuts in wages were restored in June; by August substantial improvements in the monthly trade figures were reported. By the end of 1933 the worst was over.

The years 1934–9 were good ones for the majority of brewers. 1934 was, commented the *Brewing Trade Review*, 'a remarkable one . . . on the whole things have gone well'. Trade journals rarely exceed such effusiveness. By 1937 production, although in *per capita* terms it was only half pre-1914 levels, had recovered to pre-1930 Depression levels. The habit of regular beer drinking had returned, although now in moderation as the population spent more and more on consumer goods, recreation and the football pools. The Brewers' Society believed this was due to the fact that beer was a little cheaper (certainly more money was around) and the effectiveness of the 'Beer is Best' collective advertising campaign. Temperance, after a century of advance, was at last on the run. Admittedly, the experience of different brewers was patchy. Profits were still low in the old industrial areas, but a glance in the brewing journals at the company statements of comparable brewers to Greene King in the South and East show that returns were good.

For Greene King the sharp increase in profitability in 1934–5 was maintained (see Appendix 2, Table 5). It reflected that at last agriculture was enjoying a modest prosperity. There were still anxieties for the firm: 1936 was a wet summer, causing Major Lake to lament that no brewery in England was so dependent on the weather for its success; in 1938 the upward trend was checked by rises in raw material and labour costs; a year later, in April 1939, he was 'appalled by the state of trade'. People were so much influenced by the gloomy international situation that they were, he thought, hesitant to spend. Yet however much these short term fluctuations might cause temporary difficulties, the longer term prospects—once it was realised that output would climb only *gradually* upwards—were good; that is until 1938, when impending war clouded all vision. Above all, money was cheap to borrow. This and the return to prosperity in 1933–4, meant that at last the new brewhouse could be built. Later it was regretted that the opportunity had not been taken to rebuild the entire brewery. But the brewhouse, opened in January 1939, stands as a splendid monument to the brewery's fortunes in the mid- and late 1930s.

There were other features of Greene King's success. In 1934 the wines and spirits side of the business, run since the acquisition of Clarke's from Cupola House, was strengthened by the acquisition of Thomas Peatling, a wines and spirits business centred upon Wisbech and King's Lynn. The firm, with a history dating back to 1828 in Wisbech, had long been agents for Greene King beers. Control of the new subsidiary cost £29,110. By 1937 and 1938 it was returning 15 per cent on this capital and paying dividends of 7 per cent on its ordinary shares.[17] Otherwise the process of amalgamation and rationalisation that was evident in the brewing industry nationally—the number of breweries was reduced from 4,482 in 1910 to 885 in 1939—proceeded no further with Greene King after the Rayment's takeover.[18] In fact Rayment's flourished in the late 1930s as it expanded its club trade, but the Panton Brewery in Cambridge did less well. Its profits declined by around a third from well over £20,000 in the peak of the 1929–30 boom to around £14,000 in the late 1930s. The directors bemoaned their fate and began to learn some hard lessons. They needed none about the undesirability of collecting a longer and longer string of struggling country houses, but in Cambridge their position was undermined by Tollemache's (one of the two big Ipswich breweries) acquisition of the Star Brewery, which had, during the Depression, been offered to Greene King. Tollemache's produced in Cambridge an excellent bottled beer, the growth point of the 1930s trade, and, unusually in the gentlemanly world of pre-1950s brewing, a trade skirmish developed. It led in May 1936 to talks about a merger of the two leading East Anglian firms. Sir Raymond Greene even believed this should include Cobbold's, the other large Ipswich brewery, although the deal's real basis was competition in Cambridge, Greene King's desire for a foothold in the Ipswich market, and its belief that when the head of the firm, the 74-year-old Hon. Douglas Tollemache, died, it might easily be acquired by one of the national breweries. Then Greene King envisaged a severe squeeze from Ipswich on one side and Cambridge on the other. In spite of this urgency the talks dragged on: there were fears about control of the new firm and the Lakes, who had long known the management of Tollemache's to be eccentric, on closer examination found it to be extravagant. Profit margins were tight because of irreducibly high fixed costs and the price, finally beaten down from 117,000 to 90,000 Greene King ordinary shares, allowed, they believed, little room for manoeuvre: 'in the event of trade depression or penal taxation there was so little margin in his accounts as compared with ours'. In August 1938 the deal looked near completion. The Greene King directors moved to London for a couple of days, and on the second held an unrecorded session with Collins Tootell, one of the leading brewing accounting firms of the day. They were disturbed by both Mr Collins's report and the details of the 1937–8 figures for both the Ipswich and Star Breweries. The merger collapsed on fears about Tollemache's profitability, their refusal to consider closing their London operation which appeared to be the main drag in this area, and, above all, as was so often the case in the brewing world, on personalities and management styles. Other potential deals in the mid-1930s—Phillips' of Royston revived once more in 1934, interesting offers from Shipstone's (Nottingham) and J. W. Green (Luton)—never proceeded far.

Caution and the firm's old pursuit of financial orthodoxy had prevailed. An opportunity had not necessarily been lost, for Wells and Winch (see pp. 233–8) which grew so rapidly in the inter-war years faced far severer problems than Greene King after 1948. The acquisition of Tollemache's, or indeed a string of other struggling East Anglian breweries, might well have pulled down profitability after the war and thereby inhibited Greene King's independence and survival.

Greene King therefore faced the exigencies of the Second World War with a partially rebuilt brewery, amongst the soundest finances of any brewery of its size in the country, and a growing interest in the expanding wines and spirits market. In the next section of the chapter it is necessary to look in more detail at the two key developments within the brewery in the inter-war years: the improvement of its tied houses, and the programme of re-equipment which culminated in the building of the new brew-house in 1935—8.

4

Brewing in many ways was the odd man out amongst Britain's larger industries before the 1920s. Although the size of firms grew, especially after mergers in the 1890s, modernisation proceeded very slowly. The quality of the final product had little to do with up-to-date equipment, and smallish breweries returned good profits when their outlets were right. The most delicious beers were produced in the most old-fashioned breweries. The year Greene King's Cambridge brewery carried off a string of prizes at the Brewers' Show the directors were told its 'plant generally was in a shocking condition'. Modernisation guaranteed little, so long as cleanliness and good materials remained the essentials. The nature of tied outlets in the industry meant that economies of scale in production, although they of course existed, could be circumvented to a certain extent. Moreover they achieved only small savings of labour because, as detractors of the industry always pointed out, brewing employed few people in relation to its capital. Good brewers therefore concentrated upon good house-keeping and the extension of their market by sensible public house acquisition. Considerations of these kinds were clearly uppermost in the Lakes' minds in the running of Greene King. But even in such an apparently unchanging industry as brewing things did not stand still. The demand for lighter, often bottled, beers and public house modernisation after 1918 presented new challenges to even the most conservative brewers. How did the Greene King management adapt in the inter-war years? Let us first consider its role in renewing the plant.

If one looks at the evidence on the ground now it can be concluded from the fine brewhouse, opened in 1939, and still the most notable feature of the brewery, that the management passed this test with flying colours. The reality was rather different. It must be remembered that, except for about a year in 1924, the company was always running three—four if you count the curious dual arrangement at Westgate and St Edmunds, which persisted to 1939—separate breweries in East Anglia. They each possessed their traditions and reputation, especially Cambridge; and Sudbury, with the Olivers, and Pelham, with the Lakes, were run semi-autonomously after acquisition. A pushing newcomer, working on textbook principles—rare birds in the brewing industry at any time in its history—might have rebuilt Westgate and, taking advantage of motor transport, closed the other breweries and controlled his empire from Bury alone. But the Greenes and Lakes, and the Olivers and Clarkes, who joined them after 1918, were heirs of a different tradition. They were not totally wedded to the past. When the need arose they could close breweries, but they never conceived of total rationalisation since Cambridge and Pelham held special features for them. And of course the breweries worked within capacity after 1920; the 1921–3 recession shook Greene King and the full potentialities of motor delivery were not immediately realised in its pioneering stage. Therefore they could continue, returning a handsome profit, simply by sustaining motion in the old grooves. Modernisation of plant took place only when the need arose. This was frequent in the 1920s, when, after working through the war with minimal repairs and renewal, it was in poor shape. The minute books reveal a constant succession of work. St Edmunds was especially dilapidated: in August 1919 brewing ceased for a fortnight because the plate at the bottom of the copper was burnt out; its fermenting vessels, hop-back and hot liquor tanks were all worn out; two new coppers costing £1,500 were installed in 1928, whilst two years previously the brewery walls had needed pinning when it was discovered that Fred King, in his haste to erect them seventy years previously, had done so without proper foundations.

Of course, Major Lake and Harry Clarke and B. E. Oliver at Sudbury were aware of developments in the industry. They talked to other brewers, especially at the Norfolk and Suffolk branch of the Brewers' Society, and at the Brewers' Show each autumn in London. When a new fermenting room was required at Westgate in the early 1920s, followed by a cold store in 1922 and a new yeast plant in 1925, they used either Adlams or Briggs the leading brewing engineers. But it is clear that there was always a pre-occupation with costs, and therefore new machinery was intro-duced in a makeshift way. The Chairman, Edward Greene, the most forward looking director in financial matters, niggled about the Managing Director's improvements. In 1925 he pointed out that £24,000 had been spent on their breweries in two years, and that in future work should be spread out over the years, following a properly prepared plan. A brewery architect was hired to make a report[19] and by 1927 a reserve fund of £17,000 had been created for work on the breweries and public houses. But nothing was done before recession again hit the industry in 1930.

This policy of piecemeal improvement financed out of current earnings worked worst in bottling—at least in the long run. For the demand for bottled beers in the 1920s took all breweries by surprise. After the war bottling arrangements at Westgate were somewhat primitive. There were two 12-head bottlers installed before 1914. Each machine, operated by four boys, could bottle about 500 dozen pint bottles on a good day when there was no breakdown. Bottles were still individually handled, cleansed in caustic soda and labelled. The bottling stores, in St Edmunds redundant stables, were cramped.

The aim in bottling was to produce a long-life 'bright' beer, which could only be achieved by chilling and filtering which threw out the yeast and sedimentary residues of cask beer. These processes, developed very rapidly in the 1920s as demand for bottled beer grew, were beyond the financial resources of many small breweries. Greene King was certainly well abreast of bottling technology in these years and expanded its capacity quite rapidly. The bottling store was extended in the mid-1920s, new bottlers, soakers, conditioning and pasteurising tanks were intro-duced, and the premises were enlarged yet again in 1930. The impression from the minute books is one of constant improvement with ideas taken from other breweries and the Brewers' Show, so that production at Bury alone was stepped up to over a quarter of a million dozen bottles by 1928. The trade, even in the worst years of the 1920s, constantly increased. It was the most cheering feature of the industry. But at Greene King the bottling plant grew as occasion demanded. There were no plans for a well-equipped, purpose-built store and, even in the early 1930s when in its most efficient state, it was inadequate.[20] The author of an article on Greene King's new equipment pointed out these features in *Bottling* (July 1932):

> The present bottling stores may be said to be in the nature of a makeshift . . . consequently the layout of the floor, the loading and storage arrangements, have been hampered by being forced to conform to the more or less unsuitable nature of the buildings, and it is rather in the details of the plant itself and the manner in which it is being worked, that the interest to the bottler must lie.

Developments at Bury were mirrored at Sudbury and Cambridge. Briefly the axe was suspended over Sudbury in 1923 and expenditure there was minimal afterwards. Cambridge was in a poor condition, although improvements took place there after 1928. The fact that brewing and bottling were carried out on three distinct sites, each having to be kept in reasonable working order, probably held up major reconstruction at Bury. Certainly it was well within the capabilities of the transport department at Bury to cover the region, for only coal and town deliveries at Bury were undertaken by horses after the early 1920s. Also the depression of 1931–3 put paid to long-term plans. Perhaps 'plans' is too precise a word, for the realisation—evident in the late 1920s—grew amongst directors that it was useless to push more and more new equipment into an incommodious brewery, most of which was at least seventy-five years old. But the site had always been crowded, and its poor layout was exacerbated by its curious dual nature. Now, with extended bottle and mineral water stores, it was a jumble.

Then suddenly in 1934, with the return of prosperity and the cheap money policy of the National Government, whereby money could be borrowed at 3½–4 per cent, the directors at last were galvanised into action. By issuing debentures or by selling their 35,000 unallocated ordinary shares on the market at around £4 each they could contemplate major improvements, and make savings which would virtually cover the dividends needed for additional shares. Where should they begin? That was the trouble. The Managing Director's report on the brewery was an horrific catalogue: the mash tun was cracked; the brewhouse at Westgate unsafe; loading out arrangements were totally inadequate. In the discussion which followed, Ralph King muttered about costs, but the Greenes insisted upon speedy action. A committee was formed which included Major Lake, Colonel B. E. Oliver (the head brewer), Mark Jennings (the engineer),[21] and W. Mitchell (the brewery architect). The problem was the restricted site, and after a visit to several German breweries, the plans for the present brewhouse—worked out by Colonel Oliver and Mark Jennings in consultation with their old suppliers Adlams and Briggs—were completed. It was to fit into the old coopers' yard, once the site of the almshouses and St Mary's School, between the two existing breweries. But the more the committee thought through the issues the more it realised the new brewhouse was only one area that required urgent attention. In March 1936 Major Lake presented its considerations on malting at Westgate. In this department, managed since 1918 by Harry Clarke, change had been minimal. Malting was still on five sites and, except for electrically powered hoists and elevators, Benjamin Greene would have noticed few differences over the century. The work was laborious, seasonal and extremely dusty. Major Lake was sure they did not meet Board of Trade regulations. He thought they should build new maltings capable of doing 10,000 quarters. It would effect savings in labour and carting and would largely eliminate dust. Wilkins's Theatre of 1819, currently a barrel store, should be demolished and a new spirits and tobacco store be built on its site. Edward Greene concluded, 'if the facts were as stated by the Managing Director the position was alarming'. Suddenly the brewhouse bill of around £50,000 needed trebling. Priorities therefore had to be sorted out quickly. By early summer 1936 these were agreed. The new brewhouse should take precedence. The company would issue 25,000 of its unallocated ordinary shares and run an over-draft of £50,000 with its bankers. Work on the brewhouse costing around £80,000—double early estimates—was begun in December after a tunnel under Crown Street was constructed between the Westgate brewery and the new brewhouse. Immediately difficulties were encountered: the foundations needed piles in the gravel and chalk subsoil, and, in the summer of 1937, the project ran into serious delays resulting from shortages of material supplies caused by the Government's rearmament programme.

The new brewhouse was opened at last in January 1939.[22] From the outset it worked well, which encouraged Major Lake in June to press the Board about their 'antiquated loading-out system', the wines and spirits store, which was 'a disgrace', and above all, a further unit in the bottling store. 'Our present bottling plant was working to capacity', he admitted, 'and we were never able to properly overhaul and repair it. If we had a serious breakdown [I] did not dare think how we could carry on.' The work would cost £50,000. The Chairman thought they should wait until Autumn before taking a decision. Already it was far too late, for September saw the outbreak of war. A major opportunity had been missed to rebuild the brewery at bargain prices. Why did the delay take place? The site was a problem. It was difficult to know where to begin. But the real reason was managerial. Major Lake was a tireless Managing Director, assiduous in carrying out a task to the letter, but he lacked the larger vision to force through the entire rebuilding programme. He failed to capitalise upon the company's extremely robust financial position. In the last resort he was penny pinching, suffering from the brewer's inherited conservatism. His position, moreover, in relation to the Chairman, and the wariness each possessed for the other, meant that at crucial junctures there could be damaging failures of understanding. Edward Greene had the financial grasp but he lacked the thoroughgoing commitment to push ahead with the wider schemes of improvement. The pace of modernisation, as the international situation deteriorated, was too slow. This failure to secure more than the new brewhouse was to cost the company dearly in the 1940s.

5

Except for the acquisition of houses attached to Bailey and Tebbutt's and Ogden's March Brewery, the number of tied houses did not increase in the inter-war years (see Appendix 2, Table 3). Indeed between 1919 and 1924 it showed a modest decline as licences were turned in for compensation. This process continued until the early 1930s and a number of houses doing an impossibly small trade were sold off. But it would be totally misleading to represent Greene King marking time with their tied house empire between 1920 and 1939, turning in the odd licence for compensation here, selling off the occasional house there. Of course, the days of headlong acquisition of the 1880s, 1890s and late 1910s had passed, but there were three developments which concerned all brewery directors in the management of their houses in the inter-war years: modernisation of their property; the replacement of tenants by managers; the rise of clubs. Most of the literature examining these trends has concentrated upon the market leaders, the great London, Burton and Birmingham brewers. Greene King provides, therefore, an instructive case: a largish regional brewery with an almost entirely rural market.

The springs of public house modernisation had two quite separate origins in the 1916—20 period: the state-managed houses in the Carlisle area and the Birmingham breweries, especially Mitchell and Butlers. Briefly Carlisle made the running, employing two architects of real distinction, but in both the aim was to provide better seating, eliminate the old 'perpendicular fashion' of drinking that was common to all pre-1914 houses, and provide decent living accommodation for tenants. The real problem with public house improvement was convincing licensing magistrates, to whom all plans had to be submitted for approval, that better facilities for more leisurely drinking would not encourage drunkenness. Fortunately for the brewers statistics of drunkenness showed a quite remarkable improvement in the 1920s, giving grounds for some claim that more civilised facilities led to less, not more, heavy drinking.[23] The brewers accepted they had to turn licences in to obtain some for new houses or major rebuilding. In cities such as Birmingham the process had been going on since before the war, and, as the *Brewers' Journal* of 1920 colourfully put it, there were too many of 'the hole-and-corner houses which look hungrily on each other in hundreds of our urban streets'. Modernisation, removing from public houses, at least in the southern counties, some of their finer working-class features, became a mania in the mid-1920s. It was the great subject of discussion in the journal literature. Hawkins and Pass reckon that 'between 1922 and 1930 approximately 27 per cent of the total number of public houses in England and Wales were improved in one way or another'.[24] The brewers contested genuinely that they were unsure about the profitability of the movement, but in the South and East breweries had to modernise their houses to attract trade. They had to respond to changes in consumer taste and remove the tarnished image of the public house. Some most attractive houses were built, especially by Benskins (Watford) and Whitbreads, and later by breweries in and around Birmingham and Liverpool.[25]

The Greene King houses did not lend themselves easily to this process. They were mainly rural, usually small, and enjoyed no prosperity from the new consumer goods industries or, except in Cambridge and Clacton, from what tourist trade there was in the 1920s. Nevertheless the company was aware of developments. Major and Harold Lake went to look at the new houses in the Carlisle area as early as 1919 and recommended that the company's architect and surveyor should also inspect the state houses, 'with a view to adopting some of the arrangements initiated'. In the early 1920s a determined effort was made to bring houses up to date by spending £12,000–£13,000 a year on them. The works department was expanded. It employed between forty and fifty builders, carpenters, plumbers, and painters who worked in eight gangs from Bury, going out each day up to twenty-five to thirty miles radius by lorry to renovate and modernise.[26] In addition there was some contract work. Improving 450 houses and keeping them in a good state of repair was a constant process. In East Anglia, where village houses especially were old and built in poor materials, it required quite large expenditures on individual houses every four or five years. Yet as early as 1922 the Board was assured that 'the houses belonging to the Company are now getting into an excellent state of repair'. Greene King enjoyed a good name for its houses in the region. There was less niggardliness here than in other areas of expenditure. There was a realisation that an attractive house usually ensured good trade and that first-rate tenants could only be retained by offering them modern accommodation.

Some houses were new or entirely rebuilt and since they were designed by Basil Oliver, a brother of the head brewer, and a nationally renowned architect, they brought Greene King into the front rank of public house builders. There were around half-a-dozen show places constructed in the 1920s and 1930s: two on the Essex coast, the *King's Cliff Hotel* and the *Roaring Donkey* at Holland-on-Sea; the *Rose and Crown*, Cambridge; the *Priors Inn*, Bury; the *Red Lion*, Grantchester; the *George and Star*, March. They were expensive, costing around £5,000 each without fittings, and beautifully detailed when designed by Basil Oliver.[27] The *Rose and Crown* in 1930 won an award for the best new building in East Anglia; the *Red Lion* was one of the most attractive public houses built in England between the wars. The refurbished houses carried the smart glazed stoneware plaque designed by Kruger Gray (see plate 26), and Major Lake and Basil Oliver were foremost in the movement in the 1930s to improve public house signs.[28] The company was justifiably proud of its houses. At one Annual General Meeting the Chairman invited the shareholders to view the Clacton and Holland-on-Sea houses at their busiest on a Bank Holiday, although it is difficult to conceive of a more unlikely group of day trippers to Clacton. The Licensing Justices in East Anglia do not appear to have been as obstructive as they were represented to be by the Brewers' Society elsewhere, although they could be painfully slow in their deliberations.

The direct management by breweries of their tied houses was another feature of these years. As brewers spent more and more money on them they wanted to obtain firmer control so that they could implement their ideas about improvements, especially of furnishings, and guarantee certain uniform standards. They did this by employing managers, paying them a wage and a small percentage of the profits. It created more paperwork but possessed advantages of control. The system was really pioneered by Mitchell and Butler in Birmingham, who in 1923 managed 800 out of their 1,300 on- and off-licences. Greene King, with its large number of country houses, followed a different pattern. In 1924 it had only about half-a-dozen managed houses, although twelve years later this had increased to over one hundred. There was a policy of managing the larger houses on the Essex coast and those in Newmarket, Bury and Cambridge, and in 1936 Major Lake thought the system should be extended to all houses as they became vacant, although the two Greenes dissented sharply from this view. The Managing Director believed that there were advantages in terms of stocks, furnishings and pensions and that there was a wider choice of applicants. One interesting feature is that it seems to have been, at least by the early 1930s, company policy to put employees trained in the brewery into houses which became vacant. If they had insufficient capital they were made managers. But the managers' minute book for the 1930s reveals that the system did not invariably work well. There were bad managers just as there were bad tenants. One example has the perfect 1930s ring: 'he and his wife were continually rowing, he was never in the house, she was continually at the Pictures'. Losses were made in managed houses. But it is interesting that the pressure to increase the number of managed houses also came from the tenants themselves. When they had trouble with payment for the licence and stocks they asked for a salary. Usually this was granted unless the tenant was incompetent, or the house was too small to be suitable for management. Thus in 1939 Greene King ran a mixed system. Around a quarter of its houses, including all the larger town properties, were managed; the rest were run on the old tenant system. The economics of the exercise were not entirely clear cut. But in general, large houses with a good manager returned a better profit than when tenanted; small ones, becoming increasingly tied for spirits, tobaccos and most bottled beers and stouts, still paid best with a small rental and the traditional wet rent element.[29]

Just as the nature of Greene King's properties meant that it could not absorb the full impact of the trend towards managed houses, so the other major development, the rise of the clubs, largely passed it by. There was a great growth of these after 1920. Then there had been around 9,000 registered. In 1934 there were 15,298. After 1930 the increase almost made up for the number of on-licences lost. They were largely an urban and industrial phenomenon and therefore, except for the large number of ex-servicemen's clubs which flourished after 1919, remained outside Greene King's rural experience. Since they posed something of a threat to traditional tied houses the brewers did not like them. In the 1930s the Brewers' Society ran a campaign for 'bogus' clubs to be more tightly controlled. Certainly there is evidence that Greene King found the universal arrangement, whereby clubs accepted a 'tie' in return for a loan, produced endless arguments and frequent losses. In February 1936 Major Lake, then Chairman of the Brewers' Society, was stating, 'we should never again advance money to clubs'. Only a year earlier, however, he had been greatly flattered by a Dagenham club where 'there were about 600 members, most North countrymen, who did not like the London Beers and definitely preferred the Pelham Beers'.

And it was Rayment's which really developed its club trade. The expansion was unusual. It was within the pull of North London and Rayment's realised that, except for Taylor Walker, there was no great competition for club trade. It was content 'to pick up crumbs from the rich man's table' and by excellent service it moved into this expanding market. Its policy did not meet with favour in Bury. This was

> much against the wish of many of the directors of Greene King, particularly when the clubs asked for money and that sort of thing or bars, and I was urged to give up the club trade.[30]

In 1937 there were 77 clubs on the firm's books, in 1965, 255. Since Captain Neville Lake, Managing Director after 1937, became a Catholic convert many of the new clubs were Papist. He had an outbuilding at Pelham converted into a chapel ('a better salesman than all the salesmen put together'), entertained the club chairmen and secretaries to lunch, and as a result, 'if you look at our ledger, there's a Lady of Fatima, Venerable Bede and every saint's name under the sun.' Placed, as Rayment's was, close to London, supplying good beers and an even better service, the brewery expanded and survived on the club trade after 1945.

6

When looking at Greene King's labour relations in the inter-war years it is not much use making comparisons with other firms and industries since they remained highly individualistic. They were allowed to continue in this form because unionisation in the brewing industry was minimal and because breweries were not large employers of labour. The four breweries at Pelham (25 employees), Cambridge (c. 60), Sudbury (c. 40) and Bury (c. 150) employed fewer than 300 men and boys together. This is not to deny that changes were taking place, particularly in the bottling stores, transport departments and offices. Moreover hours worked per week were reduced to around forty-four in 1920, although there continued to be a good deal of unpaid overtime working in summer months in some departments. But the size and traditions of the industry allowed the old paternalism to survive to 1939.

Major Lake gave it almost a para-military twist at Bury. Boys coming into the brewery were often recruited straight from the Boys' Brigade, and the bottled beer department was manned entirely by boys who were taken on only if they had reached the first XI of either cricket or football at their schools. The men were encouraged, especially in the late 1930s, to join the Territorial Army. In the summer of 1939—three months before the declaration of war—there were so many men at camp for a fortnight that women were introduced into the offices for the first time. And the company's private fire service, inaugurated by Edward Lake around 1890, was run on highly competitive lines to vie with the municipal service.[31] Major Lake disclosed his philosophy when he inspected the Boys' Brigade in 1921,

he was a great believer in military training of all sorts ... Discipline ... was the whole essence of Army life and discipline he would repeat was the essence of civilian life too.[32]

These beliefs, which the men—most of whom had themselves served in the First World War—expected and understood, were softened in a number of ways. And the Managing Director was not invariably taken seriously. Every Saturday morning in winter he swept briskly through the brewery in hunting pink. He was barely out of earshot before the bottled beer boys struck up a ribald version of 'A Hunting We Will Go'.

The company was inordinately proud of its labour relations. If their execution seems patronising to us, the spirit that underlay them was well intentioned and the way in which it was fostered is still instructive. Never an Annual General Meeting passed without the Chairman passing the warmest thanks to the entire staff. It rejoiced when father followed son, that already by the 1920s there were several third generation workers, and that many of the work force had never been employed elsewhere. In 1926 the General Strike claimed not a single Greene King employee. The managers, unusually employing neither girls nor women, used the bottling stores as a training ground for the brewery. There were avenues of promotion: after four years in the bottling department eighteen-year-olds went into the brewery or, more eagerly, the transport department; and as previously described tenants and managers were often drawn from the brewery work force.

Good labour relations were fostered in other ways. A large stock of housing was provided for employees.[33] In 1918–20 thirty additional cottages were bought and a further two dozen were built in the 1920s. Old properties were modernised by the brewery's own Works Department. Rents were around 5s. a week. The company ran a social service of a kind. A female social worker visited men who were sick, and widows and pensioners; Muriel Lake and her sister-in-law continued to run weekly Mothers' Meetings in their homes throughout the inter-war years. Basic wages, usually around 2s. a week above the Suffolk agricultural labourers in the 1920s, were around 7-9s. higher by the mid-1930s. And in 1929 a contributory staff pension scheme in which the company invested £25,000 was inaugurated, although since the company's inception it had paid *ex gratia* pensions to retired workers and widows. It was the company's wages bonus that best shows its paternalism. By the early 1920s it consisted of one week's wages paid after the A.G.M. and six pounds of beef and a ton of coal at Christmas.[34] The summer bonus was still paid out under the old pear tree in the brewery yard—a relic at least of Benjamin Greene's days—and the work force was addressed by the Managing Director, who provided a simplified version of the company's progress in the year. In 1924 this system was replaced by a new bonus scheme related to profits. It provided, in most years, a fortnight's additional wages. The annual address was later held in the firm's extended garage, but until the early 1960s the directors still handed the bonuses out individually.

The company's encouragement, however, went beyond matters of shillings and pence. Edward Lake's six sons all fought in the First World War and, probably uniquely, they all returned. His gratitude knew no bounds and since Sir Walter Greene's two sons also came back, he persuaded the Board to purchase 26 acres of land and open a Sports Ground to commemorate the return of most of the brewery's work force from war (twenty-one were killed). It was opened in July 1920 and when the War Memorial was unveiled he

> thought that nothing could be more appropriate than a large recreation ground where men of the present and future generations could join in those manly sports which have made the English nation what it was.[35]

Soon one of the best sports grounds in East Anglia, it was an imaginative gift. Typically Edward Lake insisted that its management was retained by the brewery. Municipalisation would be inimical to his concept of its future. At least his son Major Lake saw that it was well run. There were three cricket, soccer and hockey pitches and ten tennis courts. At first the staff of six were supervised by Walter Mead, who had played cricket for England and Essex as a professional, and, after 1927, by Vic Covill, who had headed the Minor Counties bowling averages. It was used primarily by the brewery work force but also by schools in Bury, and it became the ground of the Bury and West Suffolk Cricket Club, which was not surprising since several of its side were invariably drawn from Greene King. Matches were played midweek and selection for the team meant automatic leave from the brewery, even during its busiest periods. The brewery also fielded a league side which was extremely successful in the late 1940s and early 1950s and, when competition cricket started in Suffolk in 1970, such was the strength of the Brewery team with six or seven current or past Suffolk county players, the team finished second in the first year of the Suffolk League and won the trophy in the next two. But for most of the workers the real camaraderie was provided by events such as the Tenants *v*. Brewery matches; the vision and sound of Major Lake batting and commanding his runner; the Norwich *v*. Tottenham F.C. matches (Greene King bought their casks from the firm of the Tottenham Chairman); and those long summer evenings devoted to quiet games of bowls and tennis. In the inter-war years, as opportunities for leisure were improved by shorter hours and higher real wages, the Victory Sports Ground played a central role in the company's promotion of good labour relations at the brewery. In a sense this task was easy in that Bury was a small town where there was little competition for labour. Greene King itself was not by most standards a large employer. Since the 1850s, however, every effort had been made to identify employees closely with the brewery and the families that owned it.

7

There were, for brewers, few similarities between the First and Second World Wars. Naturally, since industrial production was controlled in both there were some sharp increases in prices and duties, and frequent shortages of brewing materials. The atmosphere, in which control and restriction was enforced by the Churchill government, however, was totally different from that generated by Lloyd George after 1915. Since drunkenness and beer consumption waned rapidly after 1920, there was no attempt to stifle beer production in a pretence to stimulate the war effort. Quite the reverse occurred. Beer production, even in terms of standard barrellage, kept up after 1940 and bulk barrellage rose by some 25 per cent between 1938 and 1944.[36] Beer drinking and the War effort were now equated. In 1940 the *Brewing Trade Review* opined: 'The inn stands as the foremost social institution in the country in peace, and as one of real value to the nation in time of war.' It would have been an unheard-of sentiment in the Great War, even from a brewing journal. The Government now accepted these views. Lord Woolton, the Minister of Food, could ease his controls of the industry in the knowledge that 'we are in the fortunate position of having a temperate nation'. Of course, his remarks reflected the fact that output in terms of standard barrels in 1939 was little over a half of its level in 1914. The need for limitation of production was therefore far less. Moreover, co-operation between the Government and the industry, largely through the auspices of the Brewers' Society, was excellent. Nevertheless there were all kinds of problems for brewers during the Second World War, even if production increased and profits were the least of their worries. Statistics of national production and descriptions of the controls themselves do not reveal how an individual brewery coped with them.

At Greene King, in terms of output and profit, the picture was rosy indeed. At Bury, annual output, which had hovered around 73,000 barrels in the late 1930s, increased to 118,600 in the peak year of 1943–4. Trade at Cambridge was, in percentage terms, even more buoyant. That year Greene King sold 155,335 barrels (including 12,300 bought from London brewers)—a rise of 60 per cent on pre-war levels. Even the most ailing subsidiary, the Ixworth cider factory, did well.[37] In June 1944 the Managing Director, introducing his accounts to the Annual General Meeting enthused,

> This is a most astonishing balance sheet, and I don't suppose we shall ever see one like it again. Everything it contains is so abnormal that comparisons become useless . . . even now the supply in no way equals the demand . . . and on average houses are only open half their permitted hours.

Profits spiralled to around three times their pre-war levels. In part this reflected the fact that expenditure in the breweries and tied properties was minimal. The Government created an Excess Profits Tax which took as its basis the average of profits made between 1935 and 1937 and then effectively creamed off any profits made over and above this average. In 1943–4 the firm set aside £210,000 for this purpose. Major Lake, aided by the Secretary, Frank Bevis, displayed conspicuous honesty in all Greene King's dealings, in war and peace alike.[38] 'We have been lucky enough', stated the Managing Director at the 1945 A.G.M.,

> to make excess profits all through the war and it is our duty, or rather mine, to see every available penny is handed over to the Chancellor to help pay for the war.'

In the year 1944–5, Greene King paid £1,477,730 in Duty, Income and Excess Profits Tax, and distributed a mere £42,100 to shareholders.

The record sales of Greene King were due to a number of factors. For the first time in twenty years there was no unemployment. Real prosperity at last reached agriculture. Wages increased and workers had few alternative outlets for their spending. Above all, East Anglia was thronged with troops, airmen and aerodrome workers. Indeed, supplies in the summers after 1942 were unable to meet demand. In August 1942 Major Lake reported as many as sixty calls a day from Army Canteens; two years later he reckoned there were a hundred. Employees still remember the queues, especially of American servicemen, forming in Maynewater Lane and Bridewell Street. Casks and bottles were in chronically short supply. Often they were simply rinsed out on return and filled up on the spot. The process was sometimes repeated for the same customers on the same day. Demands from the armed services and tied houses were more or less met because by 1943, after Government calls for reduced gravities, Greene King was in effect producing one beer. It was either 'light or dark', both tints sharing a grossly diluted 1027° gravity. It retailed at a shilling a pint, a penny below the average national price. Concentrating upon a single line undoubtedly eased production and raised profits. And Zoning Arrangements—in effect the temporary exchange of houses —with other breweries simplified transport during the war.

Situated in the midst of some of the best malting barley country in England, it might be thought that Greene King had fewer problems than other less fortunately placed brewers when quotas and import restrictions were fixed on the supply of malt, brewing sugars and hops. There is no evidence to support this assumption. Certainly in the 1930s the company brewed almost entirely (95 per cent) from East Anglian barleys. There was one shareholder, the Revd C. K. Blencowe, a grandson of Fred King, who asked the Chairman at every A.G.M. in the 1930s the proportion of English barley Greene King consumed. Indeed, it was Brewers' Society policy to aid British cereal growers by encouraging brewers to use home-grown barley. They were not entirely public spirited, for it made a good point in their collective advertising campaign. But at the outbreak of war there was no prospect of brewers turning to cheaper foreign barley supplies since the Government imposed an embargo on their use for brewing purposes. In response, farmers tended to grow more malting barley. Even so prices escalated. They reached a peak early in 1942. One week in February barley made £20 a quarter at Bury market. At these prices brewers imposed cuts in the gravity of their beers well below those enforced by the Government. In March 1942 the maximum price of barley was fixed at 27s. 6d. per cwt, and this price was held for the rest of the war. Price stabilisation cut supplies in 1943 and 1944 just as demand burgeoned. Greene King, in spite of buying the 150-acre Copdoes Farm at Great Whelnetham in 1941, and possessing some shareholders who farmed in the Bury neighbourhood, seems to have suffered similar shortages to those experienced elsewhere. Therefore the brewers, Colonel Oliver and O. H. Heyhoe, were driven to introduce a proportion of flaked barley, rye, maize and even dried potatoes (which gave drinkers terrible wind) into the mash tun. Their aim was to produce as stable and palatable a beer as their supply quotas would allow. In 1942 the Managing Director congratulated his employees for producing 'a satisfactory article out of the worst brewing materials I have ever experienced'. The 1941 barley crop had given a poor extraction, but the next three years were far worse in terms of malt substitution. The brewery was certainly doing its best in trying conditions, and customers, with no alternatives either of supply or outlets for their expenditure, remained content so long as wartime conditions prevailed.

In this atmosphere Major Lake flourished. Perpetual pressure and the unexpected crisis brought out his capacities for organisation in a way that long-term planning in calmer, pre-war days never had. For one thing the Greenes were totally immured in Leicestershire and Berkshire. Travelling restrictions meant that in some years they never saw the brewery. At last Major Lake had his head, not only in the brewery and Bury (he was Mayor throughout the war), but also in the Brewers' Society, where he was member of no fewer than ten committees, including chairmanship of the key Parliamentary committee. Few brewers had a better knowledge of Government policies, intentions and information.

At Westgate he was ably assisted by the brewers and Frank Bevis in the office.[39] Labour problems were acute. This was a direct consequence of Major Lake's cajolement of employees to join the Territorials during peacetime. Within days of the outbreak of war over sixty men had joined the Army. A year later that figure had risen to 140, many of them joining a local unit, the 58th Medium Battery Royal Artillery or the Suffolk Yeomanry. In September 1941 the Secretary calculated that Greene King had lost 75 per cent of its office staff and 62 per cent of its entire work force. At first its ranks were filled from the unemployed—forty of them were lined up in the brewery yard for inspection the week war was declared—but as this source rapidly dried up they were replaced chiefly by boys and female labour. The bottling lines were run by young women from Bury and the neighbouring villages. Even in the inner sanctum of the brewhouse, the head

28. Rayments Brewery, Furneux Pelham, Herts, from the air. It was acquired by Greene King in 1931, although it had been owned by the Lakes
and J. M. King since 1889.

29. *(left)* Sir Hugh Greene, Chairman of Greene King, 1971–8, and previously Director General of the B.B.C. 1960–69.

30. *(right)* General Sir Miles Dempsey, Chairman of Greene King, 1955–69. He was also deputy chairman of Courage, and had commanded the 2nd Army in the invasion of Normandy.

31. The Directors of Greene King in 1982. *Left to right:* Dick Lines (Secretary), Jonathan Clarke, Timothy Redman, Graham C. Greene, John Bridge (Chairman and Joint Managing Director), Martin Corke (Joint Managing Director), Bernard Tickner, Simon Redman, John Banham, Timothy Bridge.

brewer's daughter, Margaret Oliver, was brought in not only to calculate gravities and duties but also eventually to undertake the entire brewing process. There were physically demanding tasks, however, especially in malting, which were unsuited to female and young labour. And if producing virtually only one beer to un-dreamt-of standards simplified work routines, demand was so buoyant and office work so complicated by controls and the introduction of P.A.Y.E. in 1943, that the work force was fully extended. Overtime was frequent, emergencies became common-place. 'How we have been able to largely increase our output', Major Lake addressed the shareholders in 1944, 'with a staff of old men and young boys and girls astonishes me as does the way in which the office staff get through their work.' It was one of the Managing Director's best traits that he was invariably com-plimentary about the labours of his work force. And one has the impression that only a direct hit would have curtailed 'the super-human efforts' of Mr Bevis. In December 1939 he produced the half-year's balance sheet half an hour before the six-month period had ended. This was with only two men left from his original staff, 'and these were crocks from the last War who had time off at irregular intervals'.

Throughout the war the new brewhouse was a Godsend, for repairs to plant were restricted to those that could be done simply, without licences, by the brewery's own depleted maintenance staff. Bottling, as always, was the weak link in the production chain. In November 1939 the position in the bottling stores was difficult. The line was perpetually breaking down, which sur-prised no one, since it had been running constantly since the 1920s. A new 300-dozen-an-hour bottler was, after delays, instal-led by Easter 1941. It eased things somewhat, but its capacity was always inadequate, for a unit double its size had been planned in 1939. As output rose the shortcomings of both fermenting capac-ity and the loading-out bays, cramped even before the war, were highlighted. New construction was out of the question and the Directors had to live with the consequences of their hesitancy about rebuilding during the days of cheap money in 1935–7. They therefore faced the end of the war, wonderful as it had been for them financially, with a major expenditure programme both for the breweries and the houses.

7

Tradition and
Change since 1945

Most business histories fizzle out after 1945. The reasons are not difficult to appreciate. Firms are hesitant to reveal recent information. Through changes in the law in the late 1960s, a good deal of material and much general financial data are widely known from companies' annual reports and accounts. With the aid of a pocket calculator and a larding of speculation and gossip, financial journalists create the stuff of the 'business' sections of newspapers. Nevertheless firms are, not surprisingly, reluctant to make known the finer points of their planning and finances, the details of mistakes, and their views of competitors. Moreover people are loth to have their opinions about colleagues and events put into print. And if they are more willing, the views sometimes verge on libel. The business historian writing about the past forty years has therefore a difficult problem fixing a middle course, between hurtful frankness on the one hand and total blandness on the other, to provide an account that conveys reality for all those who have been recently associated with the firm. For these various reasons he walks a tightrope across recent events.

With brewing, although the general problems remain, it is essential to continue its history in some detail after 1945 because the industry has had a momentous and, as so often across the centuries, controversial record in the past forty years. It underwent a period of stagnation after the war, which lasted until the late 1950s. It then witnessed intense concentration amongst its firms brought about by the amalgamations which, between 1959 and 1964, were amongst the most spectacular and fiercest fought in the history of limited companies. The industry absorbed these, somewhat slowly at the outset, and then enjoyed a period of unparalleled prosperity from the late 1960s. Only in the last two or three years has this good fortune waned, and then much less than in industry generally. Again it is instructive to examine Greene King experiences against this national pattern, for the company escaped neither the post-1945 recession, nor the benefits of mergers and the menace of bigger marauders, nor, fortunately, the effects of the 'Beer Revolution' after the late 1960s.

I

The late 1940s and 1950s were disappointing for the brewing industry. Firms, in the heady days of victory in 1944 and 1945, were full of optimism. The war, for them, had been amazing. This was especially true of Greene King, sited in the midst of the East Anglian airfields. Its material losses had been minimal: only two houses destroyed by enemy action. In human terms fourteen employees had been killed. Dreams of a bright future for brewers, however, very different from the blighted 1920s, never materialised. Demand for beer fell away sharply after 1947. Year by year it declined until the turning point in 1959 was reached. By then output nationally was 27 per cent below that of 1945 (in terms of bulk barrels). Duty remained at high levels. From 1951 until 1959 it was four times that of 1939. Moreover the Chancellor of the Exchequer removed more profits after 1948. Some companies complained that as much as 60 per cent of their trading profits were removed by taxation. Greene King reckoned tax absorbed over half of profits, whereas before the war it had only taken a quarter. Therefore after 1948, when falling demand really began to bite into profitability, retentions for investment fell. And the Labour Governments (1945–51), in order to encourage exports and reconstruction maintained restrictions on production and building in brewing as they did in all industries. Those on output, especially between 1946 and 1948, were particularly severe but all controls seemed more pressing to brewers in peace than they had during the war itself.

Greene King's experience in these years was little different from

Table 7: Beer *produced* in the United Kingdom, 1945–82 (in bulk barrels)*

Year ending 31 March

1945	31·0	1955	23·6	1965	28·7	1975	37·5
1946	32·7	1956	24·1	1966	29·1	1976	37·8
1947	29·2	1957	24·2	1967	29·9	1977	39·1
1948	30·0	1958	24·2	1968	30·1	1978	39·5
1949	27·0	1959	23·4	1969	30·8	1979	40·5
1950	25·8	1960	25·4	1970	32·0	1980	39·6
1951	24·8	1961	26·3	1971	33·3	1981	37·7
1952	24·7	1962	27·4	1972	34·1	1982	36·5
1953	24·4	1963	27·1	1973	34·7		
1954	24·2	1964	28·2	1974	37·1		

* Source: The Brewers' Society—*U.K. Statistical Handbook* (1982).

the majority of breweries, except that its decline in production, once the airfields were closed, was steeper than elsewhere. At its lowest point in the mid-1950s it was little over a half of its wartime peak in 1944, and below the levels of the late 1930s (see Appendix 2, Table 4). Static, even declining, production was itself not a new phenomenon but peacetime restrictions and high duties, retained year after year, were. There was no room to adjust prices in this situation, and profits, ample until 1948, declined thereafter and were so eaten away by taxation that funds for the renewal of the breweries and tied properties, even when controls allowed, stayed tight.

In the short run problems at Greene King were exacerbated by the death of Major Lake in the spring of 1946. He had been the company's guiding light for over twenty-five years. Although as early as 1938 he had stated his intention of retiring when he reached sixty-five in 1945, his efforts during the war had been so extraordinary that his sudden death left the brewery stunned. It seemed a testimony to his control of its affairs that a triumvirate of Managing Directors was appointed to replace him. Given the Chairman's remoteness, it appears an odd arrangement. In fact it worked well enough as there was no serious rivalry among the three men. Colonel B. E. Oliver (1880–1960) remained, as he had been for over twenty years, head brewer, in charge of the breweries and their plant. He had brought the plans for the new brewhouse of 1938 to fruition, and he had increased production in difficult circumstances during the war. Now he was ready to implement plans for a new malting system and bottling stores. He was both forward-looking and endowed with abundant common-sense. The second joint Managing Director, Charles Wilson, had been Major Lake's right-hand man during the war. He continued to oversee properties and labour and, as a trained land agent, he supervised the company's farms at Great Whelnetham and Fur-neux Pelham. He was in poor health and retired within two years. John Clarke (1905–79), the third, and much the youngest mem-ber of the trio, had been a director since 1934. Like Colonel Oliver he had received a brewer's training, partly at Birmingham Uni-versity, partly with breweries in Bristol and Hull. He had man-aged the Cambridge brewery for most of the 1930s and returned to Bury in 1938. In 1946 he was given charge of accounts and overall control of the business. Although it is clear that he relied a good deal upon the advice of Colonel Oliver and the Secretary, Frank Bevis, he emerged as effective manager of Greene King.

His father, Harry Clarke, and Ralph King, both old men in 1939, ceased to be directors in 1948. Sir Raymond Greene had died the previous year. Latterly he had seldom made the journey to Bury, and the only shock his death gave the brewery was when 44,000 of his ordinary shares (almost 14 per cent of equity) had to be sold for death duties. Their places on the Board were partially filled by Vice-Admiral W. J. C. Lake, a cousin of the Bury Lakes, who had run the Cambridge brewery (after a seven-year spell at Rayment's) since 1938, and John Bridge (b. 1920), a great-grandson of Fred King. Two years earlier in 1946, Harold Lake, who had been Company Secretary and a director from 1922 to 1936 was brought back on to the Board on his brother's death. He was now Chairman of Wilson and Walker's (Manchester), Mor-land's (Abingdon), and the Cheltenham and Hereford Brewery. He was also, like his brother, prominent in the Brewers' Society: Chairman of its Law Committee, Vice-Chairman of the Society in 1949, and Chairman two years later.[1] He regularly attended Greene King board meetings and invariably gave the directors the benefit of his considerable experience. They were fed comparisons with Manchester and Abingdon, and pompously lectured about prices and profits. He was neither as popular as his brother, nor as devoted to Greene King affairs. The Chairman, Sir Edward

Greene, who succeeded his brother in the baronetcy in 1947, always watched him warily. In any case Harold Lake was too busy elsewhere to involve himself deeply at Bury and therefore the management settled into a quiet phase after 1946. Colonel Oliver concentrated upon brewing and bringing the plant up to date, and John Clarke, although only forty-one, had been essentially formed in the Greene King mould. By nature conservative and self-effacing, the Lake way of running a brewery—unostentatiously and with great attention to costs and good labour relations—was an integral part of his business make-up. The pattern still worked well enough in the late 1940s and early 1950s.

There were three tasks which required immediate attention in 1945: the beer, the brewery itself, and its tied property. As declining demand intensified competition, the company was well aware that it had to keep ahead of its rivals in terms of producing a good beer, running an efficient brewery, and modernising its tied houses. Greene King had adequate reserves for these purposes, built up during the war when capital expenditure was minimal. In 1946 there was some £380,000 available, plus a £67,000 rebate on Excess Profits Tax. But in all three areas improvements were seriously held up by Government restrictions.

So far as the beers were concerned the problem was that in 1946 the Government curtailed production by 15 per cent (eventually 18) of the quantities brewed in the year ending 30 September 1945. In August it imposed, in addition, a 10 per cent cut in average gravities. Limitations on production and materials were more or less retained until 1951. These caused brewers infinite headaches, especially before 1948 when demand began to slacken. In the hot summer of 1947 there were shortages of beer almost everywhere. Greene King houses in Haverhill were closed three days a week. At other times between 1945 and 1948 the firm 'rationed' its supplies and accepted no new customers.

Government restrictions on output were exacerbated in two ways. First, there were additional crucial shortages of hops and sugar, bottles and casks, in 1945–6; of electricity, oil and coal for much of 1947. Brewing was a nightmare in the notorious winter of 1947. In February electricity cuts were so severe that brewing at Westgate took place only once a week to keep the yeast alive. Second, the demand for beer was skewed. That for bottled beer continued to rise quite sharply. It was stronger, but also more convenient in modern homes and the coming of television led to a decline in the popularity of the public house in the fifteen years after 1945. Also there was a younger, constantly employed element who preferred and could afford a good, reliable bottled beer. These post-war social dimensions affected the beer market generally. For example, in March 1949 bottled beer sales at Bury were reported to be running 61 per cent above 1939 levels, while cask beer was 6 per cent down, although this latter figure obscures a massive 34 per cent fall from the previous year. Whereas in 1939 bottled beer comprised 32 per cent of trade, in 1948 it had risen to 44. Sales of cask beer, because it was so weak (around 1032° in summer and 1035° in winter), were well below those òf bottled beers in December 1948. Commenting on the Christmas trade, John Clarke said,

> The cask beer trade was poor, and until we are allowed to brew draught beer at the gravity required by the public, the prospects for sales of draught beer are not at all bright.

On the other hand bottled beer sales were 'quite phenomenal' and the orders surpassed anything he had contemplated. Of course the management was delighted as profits on bottled beers were higher, but the bottling store was under terrific strain. After 1948 there was no additional capacity for bottled beers, whereas that for cask beer was considerable. The problem was not peculiar to Greene King, for the taste for bottled beers increased nationally. But the company responded to the situation sensibly, if rather slowly. It bottled a small amount of a strong ale (*Suffolk*) each Christmas from a high gravity, vatted beer, and, since this proved popular, it was decided to market a quality beer which would stand comparison with the market leaders, Bass and Worthington. This was released in 1951 and called *Abbot*. Those who argued that tank capacity must be found in the overstretched bottling store cannot have dreamt that in the next thirty years it would become the best-known beer in the Greene King range.

When the new brewhouse was completed in December 1938 it was only the first, if major item, in a general programme of refurbishment which was totally stopped for the duration of the war. The brewhouse was a superb investment and the envy of many of the ninety members of the Institute of Brewing who visited it in 1952.[2] They were

> greatly impressed with the robust and dignified architecture of the spacious, light, and well-ventilated building, the high efficiency of the plant . . . and the superb standard of cleanliness.

It was matched by an equally up-to-date drum maltings and barley store. These had been built, in spite of restrictions, since 1945. What is surprising is that the firm achieved such extensive modernisation in these difficult post-war years. It was an uphill struggle in terms of delays, planning restrictions and shortages. The results were impressive. They stand as a monument to the quiet insistence and foresight of Colonel B. E. Oliver.

With ample reserves the firm had few financial problems. In June 1946 Colonel Oliver placed plans before the Board to spend £250,000 over the next three years on a new bottling store, maltings, boiler houses, mineral water and spirit stores and additional fermenting rooms. This schedule was blown off course by inflation, shortages of materials and building restrictions. The most significant achievement was the new malting system constructed between 1946 and 1948.

Before the war malting was carried out on five separate sites around the brewery, in decrepit buildings with minimal health provision. The old 'floor' system, which had changed so little over the centuries, was extremely labour intensive. In the 1940s, however, there were acute shortages of labouring maltsters. In this situation it was clear that malting by the old method could not continue. There was an alternative, for a far more up-to-date, mechanical 'drum' system had been introduced in the inter-war years. At Greene King it was significantly improved. The brains behind its adoption was the brewery's head maltster and chemist, F. A. Reddish. He had joined Greene King when Prentice's minute brewery at Stowmarket was bought in the trough of the 1930s depression. Possessing a sharp, practical mind, he was a first rate acquisition. He talked over the drum system with Colonel Oliver and in late 1945 he went over to Sweden to look at their Box maltings. When he returned he hit upon the device of only partly filling a drum with steeped barley and allowing it to revolve so that the sprouting grains could be turned completely. Robert Boby's drew out his plans and erected four drums in the Rink malting, the best one the firm possessed and which had been erected by Edward Greene in 1880 in Westgate. When eventually eight drums were working the system was capable of producing 18,000 quarters of malt a year, or about half more than was required in the late 1940s. 'It is interesting to note', wrote the *Brewers' Guardian* reporter,

> that this complete installation is being contained on a site which formerly produced 2,500 quarters of malt per annum on the floor system.

It also of course effected considerable labour savings. On its completion no brewery possessed a more up-to-date set of drums, kilns and air-conditioning equipment. In its first years it was visited by scores of British and foreign maltsters.[3]

In 1948 work was begun on a complementary grain store on an adjacent site (previously the Foundry maltings of the 1850s). The old barley store erected in 1913 in Sparhawk Street was, with its Topf drier, advanced for its day. By 1948, however, it was inadequate in terms of storage capacity, for the advent of the combine harvester meant that barley was available within a five- or six-week period, as opposed to the six months with the old threshing sets. The new grain store, costing £35,000, was capable of holding 8,000 quarters of barley or malt. A suction pipe, 700 feet long and 'believed to be as great in length as any yet employed in this country', delivered barley from the drying house to the silos or steeps. The 'pleasing exterior' of the building, 'preserved in more than one way the features of the old maltings and the traditions of architecture in Bury St. Edmunds.'[4]

The worst delays were experienced in the construction of an additional bottling store. This was built as a lateral extension of the existing one and occupied the site of the old loading yard. In 1946 it was planned to be completed within two or three years at a total cost of £65,000. It was certainly an immediate priority, for the existing machinery was run flat out after 1939 and was seldom stopped for proper maintenance. In the week before Christmas

1949 it processed 50,000-dozen bottles with a plant designed to complete 20,000. The new store, however, was not finally opened until 1953. The building cost three times its original estimate. There were seven years of wrangles with architects, engineers, builders and central and local government officers, conducted frustratingly against a background of increasing demand for bottled beer. At least when it was finished it contained the latest plant, set out on approved practice. When the editor of the *Brewers' Guardian* visited it on completion he was 'impressed with the smooth and rhythmic flow of operations, the congenial working conditions and the features introduced to achieve maximum hygiene'. The three bottling lines together were capable of filling 1,500-dozen half-pint bottles an hour. At last, sixteen years after work had first begun on the brewhouse, Greene King possessed, in the words of its Chairman, 'one of the most up-to-date Breweries in the Country'.

In 1945 brewers realised that one of their first priorities was to make good the enforced neglect of their public houses during the war. Improving houses had been a major preoccupation of the inter-war years, a principal plank in the brewers' campaign to make beer drinking more regular and respectable. Now after 1945, when competition became fiercer as output went once more into decline, brewers were forced to keep up a never-ending round of improvements and repairs to their tied properties. 'The amounts are formidable', reported John Clarke in 1953,

> but the management are of the opinion that unless certain of our houses are brought up to date the trade will undoubtedly suffer in competition with other Brewers' houses.

In September 1945 Major Lake and Charles Wilson began a tour of the company's tied houses, most of which they had not visited for over six years. The firm in fact could envisage few immediate major improvements, because building licences were in short supply until 1951. Minor repairs and repainting were undertaken. The stock of Greene King houses had hardly changed between the acquisition of Ogden's March brewery in 1930 and Simpson's of Baldock in 1954. Numbers marginally increased from 490 in 1931 to a peak of 506 in 1951. Turnover was not entirely static: two or three houses were purchased in most years and a similar number closed. Not until after 1951, however, when building restrictions eased, were major improvements undertaken and the occasional new house built. Then £75,000 annually was being spent on ordinary repairs (against £24,000 before the war) and an additional £45,000 a year earmarked for major alterations and seven new houses. Momentum was not entirely at the discretion of the company. By the early 1950s the local district councils and magistrates were beginning to insist upon basic sanitary and cleanliness standards. In 1950 Thingoe Rural District Council disclosed that in many of the fifty-eight public houses in its area landlords and patrons alike shared earth closets with no separate accommodation for women. In no instance was an inn connected both to mains water and the public sewer. Since Greene King owned forty-nine of the public houses in the region they felt exposed by this publicity. John Clarke sent the Clerk of the Council,

> a very strong letter . . . asking him for a complete list of the parishes where water *and* sewage were available and the dates when these amenities were installed.

There was no reply on this point and eventually the Clerk 'very much climbed down'. Thingoe was exceptional, even amongst rural districts, but it illustrates the extent of modernisation required in many country houses. Some just did not have the trade to justify a large expenditure. Moreover the company had to apportion scarce resources among new houses (eleven were built between 1952 and 1956 in the more populous centres), those with a reasonably good trade, and the large stock of rural inns that made up the bulk of Greene King property. Finance, when profits were squeezed after 1948, was tight. In 1951 dividends were reduced from 23½ to 21¼ per cent and the investment account, an historic feature of Greene King balance sheets, was run right down, and £100,000 borrowed in the spring of 1952. A start was made on modernising houses by bringing their drainage and sanitation up to date, and by installing car parks. But in the late 1940s restrictions hindered them and in the early 1950s taxation, declining profits, and sharply rising building costs, made their programme of improvement seem more daunting. The returns on modernisation and new building had never been closely costed, but increasing competition meant that the pace could not be slackened, even in harder times.

If the company found things increasingly difficult after 1948, so did its tenants. They could absorb rising costs and a dwindling trade even less readily. The response, however, was different from that adopted in the 1930s. Then many houses, often at the request of the tenant, were taken into management. To do this for some of the small houses was, in peacetime, a dubious financial proposition, and after 1948, when the Catering Act imposed minimum wages for managers, Greene King realised that many in this category could not support these new wage levels. The number of houses under management was therefore rapidly reduced from 170 (34 per cent of Greene King's stock) to 120 (24 per cent). Policy, as it had long been, was to let houses at very low 'dry' rents—the 1950 valuation reveals most in the £12–£25 per annum range. The tenant, or her husband in some cases, then took another job to make ends meet. In the late 1940s and early 1950s the company, to aid hard-pressed tenants, eased 'wet' rents by allowing tenants an increased margin on sales. Price increases, neither frequent nor extended usually over the whole range of beers in this period, were therefore shared out more equably with tenants.

2

Amalgamations of firms in the brewing industry have a long history. After 1880, when breweries scrambled to collect tied houses, the process accelerated. In that year there were around 17,000 breweries of one description or another, with an average annual output of 1,600 barrels. Sixty years later, at the outbreak of the Second World War, there were only 840, producing 30,000 barrels each year. As we have seen, Greene King had grown over the years by absorbing competitors. Its experience was entirely typical. Mergers in the industry had been negotiated, often at the instigation of the smaller party, and they were invariably conducted in an amicable, gentlemanly fashion. Even those companies, such as Ind Coope, Allsop, and Watney Combe Reid, which were active acquirers of breweries in the inter-war years, did so unaggressively. After 1950 this mood began to change. There were three reasons. First, production continued to decline until 1959 and contraction, as always, was a potent force in creating amalgamations. Second, the big London breweries, wanting to expand on this situation, began to seek additional outlets for their 'national' bottled beers. They could only do so by amalgamation and agreement. Some regional breweries—J. W. Green of Luton provides a good local example—matched their moves. It was these big breweries, examining with a new realism the assets and returns of smaller competitors, that created a more menacing atmosphere than had been known between the wars. Third, the gentlemanly brewers' world, already under strain, was shaken by an outsider's bid for Watney Mann in 1959. This, the biggest London brewery, was the result of a merger undertaken in the previous year. Sir Charles Clore, the Chairman of Sears Holdings, looked at the low return on its assets and believed that by more dynamic management he could increase turnover considerably. The bid in fact was unsuccessful, but it was much publicised and triggered off an unprecedented round of mergers and acquisitions in the next three years. In the decade after 1958 the industry was radically restructured. Before 1958 concentration within it was low. The five largest enterprises were responsible for only 23 per cent of output. Ten years later in 1968 they shared a greatly increased 64 per cent. This was achieved by a celebrated, massive takeover and merger movement which encompassed small, regional and semi-national breweries alike. How did a medium-sized brewery such as Greene King fare in these changed conditions?

At first it continued in its old ways, more or less unconcerned by events outside East Anglia. Priorities were completing the modernisation of the Westgate brewery and its public houses. With building restrictions and dwindling profits after 1948 it was a large and expensive task. The first whiff of a merger, in 1948, was similar to many of those aired in the 1920s and 1930s. Desultory explorations took place in London with representatives of Huntingdon Breweries and of Hall, Cutlack and Harlock of Ely. The initiative came from the Huntingdon Chairman, General Sir Wilfred Lindsell. Although the two breweries had an output between them of 85,000 barrels and 546 tied houses the advantages of creating a far-flung empire of over a thousand largely rural houses were unclear. But General Lindsell, a member of an old South Midlands brewing family, struck a note that was to become very familiar in the next fifteen years. He

> had come to the conclusion that the boom years were coming to an end and that the money was becoming much tighter. In addition . . . all around we were seeing big Breweries buying up the smaller ones, or amalgamations taking place.

His 'scheme whereby we could protect our mutual interests' went no further as Sir Edward Greene poured cold water upon it.[5] Although Greene King was worried by competitors buying houses at 'inflated prices' in its district, it was party to no further soundings until 1952. These concerned its Cambridge trade.

When the London brewers and J. W. Green of Luton invaded the Cambridge free trade the position at the Panton Brewery deteriorated. The situation was not new: similar conditions had prevailed in the late 1930s. Once more after 1949 sales declined as penetration of the free trade weakened. Output, not far short of 30,000 barrels in the best war years, fell to around 17,000 in 1952. Cask beer sales particularly contracted in spite of the brewery retailing good, if occasionally variable, beers at competitive prices. Greene King realised that it must either take over more Cambridge houses or close down the Panton Brewery and supply its houses from Bury. Although the new bottling stores at Bury made the latter an attractive proposition, regular debates about closing down brewing operations at Cambridge after 1952 were inconclusive because fermenting capacity at Bury was tight. The pace of brewery takeovers increased in the early 1950s. In March 1952, John Clarke stated at a board meeting:

> that we were being surrounded by Amalgamations. Messrs. Green of Luton had bought Soulby's of Alford and Phillip's of Royston, and had now bought Mowbray's of Grantham.[6]

He went on to advocate that Greene King should approach Dale's of Cambridge. Although the brewery was small, with three dozen tied houses in poor repair and an output of under 5,000 barrels a year in 1951–3, its acquisition would have partly solved problems at the Panton Brewery. Although Admiral Lake knew the owner, Colonel Guy Dale, well, the deal was not concluded. As so often in brewing it hinged on personal circumstances. Dale's mother, the only other proprietor, had her shares tied up in trust. Until she died, a not unlikely event, since she was in her eighties, nothing could be done. Greene King waited, knowing that other approaches were being made to Dale.

Greene King bided its time in the knowledge that its own affairs were improving. There was a small increase in barrellage in 1953, and both building licences and taxation were eased somewhat when the Conservative Government got into its stride. Moreover, considerable economies were derived from the modernised Westgate plant which was fully operative in that year. Dividends were raised in 1954 to their pre-1951 level and the company could take stock of the rapidly changing situation in the organisation of brewing in East Anglia. It was apparently in a good position to do so because two of its directors possessed a first-rate knowledge of the industry at the national level.

Harold Lake, as Chairman of three breweries, all of which were eventually taken over, had unrivalled access to information. He was, however, in 1953 an old and ailing man, with no clear notion of the direction Greene King should take, beyond his view that it was impossible to remain immobile in the new situation. More important in the event were the views of General Sir Miles Dempsey and Sir Edward Greene. Sir Miles, who possessed a very distinguished war record, had been introduced to the Greene King Board by Sir Edward in 1953. He was his neighbour in Berkshire and also Chairman of Simonds, the Reading brewers. Sir Miles, as a General and member of the Jockey Club, fitted easily into the exclusive upper echelons of the brewing world, which was a useful attribute in the 1950s.[7] Moreover Simonds itself had taken over half a dozen breweries after 1945. With this experience and great standing in the industry he was able to state effectively, even to E. P. Taylor, the Canadian brewer who smashed his way into the British industry in the late 1950s, Greene King's total determination to stay independent. His role in the firm was therefore a vital one between 1953 and 1969. He brought a decisiveness and professionalism to the chairmanship of the company which was lacking during Sir Edward Greene's long tenure of office.

General Dempsey's superb handling of predatory brewers was strengthened by the unanimous resolve of Sir Edward Greene and the younger directors at Bury to resist takeover. Sir Edward, now over seventy, well realised the changes that had taken place in brewing during his lifetime. Like Harold Lake he appreciated that Greene King must move forward. There was no standing still as ground was being cut from under them by aggressive competitors such as Green's of Luton. In other respects of course he harked back to an older world. He could create a rumpus when, taking refreshment in Greene King houses on his way to meetings, he found that the finer details of bar management did not come up to scratch. He could not bring himself to recognise the need for keg beer. And possessing the authentic voice of the past he could not accept the abrasive tones of pushing newcomers in the industry. Although he had no children, or indeed close Greene male relatives, he wanted Greene King both to survive and grow for he identified himself with its deep-rooted traditions in East Anglia. Had he cared less about this, the position might well have been different, although after he retired as Chairman in 1955—he remained a director for a further nine years and a principal shareholder until his death in 1966—his stance had much less significance for the firm than the perseverance of the younger executive directors at Bury, John Clarke, John Bridge and Martin Corke,[8] to resist the blandishments and manoeuvres of the brewing giants.

This collective tenacity was crucial, and a constant preoccupation in the next few years. Yet it was inadequate in itself in that the struggle for independence necessitated that the firm, as the market for beer contracted, had to expand to retain output and profitability. Common sense suggested that it should search for opportunities in the prosperous South and East Midlands. In fact subsequent events in the industry and the history of Greene King itself impose a consistency of thought and action that was in reality not present. The factors were perceived, but perceived imprecisely, for the firm, and indeed the industry generally, occupied a position in which the old traditions of brewing mergers, gentlemanliness and secrecy still existed side by side with the growing predacity of some of the larger firms. Greene King directors understood these changing forces in the 1950s, yet did not react aggressively to them. The firm believed that it should keep on good terms with its rivals, such as Wells and Winch (see pp. 232–8), calculating that it was better strategy for them to make the opening moves, because Greene King thought they were being somewhat bludgeoned by offers from other brewers. Their faith in the old customs was somewhat shaken, early in 1954, when Dale's of Cambridge was bought by Whitbreads. The latter, in an attempt to push its bottled *Pale Ale* and *Mackeson* stout, began to acquire in the 1950s equity interests in a number of breweries—large and small alike. This 'umbrella' arrangement was used to deter potential competitors. In the case of Dale's, very small fry for Whitbreads, the brewery and its houses were bought outright at what Greene King considered to be a generous price. But as was soon generally known, Whitbreads simply wanted to use Dale's brewery as a bottling depot, and, after protracted negotiation carried out on Harold Lake's advice,[9] a scheme was devised for the exchange of products in preference to Greene King's purchase of the houses. Under the 21-year agreement Greene King supplied these with cask beer in return for admitting *Mackeson* stout throughout their tied property. The deal saved Greene King heavy investment in a string of run-down houses but, although it worked well enough, the supply of around two thousand barrels of draught beer was insufficient to save the Panton Brewery. Its bottling plant was in poor shape and in 1958, inevitably, it was closed. It was reckoned that besides many hidden economies, cash savings would amount to £3,800 a year. There was little hardship since, in a situation of full employment, the work force could either be absorbed at Bury or be found work elsewhere. The employees thought the management 'had treated them very well indeed'. And the Cambridge houses, to the relief of the Bury brewer, took more quickly to the Westgate beers than had been anticipated.

Agreements like that reached with Whitbread became an increasing feature of brewing in the 1950s, as production declined and the bigger brewers extended their bottled beer sales. There were also negotiations, organised by the regional branches of the Brewers' Society, about closing uneconomic houses and proposals for the apportionment of licences for new ones. In Cambridgeshire especially, these arrangements appear to have worked well. By 1958 brewers there had agreed to close thirty-three houses in the city and thirty-two in the county. After years of dwindling trade they were totally uneconomic. In the case of two

Greene King houses, sales were less than half a barrel a week. Also of course they talked over other matters relating to the industry: routine discussions about prices and wages. Rivalry between regional brewers in the 1950s should not therefore be exaggerated. Their fears were about the motives of the bigger breweries.

In December 1954 Greene King took over Simpson's Brewery at Baldock. It provides the perfect example of how the old connections in the brewing industry still operated in a changing world. Simpson's, sited in what had once been the most famous malting county in England, was a classic country brewery with a distinguished history. In the eighteenth century it was owned successively by Robert Thurgood, who apparently built the original brewery by 1738, and, after 1799, by a well-known Hertfordshire Quaker family, the Pryors.[10] The latter had been maltsters in Baldock since around 1730 and they rented Thurgood's brewery for close on a quarter of a century before eventually purchasing it. They acquired other public houses in and around Baldock and a brewhouse and maltings in White Horse Street from James Ind, a member of the family who later formed a partnership famous in brewing history with Messrs Coope. By the 1800s there were four Pryor brothers of the third generation who, in addition to owning the Baldock Brewery and large maltings in the town, were also partners in the leading London brewery of Truman, Hanbury and Buxton and in the Hatfield brewery of Pryor Reid and Co. By 1853 the family had such extensive connections in London business life that they sold the Baldock Brewery.[11]

It had 122 tied houses and a fine looking, although by this date, slightly old fashioned, brewery powered by a 17-foot horse wheel erected, along with an equally elegant brewery house, by the Pryors in the late eighteenth century (see plate 24). The entire concern, including every stick of furniture in the house and the plants in its conservatory, was bought by two brothers named Simpson for £81,904. Sons of a Cambridgeshire landowner, they were also nephews of the Royston brewer, John Phillips. For the next century the brewery continued to remain curiously unchanged. The number of tied houses hardly increased—from 122 to around 130 in the early 1950s. Output remained similarly constant; it was exactly the same in the 1950s as it had been in the 1860s—around 20,000 barrels. Ownership was largely contained within the Simpson family, although the principals changed their name. Evelyn Simpson, the chief partner in the brewery at the turn of the century, took by royal licence that of Shaw-Hellier in 1909, shortly before succeeding to the Staffordshire estates of his maternal uncle, Colonel T. B. Shaw-Hellier of the Wombourne Wodehouse, Wolverhampton.[12] Like the Pryors before them the Simpsons/Shaw-Helliers became absorbed in county affairs. Evelyn Simpson was a J.P. in Hertfordshire and Staffordshire and was High Sheriff of the former in 1902. When he died in 1922 his estates and a major portion of the brewery, always run by family partnerships, passed to his elder daughter, confusingly also named Evelyn. After 1920 the brewery was managed by the family solicitor, T. H. Veasey, who devoted three days a week to the task. In 1936 a limited company was formed with a capital of 180,000 £1 ordinary shares. They were almost entirely owned by Miss Shaw-Hellier—the only other shareholder was T. H. Veasey. After this date the brewery returned a 10–14 per cent dividend and, except during the war, ploughed about one-third of its net profits back into property improvements and a reserve fund. By the late 1940s these profits were running at around £42,000. There was virtually no advertising, since the small range of beers possessed a good reputation and was retailed almost wholly within Simpson's houses.

To onlookers Simpson's was the epitome of all that was best in the tradition of country breweries. There were few finer-looking breweries in England than the Pryors' buildings of the 1780s. Miss Shaw-Hellier behaved exactly as a Chairman of a brewery should —generous with her employees, owning racehorses, and living in style in Staffordshire and Sicily. The brewery itself was run in a relaxed fashion by Veasey, who was given a free hand by his Chairman. Day to day control was maintained by a tireless Secretary, A. E. Pedley, who was still going strong at the age of eighty, when Greene King took over. After the war a full-time manager, John Banham, eased the brewery a little more into the modern world. A new bottling line was installed in 1950, a new beer introduced, and some of the tied houses were modernised.

As it approached its centenary, Simpson's looked good for another hundred years. Its finances and its beers were in excellent order. But in the changed situation of the 1950s soundings began to be made by other brewers. Simpson's itself had 'talked' with its nearest competitors, Phillips of Royston and Fordhams of Ashwell, but both were swallowed up by the ubiquitous J. W. Green of Luton. The weak link in the Simpson's chain was Miss Shaw-Hellier herself. Like many other brewers, she was advised to sell because heavy death duties hung over her wealth. But she had no wish to see the brewery closed by some marauding giant, so T. H. Veasey and John Banham were commissioned to find a 'friendly' brewery whose traditions and aims were not unlike those of Simpson's itself. John Banham was an old friend of John Clarke, the Managing Director of Greene King. In the summer of 1954 Greene King directors inspected Simpson's books and its properties. They liked what they saw. The firm had never been milked hard for profit and its beers and houses carried good reputations. Agreement was very quickly reached. The concern was acquired for £525,000, paid partly in cash and partly in Greene King shares.[13] The relatively low price reflected the large number of Simpson's country houses. T. H. Veasey, the only other substantial shareholder besides the Misses Shaw-Hellier, became a director of Greene King. A subsidiary directorate was set up and John Banham continued to manage Simpson's. There was a gentleman's agreement that brewing should continue for ten years at Baldock.

Simpson's under Greene King direction worked well. At first, John Clarke and Frank Bevis went across each week from Bury 'to get them into our line of working'. Although the maltings were closed, modest improvements were carried out at the brewery. A handful of the smallest houses were closed—one retailed a record low of six and a half barrels a year—and reconstruction began of those with the largest trade in the expanding towns of Luton and Stevenage. Trade and profits were above expectation and by the late 1950s Simpson's and Rayment's were doing better than the parent company. This of course reflected the fact that they were closer to Greater London which, with the development areas on its fringe such as Luton and Stevenage, was the centre of the rising prosperity of the Macmillan era. Trade accelerated sooner and faster than in rural Suffolk. After 1955 Greene King finances improved. The low point of beer sales was the year ending 31 May 1955. Between 1955 and 1960 group profits rose from £256,000 to £399,000. Although nationally beer sales did not rise before 1959, when the budget in that year led brewers to remove a long overdue 2d from the price of a pint, the acquisition of Simpson's allowed Greene King to recover sooner.

In 1958 a further small brewery in Sudbury, Mauldon's, was bought. This third-generation brewery, with twenty-two houses and a single off-licence in Sudbury and the villages on the Essex–Suffolk border, possessed an annual trade of about 2,000 barrels. Both the brewery and its houses were in poor repair and when J. C. Mauldon approached Greene King there was from the outset an understanding that neither would the brewery be kept open nor its small number of employees be taken on at Westgate (although in fact at least three were). Again negotiations were carried out on the old lines between two parties only. Mauldon told Greene King he

> had no intention of approaching anyone else until such time as he heard whether we were interested and what figure we placed on the whole concern.

For a price of £46,100 plus stock evaluation Greene King

> estimated that we should reap the advantage of the saving of competition from Mauldons, and as most of the houses are in our area there would be little additional cost for delivery.

But there was not the same appetite to swallow Daniells of Colchester in that year, 1958, although many of the considerations accepted with Mauldon's purchase were similar. With a trade of 25,000 barrels and situated well inside Greene King territory, Harold Lake and Colonel B. E. Oliver thought it should be bought and Peter Daniell was eager to join forces with Greene King. Courage in fact held a 10 per cent stake in the brewery and although General Dempsey was dispatched to talk to a senior Courage director, Greene King declined Daniell's offer.[14] Some members of the board believed the firm had modest indigestion after the Simpson and Mauldon acquisitions.

But as the industry was rocked by Sir Charles Clore's attempt to obtain control of Watney Mann and the pace of concentration accelerated in the following years, even cautious, well-mannered firms such as Greene King learnt some new lessons. In the summer of 1959 there was a full-scale discussion about

> the future of Greene King in the light of developments which are taking place or likely to take place in the brewing industry in the course of the next few years.

It arose out of a loose scheme to amalgamate Flower's, Simonds and Greene King. The plans went no further, but Greene King's response is important in understanding its position in the 1960s. Its aim was to protect itself—although it was recognised that in purely financial terms a takeover would mean that it 'should not have a great deal to lose'—its employees and its shareholders. Its strength, it believed, arose from the geographical concentration of its houses. It reckoned that no national brewery would take it over and close down Westgate Brewery because deliveries from any other centre would be impossible. In the light of Watney Mann's acquisition of Steward and Patteson and Bullards in 1963—even bigger agglomerations of even more remote houses—its reasoning, and the fact that it believed few economies could be made, proved fallacious. The weakness was that family and 'friendly' holdings in the firm were lower than the outside world believed. In 1959 these were reckoned to be about 50 per cent and 'gradually worsening'. Yet in the climate of brewery takeovers around 1960 few firms, however tightly knit their ownership, were entirely safe. Greene King stated its resolution to continue to be independent because it was the only way to protect its employees and, in the long run, its owners. It realised, nevertheless, that it might well have to allow a 'national' brewer to acquire as much as a 20 per cent holding of its voting shares in order to deter a bid from an unwelcome source. The choice, however, was not necessarily Greene King's for the activities of the big breweries, stalking their prey by unidentified holding companies, often went unrecognised.[15] Pressure might come from a company 'with whom it would be uncongenial to work'. Much of this discussion was speculation, but it reveals the inner workings of Greene King and its determination in 1960 to retain independence by a strengthening of its profits and its trading position.

Early in 1961 it acquired Wells and Winch of Biggleswade.

With 287 houses and an annual trade of around 40,000 barrels it was more than twice the size of any brewery Greene King had previously absorbed. Indeed this merger, together with the great expansion after 1968, are the central features of the company's history in the last twenty years. It is interesting in two further respects. First, Wells and Winch possessed a past that contrasts strongly in many ways with that of Greene King. Whereas a continuous theme of the latter has been total financial orthodoxy and close management, Wells and Winch provides a more unusual example of a brewery, with an old and interesting history in itself, pursuing a policy of adventurous financial management after its total reorganisation in the heady days of the 1890s. Second, after 1948 it suffered more than most breweries in the recession of the early 1950s and was therefore exposed to the attentions of the big brewers. The brief account of its history that follows underlines these two points and makes the distinction between its experience and that of Greene King after 1900.

The Wells' connection with the Biggleswade Brewery goes back to 1764. Two generations of the Wells family expanded their brewing and, after 1800, their banking interests. Sited on the Great North Road they were in a good position to do so, and when Samuel Wells II died in 1831 the brewery owned forty-eight houses, many of which were situated in Biggleswade itself. For the next sixty-eight years both the Brewery and the Bank were managed by Samuel Wells's sons-in-law and grandsons, members of the Lindsell and Hogge (Archdale) families. Like so many brewers their wealth and social connections burgeoned, and in 1899 they realised their assets in the Biggleswade Bank and Brewery.[16] This was a good year to sell a brewery with 109 tied houses. It was bought by George Winch, a Chatham solicitor, for his son, E. B. Winch, although C. S. Lindsell and G. F. Archdale retained a modest 8 per cent equity interest in the new company, serving on its Board for several years. The Winchs were a well-known Kent brewing family and in the same year that George Winch acquired Wells & Co.'s Brewery, Style and Winch, a merger of two big breweries in Chatham and Maidstone, was launched with a large valuation of £1,100,000. Biggleswade's capitalisation was, of course, much smaller at £155,000, but its management was far from unadventurous in spite of the Lindsell

—Archdale presence on the new Board. The company was dominated by its Chairman, George Winch, and in 1900, with the aid of
two debenture issues for £85,000, he almost entirely rebuilt the
brewery and purchased two small breweries—Holdens of Henlow with ten houses in 1900 for £9,000, and the Baldock Brewing
Company in 1904 with twenty-two houses for £13,000. But the
1900s were not years in which to undertake headlong expansion,
and between 1903 and 1914 profits were disheartening, especially
in 1907 and 1908 when barrellage fell to 11,500. During and
shortly after the First World War the Winchs sold off their
majority interest. The venture had been disappointing and E. B.
Winch, the Managing Director, died in 1913.

His place was taken two years later by a thrusting newcomer,
A. J. Redman. He is the key figure in Wells and Winch's twentieth-
century history and an interesting brewing entrepreneur. He had
been manager of the London properties of Style and Winch and at
first he came to Biggleswade only two days a week. By 1920,
however, he was executive chairman of the company with a 38 per
cent stake in its equity. His role at Wells and Winch was always
supported by Kenneth Walker, a director and substantial shareholder in 1899 and vice-chairman of the firm from 1917 until
1948. When Redman took over in 1915 the firm owned around
120 houses. Towards the end of the war it had a trade of only
11,000 barrels. As soon as peace was declared he instigated, in the
brief period of prosperity between 1918 and 1921, a policy of
rapid growth. He bought Day and Sons of St Neots in 1920 and
shared out their houses with Charles Wells Ltd of Bedford. Wells
and Winch retained twenty-nine. In the following year Page and
Co. of Ashwell were taken over with twenty-six houses and in
1922 Newland and Nash of Bedford with eighty. Many of the
latter were good town houses in Bedford itself. There was a pause,
with a few years of poor profits, before the process was recom-
menced. In 1928 Higgins and Sons of Bedford with 55 houses and
a large free trade (which Wells and Winch lost) was acquired; in
1931 Hudson's Cambridge and Pampisford Breweries Ltd with
fifty-eight houses; and in 1938 A. J. Wickham of Hertford with
seven. In the latter year, Wells and Winch bought their way
farther into the Cambridge area by purchasing, for £128,000,
twenty-seven houses from Barclay Perkins. By the outbreak of the

Second World War, Wells and Winch controlled 381 tied houses, compared with the 495 owned by Greene King.

A. J. Redman's experience went back to the carefree company flotations in the brewing industry of the 1890s, but his policy of expansion in the inter-war years was a remarkable one for a country brewer. Of course the process of brewery closures and company amalgamations continued between 1919 and 1939, but he pushed harder than most brewers. It was he who made the running, he who approached all the breweries named above, and he who closed them down. By 1939 his vigorous designs allowed production at Biggleswade to be quadrupled from around 14,000 barrels, when he took over in 1915, to a pre-war peak of 57,000 barrels. Expansion was achieved by enterprising financial management. In 1928 there was an issue of 85,000 preference shares and two large debenture issues of £150,000 in 1933 and £300,000 in 1938. And often the balance sheets disclosed further large loans to the company. Much of this money was borrowed very cheaply: the 1938 debentures carrying a payment of $3\frac{3}{4}$ per cent. Even so, with such gearing high yearly interest payments absorbed a fair proportion of profit. Except for two poor years between 1932 and 1934, however, net profits increased steadily from 1925 to 1939. So did A. J. Redman's share of the firm's equity. In 1938 it was 64 per cent.[17]

The war posed no problems for Wells and Winch's output or profitability. Producing little more than a mild ale, it sold 89,736 barrels and returned net profits of £59,000 in 1945—the best year so far on both counts in the company's history. In fact profitability went on increasing until 1948, the year of A. J. Redman's death. The firm then passed to the control of his two sons, D. S. Redman, the new Chairman, and Colonel J. A. Redman, the company's brewer, both of whom had been elected to Wells and Winch's Board in the early 1930s.

The years after 1946 were not easy ones for brewers and, like the vast majority of companies, the Biggleswade Brewery and its houses needed large sums spending upon them after wartime depreciation had taken its toll. Since the brewery was largely rebuilt in 1900 it was hardly extended before 1939, except that brewing and fermenting capacities were expanded to meet increased demand in the inter-war years and a bottling line was

GREENE KING

installed in 1927 in an old maltings. Now it badly required further
bottling plant as the demand for bottled beer grew after 1945, and
many of the public houses taken on so cheerfully between 1920
and 1938 needed extensive modernisation. The trouble was that
overall demand fell away sharply. In 1951 Wells and Winch sold
55,000 barrels—around the 1939 level. By 1957–8 this had fallen
to under 40,000 barrels. Net profits fell as margins tightened. The
level of £52,600 achieved in 1950 was not reached again in the
1950s. Moreover charges on loans and bills were an increasingly
worrying feature. At the end of the war, A. J. Redman had had
visions of policies similar to those he pursued in the 1920s and
1930s: approaches were made to Phillips of Royston (he had
sounded them out in the late 1920s) and Fordhams of Ashwell.
Both, however, fell to J. W. Green of Luton and nothing came of
his much more ambitious plans to merge with the Northampton
Brewery Co.[18] After 1948 schemes of this sort to take up surplus
capacity at Biggleswade were abandoned, and the struggle for
survival, in the face of very strong competition from both local
and national brewers, began.

One way was to shed uneconomic houses. From 1950 to 1961
ninety were closed. Nevertheless large sums still had to be expended to keep up the 300 or so that remained. In 1957 £111,000
was spent on repairs on them and on the brewery. Further sums
were used to acquire nine more (including five former Benskin
houses from Ind Coope in 1959 in the prosperous Watford area),
rebuild a further five and erect two new ones in the 1950s. A new
bottling store was opened in 1952, although building restrictions
were so acute that plant had to be installed in eight old hangars
re-erected on the site. Yet as trade dwindled even the bottling lines
were under-utilised and in 1956 Wells and Winch advertised its
surplus bottling capacity. It was fortunate in being able to negoti-
ate an unusually long, 21-year contract with the London brewers,
Taylor Walker. Two years later it was working so well that Taylor
Walker was installing additional plant in an extended store. In
order to bottle 30,000 barrels a year additional overtime working
was required two nights a week. Then in 1959 Taylor Walker was
taken over by Ind Coope. Its Limehouse Brewery was abruptly
closed. There were no problems at Biggleswade for Ind Coope
honoured the invaluable bottling contract (*Skol* lager was bottled

236

there until 1976) and negotiations about the sale of *Skol* in Wells and Winch houses in exchange for the five Benskin houses at a favourable price of £65,000 were concluded. But the atmosphere in which they were conducted was less friendly than that in which the Taylor Walker contract had been agreed. Colonel J. A. Redman realised that if Ind Coope acquired Wells and Winch the brewery would be closed within months. Since the Redman family had a 71 per cent holding the choice was largely theirs, except that declining trade, the terminal illness of the Chairman, D. S. Redman, the threat of death duties, and the brothers' fear of the national brewers' interventions undermined any resolve to remain independent. Colonel Redman, wanting to protect his employees, therefore began talks with 'friendly' neighbours such as Charles Wells of Bedford, McMullens of Hertford and Greene King, to seek a merger. It was the latter which showed most interest. Negotiations were on the old pattern, insofar as they could be in that remarkable year of brewing takeovers, 1960. The shock waves had reached Greene King. The other firm of which General Dempsey was Chairman, H. & G. Simonds, the big Reading brewery, was taken over by Courage. Harold Lake's Wilson and Walker was swallowed up along with Phipps Northampton Brewers Co. and Usher's Wiltshire Brewery by Watney Mann in 1960. These were only a tiny selection of firms that happened to affect Greene King directors.

Colonel Redman had known John Clarke both from rivalry in the Cambridge trade and from the Royal Artillery during the war. If he could find a place for himself and, after training, posts for his son, Simon, and D. S. Redman's son, Timothy, and obtain guarantees about the continuation of brewing at Biggleswade he was keen to sell. For Greene King the arrangement made sense. It would eliminate some competition in the Cambridge area and, more important, would open up the prosperous trade of the Bedford, Luton and Watford areas. The acquisition would buttress the resolve to retain independence. Greene King insisted that Colonel Redman should not discuss its proposals with any other brewer and that the exchange of shares should be agreed 'without independent opinion'. General Dempsey, fresh from his Simonds –Courage talks, tidied up details about the old Wells and Winch directorships and the composition of the new subsidiary Board.[19]

But since D. S. Redman died during the negotiations and Colonel Redman was ill they dragged on from November 1960 until February 1961, Nevertheless complete secrecy was observed between the Greene King and Wells and Winch directors and the two companies' Secretaries. Dick Lines at Bury remembers typing all the paperwork late at night himself. There were 'secret' meetings between the directors of the two firms in London. No valuation of Wells and Winch was undertaken, although John Clarke went round the majority of its houses to make his own notes. For Whitbread, who had acquired a 10 per cent holding in Wells and Winch, would not have stood idly by to witness Greene King filch one of its 'umbrella' companies. Even so Greene King shares advanced from 87s. 6d. to 105s. in the month before 10 February, the day the formal offer was made. It needed only half a rumour in these years to send brewery share prices rocketing, but the announcement came as a complete surprise both to Whitbreads and the City.

The basic proposals were for a straight exchange of Greene King shares for the 200,000 Wells and Winch ordinaries. *The Times* on 11 February reckoned the total package placed a value of £1,400,000 on Wells and Winch. Five days earlier there had been great excitement at Bury as the directors were thrown into the maelstrom of big brewery mergers. Not only did they work out the final details of the offer and discuss their handling of Whitbreads, but they also did their calculations about the holdings of 'Brewery Families and Friends'. If Wells and Winch were taken over the figure added up to 60 per cent and this was thought sufficient to retain independence, but such was the heat of the merger movement early in 1961 that the directors prepared themselves for 'entering into a Trading Agreement with a National Brewery'. In fact there were no hitches, for Colonel Redman had pledged 70 per cent acceptance of the Greene King offer and the big Redman holdings in fact strengthened 'family' control of the enlarged firm.[20] By early April the brewery's temperature moved towards normal as its shares fell below 100s. again.

The interesting feature of the deal is that although John Clarke raised many questions at joint meetings in London between the two companies the atmosphere of brewery mergers at this time concentrated minds wonderfully about answers. Major Lake and

Sir Edward Greene would have hesitated over the large number of country houses in poor shape, worried about the high gearing of the firm and its declining production of variable beers, and even noted that the Wells and Winch's directors' car, a Bentley Continental, did not harmonise with Greene King's more sober style. Now in the 1960–1 boom, as their Chairman, General Dempsey advised, there was no time to dwell on niceties. The merger went forward because Greene King itself was forced along in the wake of the national breweries. Its position as a strong regional brewery was much consolidated. The acquisition of 287 Wells and Winch houses gave it control of a total of over 900 tied houses. Independence was made a greater reality so long as the resolve to retain it continued unabated, and profits remained sufficiently buoyant to keep the loyalties of shareholders.[21]

3

Directors remember the struggle for Greene King's retention of its independence being 'really in all those years our one major preoccupation'. Indeeed the Chairmanship of General Dempsey (1955–69), chosen for his weight in the City and the industry, is a reminder of this central theme in policy. It would, however, be misleading to concentrate too narrowly upon it. The difficulty is that constant exposure to glossy television serials dramatising the world of big business in terms of hard fought takeover battles and fierce struggles within family firms—the stuff of at least a couple of David and Goliath type contests each winter—imposes a compelling, universal pattern. It is essential to remind ourselves that the inner reality of firms is very different. At Greene King, the daily tasks in the 1950s and 1960s, as in the past, were concerned with the more mundane, regular features of brewing and malting, houses and tenants, employees and pension funds, transport and the weather. This is not to suggest that the management did not innovate in these years, or to deny that the great concentration movement within the industry and its significance for management, finance and production affected Greene King. It clearly did. As K. H. Hawkins wrote in his *History of Bass Charrington* (1978)[22]

Those [the independent breweries] who, through luck or good

judgement, survived into the 1970s learned a great deal from the experience of the preceding decade, including the mistakes of the 'big six'. It would therefore be naïve to assume that the small independent concerns of today are exactly the same as they were in the 1950s. The tradition of family control has survived but otherwise much has changed. The management of these companies is now generally professional in character; they are concerned to improve their pubs; some have begun to brew keg and 'top pressure' beer; many use relatively sophisticated marketing techniques; it is not unknown for them to put some of their new and or improved pubs under direct management; and they use professional accountants and modern methods of financial control. The smaller companies have lived in the shadow of the 'big six' for too long either to remain untouched by the progress which the latter have made or to ignore their success in reconciling the wishes of their customers with the requirements of a modern business enterprise.

In these closing sections it remains for me to indicate very briefly some of the changes that have taken place since the late 1950s at Greene King. The time is not ripe to present a detailed history. Many of the people involved closely in events are still living. Much of the discussion would be derived from annual reports, balance sheets and comments in the financial press, for the directors' minutes are far briefer after 1958. To attempt this would be to alter the tone at quite the wrong point. Some of the figures set out simply in Appendix 2, Table 6 help to support this brief sketch.

The years since 1955 fall into two distinct periods—from 1955 to 1969 and from 1969 to 1980. These largely coincide with the chairmanship of Sir Miles Dempsey (1955–69) and the managing directorship of John Clarke (retired 1969), and after 1969 with Sir Hugh Greene's chairmanship (1971–8) and the offices of John Bridge, Managing Director since 1969 and Chairman since Sir Hugh's retirement.[23] That periods and personalities largely overlap is somewhat accidental, for the late 1950s and 1960s were years of steady recovery and modest change in the brewing industry, at least in terms of output, profits and production methods, whereas those after 1969 were of rapid expansion,

Table 8: United Kingdom Beer *Consumption* Index

Year	Million barrels	Index	Greene King sales ('000 barrels)	Index
1962	28·6	100	161	100
1963	28·3	98·9	159	98·9
1964	29·5	103·1	163	101·7
1965	29·9	104·5	172	107·0
1966	30·4	106·2	170	105·8
1967	31·3	109·4	176	109·6
1968	31·5	110·1	172	107·2
1969	32·2	112·5	181	113·0

Source: Greene King Marketing Consultants' Report (1970).

sometimes termed 'the beer revolution', in which breweries made deep incursions into the free trade and pressed much more boldly forward with developments initiated in the earlier periods.

Between 1955 and 1969 beer sales at Greene King improved. At first the growth was not very marked. There were discussions about dwindling trade as late as 1958, but after the 1959 Budget allowed brewers to remove 2d. from the price of a pint, sales advanced quite sharply. Output figures for the Westgate Brewery alone show an increase from 64,643 barrels in 1955 to 85,914 barrels in 1961. Most of this growth was achieved after 1959. Then from 1961 to 1969 group beer sales almost exactly matched the United Kingdom beer consumption index (see Table 8).

Although the picture changes from the 1948–55 recession growth, except from 1959 to 1961, was not really marked until the late 1960s. Sales of beer at Westgate indicate this. In 1955 they were worth £1.1 million: in 1961 they had advanced only to £1.38 million (prices falling after the 1959 Budget); and in 1964 they stood at £1.68 million. There was certainly no aggressive pricing policy. Invariably alterations reflected changes in duty and sharp advances in costs of labour and transport (though not those of brewing materials in the 1950s and early 1960s). Policy was to undercut by two or three pennies a pint or bottle the prices of the national brewers and keep a penny behind those of regional competitors. And if occasionally they were out of line with the latter—there was now much more open discussion of pricing in the Norfolk and Suffolk branch of the Brewers' Society—they were promptly reduced. Net profits rose steadily (see Appendix 2, Table 6), not through price increases but because of increased trade from Simpson's and from Wells and Winch, and from improved wines and spirits sales.

Although profit margins were tighter in wines and spirits, sales grew faster than those of beer after the mid-1950s. This was a constant source of surprise and rejoicing in these years. Of course it reflected the strong upward trend of national consumption, as the British middle classes took for the first time to drinking large amounts of wine regularly. Greene King was sufficiently convinced of the strength of this shift to purchase Cawdrons of Fakenham and Wells-next-the-Sea in Norfolk in 1954. It was merged with Peatling's, the wine subsidiary in King's Lynn acquired twenty years earlier, to form Peatling and Cawdron under the management of Graham Cawdron, the owner of the Fakenham business. In 1957 a further firm, Tidnam's of Wisbech, which had a renowned trade in port, was acquired. Such was the interest in wines in the mid-1950s that serious negotiations were conducted with firms in Colchester and Thetford, and several wine shops were bought in these years. The problem was, that although Peatling's occupied fine old cellars in King's Lynn, accommodation at Cupola House in Bury was extremely cramped and it was difficult to increase sales much until a new wines and spirits store, costing £35,000, was opened next to the bottling stores in 1958. Then, under the direction of Martin Corke and Graham Cawdron, this side of the business, with modest advertising, expanded well until 1964. In March of that year a consultant's report reckoned that the six-year-old building had only a further four to run before it reached capacity. The abolition of Retail Price Maintenance in the same year, however, caused a serious hiccough in the 12-year upward trend in sales. Peatling and Cawdron's profits fell sharply, and briefly the sight of people clutching supermarket carrier bags full of bottles of gin and table wines raised fears that the corner shop was finished. And in 1965–6 there was a recession in the wine trade caused by increases in the excise duty. These two features of government policy led to a rapid reappraisal of trading. Like the national brewers Greene King was able to share in the expanding wine trade because it had built up over 30 years a good subsidiary and in the 1960s it shared, through its small holding, the benefits of the Wine Traders' Consortium, which was dominated by Whitbread and Courage. In 1968 wine and spirit sales provided around 14 per cent of Greene King turnover, 2 per cent higher than that achieved by Bass Charrington.[24] It is a comparison that shows Greene King well positioned to take advantage of the further resurgence in the wines and spirits market in the 1970s.

There were, however, bigger problems at Greene King than those suffered in the mid-1960s by Peatling and Cawdron. Profits (see Appendix 2, Table 6) looked healthy, especially in comparison with the past, and dividends were well enough covered, but the firm had 930 houses after the merger with Wells and Winch. The sheer scale of modernisation in the late 1950s and 1960s was daunting. There were hundreds of country houses paying very small 'dry' rents and doing a very small trade. After the early 1950s Greene King was pressed by local authorities and licensing magistrates to improve drainage and sanitation in its country houses. In 1956 almost a third of these were still without bathrooms and water closets. And money also had to be spent on modernising tenants' accommodation and the car parks. Moreover the role of the public house itself was changing as living standards rose and a new generation of drinkers emerged. The Prices and Incomes Board (1969) stated these changes succinctly,

Until comparatively recently the pub was regarded as the social centre for those working men whose main relaxation was drinking beer in congenial company. With the coming of a more affluent society the traditional pub has had to face competition from the new entertainment industry—clubs . . . and similar places offering food and entertainment . . . This external competition requires of the brewers that they do more than maintain existing houses to a traditional standard . . . Increasingly, they are providing amenities to suit the locality, and the appropriate 'mix' of beer, wines, spirits, soft drinks, food, music, games and so on to meet consumer preferences. In practical terms this involves capital expenditure, both by brewer and licensee, not only on the maintenance of existing amenities but also on the provision of new amenities.[25]

The force of these changes was as evident in East Anglia as elsewhere. They meant that Greene King, to keep pace with competitors both in the industry itself and in the leisure market generally, had to improve the layout, decor and catering facilities of their more popular properties to conform with the new image of the public house. A series of photographs of Greene King houses taken in the early 1950s and again in the late 1960s show how numerous and extensive these alterations were. Major improvements on this scale were expensive—sometimes as much as half the cost of a new house was spent on refurbishing an old one. Therefore the company closed some uneconomic houses and concentrated funds upon bringing more profitable ones up to the standards expected in the 1960s. It was a problem not always appreciated by critics who believed that houses were shut down by some faceless accountant simply pressing the keys of his calculator. The process of closure in fact was as old as the 1887 merger at Greene King. Most years in the twentieth century had seen the demise of three or four houses—often beer houses dating from the 1830s—but the process was speeded up with the acquisition of Wells and Winch. It was a policy, of course, implemented on a far bigger scale by the national breweries. Moreover, new inns were necessary on housing estates built in Bury,[26] Luton, Stevenage and Cambridge in the 1950s. Between 1955 and 1965 Greene King built eight. By the early 1960s these were costing as much as £30,000 each, and extensions and improvements to Everards Hotel in Bury were estimated to cost £40,000. These were large sums taken together with the constant round of expenditure on plant in the breweries and the regular, mounting costs of public house modernisation, as builders' wages and materials rose sharply in these years. Between the years 1961–2 and 1965–6 capital expenditure rose from £318,000 to £570,000. As early as 1957 the position was somewhat precarious. At Westgate the cost of the additional fermenting vessels, the new wine and spirit and mineral water stores totalled around £140,000. This, together with new houses and repairs, meant that in three years, 1955 to 1958, Greene King 'would be spending on capital work £153,000 more than we had coming in'. The Chairman was not alarmed but he wanted the directors to appreciate that spending on this scale was taking the firm into deficit. The precaution was taken of liquidating the Insurance Fund to realise its assets of around £110,000 and in future capital expenditure and income reports were drawn up and discussed each year. For the next decade there was a constant lament that money was tight and taxation harsh, given the scale of the improvement problem. Yet there was no standing still as competition meant houses had to provide facilities at least equal to those of other breweries. Expenditure on fermenting vessels and bottling plant was regular and unavoidable: £130,000 was spent on a new high-speed bottling line at Bury in the mid-1960s, and a similar amount on one at Biggleswade in 1968–9.

The position was in some ways exacerbated by the acquisition of Wells and Winch, for many of their small houses were in poor shape. No fewer than sixty were closed in the decade after 1961. Of course their freehold, unlicensed value was quite high by the late 1960s and the firm sold off other property, including the two farms at Furneux Pelham and Great Whelnetham.[27] All this helped in the provision of funds, as did the shutting down and sale of Simpson's at Baldock in 1965.[28] Its closure, since it was a mere eight miles from Biggleswade, was inevitable after 1961. The 125 houses attached to it were transferred to Greene King (Biggleswade), as Wells and Winch was styled in 1963. Since unemployment levels were modest in the mid-1960s, its demise was handled amicably. The eighty employees were either offered work at Biggleswade or were paid compensation. Savings on its closure were estimated, somewhat vaguely, at £20,000 to £30,000 a year, and in the following year it was sold to Baldock Urban Council for £85,000. Some of the funds generated in this way were spent on the 340 houses attached to Biggleswade after 1965 and on the improvements at the brewery itself. Nevertheless retentions from profits after tax were inadequate for the scale of investment after 1955. Dividends were not extravagant, but they had to remain at attractive levels to retain shareholders in the years of peak merger activity. In 1965 £750,000 was raised in 6¾ per cent debentures issued at £99 per cent. The sum was sufficient to clear bank loans and provide a surplus for further investment. Nevertheless, when there was a poor summer, as in 1966, and profits slipped, the financial press could be sharp about Greene King's prospects. They suggested that sales would have to increase in order to ease pressure on margins. The *Stock Exchange Gazette* thought 'the outlook is none too bright. The present share price is mostly supported by bid hopes.'[29]

These years, 1955–69, were not easy for Greene King. Although production rose, capital expenditure increased remorselessly. It was unavoidable, but efficiency had to be sought —hence the sale of farms, uneconomic houses, the shutdown of Simpson's, and the introduction of bonus schemes in some departments. All the time its performance was being monitored by the takeover predators. Nevertheless, these pressures forced Greene King to evolve a view of itself in relation to the national brewers. In the past it had prided itself on its good management, good beers and good relations with employees and tenants. But it had not extended this image much beyond its own tied houses and its special position in West Suffolk. In short it had, like so many other small and regional breweries, concentrated upon production, not marketing. After the 1960s this was insufficient. It had to project a view of a regional brewery that provided fine draught beers and a first-rate service throughout East Anglia and its borders. In its formulation of this it was aided in the 1960s by the cohesiveness of the South-East region. It was not operating like the national breweries along very extended lines. At last real affluence came to Greene King's region. Population rose faster here than in the old industrial areas as migration of industry and offices from London took a north-easterly path. It still remained, comparatively, a low wage area, but now the rising prosperity of agriculture, industry and tourism together created an expanding regional economy. This expansion was already evident by the late 1950s in the more populous centres of the Rayment's and Wells and Winch areas. By the mid-1960s it was beginning to affect the entire Greene King area.

Although the directors understood the objectives of presenting an updated and extended image of Greene King, they did not fulfil them in the 1960s. Little use was made of advertising. At first, like all the East Anglian breweries, they blamed ITV for a drop in sales, since people left their television sets even more reluctantly. There was no determined attempt to penetrate the growing free trade after the 1961 Licensing Act opened up other retail outlets. The modest growth of these years was achieved by the rise in beer consumption and improvement of their own tied houses. As much as 90 per cent of trade was still through their own properties. This unadventurous approach, in the face of the national brewers' onslaught in the 1960s, reflected the ideas of the Managing Director, John Clarke. Then in his sixties, he found the rapid changes bewildering. It was hardly surprising. He had been trained by Major Lake in a period in which brewers believed that the tied trade was all important. If that was right and production efficient, success followed. Moreover he had carried off the acquisition of Simpson's and Wells and Winch and he was exceptionally well-liked by his employees and tenants. He represented all that was best in the brewing industry in the first half of the twentieth century. But in the 1960s he felt out of place with 'free trade penetration', computerised accounts and price-earnings ratios. He worried increasingly about details and relied upon General Dempsey, the younger executive directors, John Bridge and Martin Corke, and the Company Secretary, Dick Lines, to project Greene King's image as a major regional brewery after 1962.

Already much of the brewery life of John Clarke's youth had slipped away. The firm's last four horses were destroyed in 1958; the ton of coal doled out to each married employee was discontinued in 1963. Now the pace of change accelerated. In 1961 the T.G.W.U. visited the breweries for the first time, as part of a recruiting drive—stressing that it had no complaints to make. In the offices there were radical changes. When Frank Bevis retired as Secretary in 1958 the head office remained much as it had been in 1914; the open office was a jumble of high desks and stools; the clerks still wore black alpaca jackets; the Lake–Bevis predilection for double-entry accounts in hefty tamper-proof ledgers was totally observed. There was not a single adding machine in the office. The new Secretary, Dick Lines, quickly altered this. Machine accounting was immediately introduced and within ten years a computer had been installed. This rapid shift from the age of Dickens to that of the computer was effectively achieved with the same staff that had been trained to the fearsome standards of Bevis's quill-pen accountancy. In the brewery itself metal casks, beer cans, fork-lift trucks and pallets appeared. Mostly they were considerable improvements.

Something was even done about William Wilkins's delightful theatre built across the road from Benjamin Greene's brewery in 1819.[30] Greene King bought it in 1920 and paid off its losses. Edward Lake tried to keep it going as a live theatre but the attempt failed and by 1925 it was used by the firm as a barrel store.[31] Captain Edward Greene and Major Lake, in a rush of total philistinism in the late 1930s, wanted to demolish it so that they could construct a wines and spirits store on the site. Somehow it survived, although there were perpetual grumbles even about keeping it watertight. In 1961, a more enlightened generation of directors leased it after several years of enquiries and discussions, to the Theatre Royal Trust on a peppercorn rental and fourteen years later Greene King granted a 999-year lease, at the same traditional annual rent, to the National Trust. A surviving Regency theatre—the scene of the Company's AGM since 1973 —totally surrounded by the appendages of one of the country's busiest breweries, is unique on both counts.

In all these discussions about takeover threats and changes in the 1950s and 1960s there were lighter moments, although it is not clear from the deadpan prose of the minute books that they were treated as such. One was pure Fenland tragi-comedy. A patron at March bought some Guinness bottled by Greene King, and on drinking it found a mouse in the bottle. In a state of some shock he went to his solicitor. The story then took on a blacker turn. The lawyer, expanding on his client's experience, alleged he had had some mental disorder four years earlier and that he was now 'back to almost the same condition as he was then, through negligence on our part'. Greene King, anxious to keep the matter quiet, settled for £215. The other incident comes straight from the pages of *Clochemerle*. The unfortunately named *Cock* at Castle Camps had an ancient urinal attached to its front. The owner of the adjoining bungalow objected 'to the discharge from the urinal'. Over the years she proceeded to the law, somewhat extravagantly, employing at one time or another no fewer than three solicitors, and threatening a High Court action. Eventually Greene King had to pay £1,400 for removing the urinal to a more discreet position and the plaintiff's costs of £460.

Table 9: Beer market shares and ownership of on-licensed premises in the
mid-1970s*

Company	No. of U.K. breweries (1976)	Share of beer sales (1976)	No. of on-licensed premises (inc. clubs and hotels) (1974)	% of total
Bass Charrington	12	20	9,256	8·2
Allied Breweries	7	17	7,665	6·8
Whitbread	19	13	7,865	6·9
Watney/Grand Metropolitan Hotels	8	12	5,946	5·2
Scottish & Newcastle	3	11	1,678	1·5
Courage/Imperial Group	8	9	5,921	5·2
Guinness	1	9	—	—
Others	89	9	13,800	12·2
Free Trade	—	—	61,498	54·0
Total	147	100	113,629	100·0

* Source: K. H. Hawkins and C. L. Pass, *op. cit.*, pp. 79, 82.

4

The years between 1969 and 1974 were the most extraordinary
for the brewing industry since the 1890s. The early 1960s had
seen an intense concentration take place, and the six brewing
giants then began the rationalisation of their production and retail
outlets. Vast new breweries were built and houses closed in the
drive for increased efficiency.[32]

This oligarchy stepped up sales of a new type of beer, keg, and
pushed its lagers by extensive advertising. But these developments
were not all. The government, in its Licensing Act of 1961, eased
restrictions on off-licence and restaurant outlets so that, together
with an expanding club trade (accounting for around one-fifth of
beer sales), the free trade element in retailing beer became much
more important. Therefore the retail side of the industry was
revolutionised as much as production. The tied trade, the haven of
all brewers except Guinness since the 1880s, became less important except to the smallest breweries. The government also, in the
light of the rapid horizontal mergers within the industry, took an

extended view of these changes with a succession of referrals to the Prices and Incomes Board and Monopolies and Prices Commissions. The Erroll Committee (1972) examined the question of dismantling the framework of restrictive licensing. These investigations in some ways recalled hostility to the brewing industry in the 1900s. Their recommendations and inconsistencies have been analysed elsewhere.[33] At Greene King their findings were discussed, but there was an increasing sense of *déjà vu*, and, like other breweries, their views and statistics were channelled through their powerful trade organisation, the Brewers' Society. They came to live with attempts to control prices and dividends, changes in duty, and continuous inflation in the 1970s.

The basis of these extraordinary changes in the industry was an accelerated growth of beer, wines and spirits sales. Beer consumption, in the peak decade from 1967 to 1977, rose from 30·3 million barrels of average gravity to 40·4 million—a yearly growth of 3·2 per cent. Spirits grew by almost 8·75 per cent per annum, and wines by 8·3 per cent.[34] The share of alcohol in total consumer expenditure rose from 6·1 per cent in 1960–4 to 8·3 per cent in 1972–6—a significant shift. Other surveys indicated that drinking, by both sexes, young and old alike, was becoming more 'regular' in the 1960s and 1970s.

In this last section it is necessary to examine briefly the ways in which Greene King shared and took advantage of this growth. Between 1955 and 1964 it had been worried by the dead weight of increasingly heavy capital expenditure and was hesitant in formulating its role as a leading regional brewery. In the 1970s, however, prospects and policies changed. It emerged amongst the dozen largest companies in the industry. Greene King's beer output, that had kept step with the index of national consumption, accelerated after 1969. Throughout the 1970s it expanded at around 8 per cent per annum.[35] Growth was not even. In the years ending 20 April 1974 and 1976 it advanced by a dramatic 13 and 15 per cent respectively. Across the decade it rose, on average, at almost three times the rate of increase in national consumption. How were these remarkable figures achieved?

Performance undoubtedly reflected a deep penetration of the free trade market. In 1969 this was, except at Rayment's, which had relied on a good club trade since the 1930s, negligible. At

Bury it was a mere 6 per cent, and only 9 per cent at Biggleswade. But the free trade area of clubs, restaurants and off-licences in supermarkets and shops grew after the 1961 Licensing Act. By 1970 brewers' tied houses represented only 55 per cent of total turnover in all premises, and the figure, when turnover was accelerating fast, declined throughout the 1970s. Like the 'nationals', who had already begun their incursions into the free trade, Greene King realised that its salvation must come from this quarter. It meant a totally new marketing approach was needed. It turned to a firm of marketing consultants in 1970 whose report makes fascinating reading, for it is clear that in many ways the smart London consultants were mystified. They, of course, accepted Greene King's desire to achieve high profits in order to retain independence, and appreciated its insistence on its responsibilities to the community through its public houses, but the fact that no employee—beyond a house manager who had decamped with the furniture and stocks—had been dismissed and that donations and subscriptions to charities almost equalled revenue spent on advertising was beyond their experience. They were sceptical about the basis of Greene King's proposition that draught beer was its 'unique' sales point, suggesting that there was no evidence to support the belief that the public wanted draught rather than keg beer. They insisted that targets and plans should be rigorously defined and that the marketing structure and training of the firm must be revolutionised. Some of their recommendations were followed through. Martin Corke became Marketing Director, a senior sales executive, Simon Jamieson, was appointed, and the number of representatives in the free trade increased.[36] Detailed annual marketing plans were submitted to the Board. As early as 1971 the programme was bearing fruit, although there were those in the firm who looked on these efforts with some scepticism. In his Annual Report the Chairman announced record sales and profits. Beer sales had advanced 7 per cent by volume without any increase in the number of public houses. 'This enabled us to absorb many increases in cost', continued the Chairman, 'and thus to improve our profit margin.' This was only the beginning. By 1980, 48 per cent of Greene King sales was with the free trade. It was a remarkable penetration and the reversal of three generations of trading policy. For the number of public houses, although there was still on average a new one built each year, in fact fell.

Some of this growth was in one sense fortuitous. It was greatly aided by the expansion of population and industry in East Anglia and the South-East region which had the fastest growth rate in the country in the 1970s. Greene King informally defined its region in 1970 and did not extend its operations beyond it (see Map 2, p. 137). In this it was also helped, when it began modest television advertising after 1971, by the fact that a good portion of this area was included within the Anglia ITV region. In these respects its experience contrasted sharply with the national brewers. They had bought breweries extensively in the heat of the takeover boom and then thought about the implications of their acquisitions later. Greene King never needed extensive rationalisation because it had acquired breweries logically within its own regional sphere. In other ways the growth of the 1970s was guided by more deliberate managerial policies. There are three strands in these: their maintenance of a large range of beers, their price strategy, and their stress on service. Each is worth a moment's attention.

The company retained a large number of beers when other breweries contracted the range they offered. In the early 1970s Westgate produced three cask beers and four bottled ones; Biggleswade four draught, two keg and five bottled; and Rayment's eight different beers. The nub of promotion policy in the late 1960s and early 1970s was the production of cask or traditional draught beers in which a natural secondary fermentation was allowed to take place. An advertising feature in 1968 claimed, 'Greene King, which spans the Eastern Counties from the Wash to London, is best known as a champion of conventional draught beer.' *Abbot*, its strong bitter, first produced in the mid-1950s as a bottled beer, won the Brewers' Exhibition Championship award in 1968, and Greene King concentrated promotional efforts on this and *IPA*, when in the 1970s it began, for the first time, a properly co-ordinated, extensive advertising campaign.

In the promotion of traditional draught beers they were undoubtedly helped, in a somewhat back-handed fashion, by CAMRA (the Campaign for Real Ale). Although CAMRA was critical of Greene King's dispensing of draught beer under pressure in many of its houses,[37] their campaign for real beer benefited independent breweries such as Greene King which prided itself upon its production. For had it not been for CAMRA's publicity the national brewers might well have phased out the production of real ale, which would in the long run have had serious effects upon the independent brewers.

Although the emphasis was on draught beers, Greene King introduced a filtered and pasteurised bright beer known as *King Keg* (essentially a bottled beer in an 11-gallon barrel). Keg was first popularised by Watney Mann's *Red Barrel* and Flowers' *Keg* in the 1950s. Whereas the serving of traditional cask beer is a skilled art, that of pressurised keg is not. It obtained a rapid growth in sales because it was popular with the younger drinker and because it was consistent, easily handled and served, especially in the club trade. Greene King's keg was first brewed on any scale at Biggleswade in the early 1960s. At first barrellage was small, but by 1972 it accounted for around 10 per cent of group beer sales. The company was initially uncertain about its popularity and it followed the lead of its rivals and the pressure of consumer demand.

In the 1970s Greene King sales of lager were as buoyant as those of keg. But the cost of lager brewing and promotion was quite beyond the scope of Greene King. At first it experimented with a chilled, lager type beer, *Polar*, in 1972–3. Extensive promotion, the key to good beer sales in the 1970s, was never contemplated and the venture flopped. In 1975 Greene King took a share in the equity of *Harp*. At first its stake was a modest 1·96 per cent holding, but in 1979 when *Harp* was reorganised, Greene King increased its share to 20 per cent of the equity of the new, smaller company. By this latter date over a fifth of group beer sales were of lager. There were two other similar developments. In 1973 Greene King acquired a small stake in the Taunton Cider Company (Blackthorn), and in the same year the company ceased manufacturing its own mineral waters. The stores needed complete replacement and the scale of investment was such that Greene King decided to obtain a holding in Cantrell and Cochrane. In 1978 this firm was merged with Coca Cola (Southern) Bottlers and Greene King now hold a 10 per cent share of the reorganised firm. In these arrangements co-operation with other brewers, national and independent alike, was essential because

Greene King could not itself afford the scale of promotion of soft drinks and lager products necessary to break into the free trade.

Second, pricing strategy was a continuation of the old policy of keeping bar prices a few pence behind those of the national brewers. It was one that all the regional and smaller brewers attempted. But the concept of the traditional 'wet' rent was changed in the 1970s in favour of a much more realistic 'dry' rent and tenants being charged free trade prices. Again this was policy throughout the industry. And in fact Greene King could fix prices only in their own managed houses. Unlike the nationals, however, Greene King did not turn houses over to management aggressively. It was able to give publicans, after their association's rows with Watney Mann on this issue, the assurance that no tenant would be given notice in order to turn the house over to management and that the ratio of managed to tenanted houses, about one to five, would not alter greatly. In 1982 17 per cent of Greene King houses were managed.

Third, a constant plank of policy in the 1970s was to provide a better service both to the free and tied trades. The former was achieved by the opening of depots in Norwich, Peterborough, Rayleigh and finally London in 1980. These were entirely oriented towards free trade requirements. The firm also extended its 'back-up services'—architectural and catering advice, a cellar service, and a department that produced bars and fittings—with the free trade in mind.

In all these areas the company picked its way between the lead given by the national brewers and its own traditions. Especially in its assault on the free trade it was forced along by its heavier rivals. The free trade was not won without Greene King making it loans—again a negation of the firm's past policy—and here there was always a sense that it was being outpaced. In the supply of keg and lager similar pressures were at work. This was why good, friendly service was essential. Operating on a smaller scale Greene King drew on its own traditions at this point. There was always a realisation that the nationals' pace and tactics were not right for it. Nevertheless it was a difficult contest to judge correctly, especially in the mid-1970s when Greene King was fully extended.

Accelerating growth produced difficulties of a different kind in the breweries which were required to expand output on an

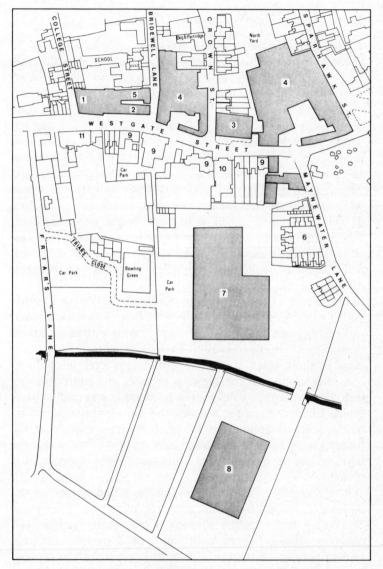

Greene King, Westgate Brewery; Bury St Edmunds, 1983

1. Maltings (drums
   fitted in Rink
   Maltings (1880) in
   1946–7)
2. Barley Store (early
   1950s rebuilding
   of 1854–5
   Foundry Malting)
3. Brew House

(1937–8)
4. Brewery
   (18th–20th
   centuries)
5. School Maltings
   (1845)
6. Maynewater
   Square (1868)
7. Wine and spirit

store (1974)
8. Draught Beer store
   (1978)
9. Offices
10. Theatre (1819)
11. Westgate House:
    Peatling and
    Cawdron's head
    offices

unprecedented scale. It was a constant battle against time to
install extra fermenting capacity and services to meet demand.
Beer output doubled in under ten years and the old Westgate
cellars were totally inadequate to meet the surge in the cask beer
trade which doubled within five years. Increasing production
demands forced Greene King into shortcuts with five-day fermentation cycles and earlier racking. Hand to mouth solutions of
these kinds, duplicated in other departments, led the company to
execute four major projects on a scale never attempted before.
The new 50,000 square feet wines and spirits store (1974), which
won a Structural Steel Design award in the following year, and
draught beer store (1978) were built on the water meadows
behind the Theatre (see the plan of the brewery, 1983, on page
255). Together they cost £3.3 million and possessed either sufficient capacity or the potential for easy extension so that their
useful life could be envisaged beyond the year 2000. Also a new
fermenting block was built on the site of the old cellars together
with a much needed new laboratory. At Biggleswade an automatic kegging plant was installed in 1976, coping with about a third
of total group beer production. There were many other innovations in these years: a five-day germination cycle in malting;
computer control of the brewing process; and 'shift' brewing
introduced in 1977 at Bury when production was pushed to its
limits. Changes in tastes and demand also necessitated adjust-
ments. The continuous growth in bottling, a feature of the
industry since before 1914, eased after the mid-1970s so that the
bottling line at Biggleswade, which needed replacement, was
closed.

It is generally held that success in the rationalisation of the
national brewing companies after the mid-1960s largely depended upon the quality of their management. As has been
explained above, Greene King had a head start in that little
rationalisation was required. Its area of operations was concentrated, and there were no frictions between a large number of
semi-autonomous breweries, which was so often the case with the
nationals. The management team at Greene King was well integrated and operated by friendly consensus. Since the directors all
represented old family interests in the company, their back-
grounds and strengths were well known. The guiding figure in the

success of the 1970s was undoubtedly the Managing Director, John Bridge—Fred King's great-grandson. He had had a long apprenticeship with the firm, stretching back to 1938, but he faced the post-1969 situation with a fresh vision. At Bury he was assisted by Martin Corke (E. W. Lake's grandson) who was in charge of the key marketing venture and by Bernard Tickner (Colonel B. E. Oliver's nephew), head brewer in 1959 and a director after 1964.[38] He kept the firm abreast of the considerable technical changes and plant expansion. Jonathan Clarke (John Clarke's son), who trained in estate management at Cambridge, was responsible for Greene King's tied houses and properties after 1968. At Biggleswade, Colonel J. A. Redman was replaced by John Banham, who continued as senior director there until 1975. Now Biggleswade is run by two Redman cousins, Simon and Timothy. After John Clarke's brief chairmanship (1969–71), he was succeeded by Sir Hugh Greene, the ex-Director General of the B.B.C. Sir Hugh had joined the Board in 1964 to keep the Greenes' association with the brewery continuous. He was a second cousin of Sir Edward Greene and a great-grandson of the firm's founder, Benjamin Greene. Like Sir Miles Dempsey, although his approach was very different, he brought a breath of the outside world to the Board. Like his father, who had been headmaster of Berkhamsted School, he had had nothing to do with brewing, but he and his brother, Graham, had a long-held interest in sampling the beers of different breweries during their holidays. He possessed a deep respect for the industry's traditions, although Benjamin Greene and his son Edward must have shifted uneasily in their graves at the prospect of William Greene's grandson heading their brewery. When he retired in 1978 he was succeeded as Chairman by John Bridge.[39]

Some things were made easier for management in the 1970s. Errors of detail at least could be avoided because constant advice was sought from professional quarters—the Institute of Brewing, the Brewers' Society, merchant bankers, stock brokers, and a variety of consultants. The independence of action of the past, enjoyed by Edward Greene and Edward Lake, was diminished. Nevertheless the firm could still rely on the two key pillars of support from their day—the tenants and the employees. Both, of course, were far better organised in the 1970s. The former were reassured by the firm's policy about managed houses and by good service and easy communications, and the latter, although entirely unionised after 1970, by continuous improvements in wages and conditions of work, bonuses, and a modest share owning scheme introduced in the last few years.

The unionisation of the work force was carried out entirely amicably. As soon as a clear majority had become members the company negotiated pay and conditions with the Transport and General Workers' Union. Its relations with union officers were good and it was amongst the earliest firms to instigate a joint management, supervisors, foremen and shop-stewards committee. Pay negotiations were undoubtedly aided by the fact that employees were represented by a single union. There has never been an official strike. This was an achievement in the mid-1970s when inflation was at its peak and the work force was fully extended in the headlong expansion of the mid-1970s, especially when this coincided with the hot summers of 1975 and 1976. The large measure of unanimity between management and employees undoubtedly aided Greene King's success in the free trade. Customers, unlike their experience with the national breweries, found deliveries were reliable because there were no serious labour disputes. Although the paternalism, so much stressed by Edward Greene and Edward Lake, has largely disappeared over the years, something of the old loyalty and continuity remains. In 1972 there were no fewer than 135 out of a total of 923 full-time employees who qualified for tankards presented on the completion of twenty-five years of service with the group.

In the 1970s, a close-knit, forward-looking management team and good tenant and employee relations have been at the heart of Greene King's emergence as a thrusting, major regional brewery. Prosperity in the future depends on these same factors. Their chances should be enhanced by the sound prospects of the region in which Greene King operates and by the considerable efficiency to be derived from major investments in plant over the past decade. It must also depend upon a continual appreciation of all that is best in their 180-year history and the time-honoured customs of country brewing.

5

In 1980 there were eighty brewery companies in the United Kingdom. Only forty years previously there had been over ten times that number. What factors led Greene King, untypically, to survive? Clearly, as this chapter has shown, a good deal of the answer rests with the decision taken by the Board in the late 1950s and early 1960s to retain independence at almost any cost. But determination in itself was not enough. The firm had to generate sufficient drive to carry through a number of innovations, especially in relation to the free trade, but also in rapidly transforming plant to extend beer, wines and spirits sales and to introduce new types of beer, so that financial performance and the range of products offered—maintaining quality was easier—would stand comparison with the national brewers. A century of total attention to the tied trade had to be relaxed. Of course, Greene King was swept along on a rising swell of consumption as real wages increased and there was a notable swing back to heavier drinking of all forms of alcohol. The trend after 1960 was not dissimilar to that which had placed Edward Greene in that league of bigger brewers between 1850 and 1880. Success of the firm in both periods, however, should not be minimised because many other breweries failed to transform themselves in comparable ways.

It is necessary to remind ourselves of Edward Greene and Edward Lake at this point, for the capacity to survive, indeed, the whole ethos of the firm, has its roots in the policies they established. They, like Fred King, were careful and efficient, and proud of their paternal role with their employees and their participation in the life of Bury St Edmunds and West Suffolk. The image of the brewery they projected was never flamboyant, but was concentrated upon tight management and a sense of service. Much of this continues today, as it did even in the 1920s and 1930s when the way forward was less clear. But before the late 1960s there was a fear of new horizons. Attempts to sell beer outside the company's tied houses were hesitant and the hotel business was generally avoided. Beliefs in efficiency and obligation, however, became so deeply ingrained that, in the heat of the merger movement in the early 1960s, they were prime factors in the determination to remain independent. Even Sir Walter Greene, who slotted so easily into the cartel of Edwardian steam-yachting, hunting, shooting magnates, and his sons, who enjoyed the smart London social round of the inter-war years, never lost their attachment to the brewery and appreciation of its wider role in East Anglia. Edward Greene, with his deep love of Suffolk and its traditions and a simple understanding of the wider political and social roles of a Victorian entrepreneur, had drummed many of his lessons into the unthinking Sir Walter. And Edward Lake and Fred King preached, in different ways, similar themes to their sons. Their traditions and views of the brewery in the community have also been handed down through five generations of brewers, the five Company Secretaries since 1887,[40] clerks, travellers, foremen and those 'families' of employees who have served the firm so loyally since the 1850s, and imbibed, in some degree, by those who have joined its management since 1917—the Clarkes, Olivers and Redmans. Together they have produced a company in which the values of loyalty and tradition are thoroughly ingrained, but which after the late 1960s fortunately have not inhibited expansion in a rapidly changing industry.

Over the years the holdings of 'family and friends' have diminished and institutional shareholders now hold an influential stake in the company. In some ways this shift in ownership has increased the drive to stay independent. Many breweries in single ownership failed through problems of inheritance and taxation. It will be interesting for the next historian of the firm to assess, from a distance, the impact of the great changes of the 1970s, to recount whether the firm retains its total family identification, and to speculate further about the continuity of its traditions.

Appendices, Notes
& Index

APPENDIX ONE
A Note on Sources

I have written this book from several sources. Its basis is, of course, the papers of the firm itself. Minute books and accounts have survived since 1887, and there is a good deal of miscellaneous material, particularly deeds and correspondence about individual public houses, from 1870 onwards. Since the firm was always efficiently run its minute books and accounts are detailed, especially between 1934 and 1958 when Frank Bevis was Secretary. But undoubtedly a great deal of material was destroyed by E. L. D. Lake and the Secretary during the Second World War. Their zeal for the War Effort was such that they obeyed government salvage drives to the letter. Greene King absorbed Simpson's of Baldock in 1954 and Wells and Winch of Biggleswade in 1961. Material concerning the former, except for a series of partnership and property deeds and a superb valuation of 1858, is sparse for the period before 1934. Wells and Winch's papers have survived more fully, especially for the years after 1899. Ken Page at Biggleswade has sorted these out and added much ancillary material. Mr J. Collett-White of the Bedfordshire Record Office has compiled an invaluable guide to the pre-1900 legal records which Greene King (Biggleswade) deposited there. Unfortunately, little correspondence concerning any of these three breweries remains.

I have also used oral evidence where I could reconcile it with the written record. Mr R. H. Hempstead made a series of recordings with the following in the mid-1970s: Mr F. W. Andrews, Mr R. G. Baldwin, Mr J. Borley, Mr A. Brazier, Major John Clarke, Mr C. Coe, Mr and Mrs V. J. Covill, Mr S. Fuller, Dr Raymond Greene, Mr H. Hargreaves, Mr O. H. Heyhoe, Mrs E. Hoxley, Mr J. Jacobs, Captain H. N. Lake, R.N., Mr W. H. (Tim) Lovelace, Mr R. Sandry, Mr J. Scott, Mr H. Sparrow and Mrs I. Whiting. In some cases their memories went back before the Great War. I also made further recordings with Mr Heyhoe and Captain Lake, and I have talked to another generation of directors and employees of the firm. No footnote references are given to these recordings and interviews or to the internal business records of Greene King.

Because the pre-1887 period was covered so scantily by the brewery's own records I was forced to use other sources which, in the event, produced a far better return than I had anticipated. Even so there were disappointments. Few papers of the senior branch of the Greenes (the Baronets) or Benjamin Buck Greene have, to my knowledge, survived. Those that do have been collected over the years by the late Dr Raymond Greene and his uncle, the late Sir Graham Greene. They are very miscellaneous, including stray letters and press cuttings, much genealogical material and some papers relating to the St Kitts estates. The King side of the enterprise was easier to reconstruct as most of Fred King's voluminous legal papers have been retained by the firm's solicitors, Partridge and Wilson. They also keep, and regularly use, the documents created each time Greene King took over another brewery or made a debenture issue. Greene King's London accountants, first appointed by Fred King in 1868, also hold a few early balance sheets and financial compilations.

In addition to these business and family papers I had to rely heavily upon the Bury newspapers between 1800 and 1914. Especially when Edward Greene (1815–91) was M.P. for Bury almost continuously after 1865—the golden age of extended reporting in the provincial press—they contained an enormous amount of information about his family, politics and brewery. Mrs Ann Reeve collected card index notes from the newspapers for many of the years between 1800 and 1914. The Bury St Edmunds rate-books, church and chapel records and, on a wider scale, some of the Parliamentary Papers relating to the brewing industry and the West Indies were invaluable. With these, and

family papers of the Blakes and Molineux-Montgomeries, I was
able to reconstruct the affairs of Benjamin Greene and his sons in
far greater detail than I had thought possible.

I also read the volumes of the *Brewers' Journal* for 1870 to the
mid-1950s, and, when these seemed less useful for my purpose,
the *Brewing Trade Review*. This was necessary because there is, at
the moment, no extended history of brewing after 1830. Peter
Mathias's volume, which covers the 1700–1830 period, is a
remarkable book and although Tom Corran is now writing a
second volume, sponsored by the Brewers' Society, to cover the
years between 1830 and 1969, it will not survey the industry on
Mathias's grand scale. I have also found the work of J. E. Vaizey
and the more recent publications of K. H. Hawkins useful.* My
volume is intended to fill the gap of a sound history of a major
regional brewery.

---

* See P. Mathias, *The Brewing Industry in England 1700–1830* (1959); J. E.
Vaizey, *The Brewing Industry, 1886–1952* (1960) and 'The Brewing Industry' in
P. L. Cook and R. Cohen (ed.) *Effects of Mergers* (1958); K. H. Hawkins, *A
History of Bass Charrington* (1978) and (with C. L. Pass), *The Brewing Industry,
A Study in Industrial Organisation and Public Policy* (1979).

APPENDIX TWO

Tables

Table 1: Bushels of malt brewed in Suffolk, 1830–90*

Year	[1] No. of common brewers	Bushels of malt brewed by [1]	[2] Total licensed victuallers	[3] No. of [2] who brewed own beer	Bushels of malt brewed by [3]	[4] Persons licensed to sell beer (beer houses)	[5] No. of [4] who brewed own beer	Bushels of malt brewed by [5]	% brewed by [1]	% brewed by [2]	% brewed by [5]
1830	20	87,572	674	234	141,092	402	191	43,325	32.2	51.9	15.9
1840	26	100,927	701	256	154,062	577	229	48,077	33.3	50.8	15.9
1850	32	127,704	688	232	125,970	492	221	53,851	41.5	41.0	17.5
1860	21	163,445	648	158	81,592	432	155	21,299	61.4	30.6	8.0
1870†	23	139,690	514	65	36,693	343	46	4,316	77.4	20.1	2.5
1880‡	26	181,778	498	27	10,427	312	17	1,897	93.6	5.4	1.0
1890	23	264,522	675	40	21,921	388	15	3,228	91.3	7.6	1.1

* Compiled from 'Accounts and Papers', 1831–2, XXIV, 27, etc.

† Too much should not be read into the decline in malt consumed in 1870 for the excise collection district was changed from 'Suffolk' to 'Ipswich' and part of the original area was possibly included in neighbouring districts.

‡ After 1880 the figures became increasingly unreliable as indicators of brewing production. Gladstone's 'freeing of the mash tun' from excise control in 1880 allowed brewers to use increasing amounts of brewing sugars to supplement malt.

Table 2: The partnership of Edward Greene and Son, 1876–86*

(a) *Capital profits and loans* (in £s)

Year ending 31 May	[a] Capital Account	[b] Mortgage Account	[c] Total† Profits	[c] as % of previous year's capital [a]	[d] To partners' accounts	To capital account	'Cash left in Bank'	Balance in credit/overdrawn
1876	144,082	—	—	—	—	—	—	—
1877	146,634	3,850	23,104	16·0	19,682	2,552	870	—
1878	151,496	2,650	22,273	15·2	16,223	4,861	72	1,986
1879	165,601	3,950	23,141	15·3	12,975	14,105	—	-1,913
1880	180,042	3,950	24,699	14·9	17,643	14,441	—	-7,999‡
1881	175,727	3,950	23,333	13·0	19,281	-4,316	368	—
1882	181,291	3,950	24,555	14·0	19,407	5,464	52	—
1883	191,467	4,250	24,718	13·6	16,545	10,570	-2,346	—
1884	193,671	24,250§	24,856	13·0	19,993	2,396	181	—
1885	190,543	12,700	24,020	12·4	17,674	8,533	-2,005	—
1886	195,963	9,600	26,767	14·0	21,209	5,420	137	—

* Source: Private Ledger No. 1.

† Brewery profits (see table 2b, column f) were shared between E. Greene, E. W. Greene and E. W. Lake in the ratio of 9 : 2 : 1 and the much smaller maltings profits 8 : 2 : 1 : 1 (Pead).

‡ The overdraft in the Balance Sheets was covered by a bank loan of £2,359, the sale of houses £1,300 and cash lent by E. Greene, £5,642.

§ Stowmarket Brewery was purchased in 1883–4 for £26,450.

Table 2: The partnership of Edward Greene and Son, 1876–86
(b) *Sales of beer, profits and costs* (in £s)

Year ending 31 May	[a] Sales of beer	[b] Other items*	[c] Cost of malt brewed	[d] Other items†	[e] Stocks of beer and materials	[f] Net Profit
1876	—	—	—	—	11,232	—
1877	79,627	2,957	30,221	31,696	12,099	21,420
1878	80,002	3,568	31,665	30,674	11,319	20,450
1879	82,854	4,030	39,054	29,652	14,017	20,966
1880	81,476	4,082	33,936	31,451	15,991	22,055
1881	82,922	4,374	25,462‡	41,372	16,381	20,852
1882	82,965	4,480	18,379	46,606	16,889	22,968
1883	90,173	5,349	19,348	52,509	16,002	22,778
1884	94,794	6,426	19,855	59,708	16,478	22,132
1885	90,058	6,643	19,503	57,445	18,071	21,346
1886	86,193	6,838	18,165	49,792	17,346	24,358

* Chiefly rents and sales of spent grains. Wine and spirit profits were negligible.

† Includes sugar, hops, keep of horses, Beer Duty (after 1880), interest, depreciation and a large item, 'Incidental Expenses', which must have included labour.

‡ The Malt Tax was replaced in 1880 by Beer Duty and the fall in malt costs, 1880–2, reflects this fact.

Table 3: Greene King and Sons: public houses, 1887–1954*

Year ending 31 May	[1] Owned	[2] Bought in year	[3] Sold or licence surrendered or dropped	[4] Leased	Total of all tied houses [1] + [4]
1887	148	—	—	—	—
1888	189	41	0	—	—
1889	202	13	0	50	252
1890	210	8	0	50	260
1891	218	11	3	46	264
1892	229	14	3	45	274
1893	238	9	0	45	283
1894	262	25	1	45	307
1895	262	3	3	43	305
1896	278	16	0	42	320
1897	286	10	2	37	323

APPENDIX 2

Table 3 (*contd*)

Year ending 31 May	[1] Owned	[2] Bought in year	[3] Sold or licence surrendered or dropped	[4] Leased	Total of all tied houses [1] + [4]
1898	306	20	0	34	340
1899	320	14	0	31	351
1900	326	6	0	29	355
1901	336	10	0	30	366
1902	351	15	0	27	378
1903	347	1	4	25	372
1904	347	3	3	25	372
1905	365	18	0	24	389
1906	363	0	2	24	387
1907	356	0	7	24	380
1908	358	3	1	21	379
1909	353	1	5	18	371
1910	349	1	5	18	367
1911	344	0	5	18	362
1912	345	4	3	19	364
1913	347	6	4	16	363
1914	344	2	5	15	359
1915	341	0	3	15	356
1916	344	7	4	14	358
1917†	353	18	9	27	380
1918‡	389	57	21	26	415
1919§	436	55	8	24	460
1920	437	6	7	20	457
1921	433	7	11	18	451
1922	431	4	6	17	448
1923	429	4	6	16	445
1924	426	4	7	16	442
1925	472**	49	3	20	492
1926	467	2	7	20	487
1927	470	6	3	18	488
1928	466	1	5	19	485
1929	465	2	3	17	482
1930	463	3	6	16	479
1931	490††	29	2	23	513
1932	492	2	0	20	512
1933	490	6	8	20	510
1934	490	4	4	20	510
1935	493	6	3	20	513
1936	490	1	4	19	509
1937	491	2	1	21	512

270

APPENDIX 2

Table 3 (*contd*)

Year ending 31 May	[1] Owned	[2] Bought in year	[3] Sold or licence surrendered or dropped	[4] Leased	Total of all tied houses [1] + [4]
1938	495	8	4	19	514
1939	495	3	3	18	513
1940	496	2	1	19	515
1941	501	7	2	20	521
1942	498	6	9	20	518
1943	499	1	0	20	519
1944	499	0	0	19	518
1945	499	0	0	19	518
1946	501	3	1	18	519
1947	499	0	2	17	516
1948	502	3	0	14	516
1949	505	4	1	11	516
1950	504	0	1	11	515
1951	506	4	2	10	516
1952	505	3	4	10	515
1953	505	3	3	9	514
1954	505	2	2	9	514

* Taken from the Directors' minute books, and annual stock books.

† Messrs Clarkes' Risbygate Brewery was taken over in 1917. It owned 15 public houses and leased 13.

‡ Christmas's Haverhill brewery was bought with 49 houses.

§ Oliver's Sudbury brewery was taken over on 1 May 1919 with 51 houses.

** In 1925 Bailey and Tebbutt's Panton Brewery, Cambridge, was purchased. It had 48 licensed houses and a 'large free trade'.

†† Ogden's Brewery at March (Cambs.) was bought with 28 freehold and six leasehold houses for £50,500 in October 1930.

In 1954 Simpson's of Baldock was bought with 130 houses and in 1961 Wells and Winch with 287 houses. In October 1971 there were 452 licensed houses and 44 off-licences served from Bury; 337 and five respectively from Biggleswade and 28 and one respectively from Rayment's—a total of 866 outlets. At its peak in the early 1960s there were over 930. In 1981 this number had fallen to 730.

Table 4(a): Greene King and Sons: beer sales, 1887–1919*

Year ending 31 May	Bulk barrels	Value of beer sales (£,000s)	Year ending 31 May	Bulk barrels	Value of beer sales (£,000s)
1887	63,646†		1904	74,172	138
1888	62,310	117‡	1905	73,082	135
1889	59,745	113	1906	73,550	135
1890	63,335	120	1907	73,568	135
1891	63,189	120	1908	71,169	131
1892	63,429	121	1909	71,324	131
1893	63,394	121	1910	70,450	130
1894	61,823	118	1911	70,098	130
1895	61,764	117	1912	73,198	139
1896	63,507	119	1913	72,364	138
1897	63,079	119	1914	75,142	144
1898	65,602	123	1915	76,071	170
1899	71,050	132	1916	71,759	190
1900	72,056	134	1917	63,665	197
1901	73,212	136	1918	61,141	235
1902	74,004	138	1919	58,659	224
1903	75,378	140			

* Source: Private Ledger and Annual Stock Books.

† In the year preceding the merger Greene's output was 43,593 barrels, King's 20,053 barrels.

‡ Profits from beer sales provided a high proportion of total gross profits: for the years 1890–94 they averaged 88·2 per cent; 1900–4, 82·4; and only by 1920–4 had they fallen to 77·8 per cent. The rest was chiefly made up from rents, wine and spirit and mineral water sales.

Table 4(b): Greene King and Sons: beer sales, 1919–32 (bulk barrellage unless otherwise stated)*

Year ending 31 May	Bury	Value of Bury sales (£,000s)	Haverhill	Sudbury	Cambridge	Total
1919	58,659	224	?	?	—	86,589
1920	77,057	382	10,987†	21,284	—	109,328
1921	67,440	423	9,510	19,786	—	96,736
1922	59,457	386	8,383	17,303	—	85,143
1923	47,482	304	6,751	14,122	—	68,355
1924	49,154	268	3,480	14,589	—	67,223
1925	53,429	290	—	14,976	3,885	72,290

Table 4(b) (*contd*)

Year ending 31 May	Bury	Value of Bury sales (£,000s)	Haverhill	Sudbury	Cambridge	Total
1926	55,987	310	—	14,736	12,625	83,348
1927	57,719	323	—	14,237	13,271	85,227
1928	55,920	313	—	14,941	12,771	83,632
1929	55,517	314	—	13,554	12,356	81,427
1930	56,134	321	—	13,643	12,340	82,117
1931	58,781	336	—	12,948	11,024	82,753
1932	51,356	322	—	10,829	9,029	71,214

* Source: Directors' minute books and annual stock books.

† The Sudbury and Haverhill Brewery figures were presented separately from 1 January 1920. Haverhill was closed 1923–4. The Panton Brewery (Cambridge) figures are included from 1 February 1925. Sudbury Brewery was closed June 1932.

Table 4(c): Westgate (Bury) beer sales and duty paid, 1933–61*

Year ending 31 May	Bulk barrels	Value of sales (£,000)	Duty paid (£,000)	Year	Barrels	Value of sales (£,000)	Duty paid (£,000)
1933	56,893	372	183	1948	96,220	1,306	831
1934	61,356	333	144	1949	82,688	1,296	850
1935	65,690	359	153	1950	75,891	1,133	687
1936	68,592	375	154	1951	68,879	1,058	622
1937	70,981	391	165	1952	66,954	1,103	599
1938	74,657	411	171	1953	67,649	1,142	601
1939	73,568	405	166	1954	66,305	1,124	583
1940	73,568	461	224	1955	64,643	1,110	544
1941	85,283	726	426	1956	68,147	1,186	558
1942	93,913	847	486	1957	66,296	1,207	548
1943	96,323	1,131	678	1958†	68,533	1,260	539
1944	118,682	1,515	867	1959	75,864	1,367	580
1945	112,779	1,440	890	1960	81,428	1,309	496
1946	107,284	1,368	866	1961	85,914	1,379	532
1947	93,202	1,126	704				

* Source: Annual stock books and private ledger. The Cambridge Brewery and Rayment's figures have apparently not survived for much of this period. They were not recorded by the main Board, nor of course included in the Westgate (Bury) ledgers. Together the two small breweries contributed around 20–25 per cent of total production.

† Even in the late 1950s beer profits were still contributing well over 75 per cent of total gross profits, which shows how reliant Greene King were upon selling beer in their own tied houses.

Table 5: Greene King and Sons: profits and dividends, 1887–1947 (£,000 unless otherwise stated)*

Year ending 31 May	[a] Net assets	[b] Profits net of depreciation	[c] Return on capital employed [b] as % of [a]	[d]† Allocation of profits				% dividend on nominal value of equity	[e] Accumulated balance of general reserves
				Interest	Dividends before tax	To general reserves	Other named reserve funds		
1888	573	36	6·3	6	27	3	—	9	3
1889	573	34	5·9	6	25·5	2·5	—	8	5·5
1890	578	36	6·2	6	25·5	4·5	—	8	10
1891	580	33	5·7	6	25	2	—	8	12
1892	591	33	5·6	6	25	1	—	8	13
1893	589	35	5·9	6	25	3	—	8	16
1894	608	35	5·8	7	25	3	—	8	19
1895	611	35	5·7	7	25	3	—	8	22
1896	619	40	6·5	7	25	8	—	8	30
1897	632	45	7·1	7	25	12	—	8	42
1898	644	44	6·8	7	25	13	—	8	55
1899	665	53‡	8·0	7	25	11	—	8	66
1900	677	54	8·0	7	26	20	—	9	86
1901	696	52	7·5	7	26	14	5	9	100
1902	711	52	7·3	7	26	15	3	10	115
1903	727	53	7·3	7	28	16	2	10	131
1904	745	55	7·4	7	28	7	13	10	138
1905	748	52	7·0	7	28	16	—	10	154
1906	763	50	6·6	7	28	16	—	10	170
1907	812	53	6·8	7	28	18	—	10	188

274

1908	825	51	6·4	7	28	15	—	10	203
1909	839	51	6·3	7	28	16	—	10	219
1910	825	48	5·8	7	28	13	—	10	232
1911	839	49	5·8	7	28	16	—	10	248
1912	646	50	7·7	6	28	15	—	10	93
1913	651	44	6·1	5	28	12	6	10	105
1914	651	47	7·2	5	28	8	4	10	113
1915	660	51	7·7	4	27	15	12	9	128
1916	670	41	6·1	4	23	2	—	12	140§
1917	699	48	6·9	3	26	15	10	12	186
1918	744	56	7·5	5	26	30	30	12	171
1919	821	78	9·5	4	41	20	5	12	152
1920	810	84	10·4	4	50	—	—	12	189
1921	814	62	7·6	4	50	5	5	12	179
1922	813	65	8·0	4	54	—	5	14½	170
1923	812	61	7·5	4	46	5	8	12	164
1924	809	61	7·5	4	53	16	17	14½	168
1925	859	61	7·1	4	46	10	24	16	168
1926	881	89	10·1	4	53	10	25	17	188
1927	913	97	10·6	4	57	10	20	18	244
1928	1,039	104	10·0	4	66	6	21	18	257
1929	1,059	107	10·1	4	73	—	30	18	262
1930	1,067	108	10·1	4	73	—	25	16	249
1931	1,063	108	10·2	4	73	5	14	16	243
1932	1,063	97	9·1	4	68	—	21	16	252
1933	1,065	91	8·6	4	68	—	30	18	261
1934	1,075	93	8·7	4	68	6	15	18	265
1935	1,096	109	9·9	4	75				281
1936	1,103	118	10·7	4	75				349

Table 5 (contd)

276

Year ending 31 May	[a] Net assets	[b] Profits net of depreciation	[c] Return on capital employed [b] as % of [a]	[d]† Allocation of profits — Interest	Dividends before tax	To general reserves	Other named reserve funds	% dividend on nominal value of equity	[e] Accumulated balance of general reserves
1937	1,216	122	10·0	4	80	—	36	18	341
1938	1,208	119	9·9	4	80	—	33	18	295
1939	1,166	120	10·3	4	80	—	34	18	305
1940	1,179	121	10·3	4	80	—	35	18	348
1941	1,219	120	9·8	4	80	—	38	18	415
1942	1,288	121	9·4	4	80	—	27	18	464
1943	1,347	121	9·0	4	80	—	32	18	388
1944	1,279	122	9·5	4	80	—	25	18	410
1945	1,315	122	9·3	4	80	—	27	18	618
1946	1,368	140	10·3	—	49**	—	98	21	679
1947	1,544	154	10·0	—	56	—	135	23·5	736

* Source: Directors' minute books and private ledgers.

† If the total of [d] does not equal [b], the difference is accounted for by the balance carried forward in the accounts.

‡ An additional £10,000 was 'written off Plant, Machinery etc.'

§ After 1916 this column represents total reserves, but not the large sum set aside for Fire Insurance, License and Workmen's Compensation Funds. Large upward movements as in 1917, 1927 and 1936 are accounted for by premiums on share creations, between 1941 and 1947 by reserves against tax, reconstruction and repairs.

** Dividends for 1946-7 were tax deducted at source.

APPENDIX 2

Table 6: Greene King and Sons: financial results, 1948–81*

Year ending 31 May	[a] Trading profit before tax† (£,000)	[b] Tax (£,000)	[c] Dividends less tax (£,000)	[d] Retained profits (£,000)	[e] Total net assets (£,000)	[f] Return on capital employed [a] as % of [e] (£,000)
1948‡	350	172	56	122	1,706	20·5
1949	254	123	56	75	1,756	12·8
1950	203	104	56	43	1,722	11·8
1951	195	102	50	43	1,719	11·3
1952	215	117	49	49	1,737	12·4
1953	217	117	52	48	1,785	12·2
1954	229	117	56	56	1,794	12·7
1955	256	142	64	50	2,400	10·7
1956	290	166	65	59	2,434	11·9
1957	311	182	68	61	2,510	12·4
1958	331	183	68	81	2,561	12·9
1959	354	165	85	104	2,614	13·5
1960	399	183	100	116	2,779	14·4
1961	433	213	105	115	4,107	10·5
1962	626	323	150	153	5,147	12·2
1963	621	319	150	152	5,281	11·8
1964	719	376	176	167	5,499	13·1
1965	801	375	190	236	5,818	13·8
1966	750	277	260	213	6,658	11·3
1967	787	315	319	153	6,967	11·3
1968	803	319	299	185	7,129	11·3
1969	892	363	311	218	7,351	12·1
1970	923	376	343	204	7,622	12·1
1971	1,073	400	386	287	8,006	13·4
1972	1,277	479	461	337	8,797	14·5
1973	1,674	658	384	632	9,810	17·1
1974	1,838	832	345	661	11,311	16·2
1975	2,003	829	366	808	12,443	16·1
1976	2,774	1,344	577	853	13,426	20·2
1977	3,613	1,773	669	1,171	17,528	20·6
1978	4,252	2,134	746	1,372	19,568	21·7
1979	5,089	1,893	971	2,225	22,796	22·3
1980	5,802	2,082	1,131	2,589	26,288	22·1
1981	6,561	1,572	1,299	3,690	29,148	22·5

* Source: Directors' reports and accounts.

† But after deductions of debenture and loan interest, and depreciation.

‡ After 1948 accounts were presented differently to comply with the Companies Act of 1947.

Table 7: Greene King and Sons: Tree of brewery acquisitions (number of houses attached, free and leasehold, in parentheses)

Left	Year	Year	Right
		1961	WELLS & WINCH LTD Biggleswade, Beds. (287)
MAULDON & SONS LTD Sudbury, Suffolk (23)	1958		
HERBERT CAWDRON & CO. LTD* Fakenham, Norfolk (Merged with Thos. Peatling to form Peatling & Cawdron)	1954	1954	SIMPSON'S BREWERY LTD Baldock, Herts. (130)
THOMAS PEATLING & CO. LTD* King's Lynn, Norfolk	1934		
THOMAS PRENTICE & CO. Stowmarket (0)	1933		
		1931	RAYMENT & CO. LTD Furneux Pelham, Herts. (28)
OGDEN & SONS March, Cambs. (34)	1930		
		1925	BAILEY & TEBBUTT LTD Panton Brewery, Cambridge (48)
OLIVER BROS. Sudbury Brewery, Suffolk (51)	1919		
		1918	F. C. CHRISTMAS & CO. Haverhill Brewery, Suffolk (49)
CLARKE BROS. Risbygate Brewery Bury St Edmunds, Suffolk (28)	1917		
OLIVER GOSLING Bocking Brewery Bocking, Essex (19)	1904		
		1902	SNELL & RAVEN Wethersfield, Essex (15)
MOODY'S BREWERY Newmarket, Suffolk (10)	1896		
Colchester Brewery of STEWARD & PATTESON (28)	1893		
JABEZ RANKIN Orange Tree Brewery Braintree, Essex (8)	1891	1891	CHARLTON'S BREWERY Fakenham, Norfolk (11)
		1887	JENNERS BREWERY Kedington, Suffolk (22)
E. GREENE & SON at Westgate Brewery since 1806	1887		F. W. KING & SON St Edmunds Brewery founded 1869

* Non-brewing companies.

APPENDIX THREE

The Genealogies

The following pages trace the Greenes, the Kings and Maulkins, and the Lakes from their earliest known dates to the present day. As it is not feasible to show the entire family on one page, except in the case of the Lakes, the names of the leading individuals in this history and directors of the breweries are shown in bold, to enable the reader to follow the connections with the brewery more clearly.

On page 282 Thomas Greene of Oundle was the son of Benjamin Greene II and Sarah Baggerley. On page 284 Edward Greene was the third son of Benjamin Greene III, and on page 286 William Greene was the fifth son of Benjamin Greene III.

The abbreviations d. = daughter; *b.*, *m.*, *d.* = born, married, died, respectively.

THE GREENES

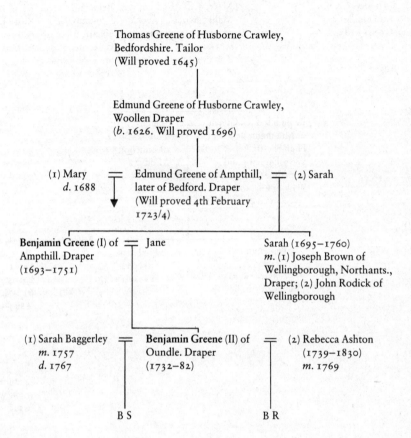

Thomas Greene of Husborne Crawley,
Bedfordshire. Tailor
(Will proved 1645)

Edmund Greene of Husborne Crawley,
Woollen Draper
(b. 1626. Will proved 1696)

(1) Mary ══ Edmund Greene of Ampthill, ══ (2) Sarah
d. 1688   later of Bedford. Draper
             (Will proved 4th February
             1723/4)

Benjamin Greene (I) of ══ Jane   Sarah (1695–1760)
Ampthill. Draper   m. (1) Joseph Brown of
(1693–1751)   Wellingborough, Northants.,
                                        Draper; (2) John Rodick of
                                        Wellingborough

(1) Sarah Baggerley ══ **Benjamin Greene** (II) of ══ (2) Rebecca Ashton
m. 1757   Oundle. Draper   (1739–1830)
d. 1767   (1732–82)   m. 1769

B S   B R

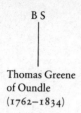

B S

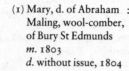

B R

Thomas Greene
of Oundle
(1762–1834)

(1) Mary, d. of Abraham
Maling, wool-comber,
of Bury St Edmunds
m. 1803
d. without issue, 1804

= **Benjamin Greene** (III) of Bury St
Edmunds, later of Russell
Square, Bloomsbury, London.
Co-owner of Buck & Greene's
brewery, 1806–36
(1780–1860)

Benjamin Buck Greene
of Midgham, Berks. J.P.
High Sheriff
1865. Director and
sometime Governor of the
Bank of England
(1808–1902)

= Isabella, d. of
Thomas Blyth
of Limehouse,
Middx.
(1811–88)

Benjamin
Greene
(1839–1916)

Frederick
Greene
(1841–1914)

Henry David
Greene,
Barrister, Q.C
J.P., M.P.
(1843–1915)

4 children,
none with
issue

(2) Catherine, d. of Rev. Thomas
Smith (1749–1801), Minister, Howard
Chapel, Bedford, by his wife Elizabeth
(1750–92), only d. of Zachariah
Carleton of London, Banker. *m.* 1805
(1783–1855)

John Greene = Elizabeth
of Birmingham, Carleton
Banker Smith
(1777–1844) (1777–1825)

John Greene = (1) Margaretta, d. of
of Bury St Rev. H. Y. Smythies
Edmunds, Attorney. of Stanground,
J.P. Hunts.
Twice Mayor *m.* 1836
of Bury (1812–53)
(1810–67)

(continued on p. 284)

Harriet, d. of John Jones   2 d.   John Smythies
of Grove, Church   un-*m.*   Greene of Bury
Stretton, Salop,   St Edmunds,
Banker   Solicitor
m. 1879   (1842–84)

John Wollaston
Greene, Solicitor
(1869–1925)

(1) Emily, 4th d. of		Edward **Greene** of Nether		(2) Dorothea, d. of
Rev. H. Y. Smythies	=	Hall, Thurston, Suffolk,	=	C. Prideaux-Brune
m. 1840		M.P., D.L.; Owner of		and widow of
(1820–48)		Greene's Brewery after		Rear-Admiral Sir
		1836. First Chairman,		William Hoste, Baron⊸
		Greene King, 1887–91		*m.* 1870
		(1815–91)		(1827–1912)

Sir (Edward) Walter Greene, of
Nether Hall, Baronet (created
1900), M.P., J.P. and D.L. for
Suffolk and Worcestershire.
High Sheriff of Suffolk 1897.
Chairman, Greene King, 1891–1920
(1842–1920)

Emily Smythies (1841–1924)
m. 1864 Frederick
Machell Smith

3
oth⊸
d.

**Sir Walter Raymond
Greene**, Baronet,
D.S.O., M.P. Director,
Greene King 1891–
1947, Chairman 1922–3
(Unmarried)
(1869–1947)

**Sir Edward Allan
Greene**, Baronet,
M.C., T.D. Director,
Greene King 1920–
1964, Chairman 1923–55
(*d.* without issue)
(1882–1966)

Kathleen Smith,
m. Lt. Col. F. B.
Isherwood

Christopher Isherwood
(*b.* 1904)

(continued on p. 286)

(Henry) Charles Greene (1821–40)	William Greene (1824–81)	Charlotte, d. of T. W. Smith of Wrawby, Lincs. *m.* 1854 (1831–1904)

Sir William Graham Greene of
Harston House, Cambs., K.C.B.,
J.P. Permanent Secretary to
the Admiralty 1911–17;
Permanent Secretary,
Ministry of Munitions 1917–20
(1857–1950)

(Charles) Raymond Greene,
M.A., M.D., F.R.C.P.,
Endocrinologist.
Senior Medical Officer,
Mount Everest Expedition,
1933
(1901–1982)

(Henry) Graham Greene,
C.H., B.A., Hon. D.Litt.
Author. (*b.* 1904)

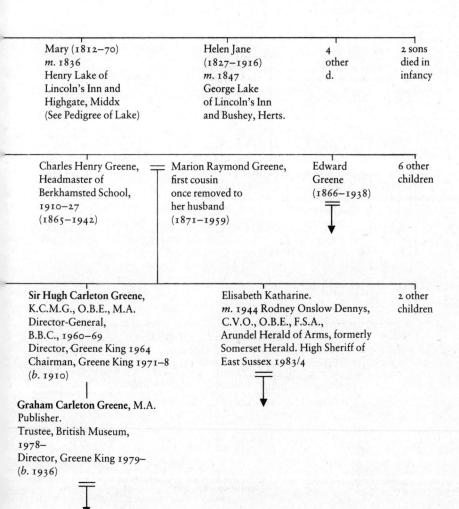

Mary (1812–70)
m. 1836
Henry Lake of
Lincoln's Inn and
Highgate, Middx
(See Pedigree of Lake)

Helen Jane
(1827–1916)
m. 1847
George Lake
of Lincoln's Inn
and Bushey, Herts.

4
other
d.

2 sons
died in
infancy

Charles Henry Greene,
Headmaster of
Berkhamsted School,
1910–27
(1865–1942)

Marion Raymond Greene,
first cousin
once removed to
her husband
(1871–1959)

Edward
Greene
(1866–1938)

6 other
children

Sir Hugh Carleton Greene,
K.C.M.G., O.B.E., M.A.
Director-General,
B.B.C., 1960–69
Director, Greene King 1964
Chairman, Greene King 1971–8
(b. 1910)

Graham Carleton Greene, M.A.
Publisher.
Trustee, British Museum,
1978–
Director, Greene King 1979–
(b. 1936)

Elisabeth Katharine.
m. 1944 Rodney Onslow Dennys,
C.V.O., O.B.E., F.S.A.,
Arundel Herald of Arms, formerly
Somerset Herald. High Sheriff of
East Sussex 1983/4

2 other
children

THE KINGS & MAULKINS

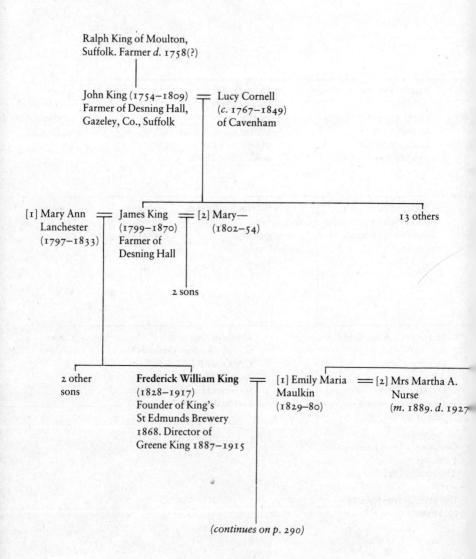

Ralph King of Moulton,
Suffolk. Farmer *d.* 1758(?)

John King (1754–1809) ══ Lucy Cornell
Farmer of Desning Hall,   (*c.* 1767–1849)
Gazeley, Co., Suffolk   of Cavenham

[1] Mary Ann ══ James King ══ [2] Mary—   13 others
Lanchester   (1799–1870)   (1802–54)
(1797–1833)   Farmer of
               Desning Hall

2 sons

2 other   **Frederick William King** ══ [1] Emily Maria ══ [2] Mrs Martha A.
sons   (1828–1917)   Maulkin   Nurse
             Founder of King's   (1829–80)   (*m.* 1889. *d.* 1927)
             St Edmunds Brewery
             1868. Director of
             Greene King 1887–1915

(continues on p. 290)

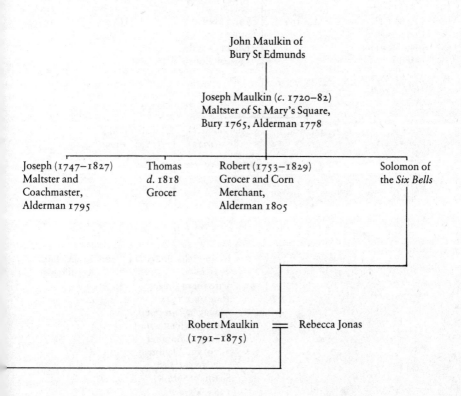

John Maulkin of
Bury St Edmunds

Joseph Maulkin (*c.* 1720–82)
Maltster of St Mary's Square,
Bury 1765, Alderman 1778

Joseph (1747–1827)   Thomas   Robert (1753–1829)   Solomon of
Maltster and   *d.* 1818   Grocer and Corn   the *Six Bells*
Coachmaster,   Grocer   Merchant,
Alderman 1795   Alderman 1805

Robert Maulkin ══ Rebecca Jonas
(1791–1875)

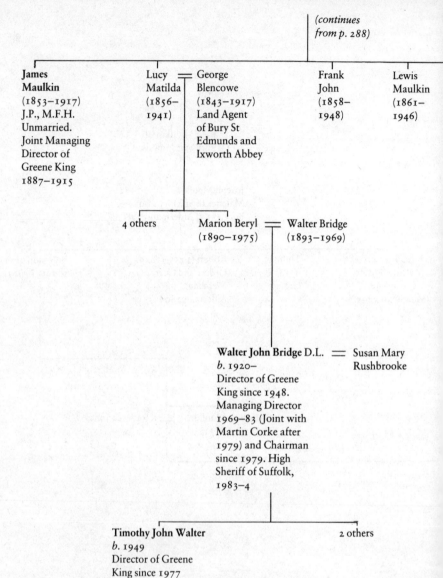

(continues from p. 288)

James Maulkin (1853–1917) J.P., M.F.H. Unmarried. Joint Managing Director of Greene King 1887–1915

Lucy Matilda (1856–1941) = George Blencowe (1843–1917) Land Agent of Bury St Edmunds and Ixworth Abbey

Frank John (1858–1948)

Lewis Maulkin (1861–1946)

4 others

Marion Beryl (1890–1975) = Walter Bridge (1893–1969)

Walter John Bridge D.L. = Susan Mary Rushbrooke
b. 1920–
Director of Greene King since 1948. Managing Director 1969–83 (Joint with Martin Corke after 1979) and Chairman since 1979. High Sheriff of Suffolk, 1983–4

Timothy John Walter
b. 1949
Director of Greene King since 1977

2 others

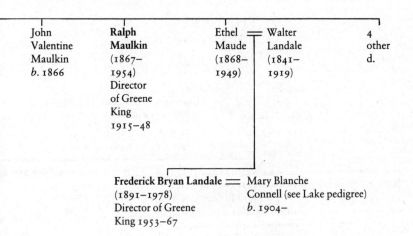

| John Valentine Maulkin *b.* 1866 | **Ralph Maulkin** (1867– 1954) Director of Greene King 1915–48 | Ethel Maude (1868– 1949) | Walter Landale (1841– 1919) | 4 other d. |

Frederick Bryan Landale ══ Mary Blanche
(1891–1978)   Connell (see Lake pedigree)
Director of Greene   *b.* 1904–
King 1953–67

THE LAKES

Henry Lake
of Lincoln's Inn and
Highgate. Solicitor

＝

Mary (1812–70) d. of
Benjamin Greene of Bury St Edmunds,
Suffolk. *m.* 1836

H. J. Lake
[3rd son]
Barrister

Edward William Lake
[6th son] (1851–1922)
J.P. Partner of E. Greene & Son,
1875–87. Managing Director of
Greene King 1887–1919.
Chairman 1920–22. 6 times
Mayor of Bury

＝

Blanche Frampton Dewé
m. 1877, *d.* 1913

**Vice-Admiral
W. J. C. Lake**, C.B.E. *d.* 1952
Manager of Rayment's
1931–38, of the Panton
Brewery 1938–48. Director
of Greene King 1946–52

Mary Blanche
(1878–1904)
m. 1902
Charles Connell

**Edward Lance(lot)
Dewé Lake**
(1881–1946)
J.P. Un-*m.*
Managing Director,
Greene King, 1919–46.
Chairman, Brewers'
Society 1934–36.
9 times
Mayor of Bury

Muriel Dewé
(1881–1971)
[twin with
Lance]

Harold Walter Lake
(1882–1960) M.C., J.P.
No issue. Director,
Greene King
1922–37 and
1946–60. Chairman,
Brewers'
Society 1951–52

Mary B. D. Connell
m. **F. B. Landale**
d. 1978. Director,
Greene King (1953–67)
b. 1904, *m.* 1925

↓

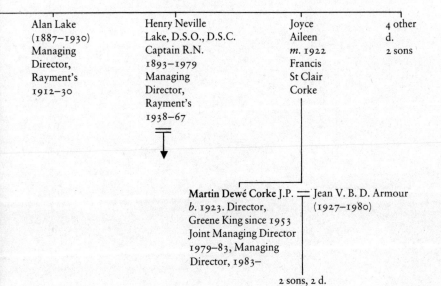

┌─────────┐
5 others and
several
who died
young

Alan Lake
(1887–1930)
Managing
Director,
Rayment's
1912–30

Henry Neville
Lake, D.S.O., D.S.C.
Captain R.N.
1893–1979
Managing
Director,
Rayment's
1938–67

Joyce
Aileen
m. 1922
Francis
St Clair
Corke

4 other
d.
2 sons

Martin Dewé Corke J.P. ══ Jean V. B. D. Armour
b. 1923. Director,   (1927–1980)
Greene King since 1953
Joint Managing Director
1979–83, Managing
Director, 1983–

2 sons, 2 d.

Notes

1. Benjamin Greene, Bury and Brewing, 1799–1836

1 On the other side of the road, let into the wall, is a date stone marked 'Westgate Brewery Founded 1800'. The carving of the letters looks contemporary, but it is not supported by the documentary evidence of the rate books.

2 *Bury and Norwich Post*, 29 April 1806.

3 *Ibid.*, 17 April 1875. It is possible that the details of the 'legend' had been assembled by John Greene (1810–1867), Benjamin Greene's second son.

4 Already by the 1840s when Benjamin Greene had retired to London, his carriage and silver sported the Greenes of Drayton crest.

5 In the seventeenth and early eighteenth century the brewery was amongst the largest in London and its owners prominent in the city's affairs. It was sold in 1789 to a firm that eventually became Watneys. There is apparently no connection between the London and Bury Greenes. See Harford Janes, *The Red Barrel: A History of Watney Mann* (1963), p. 26.

6 Edmund Greene's grandfather Thomas was a tailor who died in 1645. It seems he had settled in Husborne Crawley from Wavendon (Bucks), where connections of the Greenes of Drayton held the manor in the fifteenth and early sixteenth centuries. The wills of these early Greenes show that the family's property at Husborne Crawley grew, modestly and continuously, across the seventeenth century. This is the reality behind the family's recollection in 1875 of their movements in the South Midlands across three centuries.

7 See H. G. Tibbutt, 'The Minutes of the First Independent Church (now Bunyan Meeting) at Bedford 1656–1766', *Publications of the*

Bedfordshire Historical Society, Vol. 55 (1976). Only the minutes survive before 1766; the register of births, baptisms and burials dates from 1785. Benjamin Greene (1693–1751) appears to have been the only male member of his family to be a member of the Congregation. From the evidence that his uncle Francis Greene was Vicar of East Claydon (Bucks) for over sixty years before his death in 1741 it seems that the rest of his family were Anglicans.

8 *The Gentleman's Magazine*'s list of Bankruptcies for August 1751 lists 'Benjamin Greene of Ampthill, Bedfordshire, draper'.

9 According to his will proved in 1779. The Rodicks again were Independents. Archibald Rodick, John's nephew and heir, was a country banker in Wellingborough.

10 Clifton's diaries covering the period 1763–1784 are deposited in the Northamptonshire Record Office.

11 He wrote *Reminiscences of the Revd. Robert Hall* (1832). Hall was a Baptist minister in Cambridge and an enlightened reformer. Both Hall and John Greene adopted a very different stance on slavery from Benjamin (see Chapter 2).

12 *Parliamentary Papers*, The Use of Molasses in Breweries and Distilleries, 1831, vii, p. 22.

13 Bailey's *Universal Directory* (1784) lists B. Green, Southgate as a yarn manufacturer. He was a member of the Corporation and eventually Alderman. There was also a John Green in Risbygate Street whom the rate books indicate was a substantial yarn maker in the 1800–20 period. Their names never appear spelt otherwise than 'Green', whereas Benjamin Greene's family—and this was unusual in the eighteenth century—were meticulous in employing the final 'e' in spelling their name. There was also a William Greene who was a bookseller and printer in the town. It is possible, but I have no proof, that he was a relative of Benjamin Greene.

14 Add. Ms. 41267B, Vol. 8, Clarkson. S. J. Maling to C. Clarkson, 18 July 1804.

15 And no connection of Clarke's Risbygate Brewery which was amalgamated with Greene King in 1917.

16 The sale note appears in the *Bury and Norwich Post*, 12, 19 Dec. 1792. Details of its subsequent changes of hand appear in the St Mary's rate books. In the 1820s under Stutter and Gallant's management, it was the largest brewery in Bury. When sold by them in 1829 it had 11 tied houses (*Bury and Norwich Post*, 20 May 1829). Although it was still in operation in the late 1830s, under Henry Everard, its houses had been sold off and it had been overtaken both by Greene's and Braddock's breweries.

17 Before 1900 more members of the Apostles Society in Cambridge were scholars at Bury Grammar School than Winchester College.

18 Arthur Young reckoned its population in 1775 at 7,135. The census figure of 1801 (usually considered an underestimate of at least five per cent) was 7,655. By 1821 the population had increased to 9,999. There is no extended modern account of the West Suffolk yarn industry. Unwin's essay in the *Victorian County History of Suffolk*, 2 vols (1907–11) provides an introduction. There is a lot of scattered information in Arthur Young's writings and stray references in the *Bury and Norwich Post*. James Oakes's own calculations of the Suffolk manufacturing industry in 1784 appear in A. Young, *General View of the Agriculture of the County of Suffolk* (1794), pp. 232–3.

19 In 1793 William Buck's daughter Catherine wrote to Henry Crabb Robinson, presumably with the experience of Bury in mind, 'the commerce of the country is gone and the manufactures will soon be transported to distant climes', quoted in J. M. Baker, *Henry Crabb Robinson* (1937), pp. 59–60.

20 *Bury and Norwich Post*, 20 July 1831.

21 S. Tymms, *A Handbook of Bury St. Edmunds* (1872 ed.) is the first guide to recount the industrial reawakening of Bury in the 1860s. Besides numerous maltings and the two Westgate breweries—both relatively small employers of labour—Tymms noted Boby's agricultural implement works employing 200 men.

22 The 11 volumes of the diaries (S.R.O. HA 521/3) cover the years 1778–1827.

23 No. 81, now occupied by Bankes Ashton, solicitors.

24 There is no good printed history of either the Corporation or its parliamentary representation. General works provide some references, but the Oakes's diaries, the Corporation court books and the Bury press alone give the essential flavour of Bury's politics in the 1780–1830 period.

25 *Bury and Norwich Post*, 14 February 1827.

26 *A Topographical and Historical Description of the County of Suffolk* (1829), p. 387. The 'County Ball' continued in Bury until around 1950. Attendance, until its demise, was by invitation of the Stewards only.

27 *Ibid.*, 1821 ed., p. 88.

28 *The Oxford Dictionary of Quotations* (1962 ed.), p. 274.

29 P. Mathias, *A History of Brewing in England, 1700–1830* (1959), provides an excellent survey of these developments in London and of the malt trade. But its discussion of country breweries in the period is much less extensive. See also E. Sigsworth, 'The Brewing Trade during the Industrial Revolution: the Case of Yorkshire', *Borthwick Papers*, 31 (1967).

30 W. Ford, *An Historical Account of the Malt Tax Laws* (1849) p. 50 reckons one-fifth of the whole consumption of beer was privately

brewed. The proportion was estimated to be one-half 150 years earlier.

31 Much of the information for this and the following paragraph is taken from *P.P.* Report from the Committee on Public Breweries, 1818 iii. Report from the Select Committee on the Sale of Beer by Retail, 1830–1.

32 I am grateful to Dr J. D. Murphy for the information about Lacons.

33 *P.P.* 1826 XXI, 199. See Appendix 2, Table 1.

34 See Payne's 1833 'Particulars of the Lands in Bury St. Edmunds'. (Suffolk Record Office, E/8/2/1). There were about a dozen maltsters in Bury in the early 1830s. Two of the largest, Henry McL'Roth and Robert Maulkin owned 11 public houses between them. A further 12 public houses were owner-occupied.

35 *Bury and Norwich Post*, 12 September 1798. The number of 'public houses at present annexed to the same' was not stated. Wright was amongst the largest rate-payers in the town, occupying besides the brewery a malthouse in Southgate Street and farming with his brother and brother-in-law (John Fairfax) a good deal of land scattered across St Mary's parish.

36 The following account is based upon J. Duncan 'The Origins of the Free Churches in Bury St. Edmunds' (1955) vol. 3, in the West Suffolk Record Office and the Accounts, Finance books, Sunday School book etc. of the chapel in the same place, FK.302/2.

37 Benjamin Greene's great friendship with Abraham Maling survived his second marriage. When the latter died in August 1828 the *Bury Herald*, then owned by Greene, carried an unusually long and warm obituary. 'He was an Israelite indeed, in whom there was no guile; and having lived the life of the righteous his latter end was like his. His true piety, perfect rectitude and genuine benevolence, joined with the greatest amenity of manner, will for ever endear his memory to all who knew him.'

38 Add. Ms. 41267B, Vol. 8 Clarkson: S. J. Maling to C. Clarkson, 6 July 1804 and 18 July 1804.

39 A letter (*ibid.*, 17 May 1807) between the same correspondents suggests his capacity for friendship, 'It gives me great pleasure that Mr. Greene has shown himself so friendly. He has a great deal of feeling—that is he is very capable of feeling and no man would exert himself more in any case which interested him.'

40 Benjamin's brother John (1777–1844) married the eldest daughter of the Reverend Thomas Smith. See J. B. Brown, *Memoirs of the Public and Private Life of John Howard, The Philanthropist* (1823), p. xv.

41 J. Hunter, 'Familae Minorum Gentium', *Publications of the Harleian Society*, XL (1896), pp. 192–5. His brother Samuel was Recorder of Leeds and grandfather of the first Viscount Halifax.

42 His will is in P.R.O. 1R/1619/363. His estate was sworn under £20,000.

43 The voluminous letters, diaries, journals etc. of Samuel Taylor Coleridge, William and Dorothy Wordsworth and Henry Crabb Robinson all show their warm regard and long, close friendships with Catherine Clarkson. She was also well known to the leading Norwich Dissenters, Amelia Opie and William Smith, M.P.

44 Information about the *Theatre Tavern* and many other details in the next pp. are taken from St Mary's parish rate books, N3/3/6.

45 Greene was somewhat vague, he spoke 'only from memory' and reckoned that consumption had risen by a third since trade was freed in 1830–1. In 1875 Edward Greene, perhaps wishing to emphasise his achievements, maintained that in 1836 production was a mere 2,000 barrels a year. National figures suggest that in 1799 the average output of common brewers in England and Wales was 3,000 barrels of strong beer and 800 barrels of small. There are no figures for the number of common brewers in 1830, although the output of strong beer had declined by almost 10 per cent between 1799 and 1830.

46 Stutter and Gallant's was described as 'old-established' when sold in May 1829. Beside a 'capital malting' in St Andrew's Street, the brewery owned 11 country inns. Not until 1837 did the brewery commence operations again. It was then under the direction of Henry Everard. When Henry Braddock's brewery was sold on his death in July 1868 it had 11 tied houses attached, including the celebrated *Bull* at Long Melford. Edward Greene bought several (see p. 116).

47 Sometimes he combined both. In 1807 he gave a boiled beef and plum pudding dinner in the brewery for 130 Sunday school children from the Independent Chapel.

48 Knowledge about practices was widespread. Ree's *Cyclopaedia* in its article on brewing had recipes for 'brewers balls' for 'fining, feeding, preserving and relishing beer'. It even suggested the use of sycamore or birch sap as a malt substitute.

49 See especially *P.P.* Minutes taken before the Committee to whom the Petition of several inhabitants of London and its vicinity complaining of the high price and inferior quality of beer was referred, 1819, V, pp. 453–557, upon which this paragraph is based.

50 *P.P.* Report from the Select Committee on the Use of Molasses in Breweries and Distilleries, 1831 vii, pp. 14–24. See also the *Bury and Norwich Post*, 6, 20 April 1831.

51 The best account is to be found in Brian Harrison, *Drink and the Victorians* (1971), pp. 64–86.

52 See the per capita malt consumption table in Harrison, p. 72.

53 *Bury and Norwich Post*, 10 February 1830.

54 *Ibid.*, 17 March 1830. See also his very long letter on the repeal of the malt tax in *Bury and Suffolk Herald*, 23 December 1829.

55 *Ibid.*, 12, 26 May 1830.

56 *Ibid.*, 6 October 1830.

57 Ronald Fletcher, (ed.), *The Biography of a Victorian Village* (1977), pp. 151–2.

58 On the Use of Molasses in Breweries and Distilleries (1831) and On the Sale of Beer (1833).

2. *The Greenes' West Indian Venture*

1 This section on the Blakes is compiled from a number of sources: their wills in the P.R.O.; a box of deeds marked 'Sir Patrick Blake's Marriage Settlement' at Partridge and Wilson, Bury St Edmunds; a number of deeds, wrongly described, in the West Suffolk Record Office 1011/1/1 and 2753/29/1 and some papers kindly loaned to me by Mrs Anstace Gilson-Taylor. I stumbled across the Blake connection, quite unknown in the Greene family, when reading through the Bury rate-books and newspapers.

2 P.R.O., IR 26/769.

3 It was possibly with this money and the knowledge of his role in Lady Blake's will that he bought the fine house William Wilkins had erected next door to the Theatre in Bury (see pp. 20–1). The grey brick house, the family home of the Greenes and Lakes for over a century, still belongs to the brewery.

4 In 1825 Robert Maulkin of Bury St Edmunds (see p. 98) was holding a mortgage of £8,500 on the Langham and Bardwell estates.

5 This continued until 1834 for the Suffolk estates and until the early 1840s for the St Kitts and Montserrat properties.

6 Presumably very cheaply. It had been known as the *Suffolk Herald*; on 2 July 1828 this was changed to the *Bury and Suffolk Herald*. It continued to be printed by T. D. Dutton in College Street until 1830 when he was succeeded by W. B. Frost. The proprietorship is difficult to sort out. Greene was most probably not the sole owner: in 1831 John Benjafield was a co-partner and in 1833 Frost, Blencowe, John Greene and Patrick McIntyre, a surgeon in Bury, were given as owners. Greene seems to have remained one until 1832. Then he was replaced by his son John Greene, still a minor, and the latter was succeeded by Edward Greene, also a minor, in December 1833. But it is clear that in reality, if not in name, Benjamin Greene was the managing proprietor at least until 1834.

7 *Bury and Suffolk Herald*, 11 March, 23 September, 7, 21 October 1829, 4 August 1830.

8 *Bury and Suffolk Herald*, 29 December 1830.

9 See both the *Bury and Suffolk Herald* and *Bury and Norwich Post* in April, May 1831 for this lively election.
10 *Bury and Suffolk Herald*, 5, 12 October, 30 November, 7, 14, 21 December 1831.
11 *Ibid.*, 19 February 1834. King Eagle had married a sister of Sir Henry Bunbury, Bt.
12 *Bury and Suffolk Herald*, 28 November 1832; 13 November 1833.
13 The best modern account of the anti-slavery movement is in H. Temperley, *British Anti-Slavery 1833–1870* (1972). Sir G. Stephen, *Anti-Slavery Recollections* (1854) is good on the main participants in the movement.
14 *Bury and Suffolk Herald*, 6, 27 February, 17 March, 2, 23 April 1828, letters signed N(orth) E(ast).
15 Benjamin organised a petition from 70 of the 'most respectable and intelligent members of his town' praying for a commission 'for the purpose of comparing the conditions of the slaves in those islands with the labourers of this country.' (See *Bury and Suffolk Herald*, 23 July 1828).
16 *Bury and Suffolk Herald*, 3, 14, 28 May; 4, 25 June; 9, 16, 30 July; 27 August; 10, 24 September; 8, 22 October.
17 *Ibid.*, 10 September 1828.
18 *Ibid.*, 5 November 1828; 14 July 1830.
19 *Ibid.*, 17 November 1830.
20 *Bury and Norwich Post*, 24 November 1830. See also 1 December and the *Bury Herald*.
21 *Bury and Norwich Post*, 6 February 1833; 2 April 1834; *Bury and Suffolk Herald*, 4 September 1833; 26 March 1834.
22 The amounts of slave compensation for St Kitts are given in *P.P.* 1837–8, XLVIII (215), pp. 89, 135, 202, 310, 319. Benjamin Greene was paid £3,934 for 216 slaves; Sir Henry Blake £5,157 for 309 and C. Molineux £2,838 for 175.
23 See R. Sheridan, *An Era of West Indian Prosperity 1750–1775* (Barbados, 1970). Elsa Goveia, *Slave Society in the British Leeward Islands at the End of the Eighteenth Century* (1965) and D. Hall, *Five of the Leewards 1834–1870* (Barbados, 1971) provide excellent introductions to the economic history of St Kitts from 1783 onwards.
24 *P.P.* 1831–2, XX (381) Report from the Select Committee on the Commercial State of the West Indian Colonies.
25 *P.P.* 1847–48 (123) XXIII Select Committee on Sugar and Coffee Planting in East and West Indies and Mauritius. Much of the information that follows is from the superb evidence B. B. Greene gave to the Committee.
26 The figures are given in *ibid.*, Q.6117. But all plantation accounts give problems at this period since capital and current costs were

inextricably muddled. The apprenticeship system in St Kitts is discussed in R. Fracht 'Emancipation and Revolt in the West Indies: St. Kitts, 1834' in *Science and Society*, 39 (1973), pp. 199-214.

27 *Bury and Norwich Post*, 23 February 1836.

28 Phillips (Phipps) and Spooners in Nicola Town; Cranstoun and Belle Tete at Sandy Point. See W. McMahon, *A New Topographical Map of the Island of Saint Christophers* (1828).

29 From Lloyds *Register of Shipping* (1844)

Name of ship	Place & date of building	Tonnage	Classification
Benjamin Greene	Sunderland 1838	318	AE1
Catherine Greene	Shields 1839	349	A1
Conservative	Sunderland 1840	345	A1
Houghton-Le-Spring	Sunderland 1837	283	A1
St Vincent's Planter	Bristol 1820	256	AE1

Shipping provision for the island increased with the Greenes' entry. In 1835, 18-19 ships carried the island's produce, in 1840, 24 and in 1845, 32. Many of the imports were from North America but the trade was still controlled by the Navigation Laws. P.R.O., CO243/23 -33.

30 The original manuscript has not survived. A copy of it was made by his son, Sir Graham Greene, and either then or earlier substantial sections, presumably about Charles Greene, were removed.

31 See R. W. Elliott, *The Story of King Edward VI's School, Bury St Edmunds* (1963) and C. B. Johnson, *William Bodham Donne and His Friends* (1905).

32 This paragraph is largely based upon William Greene's curious journal, written in 1853, now in the possession of Mr Oliver Greene.

33 H. C. Greene, 'On the track of Great Uncle Charles', *History Today*, xx (1970), pp. 61-3.

34 Much of this section is taken from the minutes of evidence from the Report . . . on Sugar and Coffee Planting (1848) and D. Hall, *op. cit.* and for the post-1865 period from R. W. Beachey, *The British West Indies Sugar Industry in the Late 19th Century* (1957) and F. Watts, 'A Review of the Sugar Industry in Antigua and St. Kitts-Nevis during 1881-1905' in *West Indies Bulletin*, vol. 6, part 4 (1906), pp. 373-86.

35 Benjamin Buck's eldest sister had married Isabella's brother Alfred in 1830. The latter built up an important iron foundry and steam boiler making business in Limehouse. He probably supplied steam engines for the Greenes' St Kitts property and the one installed in the brewery in 1836. Around this period the Greenes began their connections with the Lakes. They were solicitors with clients in St Kitts. Mary

Greene (1812–70) married Henry Lake in 1836; Helen Jane (1827 –1916) married George Lake in 1847. They were solicitors in New Square. Together the Greenes, Blyths and Lakes formed a closely woven net of family and business interests.

36 Report . . . on Sugar and Coffee Planting, Qs., 3035, 3076. James Blyth's evidence like his brother-in-law's was full and outspoken.

37 A brief history of the firm exists: A. Muir, *Blyth, Greene, Jourdain & Company Limited 1810–1960* (1961).

38 This paragraph is based on bundles of the Molineux-Montgomerie family papers kindly loaned to me by their descendant Mrs Rosemary James.

39 His estate in England was sworn under £80,000.

40 Amongst the family papers of Dr Raymond Greene. All this material on William Greene and his family is taken from his collection.

41 Graham Greene, *A Sort of Life* (1971), pp. 93–4.

42 R. W. Beachey, *op. cit.*, pp. 40–60, 137–74.

43 Their affairs revived in the 1890s. This was due in large measure to the efforts of her sons, Graham and Edward. The former had a long career in the Admiralty, was Permanent Secretary to the Admiralty (1911–17) and the Ministry of Munitions (1917–20). 'One of the ablest civil servants of his generation', he had trained at Westgate Brewery (1875–9), but went into the civil service in 1881. He began to collect Greene family material on his semi-retirement after 1920 (see *Dictionary of National Biography 1941–1950* (1959), pp. 323–4). Charles Greene, the second son, was Headmaster of Berkhamsted School, 1910–27. He was the father of Raymond Greene, who continued his uncle's collection of family papers, Graham Greene, the novelist, and Sir Hugh Carleton Greene (see below p. 257). Edward Greene the third son (1866–1938) was eventually Chairman of E. Johnston & Co., coffee importers. See also Graham Greene, *A Sort of Life* (1971).

44 In 1836, the daughter of the Revd H. Y. Smythies, Rector of Stanground, Hunts. Edward Greene married her younger sister in 1840. See Burke's *Landed Gentry* (1965 ed.), 'Greene formerly of Harston House'.

45 *Bury and Norwich Post*, 29 January, 5 February 1867. The legal firm, now Greene and Greene, was carried on by J. W. Greene (1842–84), a zealous churchman, and in the third generation, J. W. Greene (1869–1925). He was registrar of the new Ipswich and St Edmundsbury diocese and clerk to the Bury sessions for 30 years. His wife, the daughter of Sir George Boughey, carried on tirelessly the Greene traditions in Bury when Sir Raymond Greene left Suffolk in 1920. She was the first woman Justice of the Peace, member of the borough council and Mayor. This branch of the family had little connection

with the brewery. When around 1880 J. S. Greene terminated his connection with George Partridge to found Greene and Greene both the Greene and King breweries kept their attachment to Partridge, now Partridge and Wilson.

46 James Blyth (1800–73) was also a director of the London Assurance Corporation, Chairman of the Oriental Bank Corporation and the East and West Indian Dock Company (as was Benjamin Snr). Blyth was a self-confessed addict of statistics, his letters overflow with calculations about sugar etc.

47 James Pattison Currie married James Blyth's daughter. Like Benjamin he was a director and Governor of the Bank of England.

48 Quoted by L. S. Pressnell in 'Gold Reserves, Banking Reserves, and the Baring Crisis of 1890' in C. R. Whittlesey and J. S. G. Wilson (eds) *Essays in Money and Banking* (1968), pp. 167–228. This gives the best, albeit brief, account of B. B. Greene's activities. See also J. H. Clapham, *The Bank of England: A History*, Vol. II (1944), Chapter VI. Professor Pressnell wrote to the author, 'It appals one that a man of such evident influence on the Bank of England has received so little attention ... it was something to be the first Bank Governor to steer the City of London clear of a major European financial crisis, that of 1873.'

49 Copies of the Resolutions of the Court of Directors provided by the Bank for Dr Raymond Greene.

50 *The Burian* for May 1903.

51 His partner and brother-in-law James Blyth had a few years previously bought the neighbouring Woolhampton estate with 2,200 acres. In their correspondence they referred to them as 'the happy valley'. Blyth, like Greene, was a model landowner.

52 'Luncheon with Uncle Benjamin at Kensington Palace Gardens' in Dr Greene's papers.

53 Valued for probate at £467,000.

54 From the *Directory of Directors* (1880–1910).

55 John Jones of The Grove, Wistanstow, Shropshire. He owned 2,200 acres there and was Chairman of the City Bank. Henry Greene left £167,076 in 1915. Except for bequests to his servants and his *masseuse* his estate passed entirely to his wife.

3. *Edward Greene, 1815–91*

1 *Bury and Norwich Post*, 17 April 1875.

2 *Ibid.*, 8 March, 16 August 1836, 13 May, 12 July, 26 September, 11 October 1837, 2 April 1838.

3 *Ibid.*, 18 July 1863.

4 Suffolk Record Office (Bury St Edmunds), E8/2/1. Payne's 'Particulars of the Lands in Bury St. Edmunds' (1833), shows Greene's

owning only one public house. The rate-books of the two parishes in Bury confirm this. It is possible they owned some in the county, but these are not included amongst the very numerous and public house sale notices in the press.

5 Infusion of malt before it is fermented into beer.

6 It was still in working order in 1920. O. H. Heyhoe remembers its date-plate clearly.

7 As late as the 1930s brewers mashed with 'false' thermometers so curious rivals could not easily establish the exact temperature at which they brewed.

8 J. Richardson, *Philosophical Principles of the Science of Brewing* (3rd ed. 1805) and W. Black, *Practical Treatise in Brewing* (1849). A. Rees and E. Chambers, *Cyclopaedia* (1778–86) gives a good impression of the unscientific state of brewing around 1780. The best modern accounts are in P. Mathias, *The Brewing Industry in England 1700–1830* (1959), Chapter 3; E. W. Sigsworth, 'Science and the Brewing Industry, 1850–1900', *Economic History Review* (1965) xvii, pp. 536–50 and H. S. Corran, *A History of Brewing* (1975).

9 William Nethercote, *Brewing* (Bury St Edmunds, 1829), p. 2.

10 J. Baverstock, 'Observations on the State of the Brewery' in *The Pamphleteer*, 2 (1813), pp. 478–94.

11 Somewhat improved by 1884 they were then described as consisting of 'a series of hollow corrugated surfaces, the cold water passing from end to end inside and the wort outside. The cold water enters at one end of the refrigerator and the hot wort at the other. In passing each other, separated by the corrugations they simply exchange heat, the cold water passing out hot and the hot wort passing away cold.'

12 The two periods are difficult to compare exactly for in the 1830s home brewing, which in some measure evaded the malt duty (from which all beer production figures for 1831–80 are compiled) was much more prevalent than in the 1870s. See G. B. Wilson, *Alcohol and the Nation* (1940), pp. 332, 369.

13 I.e. by around 11 per cent between 1851 and 1901 from 337,215 to 373,353, which was way below the national average (81 per cent). Between 1851 and 1861 it fell marginally, and many villages, especially in West Suffolk, suffered continuous decline after 1851.

14 *Bury and Norwich Post*, 17 April 1875.

15 It was assessed for rates on a gross estimated rental of £100, whereas the brewery (which included the original malting office) was only £160. The information on Edward Greene's maltings is taken from the St Mary's rate-books.

16 *Bury and Norwich Post*, 9 December 1845.

17 *Ibid.*, 9 November 1858. The Foundry Maltings were demolished in the early 1950s to make way for the grain store.

18 *Bury and Norwich Post*, 9 October 1866.

19 At the Risbygate Foundry. The firm did Greene's engineering work in the 1850–80 period. Boby's were successful agricultural engineers, best known for their malt screens.

20 Reprinted in full in the *Bury and Norwich Post*, 17 April 1875.

21 *Ibid.*, 4 March 1884.

22 *Ibid.* This accounts for what seems an impossibly large number of brewings: in 1883 there were 373 separate brewings.

23 Shown especially in the influential W. Black, *Practical Treatise in Brewing* (1849).

24 The Stock Book between 1887 and 1914 reveals beer stocks of between 11,000 and 14,000 barrels. There was a tendency for the figure to decline over the years as the taste for vatted strong ale decreased.

25 Total capital employed in 1877 was £146,634. It rose to £196,963 at the last valuation of Greene's brewery in May 1886, see Table 3.

26 E. Greene, *The Christian Man of Business: An Address Delivered by Edward Greene Esq. to the Young Men's Christian Association, Bury St. Edmunds*, n.d.

27 *Bury and Norwich Post*, 9 October 1866. See also *Bury Free Press*, 28 September 1878 for Edward Greene's 50th Jubilee celebrations at the Brewery.

28 *Bury and Norwich Post*, 9 November 1858.

29 *Ibid.*, 17 April 1875.

30 Although cash bonuses were introduced in the 1880s, the Christmas beef was continued until the early 1920s. It was then replaced by an additional 10s. in the men's wage packets.

31 *Bury and Norwich Post*, 21 April 1891.

32 Speech made in 1865, quoted in *Bury and Norwich Post*, 21 April 1891.

33 *Suffolk*, a bottled strong beer, is still made in the traditional way by storing a XXXX stock ale—about as strong as can be brewed—in an oak vat for a year or more before blending with weaker BPA. The process has now almost disappeared from modern brewing practice.

34 Quoted both in his obituary in the *Brewers' Journal* and the *Bury and Norwich Post*, 21 April 1891.

35 *Ibid.*, 4 March 1884.

36 *Ibid.*, 17 April 1875.

37 This continued throughout the rest of his life, usually going beyond the involvement of the average, wealthy brewer. He was a prominent supporter of St Mary's church and the Suffolk Hospital in Bury. In 1866 he raised £2,300 for reseating and a new organ in the former and he was a generous governor of the latter. The East Counties Lunatic Asylum, the R.S.P.C.A., Friendly Societies and Sunday

School in Bury and Ixworth and Pakenham all looked to him for help. Less formally he regularly provided gifts of money and goods to aid the unemployed, aged and widows in the two villages he resided in after 1865. 'In Bury and throughout West Suffolk', his obituary recalled, 'his kindness, thoughtfulness and generosity is everywhere extended, and his charitable acts were performed in a hundred ways, of which the world knew nothing.' His charitable efforts were continued by Greene King long after his death.

38 *Bury and Norwich Post*, 17 April 1875.

39 *Bury and Norwich Post*, 18 July 1865. The *Post* covered the election in great detail as it did Edward Greene's subsequent career as an M.P. He spoke at many functions in Suffolk in the late 1860s. See the newspaper for 22 October 1867 and 17 November 1868 for two typical examples.

40 Much of this section on Edward Greene's political career is based upon a volume of press cuttings, mostly extracted from the Bury newspapers by Lady Hoste in the 1870s. It is in the possession of Dr Raymond Greene.

41 *Bury Free Press*, 25 August 1883.

42 *Bury and Norwich Post*, 22 June 1886. See also 29 June; 6, 13, 20 July, and the *Bury Free Press* for this election.

43 *Bury Free Press*, 21 June 1890.

44 *P.P.* 1873 (325) XIV.

45 Letter of S. H. Nuthatch to Lady Hoste, 3 December 1878, stuck in a volume of press cuttings of Edward Greene's speeches in the 1870s.

46 *The Letters of Disraeli to Lady Bradford and Lady Chesterfield*, Vol. II (1929), p. 62. He was strongly anti-Roman Catholic, detesting the introduction of ritualism and confession into the Anglican Church and, in a speech to the Commons, he maintained that the inmates of convents were often in a worse situation than those in lunatic asylums.

47 Proceedings at the meetings were always fully reported in the Bury press. Two of Edward Greene's lectures survive, those on 'Sheep and Bullocks' (1890) and an MS. lecture on 'Steam Cultivation'.

48 *Bury and Norwich Post*, 22 October 1867.

49 *Bury and Norwich Post*, 20 June, 26 December 1865; 27 February, 26 August 1866; 5 March, 3 September 1867; 25 February, 25 August 1868; 2 March, 16 November, 21 December 1869. *Bury Free Press*, 15 February 1873; 6 February 1875; 3 March, 8 September 1877; 31 August 1878.

50 D. I. Gordon, *A Regional History of the Railways of Great Britain*, Vol. V: *The Eastern Counties* (1968), pp. 159–63.

4. *Fred King and the Amalgamation of 1887*

1 Until 1849. She lost three daughters within eight months in 1824–5, two being buried on the same day. The material for this section is taken from Gazeley and Bramfield Parish Registers, directories, censuses and information supplied by Miss King of Higham.

2 Fred's cousin, W. N. King of Great Barton Place, was a leading Suffolk farmer, prominent in every aspect of its agricultural life in the latter half of the nineteenth century. Another cousin, Robert King, was a landowner, farmer and maltster at Brinkley Hall, beyond Newmarket. Yet another cousin farmed at Denham Castle near Gazeley, and his brother John King farmed at Thorpe Abbotts Hall, near Diss.

3 This section on the Maulkin family is reconstructed from directories, stray newspaper notices, their wills in the Public Record Office, Bury Corporation minutes, the Poor rate-books, James Oakes's diaries, a box of Maulkins' papers at Partridge and Wilson, and information kindly supplied by Mrs Gwenever Pachent.

4 Bailey's *British Directory* (1784), described him as 'a brewer'. But everywhere else he is described as a maltster, coal proprietor, etc. For their wills, see P.R.O. Prob. 11/1743, 1757 and IR 26/1134.

5 In 1795 and 1805 respectively.

6 The bulk of the elder Robert Maulkin's property—sworn for estate duty under £25,000—passed to his grandson Robert Maulkin Lingwood (1814–87). Although he graduated from Cambridge University in 1836 he did not follow his grandfather's wish and enter the church. He was High Sheriff of Herefordshire in 1848. Later after meeting with 'a severe reverse of fortune' he lived in Devonshire. His younger brother, Thomas, was an Anglican priest. See J. A. Venn, *Alumni Cantabrigiensis*, Part II, Vol. IV, p. 175.

7 Payne's 1833 survey shows the St Mary's Square-Sparhawk Street premises extending over 1½ acres and including 'A House, warehouse, stable, chaise-house, cow-house, Barns, Lodges, Office, Yards, orchard, garden, Hot-house, Malt-offices.' The house was demolished when the present barley stores were built.

8 They farmed at Chrishall Grange, Ickleton. Samuel Jonas wrote the prize essay on Cambridgeshire farming published in 1846. See *V.C.H.* Cambridgeshire and Isle of Ely, Vol. VI (1978), pp. 237, 240, 246.

9 *Bury and Norwich Post*, 6 December 1836.

10 The section that follows, on King's brewery and its public house acquisition, is taken from the four large deed boxes of Fred King that have survived at his solicitors, Partridge and Wilson. The papers are very miscellaneous, but they include stray letters, bills and calculations as well as a mass of deeds, testamentary and trust material.

11 Capital, though tight, was not pressing, although the resources of his malting and wine and spirits business were heavily tied up in stocks. In 1869 the capital value of his enterprise was reckoned to be £14,563, in 1871, £19,034. The bankers, Oakes, Bevan & Co., allowed him an overdraft of around £2,000 in these early years. He only employed six men in 1870.

12 *Bury and Norwich Post*, 16 June 1868. Messrs Phillips rented the Stowmarket brewery with nine public houses and a store in Yarmouth. The premises were advertised for sale at the expiration of their lease in 1865 in eleven lots, but Phillips continued brewing there until their bankruptcy in 1872. Greenes acquired the brewery, 35 pubs and the Stowmarket Water Company in 1883. (See pp. 118, 312.) Another Phillips was a partner in Moody's Newmarket brewery.

13 Identical prices to those in the Greene King stock books between 1888 and 1896. See *Bury Free Press*, 30 April 1870 and 17 March 1877.

14 *Bury Free Press*, 12, 19 December 1874.

15 K. H. Hawkins and C. L. Pass, *The Brewing Industry* (1979), p. 25.

16 In 1871 he owned seven freehold houses, three of which were bought on mortgage (one from the Eastern Counties Building Society). Profits rose fast in the first three years of trading. In 1871 net profits were £2,754. Unfortunately only the balance sheets for 1869–71 and 1886–7 survive.

17 Certainly this is not revealed in the 1886 balance sheet. Partners' capital was valued in 1885 at £46,115. (This did not include 39 houses Fred King rented to the partnership, although it accounted for 13 that were.) Net profits in 1886 were £10,012.

18 Lewis Maulkin King later worked at the Centennial brewery, Leichhardt, New South Wales. He had none of his father's business acumen, and there was never any discussion about his joining Greene King, although he was assisting his elder brother in the St Edmunds Brewery in the mid-1880s.

19 King's Brewery and, later, Greene King ran this farm until 1917.

20 He lived there himself after 1880 and merged his farming accounts with those of the brewery so that he could enjoy his great recreation, shooting, and the pleasures of farming and country life without worrying too much about returns on his capital.

21 Blencowe was a partner in the leading Suffolk auctioneering firm of Biddell and Blencowe. He was very successful and possessed a vast knowledge on all agricultural matters (see the *Bury Free Press*, 7 December 1917). George Blencowe was the grandfather of the present Greene King Chairman, John Bridge.

22 The firm was Coles, Shadbolt and Co. Frank became a director

although typically his father stated in some notes on the draft of his 1886 will, 'my son Frank's name appears as Partner but I am really the Partner and all the monies are mine'. In 1887 the business was stated to be doing well. Fred King's investment stood at £18,000 and his interest on loans and share of the profits returned him £2,390. However the King interest was dispersed soon after this date for it is not mentioned in his will of 1889. In 1896 Frank was described as 'of Bury gentleman' (later he lived in Sussex), presumably involved in management of the family's farms. John and Ralph the youngest, were listed as 'merchant' and 'stockjobber' respectively in a deed of 1896, although neither was apparently doing well, for their father in his will of that year was concerned about the possibility of their bankruptcy, whilst a draft codicil of the previous year was written with the special intention 'to assist John in his difficulties'.

23 He was paid £200 a year and brought some money into the firm. But a surviving letter about accounts for the 1870s suggests he was inadequate. Struggling over the firm's books he wrote to Josiah Beddow, 'I get in a maze and somewhat fuddled.'

24 *Bury Free Press*, 17 March 1917.

25 This, and subsequent, material about (Sir) Walter Greene is taken from the mass of Bury newspaper notices about his exploits and less frequent forays into politics between 1864 and 1906. A résumé is provided in his obituaries in the Bury press on 5–6 March 1920. His daughter's (Mrs C. M. Pell) diaries and manuscript autobiography include many references.

26 Most probably Tamplin's Brewery.

27 Captain in the Suffolk Militia and later Major in the Loyal Suffolk Hussars Yeomanry and Hon. Colonel of the 3rd (Special Reserve) Battalion of the Suffolk Regiment.

28 A long article in the *Bury and Norwich Post*, 13 December 1881, reprinted from *The Country Gentleman*, provides detailed information about his hunting exploits.

29 *Bury Free Press*, 6 March 1920. For nearly sixty years the press had recorded his exploits in the saddle, even when he hunted in Worcestershire. He had a penchant for making silly speeches each year at Hunt dinners (e.g. *Bury and Norwich Post*, 10 April, 1 May 1866 and 7 May 1867). None was worse than that made in 1885, at the height of the agricultural depression, when he told the Croome Hunt puppy show, 'nothing taught farming better than fox-hunting'.

30 From his obituary in the *Bury Free Press*, 4 April 1903.

31 There is a brief account of Fred and Emily Machell Smith's relationship by their grandson, Christopher Isherwood, in *Frank and Katherine* (1971). Fred Smith was a loyal aide of Edward Greene in political and agricultural affairs in the county, often deputising for

him at meetings. But he never seems to have been taken very seriously at these events. His wine business flourished in the 1880s. In 1882 it opened a branch at 432 West Strand, London.

32 From 'Fifty Years in Public Life . . . an Exclusive Interview' in the *Bury Post*, 6 June 1919.

33 In July 1886, within three days of the death of the owner of the *British Lion* beer house, Lacy Scott were writing to Greene's solicitors that the property was to be advertised for immediate sale.

36 The first draft lease to survive dates from 1868. It is riddled with corrections which suggests the firm and its lawyers had become unused to drafting this straightforward document. Later, tenants had to complete a standard printed form.

37 Of course many other public houses which had been leased to the firm were purchased in the fifteen years before amalgamation. The 1887 list of leases gives only the unpurchased residue.

38 This and the other details below in this paragraph are taken from the 'Sale Particulars' of the Maulkin Trust houses on 4 August 1875.

39 *Bury Free Press*, 20 June 1903, for details about Robert Spalding (1837–1903). See also *Bury and Norwich Post*, 4 March 1884.

40 For the general background see H. A. Shannon, 'The Coming of General Limited Liability' and 'The Limited Companies of 1866 –1883' in E. M. Carus-Wilson (ed.), *Essays in Economic History* (1954), pp. 358–405 and P. L. Payne, 'The Emergence of the Large-Scale Company in Great Britain, 1870–1914', *Economic History Review*, XX (1967), pp. 519–42.

41 The number of common brewers fell from 17,000 in 1881 to 12,000 in 1890 whereas in the same period the number of middle-sized brewers producing 20,000–30,000 barrels a year grew from 88 to 130; 30,000–50,000 barrel producers from 63 to 72; 50,000– 100,000 producers from 32 to 53. Source: *Brewers' Guardian* (1891), p. 81.

42 They were then legally public companies although many of them, such as Greene King, remained 'private' in practice with shareholding and direction entirely limited to the existing families who controlled them.

43 *Bury and Norwich Post*, 25 July 1882.

44 The brewers' investment in public houses is reckoned to have increased from £30 million to well over £200 million between 1869 and 1900. By the latter date only 10 per cent of the total number of houses were 'free'. Hawkins and Pass, *op. cit.*, p. 27.

45 A partner in Lake, Beaumont and Lake of 10 New Square, Lincoln's Inn.

46 Josiah Beddow and Son. Greene King still uses them.

47 Not quite so. A Haverhill solicitor wrote on 14 May to enquire on

behalf of a client, 'whether there is room for another Brewery in the projected undertaking'.

48 Greene King capitalisation was quite different from one of its competitors, Bullards of Norwich. When they sought limited liability in 1895, £360,000 of their £650,000 capital was raised in debenture stock offered to the public. H. H. Bullard, *Sir Harry Bullard, M.P.* (1902), pp. 150–1.

5. *The New Company and Edward Lake's Regime, 1887–1920*

1 The fact that there was ample capacity was yet another reason for continuing tied house acquisitions after 1887.

2 For a full discussion of these points see A. E. Dingle, 'Drink and Working-Class Living Standards, 1870–1914', *Economic History Review*, XXV (1972), pp. 608–22.

3 After 1887 the Directors' Minute Books, Stock Books, Ledgers, Share Registers and some Balance Sheets have survived. They provide the backbone of source material for the next three chapters. Since there is no extended survey of the brewing industry after 1830, I continue to use the *Brewers' Journal* and in the later period (i.e. after 1930) the *Brewing Trade Review* to provide me with a background to the industry. J. Vaizey, *The Brewing Industry 1886–1951: An Economic Study* (1960) provides a brief introduction to its history between the 1880s and 1940s. Hawkins and Pass, *The Brewing Industry* (1979), carry it forward to the later 1970s.

4 They gave even greater weight to 'the vast increase in private Brewing', which is surprising because most accounts reckon it to have been far in decline by the last quarter of the nineteenth century. Presumably its brief resurgence between 1887 and 1894 depended upon rural recession and the very low price of malt. The 1891 returns included in the Ipswich District 518 private brewers liable to duty and 1,116 who were not. This, compared with other areas in England, was a very high figure. It also confirms my impression that private brewing was more common in Suffolk than elsewhere before the 1890s.

5 A good deal of the material for this section on the brewing industry between 1890 and 1914 comes from the annual review of trade provided by the volumes of the *Brewers' Journal* in these years.

6 The *Journal of the Society of Arts* quoted in the *Brewers' Journal* (1906), pp. 11–14.

7 K. H. Hawkins, *A History of Bass Charrington* (1978), pp. 49–54.

8 Quoted in G. B. Wilson, *Alcohol and the Nation* (1940), p. 87.

9 In 1902 the firm owned 61 public houses in Bury and 181 in the 'country trade': 9 and 18 houses respectively were leased in the two areas. These figures are taken from 'Trade: Half Yearly Abstract,

1902–1910' which has survived. It covers only the 1 June–30 November period. The six months period in 1903 shows the following division of trade:

	Beer (barrels)	Spirits (gallons)
Country Houses	15,984	3,772
Town Houses	7,404	1,253
Sundries	43	
Agents	1,608	
Stores	11,594	2,090
Private	1,995	334
Bottled	809	
	39,437	7,449

10 With the exception of Fakenham and Colchester they were brought into the firm by the Greenes, who also ran a London store in the late 1870s and 1880s. Indeed, the managing directors in the honeymoon fervour of the merger bid up to £41,000 for Cullingham's London brewery in July 1888. They were not successful and then seem to have abandoned all pretence of a London trade until the inter-war years. Perhaps they were fortunate, for the London trade had become so highly competitive by the 1880s that even the Burton brewers were experiencing problems.

11 For example Greene King proposed paying £4,000 for *The Marquis of Granby* at Newmarket in 1904. It was sold to Watneys for £4,600.

12 This firm had always owned many houses in the Lowestoft area and the Waveney Valley.

13 Brewing at Bocking was continued for some years after 1905 because no purchaser could be found and it was thought that it could be sold more readily if still in working order.

14 *Brewers' Journal* (1869), p. 157.

15 See S. & B. Webb, *The History of Liquor Licensing in England* (1908). G. B. Wilson, *Alcohol and the Nation* (1940) provides a detailed statistical account of licensing as well as other aspects of the drink trade.

16 See Table 25 in G. B. Wilson, *op. cit.*, pp. 394–97.

17 In the latter year there was one liquor licence to every 170 persons, almost twice the national average.

18 In January 1903 Greene King offered not to renew licences on two Bury houses after the magistrates had called upon them to reduce the number of licences, although in March they, and most of the neighbouring benches, decided to renew all licences for a further 12 months.

19 Between 1905–35 an average of 601 on-licences were closed each

year under the Act, although in the first five years of its operation it was 1,061. See G. B. Wilson, *op. cit.*, p. 111.

20 In 1887 Sir Wilfred Lawson M.P., the Temperance veteran, asked the Home Secretary if it was true that 3 out of 5 new magistrates in Bury St Edmunds and half the active members of the Bench were engaged in the liquor trade. *Country Brewers' Gazette*, IX (1887), p. 283.

21 In 1914 Edward Lake reckoned that the value of three of their West Suffolk licences referred for compensation was £2,179, whereas the local compensation authority had offered £1,918 and Somerset House, £2,140.

22 As early as 1906 Edward Lake found the 1904 Act working well. Of six houses delicensed, which had originally cost the firm £3,350, the authority had paid £4,702 and their freehold value was still between £150 and £250 each.

23 The *Brewers' Journal* (1906), p. 730. Between 1905 and 1914 he went across to Cheltenham monthly. The Lake connection with the Cheltenham Brewery continued with E. L. D. and H. W. Lake after their father's death in 1922.

24 K. H. Hawkins, *op. cit.*, p. 38. Net profits at Greene King averaged around £35,000 in 1887–90. Therefore goodwill expressed as the number of years' purchase of earnings was five. General practice was that goodwill should not exceed more than two years' purchase of company's net profits.

25 Of the £41,000 issued in debentures, above the £140,000 allotted to the Greene and King families in 1887, £15,000 was raised in 1887 to pay for the Kedington brewery, £10,000 in 1891–2 for the Fakenham brewery and £10,000 in 1893 for the acquisition of Steward & Patteson's Colchester houses. It should be also remembered that the new company had only £8,150 outstanding in mortgages. These were paid off over the next decade and only the Orange Tree Brewery, Braintree was bought with the aid of a £4,300 mortgage redeemed within three years.

26 In 1886 he had already built up a personal portfolio valued at £24,370.

27 Many of the investments were sold between 1917 and 1920. In May 1920 they were valued at £52,540. They were maintained at around this level throughout the inter-war years. In the Second World War they reached their highest book values (c. £195,000 in 1947) after the purchase of War Loan. The fund was quickly run down in the early 1950s.

28 The purchases made after the 1904 A.G.M. were not untypical: £20,000 in five North American and Indian railway companies; in 1907: £2,998 in Canadian Pacific 4% debentures, £2,078 in Lake Shire and Michigan Southern 4% bonds, £2,895 in Norfolk and

Western Pocahontas Coal Co. Joint bonds, £3,204 in Great Central 5% Convertible Preference shares.

29 It was continued until 1957 when commercial insurance was arranged for the entire Greene King properties. The fund, never really increased in real terms between 1918 and 1957, had been invested in low return Government stocks, and, after 1940 especially, had failed to keep pace with building costs. It was a victim of unadventurous financial management. In one sense it continues with the Greene King private fire service. The firm always ran its own fire service. In addition to tending its own properties it also aided, and often exceeded in enthusiasm and equipment, the Bury and West Suffolk service.

30 The best brief historical survey is E. M. Sigsworth, 'Science and the Brewing Industry, 1850–1900' in *Economic History Review*, XVII (1964–5), pp. 536–50.

31 I.e. in scientific terms the brief entries in the minute book are unclear. Only a full letter book would provide a more complete answer.

32 *Bury Free Press*, 21 January 1899; *Bury and Norwich Post*, 17 January 1899. The disputed figures were an assessment of £10,453 for the buildings at Westgate and £6,587 for plant, £1,050 for the mineral waterworks and £9,186 for St Edmunds brewery and £2,630 for plant. It is impossible to extract the figures from composite totals in the firm's balance sheets. But stray figures suggest even the new valuation was low.

33 The brewery consumed an average of about 1200 tons of coal annually in the 1890s, all carted from the station as well as the barley, hops or beer transported. In 1898 the firm employed 46 horses in Bury.

34 The proportion of 'old' beer stored in vats, once a great speciality of the brewery, had now fallen to 10–15 per cent of output.

35 But he was sufficiently impressed with Heyhoe's work and attitude to increase his salary by £50 a year the next morning.

36 The *Brewers' Journal* (1890), p. 7.

37 J. Vaizey, *The Brewing Industry 1886–1951* (1960), p. 5. Brewers were imitating their Burton rivals. According to K. H. Hawkins, *op. cit.*, p. 51, Bass brewed an 'average of 770,000 barrels of pale ale a year for the home trade, approximately 75 per cent of which was in bottled form'.

38 Greene King had experimented in 1893 with delivering beer to Haverhill and Stowmarket by traction engine, but the scheme was dropped for some reason. In 1913 a critical shareholder of the Colchester Brewing Company attacked it as 'being antiquated and more or less referring to the time of Adam than the present day'. An instance he cited was their failure to use motor transport. The *Brewer's Journal*, XLIX (1913), p. 555.

39 In 1913 there were still 59 horses at Westgate, but by 1924 only 10. They had been replaced by 18 lorries and vans.

40 His untaxed income from his Greene King shares was around £18,000 after 1900. I have never seen papers disclosing his income from other sources. But his daughter (Mrs C. M. Pell), when she lived with him during the First World War, commented about the extremely healthy state of his finances after the accountant's visit each year. On his death in 1920 his 'resworn' estate was valued at £443,748 for death duties.

41 This was replaced by the 500-ton *Agatha* in 1911, which was requisitioned as a patrol vessel during the First World War. He was a member of the Royal Yacht Squadron and had been interested in sailing since his youth. In Suffolk he was a Justice, Deputy-Lieutenant and Colonel in the militia, in London a member of Boodles and later the Carlton Club.

42 See H. R. Barker, *West Suffolk Illustrated* (1907), pp. 356–8; E. Farrer, *Portraits in Suffolk Homes* (1908) and the *Bury Free Press*, 31 July 1920.

43 Christopher Isherwood, *Kathleen and Frank* (1971), p. 242.

44 *Bury and Norwich Post*, 6 December 1898.

45 Edward Lake, a successful Mayor of Bury in the 1887 jubilee year and a staunch and able Conservative was mentioned as a candidate, but he had to give way to the political pretensions of his cousin, whom he loyally supported in the contest. (*Bury Free Press*, 18 April 1891.)

46 The following account is taken from the files of the *Bury and Norwich Post* and *Bury Free Press*, April–May 1891.

47 The figures were 4,346 votes to 4,132.

48 See the *Bury Free Press*, September–October 1900 for this election.

49 From 1895 to 1909 he was still involved in farm partnerships at Fornham All Saints and Bridge Farm, Pakenham with his son, F. J. King, and Robert and Reginald Burrell. In addition to owning the great tithes at Pakenham he had bought some land there from the Newe Hall estate in 1881.

50 Emily King died in 1888. Three others had died in infancy.

51 The *Country Gentleman*, 23 November 1889.

52 *Bury Free Press*, 20, 27 January 1917.

53 In 1916 the State took over the breweries and public houses of the Carlisle–Gretna area to limit a sharp rise in drunkenness, which occurred when an army of 10,000 workers was building a local explosives factory.

54 The brewery had been founded in the early 1840s by Harry Clarke's grandfather. Its beers had a good reputation and it was Greene King's only serious competitor in Bury. Brewing there was immediately

discontinued in 1917. Clarke's were paid £29,615 in various shares and war stock.

55 Messrs Oliver received 3,000 £10 ordinary shares and £39,000 in cash.

56 He died in August 1922. After Sir Walter Greene's death in March 1920 he was Chairman of the Company.

57 A long 'exclusive interview' with E. W. Lake appeared in the *Bury Post*, 6 June 1919.

58 *Bury Free Press*, 15 January 1909.

59 The stormiest was over the dismissal of the Borough Surveyor in 1902. See *Bury Free Press*, 16 August 1902.

60 *Bury Free Press*, 5 August 1922.

61 *Bury Free Press*, 15 January 1909.

62 *Brewing Trade Review*, XXXVI (1922), pp. 351–2.

6. *Peace and War, 1920–45*

1 *The Social and Economic Aspects of the Drink Problem* (1931), pp. 44–5.

2 In a pamphlet prepared for the Labour Party in 1924 on the drink question he had written, 'Everybody admits the Trade has become a menace to the public life of the country and it corrupts public life.'

3 R. M. King was not a major shareholder, for his brother had left his shares to a nephew and the King Trust in 1917. Nevertheless he represented King interests on the Board.

4 Harold Lake (1882–1960), second son of E. W. Lake. Educated Uppingham and Oxford. Practised in Lincoln's Inn as a solicitor until 1912, when he went to Rayment's Brewery. Member of West Suffolk County Council, 1920–37. Director of Greene King 1922–37. Left Greene King to become assistant managing director at Benskin's (Watford), and in 1939 he became chairman and managing director of Morland's Brewery, Abingdon. For his later career, see p. 215.

5 He had succeeded to the baronetcy in 1920.

6 Although long before 1914 he was always a poor attender of Board meetings.

7 Even their clubs mirrored the gap: the father was a member of the Carlton, Cavalry and the Royal Yacht Squadron; the son belonged also to the Carlton—obligatory for Tory M.P.s—but also Whites and Pratts.

8 He served with the Suffolk Yeomanry and won the Military Cross.

9 During a visit in 1949 she 'spent the day with Edward, entertaining me with seeing his house, his "curios" of every description and all the charming family, hunting paintings by Smythe—besides innumerable snapshots of himself with exalted friends about whom "we don't talk" meaning Royalties, Dukes and Duchesses . . . I could only feel,

with all their wealth, possessions and advantages how much these two uncles might have done for their two charming Pell nieces living in London, but never included in any of their house parties or yachting parties'. She had little cause for complaint, living through the 1920s and 1930s at 2, Onslow Square on a very comfortable income derived largely from the brewery and, without their uncles' aid, her daughters both married into the baronetage.

10 Like her father and brother (for whom she acted as Mayoress) she was elected Honorary Freeman of the Borough in 1946. This was in recognition of her services during the war. For almost 50 years after her mother's death, she ran the weekly Mothers' Meeting for brewery wives.

11 In 1920–1 Stowmarket waterworks, acquired with the brewery there in 1883 and run by Greene King for the town for almost 30 years, were sold to Stowmarket Urban District Council for £10,000. The beer store there was closed in 1920.

12 I.e. in 1929 the *Brewers' Journal* reported that Youngs, Crawshay & Youngs, and Morgans in Norwich paid 10 and 15 per cent respectively; the Hull Brewery 13¾ and the Cheltenham O.B.C. 12½ per cent.

13 Greene King policy contrasts strongly with Wells and Winch's. See pp. 234–5.

14 Mrs Pell was an exception. She bought 1,000 at 43s. each by 'family preference'. They were (12 November 1927) 45–46s. on the market. Exactly a year later they were, she noted with glee, 52s. 9d.

15 J. M. King withdrew in 1912 and the company was then run by E. W., E. L. D., H. W. and A. H. Lake. The latter managed it from 1912 to 1931.

16 Edward Greene argued on these lines at the 1933 Annual General Meeting, 'In effect this new system is considerably more advantageous to those breweries which sell a large proportion of high priced beers in urban districts than to a Company like ours which has to sell more of the lower priced beers in endeavouring to cater for a public with less money to spend.' He was developing a point made by the Managing Director in May. The *Brewing Trade Review* calculated that a beer of 1055° would pay 80s. (a reduction of 34s. on the old duty). Of course hardly any beer in 1934 was of this strength, but the evidence quoted here refutes the popular idea that the change in duty systems encouraged weaker beers.

17 A second and much smaller wine business, Scruby's of Saffron Walden was acquired for £6,400 in 1936, and performed a similar function to Peatling's for the Rayment's subsidiary.

18 There was one minute exception: Prentice's of Stowmarket was acquired for £1,250 in 1934. It had only four employees and no tied houses. The brewery was extremely antiquated, a lone survivor of the

numerous little breweries of early nineteenth century Suffolk. Its trade was mostly private—farmers and labourers especially at harvest time. The chief acquisition turned out to be its brewer, F. A. Reddish, see pp. 218–19.

19 I have not seen this. Since it was never discussed on its receipt it is possible it was never undertaken.

20 Nevertheless it was one of the wonders of its day in Bury, and a film of it was shown in the local cinemas in 1927–8. There was one problem not effectively solved before 1939—a slight 'haze' in the bottles caused by pasteurisation. But the 1932 article quoted shows that Greene King was an early convert to and experimented with the pasteurisation of bottled beer.

21 Mark Jennings was a protégé of E. L. D. Lake. He set up a successful firm of brewing engineers in London, and was always consulted by Greene King after 1930.

22 Greene King proudly issued a 12-page illustrated brochure about the brewhouse in August 1939. The brewhouse possessed two great advantages: it was spacious, and had so much spare capacity that even today, when output had risen to roughly three times the output of 1939, there are no plans to replace it. Even so, close attention was paid to economy in its details.

23 In 1913 there were 50 prosecutions per 10,000 of the population, in 1922, 20, and in 1932 only 7·5.

24 Op. cit., p. 47.

25 See B. Oliver, The Renaissance of the English Public House (1947).

26 They were supervised by W. Wayman, a surveyor, who worked full-time for the company. The major improvements were designed by W. Mitchell, Colonel Hooper or Basil Oliver.

27 See his Renaissance of the English Public House (1947) for illustrations and plans of these houses.

28 Major Lake and Basil Oliver were Vice-Chairmen of the committee which organised the Inn Signs exhibition in London in 1936. Of the 250 signs shown 15 came from Greene King houses.

29 The managers' minute books reveal a warm relationship between the company and its tenants. Widows succeeded husbands, sons followed their fathers. Harry Clarke and the head traveller, A. T. Colman (remembered by the late R. G. Saunders as 'the dead image of Edgar Wallace . . . he had a long cigarette holder and spats, he looked a real gentleman') kept a regular surveillance, although miscreants were summoned to the Head Office for a 'stern' word from Major Lake. But his bark was far worse than his bite. He was easily moved by a 'pathetic' letter and only when the position was hopeless, after repeated warnings, was a tenancy terminated. Temporary financial aid was often granted.

30 This paragraph is based upon a recording made by the author with Captain Neville Lake in April 1977.

31 Practices were frequent and the tenders, especially after they were motorised in the late 1920s, were a regular feature at events in West Suffolk. The men were rewarded with long service medals. As one director put it, 'some firms have brass bands, we have our fire service'.

32 *Bury Free Press*, 14 May 1921.

33 In the 1951 valuations there were 165 cottage properties in Bury and 38 at Cambridge.

34 The boys in the bottled beer store around the First World War remember a tougher system. A shilling a week was stopped from their wages as 'Good Conduct' money, and was paid to them in a lump sum at the end of the year if they had broken no windows playing football, etc.

35 *Bury Free Press*, 10 July, 12 October 1920. In 1975 it was sold to St Edmundsbury Council on terms which allowed the brewery work force as well as the town to use it.

36 *Home Production of Beer (U.K.)*

Excise Year	1938–9	1939–40	1940–1	1941–2	1942–3	1943–4
Standard barrels (m.)	19·1	17·9	18·8	18·6	18·7	19·6
Bulk barrels (m.)	25·7	26·9	28·2	29·6	29·8	31·2

Source: *Brewing Trade Review* (1945), p. 372.

37 The company was acquired for £5,000 in 1927 jointly with A. & E. Hunter, wines and spirits merchants in Bury. It continued in existence until 1956. Always lacking investment and proper advertising it returned low profits except during the war.

38 In 1943 the firm gave £20,000, 'to give the town a lead' and enough to buy a 'Mosquito' fighter, during War Savings Week.

39 Besides Colonel Oliver, the only other executive director was Major C. S. Wilson. He was the first 'outside' director, a one-time land agent and Suffolk County cricketer, who was appointed in 1940 to help the Managing Director with properties. Neville Lake maintained that he was given the job so that his brother had someone to talk to about cricket. He resigned through ill health in 1948.

7. Tradition and Change since 1945

1 Instead of the customary two years, he served, through ill health, only one year in office, resigning in 1952.

2 The articles on 'Modern Pneumatic Drum Malting', 'A Modern Bottling Store', and 'A Modern Brewery' appeared in the *Brewers'*

Guardian, August, October, 1952. Greene King reprinted these and distributed them to shareholders in 1953.

3 In 1951 an Australian firm, Carlton and United Breweries of Melbourne, made Mr Reddish 'an offer of employment he could not refuse'.

4 See note 2 above.

5 Huntingdon Breweries and Hall, Cutlack and Harlock merged in 1950 as East Anglian Breweries. They were taken over by the Norwich brewers, Steward and Patteson, in 1957. This big East Anglian combine was acquired by Watney Mann in 1963. Nine years later Watney Mann was acquired by Grand Metropolitan Hotels which had in 1971 acquired Truman, Hanbury and Buxton.

6 In 1954 Greens merged with Flowers of Stratford and retained the latter's name. Bernard Dixon, a director of Greens, was one of the leading takeover exponents of the 1950s and one of the first brewers to introduce keg beer. He was head brewer at Greene King's Panton Brewery in 1931 when it won the Champion Challenge Cup at the Brewers' Exhibition. He was Chairman, Managing Director and head brewer of Flowers Breweries Ltd in the late 1950s.

7 General Dempsey (1896–1969) commanded the 2nd Army in the invasion of Normandy and North West Europe. He was eventually C-in-C, Middle East, 1946–7. Montgomery, who divided his generals into *grand-cru* and *vin-ordinaire* classifications placed Dempsey very highly amongst the former. His entry into the brewing world was eased by his chairmanship of the Racecourse Betting Control Board, 1947–51. He was Chairman of H. and G. Simonds (Reading), 1953–63 and Deputy Chairman of Courage, Barclay and Simonds, 1961–6, after Courage's takeover of Simonds. He was Chairman of Greene King from 1955 until his death in 1969.

8 Martin Corke, a grandson of E. W. Lake, was elected a director in 1953. He managed Greene King's Cambridge brewery 1948–55. F. B. Landale, who also became a director in 1953, held similar views. He bridged the King–Lake interests. He had inherited most of his considerable shareholding from his uncle, J. M. King, and he had married a grand-daughter of E. W. Lake.

9 One of the twenty or so breweries included under the 'umbrella' was Morlands of Abingdon of which Lake was Chairman. Whitbread still has an almost 40 per cent holding in Morlands.

10 See Burke's *Landed Gentry* (1937 ed.) 'Pryor of Weston' for details and also G. Curtis *A Chronicle of Small Beer* (1970), a book based upon the diary of John Izard Pryor (1774–1861) which provides many details about the Baldock brewery and a first-rate view of the life of a wealthy country brewer in the first half of the nineteenth century.

11 But, having abandoned their Quakerism, they still retained interests in Hertfordshire as landowners and clergymen.
12 For details see Burke's *Landed Gentry* (1937 ed.) 'Shaw-Hellier of the Wombourne Wodehouse'.
13 Simpson's was paid for by the creation of a further 100,000 ordinary shares of £1 each: 45,600 of these were issued in part payment for the share capital of Simpson's. £500,000 four per cent debenture stock was also issued at £97 10s. per cent to redeem the outstanding £100,000 debenture stock and raise the cash to pay Simpson's five shareholders.
14 It was taken over by Truman, Hanbury and Buxton.
15 Notification of substantial shareholdings under section 33 of the Companies Act (1967) revealed that both Canadian Breweries (G.B.) Ltd and Bass Charrington jointly held 11·2 per cent of Greene King equity. These shares were sold by 1971. On the other hand, Guinness held for many years an 8 per cent stake in Greene King, and this was always regarded as a 'friendly', protective holding.
16 The Bank was sold in 1894 to the Capital and Counties Bank, of which A. K. Lindsell became a director. A chronology of the Wells and Lindsell families is provided in Burke's *Landed Gentry* (1937 ed.), 'Lindsell late of Fairfield', although far more useful is 'the Introduction to G. K. Collection' compiled by J. Collett-White of the Bedfordshire Record Office from the Wells and Winch deeds deposited by Greene King.
17 He was also a director of H. & G. Simonds (Reading) in the inter-war years.
18 These plans were revived in 1956 when Wells and Winch sounded out the Northampton Brewery Company about amalgamation with a scheme to brew at Northampton and bottle at Biggleswade (where Wells and Winch were already bottling Guinness for them). The Northampton Brewery Company merged with Phipps in the following year.
19 Colonel J. A. Redman joined the main Greene King Board. He continued as Managing Director on the Greene King (Biggleswade) Board as it became known in 1963. Other members were E. C. Doresa, A. J. Redman's son-in-law, from the old Wells and Winch Board, S. J. B. Redman, Sir Miles Dempsey (Chairman), T. H. Veasey and John Banham from Simpson's. Until his death in 1966 Colonel Redman continued to run Biggleswade on similar lines to those of the past.
20 Wells and Winch was paid for by the issue of a further 200,000 £1 ordinary shares and 450,000 £1 5 per cent preference shares.
21 The holdings of 'family and friends' remained well above 40 per cent of equity in the 1960s. Greene King profits in these years did not

compare unfavourably with those of the national brewers because the latter, rather painfully organising themselves after the takeovers of 1959–62, reaped the benefits of scale and investment only after 1968.

22 p. 217.

23 John Clarke was briefly Chairman, 1969–71. John Bridge has been joint Managing Director with Martin Corke since 1978.

24 In 1964 wines and spirits totalled 34 per cent of group sales, but even at this high level they only contributed 12½ per cent of profits.

25 National Board for Prices and Incomes, Report No. 136 *Beer Prices*, Cmnd. 4227, HMSO (1969), pp. 4–5.

26 At last Bury's population began to expand. It remained static at around 16,500 from 1900 until 1940. By 1975 it was estimated to have grown to 27,600. Under the Towns Development Act (1952) it was agreed with the Greater London Council to receive 10,000 from the London area. Thetford and Haverhill experienced a proportionally greater expansion under the same terms.

27 Lodge Farm, Pelham realised £22,500 in 1959; Copdoes Farm, Whelnetham £57,000 in 1965. It was the end of a 110-year tradition that had combined brewing with farming.

28 Although listed, the brewery was demolished (its two fine houses remain) and its site cleared to provide a housing estate. It was a sad loss. Simpson's would have made a splendid Country Brewing Museum.

29 29 July 1966. See also similar comments made in the *Investors' Chronicle*, 15 July 1966.

30 See Iain Mackintosh's splendid, *Pit, Boxes and Gallery. The Story of the Theatre Royal, Bury St. Edmunds 1819 to 1976* (The National Trust, 1979).

31 In 1951 it was valued at £500 as a crate store.

32 There were proposals, never very seriously considered, in late 1971 for a merger between Trumans (which had recently been acquired by Grand Metropolitan Hotels) and Greene King.

33 K. H. Hawkins and C. L. Pass, *op. cit.*, pp. 79–149.

34 A note of caution is necessary here. The growth of wines and spirits sales were proportionally far greater, but margins for brewers, who of course handled only a fraction of wines and spirits sales, were extremely tight. It took only a modest rise in beer production, the source of the brewers' biggest profits, to increase the prosperity of the industry.

35 Group turnover, a more problematic indicator because of inflation, grew from £8·6 million in 1969 to £55·8 million in 1981.

36 This side of the enterprise was strengthened by the appointment of Timothy Bridge, John Bridge's son, as director in charge of free trade

in 1977. He came to Bury after taking his degree at Exeter University, a period with Fine Fare's marketing division and running Rayment's in the mid-1970s.

37 Top pressure kits were installed in most Greene King houses after the late 1960s. In 1978 CAMRA reckoned Greene King was serving its beers by traditional methods (i.e. not using extraneous gas) in less than one-third of their houses.

38 John Bridge and Martin Corke have continued the firm's tradition of service in West Suffolk. The former was an alderman of the old West Suffolk County Council before reorganisation in 1974, and is High Sheriff of Suffolk, 1983–4, and a Deputy-Lieutenant. Martin Corke's involvement would have brought joy to his grandfather, E. W. Lake, and Major Lake. He was captain of Suffolk County Cricket Club for several years, and is currently Chairman of the District Health Authority, Chairman of St Edmundsbury Magistrates, Chairman of the Suffolk Hunt and Chairman of the Theatre Royal Management.

39 The Greene name is represented today by his son, Graham C. Greene, Managing Director of the publishers Jonathan Cape, and a non-executive director since 1979. Since his mother was a member of the Guinness family, he has double links with the brewing world.

40 W. Pead, Edward Lake, Harold Lake, Frank Bevis and, since 1958, H. G. Lines.

INDEX

Hargreaves, H., 264
Harwich, 62
Haverhill, 83, 104, 136, 138, 154, 168, 216
Hawkins, K. H., 200, 239, 265
Hempstead, R. H., 263
Hervey, Lord Alfred, 85
Hervey, Lord Francis, 86
Heyhoe, O. H., head-brewer, 150–2, 210, 261, 305
Higgins and Sons, brewers, Bedford, 234
Higham, 96
Holden's Brewery, Henlow, 234
Holland-on-Sea, Essex, 201
Home brewing, 12–13, 305
Hops, 23–4, 122, 184
Horses, Lords Committee on the Supply of (1873), 90
Hoste, Dorothea, Lady Hoste (Mrs Edward Greene), 87–8
Hoste, Rear-Admiral Sir William, Bart, 87
Howard, John, prison reformer, 6, 18
Hoxley, Mrs E., 264
Huddleston, Cooper, Greene and Co., bankers, 75–6
Huddleston, Peter, banker, 95
Hudson's Brewery, Pampisford, 185, 234
Hull Brewery Company, 134
Huntingdon Brewery, 188
Husborne Crawley, 3
Hydrometers, 12, 65, 67–8

Ind, James, 228
Ind Coope, brewers, 125, 133, 222, 228, 236
Institute of Brewing, 218, 257
Ipswich, 95, 192
Isherwood, Christopher, 158
Isinglass, 25

Ixworth, 138
Ixworth Cider Factory, 208, 314
Ixworth Farmers' Club, 92–3

Jacobs, J., 264
Jamieson, Simon, 251
Jenner's Brewery, Kedington, 278
Jennings, Mark, 197, 313
Johnson, Samuel, 12
Jonas, Alfred, 110
Joyson-Hicks, Sir W., 174

King, Emily (nee Maulkin), 97, 99–100
King, Frank, 107, 310
King, Frederick William, (1828–1917), 125, 129, 135, 155–6, 194, 215, 259, 264; amalgamation with Greenes, 108, 124, 127–8; assets, 106–7, 127; begins brewing, 100–1; business techniques, 108–11; cement making, 107, 304; death, 110, 162; family, 106–8; family origins, 96–7; farming, 97, 106–7, 316; founds St Edmunds Brewery, 96; income, 148, 161–2; investments, 148; later career, 160–3; malting, 100; partnerships, 101, 107; performance of brewery, 126; public houses, 103–6, 116–17; second marriage, 109; shooting, 110, 162; wills, 97, 107–8
King, F. W., and Son, 278
King, James, 96–7
King, James Maulkin, 105–6, 108, 126, 129, 135, 148, 151, 155–6, 162–3, 165, 188
King, John, 96
King, John Maulkin, 107, 310

King, Ralph Maulkin, 197, 215,
310, 317
King family, xi, 96–7, 187
King Securities Realisation Trust,
161–2
King's Lynn, 14, 242
Kinsey, William, publican, 121
Kirtling (Cambs.), 97, 100

Labour, 203–5
Labour Government, attitude to
drink, 174
Labour Governments (1945–51),
213, 216–17
Lacon's Brewery, Great
Yarmouth, 14, 105
Lager, 69
Lake, Alan, 189
Lake, Benjamin, solicitor, 125–7
Lake, Major E. L. D., 152, 165,
171, 176, 178–9, 220, 238,
247–8, 263, 319; career,
180–2; death, 214; inn signs,
201; managed houses, 201–2;
managing-director, 182–98;
modernises brewery, 214–22;
modernises public houses,
199–201; recruitment of
labour, 204–5; Second World
War, 208–11; sport, 204–6
Lake, Edward W., 78, 115, 152,
154–6, 175–6, 179, 181–2,
186, 188–9, 205, 247, 258–60,
310; annual reports, 132;
career, 168–71; Cheltenham
Brewery, 145; entrepreneurial
qualities, 126; financial
management, 131, 144–9; First
World War, 165–8; income,
148; licences, 142–4; politics,
169–71; public houses,
135–40; wife, 169

Lake, Harold, 176, 200, 215–16,
226, 227, 231
Lake, Muriel, 181, 205, 232
Lake, Capt. Neville, R.N., 180,
182, 189, 203, 264
Lake, Vice-Admiral W. J. C., 189,
215, 224
Lake family, 186–7, 194, 296–7
Landale, F. B., 321
Langham (Suffolk), 33–5
Last, William, traveller, 121
Lawson, Sir Wilfred, M.P., 314
Leland, John, 8
Liberal party, attitude to brewers
and drink, 124–5, 130, 135,
142, 144, 163
Licence duty, on public houses,
144
Licensed victuallers, 120, 267
Licensing Act: (1872), 140–1;
(1902), 141; (1904), 133,
140–4, 314; (1921), 172;
(1961), 245, 249–51
Licensing Bill: (1871), 140;
(1908), 135
Licensing Laws, 117–18
Licensing Laws, Royal
Commission on the (1899),
133, 141; (1931), 174–5
Licensing magistrates, 141, 199,
201, 243, 307
Licensing restrictions, 124, 140–2
Limited liability, 125
Lindsell, C. S., 233
Lindsell, General Sir Wilfred,
233
Lindsell family, 224, 316
Lines, H. G. (Dick), 238, 247
Liverpool, 141, 200
Lloyd George, 163–4, 176, 207
Lloyds Bank, 185
Local Option, 175
Loft, Capel, 20

Oakes, James, banker, 7–11, 13,
98, 297
Oastler, Richard, 39
Ogden's Brewery, March, 187–8,
198, 220, 271, 278
Oliver, Colonel B. E.,
head-brewer, 180, 195, 197,
210, 214–16, 218, 231, 257
Oliver, Basil, architect, 201, 319
Oliver, J. H., 179
Oliver, Margaret, 211
Oliver family, 186–7
Oliver's Brewery, Sudbury, 138,
168, 183, 194, 260, 271–3,
278
Opie, Amelia, 299
Orton, Rev. J., 41–3
Oundle, 3–6, 18

Page, Ken, 263
Page's Brewery, Ashwell, 234
Page's (Brewery) Framlingham,
136
Pakenham, 107, 157
Panton Brewery, Cambridge
(formerly Bailey and Tebbutt's),
152, 178–9, 183, 186–7, 191,
193–4, 196, 203, 227, 272–3
Parr, Katherine, 2
Partridge and Wilson, solicitors,
110, 127, 264
Pass, C. L., 200
Pasteur, Louis, 68, 149
Paul, George, ironmonger, 17
Pead, William, 78, 114, 126–7,
129
Peatling, Thomas, and Co. Ltd,
191, 278
Peatling and Cawdron, 242–3
Pedley, A. E., 29
Pell, Mrs C. M., 158–9, 166, 178,
317–18
Peterborough, 254

Phillips, Francis, 101, 109
Phillips, John, 228
Phillips, Joseph, 41
Phillips of Royston, brewers, 172,
188–9, 224, 230, 236–7
Phipps, James, 33
Phipps's Brewery, Northampton,
127, 134
Pickwoad, Edwin, 45, 49–50
Pinchin's Brewery, Fakenham,
136
Porter, 26
Prentice's Brewery, Stowmarket,
218, 278, 318–19
Pressnell, L. S., 56, 304
Prices and Incomes Board, 243,
250
Prohibition, 174–5
Pryor, John Izard, 321
Pryor, Reid and Co., brewers,
Hatfield, 228
Pryor family, 228
Public houses, 21, 27–8, 103–5,
116–22, 138, 175, 193,
199–202, 220–1, 230, 235–6,
243–4; (individual houses in
Bury St Edmunds unless
otherwise stated), *Angel Hotel*,
22, 98; *Bushell*, 120; *Castle*,
99, 119; *Cock*, Castle Camps,
248; *Crown*, Fornham, 105;
Crown, Great Barton, 109;
Dog, 20; *Dog and Partridge*,
35, 73, 116; *Everards Hotel*,
244; *George and Star*, March,
201; *Greyhound*, Whepstead,
120;*Horse and Shoes*, Stanton,
120; *King's Cliff Hotel*,
Holland-on-Sea, 201; *Manger*,
Bradfield Combust, 120;
Pickerell, Ixworth, 93; *Prior's
Inn*, 201; *Red Lion*,
Grantchester, 201; *Roaring*

Sport, 115, 205–6
Stag Brewery, Westminster, 2, 295
Star Brewery, Cambridge, 188, 192
Steam engines, 45, 151, 302
Steam ploughing, 93–4
Steggles, William, 81
Stephen, Sir George, 41
Stephen, James, 40
Steward and Patteson, brewers, Norwich, 14, 105, 138, 153, 232, 278
Stope's Brewery, Colchester, 125
Stowmarket, 83, 136, 154
Stowmarket Brewery, 101, 117–18
Stowmarket waterworks, 318
Stutter and Gallant's Brewery, Bury St Edmunds, 22, 296, 299
Style and Winch's Brewery, Chatham, 233–4
Sudbury, 62, 231
Sudbury Brewery (Oliver's), 88, 183–4, 194, 196, 203
Suffolk, 2, 21, 27, 29–30, 45, 61, 66, 70–1, 86, 90–5, 105–6, 113, 117, 131–2, 158, 206, 230, 267
Suffolk Assurance Company, 98
Suffolk and General Insurance Company, 19
Suffolk Hunt, 113, 162
Suffolk, North-West, constituency, 89, 159
Suffolk, textile industry, 18
Suffolk, West, 10, 72, 185, 246, 259, 297
Suffolk, West, Chamber of Agriculture, 93
Suffolk, West, hospital, 170
Suffolk, West, magistrates, 143
Sugar, 26, 49–50

Sugar beet, 53
Sugar and Coffee Committee (1848), 45, 49–50
Sugar Duties Act (1846), 49–50
Sugar prices, 44
Sugar production in St Kitts, 44–54
Sunday closing, 175
Sutton stores, 83, 136
Swing Riots, 37
Symonds, R. J., 115, 129, 132

Taunton Cider Company, 253
Taylor, E. P., 225
Taylor Walker, brewers, London, 154, 203, 236–7
Television, 246, 252
Temperance Movement, 131, 134, 140, 143, 164, 174, 190, 314
Territorial Army, 204, 210
Theatre Royal, Bury St Edmunds, 22, 247–8, 300
Theatre Royal Trust, 248
Thermometers, 12, 56, 67
Thetford, 62, 136, 242
Thingoe Rural District Council, 221
Thrale's Brewery, 12
Thurgood, Robert, 228
Thurgood's Brewery, Baldock, 228
Tickner, Bernard, 257
Tidman's, Wisbech, 242
Tollemache, Hon. Douglas, 192
Tollemache's Brewery, Ipswich, 105, 192–3
Transport and General Workers Union, 247, 258
Truman, Hanbury and Buxton, brewers, 228

337